D0631594

LEO TOLSTOY

VOLUME

I

VINTAGE *RUSSIAN* LIBRARY

Advisory Committee

VINTAGE *RUSSIAN* LIBRARY

LEO TOLSTOY

VOLUME

I

The Years of Development

1828–1879

BY

ERNEST J. SIMMONS

1 9  6 0

VINTAGE BOOKS : NEW YORK

Published by Vintage Books, Inc.

Reprinted by arrangement with Little, Brown and Company, the original publisher of the book in association with The Atlantic Monthly Press.

 Manufactured in the United States of America. Published simultaneously in Canada by McClelland & Stewart Ltd.

FIRST VINTAGE EDITION

To

WINK AND DICK

Author's Note

TO THE VINTAGE EDITION

LEO TOLSTOY was eighty-two years old when he died in 1910. Hence the full narrative of his absorbing life, during which he became, not only one of the world's greatest novelists, but also one of the most celebrated moral thinkers of his time, is necessarily a lengthy one. Accordingly, in making the original book available in an inexpensive edition, for technical reasons Vintage Books has been obliged to reissue it in two volumes. The first volume covers the period from his birth, in 1828, to 1879, at which point he had completed the long spiritual struggle that radically transformed the remaining years of his life. The second volume continues with the record of his existence from 1880 to his death. During these last thirty years, besides writing many significant works of art, he engaged in the vigorous advocacy of his philosophy of life, which, he firmly believed, would make the world a better place if its precepts were accepted and practised by mankind.

The extensive apparatus of footnotes, concerned almost entirely with citing the Russian sources from which translations in the text have been made, and the "Bibliographical Survey" are omitted in this reissue. Readers who are curious about such sources and bibliography are referred to the original annotated edition, Little, Brown and Company, Boston, 1946.

ERNEST J. SIMMONS

Preface and Acknowledgments

THE PRESENT BOOK has made full use of the vast amount of new manuscript and printed material about Tolstoy that has become available during the last twenty years in Russia. This material has significantly increased our knowledge of the man—of his life and thought and writings.

All dates are given in the "old style": that is, they accord with the Julian calendar in use in Russia until after the 1917 Revolution. The Julian calendar was twelve days behind the Gregorian calendar in the nineteenth century, and thirteen days behind in the twentieth century.

Italicized words in the original Russian are preserved in the translations.

I am indebted to the Oxford University Press and to the executors of the Maude estate for permission to quote from *The Life of Tolstoy* by Aylmer Maude, from *Essays and Letters* translated by Aylmer Maude, and from *Tolstoy Centenary Edition* translated and edited by Aylmer Maude. I am also indebted to the Yale University Press for permission to quote from *The Tragedy of Tolstoy* by Alexandra Tolstoy.

E. J. S.

1946

Contents of Both Volumes

Volume I, 1828–1879

Volume II, 1880–1910

I clearly realized that my biography, if it suppressed all the nastiness and criminality of my life—as they customarily write biographies—would be a lie, and that if one is going to write my biography, one must write the whole truth.

TOLSTOY

PETER ANDREYEVICH TOLSTOY (1645–1729)
Favorite of Peter the Great. Exiled shortly before death of Catherine I because of his participation in murder of Peter's son Aleksei.

IVAN PETROVICH TOLSTOY (1685–1728)
Went into exile with his father where he died.

ANDREI IVANOVICH TOLSTOY (1721–1803)
Restored family fortunes. 23 children born to him in 25 years. Household called "The Great Nest."

ILYA ANDREYEVICH TOLSTOY (1757–1820)
Governor of Kazan. Probably the model for Old Rostov in WAR AND PEACE.

m.

PELAGEYA NIKOLAYEVNA GORCHAKOV (1762–1838)
Guardian of Leo and his brothers and sisters.

NIKOLAI ILYICH TOLSTOY (1795–1837) *m.*
Model for Young Rostov in WAR AND PEACE. Went on 1812 campaign against Napoleon.

NIKOLAI NIKOLAYEVICH TOLSTOY (1823–1860)
Leo's favorite brother and the founder of the Ant Brotherhood.

DMITRI NIKOLAYEVICH TOLSTOY (1827–1856)
Black sheep of family. Probably model for the brother of Levin in ANNA KARENINA.

SERGEI NIKOLAYEVICH TOLSTOY (1826–1904)
"dandy"

m.

MARYA MIKHAILOVNA SHISHKIN (1832–1919)

SERGEI LVOVICH TOLSTOY (1863–1947)

TATYANA LVOVNA TOLSTOY (1864–1950)
"Tanya"

ILYA LVOVICH TOLSTOY (1866–1933)

LEO LVOVICH TOLSTOY (1869–1945)
"Lyovka"

MARYA LVOVNA TOLSTOY (1871–1906)
"Masha"

PETER LVOVICH TOLSTOY (1872–1873)

The Tolstoy Family

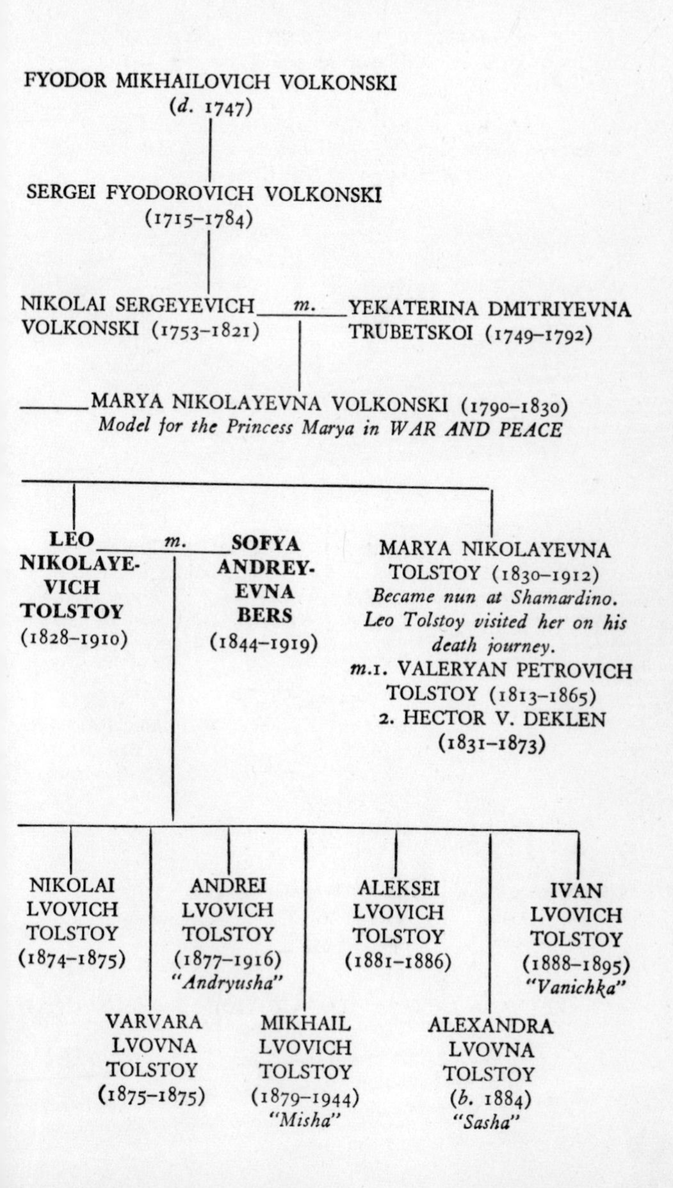

PART ONE

"Innocent,

Joyous, Poetic Childhood'

I

Princes, Generals, and Scoundrels

On the walls of the large dining room of the Tolstoy home at Yasnaya Polyana hung blackened ancestral portraits—seventeenth- and eighteenth-century men in wigs, uniforms, ribbons, and decorations, and women in their stiff gowns, laces, and powdered hair. At first the Tolstoy children were rather alarmed by these painted spectators from a mysterious past, but once the youngsters got accustomed to eating with the grownups the portraits ceased to bother them.

The only source of information, and one not wholly reliable, about the ancient founder of the Tolstoy family is the *Book of Nobility* (1686). In this account, medieval annals are cited to the effect that the Tolstoys derive from a certain Indris who in 1353 came to Russia from the West with his two sons and three thousand retainers. He was well received by the ruler of Chernigov in the Ukraine, where he adopted the Russian Orthodox faith. His great-grandson settled in Moscow and was honored by the reigning Grand Duke, who bestowed upon him the surname Tolstoy, which means "fat" in Russian. Leo Tolstoy seems to have been of the opinion that his family was of German origin, and that his name was a translation of the German family name *Dick* ("fat"). But it is more likely that Indris, from whom Leo Tolstoy descended in a direct line in the twentieth generation, was of Lithuanian origin.

The first eleven generations of Tolstoys are known only by name, and it is not until the time of Peter I that history begins to record their activities. Leo Tolstoy's great-great-

great grandfather, Peter Andreyevich Tolstoy, was a cowardly, cruel, and treacherous individual, but clever in the ruthless tactics of court intrigue and in what then passed for diplomacy. At first a partisan of Peter's half-sister Sophia, he quickly deserted her for the Tsar when she was defeated in the struggle for the throne. His subsequent career was a varied one: he fought in the Azov campaign of 1696; was sent abroad with others to study naval science in 1697 and returned a confirmed Westerner. In 1701 Peter appointed him first Russian ambassador to Constantinople.

When war broke out between the two countries in 1710, the Sultan, who had little regard for diplomatic immunity, promptly threw the ambassador into the prison of the Seven Towers, and there he languished for almost two years. This disaster ultimately provided him with a device for the family coat of arms, which displays the seven towers, supported by two wolfhounds rampant. When he returned to Russia in 1714 Peter rewarded him for his services by making him a Minister of State. He accompanied the Tsar abroad in 1716, and his growing reputation for learning, unusual in those days in Russia, further endeared him to the pedantic Peter.

In 1717 Tolstoy won the special favor of his master by tricking Aleksei, the unhappy heir to the throne who had fled the country, into returning to Russia. Not only was Tolstoy a member of the tribunal that condemned the Tsarevitch, but there is much reason to believe that he helped to suffocate him with pillows in his prison cell.

The headship of the Secret Chancellery, large estates, and the title of Count were Tolstoy's rewards for his part in this sorry business. He became a close adviser of the Tsar, but despite his position of trust, or perhaps just because of it, Peter did not place much faith in the loyalty of his cunning counselor. The Tsar is said to have remarked to the French minister that Tolstoy was a very able man, but in doing business with him "it was necessary to take the precaution of keeping a stone by you in order to smash his teeth in should he be disposed to snap." And in his cups Peter would fondly pat Tolstoy's head and say: "Head, head, if you were not so clever, I should long ago have ordered you cut off."

Indeed, in the end the clever Tolstoy reaped the whirlwind. Because he feared the young son of the murdered Aleksei—from whom he could expect no mercy—would become Tsar after the death of Catherine I, he plotted with a group to bring about the accession of Elizabeth, the daughter of Peter. The ruling favorite Menshikov, whose own daughter was betrothed to the Tsarevitch, learned of the conspiracy and had Tolstoy and others arrested.

The trial was rushed, and shortly before the death of Catherine, Menshikov persuaded her to deprive Tolstoy of his rank and of all his orders and estates, and to sentence him to the Solovetski Monastery, that bleak prison in the White Sea to which Tolstoy himself had condemned victims of Peter's wrath. An old man of eighty-two, he set out under escort on his long journey, accompanied by his son who had been convicted with him. After a year on this desolate island the son died, and Tolstoy himself died a year later (1729).

The family fortunes were considerably repaired by Peter Tolstoy's grandson, Andrei Ivanovich Tolstoy. He served in the army and held several high administrative posts, and in 1760 the Empress Elizabeth restored to him the title of Count as well as some of the confiscated estates of his grandfather. Little is known about his personal life, but he appears to have been a most exemplary husband. One evening his wife (she was probably only fourteen at the time) departed for a ball without her husband, who was unable to attend. On the way she suddenly remembered that she had neglected to bid him the usual farewell, and she at once returned only to find him in tears over this lapse of wifely devotion. Nevertheless, she was apparently a model spouse, for she bore him twenty-three children over the space of twenty-five years, an accomplishment that won for their household the nickname of "the great nest."

One of this nest of children was Ilya Andreyevich Tolstoy (1757–1820), the future grandfather of Leo. His round, fat, good-natured face among the stern-visaged ancestral portraits on the dining-room walls at Yasnaya Polyana seems to reflect the pleasure that he always found in the company of amiable guests. Leo Tolstoy said of him that he was "a man of limited intelligence, very gentle and merry, and not only generous but senselessly prodigal, and above all very confiding."

In the characterization of old Count Rostov in *War and Peace,* Tolstoy has reproduced the essential traits of his grandfather, the peccadilloes softened somewhat and the nature rendered more lovable to suit the artist's purpose. A continuous round of feasting, theatrical performances, balls, outings, and card playing ended in the financial ruin of the grandfather. He could not bear to refuse a petitioner, for generosity was as instinctive as it was indiscriminate in him. Even the fortune of his wealthy wife, Princess Pelageya Nikolayevna Gorchakov, was sacrificed because of her husband's extravagances. Finally, in order to secure a means of livelihood, he obtained the post of Governor of Kazan. Luxurious habits, however, are easier to acquire than to dispense with, and grandfather Tolstoy continued to lead his prodigal existence—he ordered sturgeon for his table from Astrakhan, sent his linen to Holland to be washed, and maintained a domestic theater and orchestra.

Although he was the soul of probity for a Russian governor of the time, grandfather Tolstoy's administration of Kazan was soon being furtively whispered about among the local gentry. He never took bribes (except the traditional ones from the liquor monopolists), a practice to which his more realistic wife was not averse. Perhaps it was his unconventional honesty as a government official that resulted in his being reported to his superiors in Petersburg for malfeasance. He was advised to resign, and an investigator was sent to Kazan to report on the conduct of his office. The kindly old man was so shaken by the charges that he died in less than a month after the order for his retirement.

2

Nikolai Ilyich Tolstoy (1795–1837), the older son of Ilya Andreyevich,[1] became the father of Leo Tolstoy. He was of medium height, well-built, active, with a pleasant face but with eyes that seemed always sad. Brought up as he was in a pleasure-loving household, his mind and tastes were formed to the lax social pattern of gentlemanly pursuits and occasional license common among the landed gentry. To promote his physical well-being—or so it was imagined—his parents arranged a liaison between their sixteen-year-old son and a pretty serf girl. "That union," Tolstoy records, "resulted in the birth of a son, Mishenka, who became a postilion and who, while my father was alive, lived steadily, but afterwards went to pieces. Often when we brothers

[1] There were three other children, a younger son who died and two daughters: Alexandra (1797?–1841) married Count K. I. Osten-Saken, and the younger, Pelageya (1801–1875), married V. I. Yushkov.

were grown up, he used to come to us begging for help. I remember the strange feeling of perplexity I experienced when this brother of mine, who was very much like my father (more so than any of us), having fallen into destitution, was grateful for the ten or fifteen rubles we would give him."

Before he was eighteen, and over the protests of his parents, Nikolai entered the army at the time of Napoleon's invasion of Russia. Since a near relation of his mother was Minister of War, the young soldier encountered no difficulty in eventually obtaining the post of adjutant to another relative, a general in command of part of the active army. He saw action in most of the important engagements of the bitter campaign, but he soon lost his zeal for war. In October 1813, he was sent with dispatches to Petersburg, and on the way back to rejoin the army he and his orderly were captured by the French and sent under guard to Paris.

At the moment of capture, the orderly had the presence of mind to slip all his master's money into his boots. During the long journey to Paris, which took several months, the orderly never once dared to remove his boots, although he suffered extreme pain from the concealed coins. This devotion enabled his master to support the trials of captivity in Paris in relative comfort. Not until the Russians entered the French capital in March 1814 was he released.

Although Nikolai Tolstoy may have disliked the horrors of war, the army in times of peace was a pleasant enough haven for the next five years. He retired with the rank of lieutenant colonel in 1819, went to Kazan where his father was governor, and soon entered the civil service. His father's death in 1820 left him with an estate so encumbered with debt that he refused to accept his inheritance. The salary of a civil servant was now entirely inadequate to meet the new demands thrust upon him—the care of a distant relative and of a mother and sister who were accustomed to every luxury.

In such a situation the natural way out for a brilliant young man with a name and important connections was an advantageous marriage, and one was soon arranged. He married the wealthy Princess Marya Nikolayevna Volkonski in 1822, retired from the service, and settled down on his wife's estate at Yasnaya Polyana ("clear glade") to enjoy a large income from the efforts of some eight hundred serfs.

Despite his bride's wealth and the fact that he was virtually penniless when he married her, Nikolai's close bachelor friends must have wondered at his choice. Marya Volkonski (1790–1830) was already thirty-two, five years older than her husband, a ripe old-maid age in those days. Added to this disqualification was her very plain appearance; some even called her ugly. She was the only daughter of Prince Nikolai Sergeyevich Volkonski, whose portrait on the dining-room wall filled the Tolstoy children with awe. It presented an impressive figure in a red caftan and gray wig, with a high forehead, thick overhanging eyebrows, and a piercing glance. His face bore a close resemblance to that of his famous grandson.

The Volkonskis traced their ancestry back to the Scandinavian Rurik, the traditional founder of Russia's first ruling dynasty. Nikolai Volkonski was an illustrious member of this proud line. In the reign of Catherine II he held high military and court positions, took part in the campaign against the Turks in 1780, and accompanied the Empress on her trip to the Crimea in 1786. When Volkonski had already achieved the lofty rank of general-in-chief, he lost it because he refused to marry Varvara Engelhardt, the niece and mistress of Potyomkin, who at that time was the Empress's chief favorite. Volkonski is said to have replied to Potyomkin's proposal: "What makes him think I would marry his strumpet?" According to another account, he lost favor in the Emperor Paul's reign because he incurred that mad monarch's displeasure by not appearing at a regimental review; he was dropped from the service but restored the next year (1798), when he was appointed Military Governor of Archangel. The prototype of Prince Bolkonski in *War and Peace,* he was a stern but wise landowner, opposed to the cruel punishments inflicted on serfs, and managed his large estate with an eye to the practical advantage of both himself and his peasants.

Yasnaya Polyana had been inherited by Volkonski from his father. The estate is a hundred and thirty miles south of Moscow and is situated in the Krapivenski district, about ten miles from the city of Tula. Volkonski had made many improvements: he built the original large manor house in which Leo Tolstoy was born, the two buildings that now serve as wings to the present central dwelling, and fine accommodations for his serfs. He saw to it that they always had enough to eat and sufficient clothing to wear—considerations of little concern to many landowners—and on holidays he provided them with recreation, such as games and village dances. The buildings he planned reflected his excellent taste and sense of beauty. Unlike the average Russian country gentleman of the time, he had no use for hunting, but he was well read in French literature and loved music. In the morning he would stroll along his lime-tree avenues, listen to the playing of his domestic orchestra, and enjoy the flowers and plants of his greenhouse.

Tolstoy's mother was severely brought up by her father. He tolerated no girlish nonsense in his deep affection for her, and himself taught her unwelcome lessons in mathematics, physics, geometry, and geography.

She was unusually well educated for a time when women were supposed to eschew learning as a social encumbrance. Perhaps her stern parent made the common mistake of trying to bring up as a boy the unfortunate only child that turned out to be a daughter, and one doubly unfortunate in that she was only two years old when her mother died.

Young ladies in aristocratic circles often knew French much better than their native language, but Tolstoy's mother spoke and wrote Russian correctly, and she also knew French, German, English, and Italian. Nor were practical matters concerning the management of the estate neglected in her rigorous training. On a visit to Petersburg when she was twenty her father obliged her to tour a number of factories, as well as museums, art galleries, and famous churches and palaces. She shared his love for music, played the piano well, and was credited with a unique talent for inventing folk tales and narrating them to children and grownups.

Unusual moral and spiritual qualities endeared Tolstoy's mother to all who surrounded her. Although quick-tempered, she exercised the utmost self-control. When provoked to fierce anger, her maid once told Tolstoy, she would go quite red in the face and even begin to weep, but she would never say a rude word—she did not even know any. Sincerity and simplicity dignified all her relations with people. Modesty was so deeply ingrained in her nature that she seemed literally ashamed of her own mental, moral, and spiritual superiority. Large, beautiful eyes transfigured her homely face and reflected the spiritual depths within.

Although an heiress and a member of a most prominent family, Princess Volkonski does not appear to have had many suitors. Her plain appearance and perhaps the jealous love of her severe father served to discourage them. As a mere girl she had been engaged to one of the sons of Prince Sergei Fyodorovich Golitsyn, who had married that same Varvara Engelhardt, mistress of Potyomkin, whose hand Volkonski had spurned. This coincidence, however, did not affect the friendship of the two princes, and the engagement of their children increased the intimacy of the two families. Before the marriage could take place the fiancé fell ill and died. Tolstoy observed that his mother's love for her deceased betrothed remained always in her memory as that poetic love which girls experience only once. As the years passed and the prospects of marriage faded, one may be certain that the belated proposal of Nikolai Tolstoy was utterly without benefit of "poetic love" in the eyes of Marya Volkonski.

Like many Russian families in the restricted circle of nobility, the Tolstoys in both the male and the female branches were related through intermarriage to nearly every family of consequence in the nineteenth century. In general, they belonged to the landed gentry, and most of them went into government service. Their names fill the pages of Russian history and literature and adorn the honor roll of famous artists. In literature alone Tolstoy could claim kinship with famous authors whose names every Russian schoolboy would know—Pushkin, Chaadayev, A. K. Tolstoy, Odoyevski, and Tyutchev.

Obviously, the conglomerate strains that contribute to the Tolstoy line discourage the customary pious occupation of biographers of tracing "racial influences." Lithuanian, Scandinavian, and Tatar blood are mingled with the Slavic. Leo Tolstoy would have dismissed any such attempt with the proud assertion that he was a Russian. If God had favored him with a second choice in the matter, he once thoughtfully admitted, he would choose to be an Englishman.

⁂ 11 ⁂

II

Tubbed and Swaddled

FROM THE DEEP well of memory Tolstoy brought to the surface recollections of his purely infant existence. He recalled a not unpleasant smell, probably from the bran with which his nurse rubbed him in the bath. His sensations on this occasion returned to him sharply across the years—the sudden awareness of his own tiny body with its visible ribs, the smooth dark wooden tub, the bare arms of his nurse, the noise of the warm, steaming, swirling water, and the smooth feel of the wet rim of the tub as he passed his little hands along it. Then there was the recollection of the family bogey name "Eremeyevna" that filled him and his sister with mingled fear and pleasure when whispered in a gruff, mysterious voice; and he remembered his agitation and tears over the depraved manner in which the family tutor kicked up his legs when they all danced in a circle.

It was this shadowy region between the unconscious and the conscious that principally occupied his thoughts in the few autobiographical notes that he jotted down in 1878 and added to in his *Recollections* twenty-five years later. The meager catch in the net of memory only served to stimulate his speculation over the enormous chasm between the embryo and the newborn babe and the utter incomprehensibility between nonexistence and an embryo. Autobiography was quickly sacrificed to the ineluctable difference between being and non-being.

Genius has no ancestors or descendants; it is an accident of nature and hence inexplicable in terms of human influences. The man who possesses genius, however, is subject to all the ordinary factors and circumstances that influence the average person. Tolstoy's heightened sensibilities made him even more susceptible to such influences, and among them his mother must be accorded a significant place. Although she died before he was two years old, her moral and spiritual influence persisted to an extraordinary degree throughout his long life. The absence of any real memory of her only served to contribute to the idealized memory that his vivid imagination evoked.

Tolstoy heard about his mother from aunts and old family servants. Some of her extant letters and her diary provided additional information, but he was rather glad that no portrait of her existed (only a silhouette has been preserved), for it left his own beautiful image of her uncontaminated by reality.

Feminine sympathy, help, and love were essential to Tolstoy, and he sought them all his life. Everything he learned of his mother seemed to contribute to his imaginative conception of her as the very quintessence of feminine solicitude and no doubt intensified her spiritual influence over him. Three sons were born before him—Nikolai, Sergei, and Dmitri. Nikolai, who possessed unusual qualities, both as a child and as a man, was her favorite, and she lavished on him all the abundant affection of her loving nature. When Leo—often called by his pet name Lyovochka—came along on August 28, 1828, he displaced Nikolai, who was now old enough to be given over to the care of the family tutor, as his mother's favorite. She had to love someone, and the one love replaced the other. Her latest born she called *"mon petit Benjamin."*

The children's early education was undertaken by their mother, who in the matter of moral direction derived hints from Rousseau's *Émile*. At the end of the day she graded the children's progress or lack of it on "tickets" and kept a diary in which she recorded her reactions to the lessons and behavior of her charges.

The diary of Tolstoy's mother contains an interesting account of her efforts with Nikolai. "That diary," Tolstoy remarked, "portrays her passionate wish to do everything to educate Koko [Nikolai] in the best possible way, and at the same time how very obscure a perception she had of what such an education should be. She reproves him, for instance, for being too sensitive and crying over the sufferings of animals when he witnessed them. A man, in her view, had to be firm. Another defect she tried to correct in him was that he was absent-minded and said *'Je vous remercie'* to grandmamma instead of saying *'Bonsoir'* or

'Bonjour.'" In general she tried to encourage in her son manly and patriotic virtues, but moral and spiritual instruction took precedence over the practical. A kind heart pleased her more than a quick mind.

"I think that my mother was not in love with my father," Tolstoy wrote, "but loved him as a husband and chiefly as the father of her children." No more could be expected from this *mariage de convenance*. Morally and spiritually inferior to his wife, he could not understand her radiant nature, yet he proved an excellent husband in everything that made for happiness and prosperity in the household. Tolstoy's mother died on August 7, 1830, some five months after the birth of her only daughter, Marya (Masha), and after barely nine years of married life. The moving description of the death of the hero's mother in *Childhood* was unquestionably suggested by the accounts Tolstoy had heard of his own mother's death. The boundless love of a soul always striving towards the infinite, the eternal, and hence never at peace, is the dominating trait that runs throughout the whole characterization. Tolstoy believed boundless love to be the chief attribute of his mother's nature. In later life he rarely spoke of her to his own children, but when he did it was always with such tenderness and reverence that they thought of her as a saint.

2

Tolstoy did not love his father as he did his mother, perhaps for the simple reason that the mystery that nourished her moral and spiritual influence was lacking. When he was old enough to be conscious of his surroundings, however, his father occupied first place in his esteem. His personality and even his handsome appearance in a frock coat and narrow trousers made an ineffaceable impression on the boy.

Nikolai Tolstoy was the original for the characterization of Nikolai Rostov in *War and Peace*. After his marriage he settled down at Yasnaya Polyana and managed his agricultural affairs with competence, just as young Rostov did at Bald Hills after he married Princess Marya. And some of the details of his existence as a country gentleman, such as his zeal for hunting, reappear in the novel. Unlike Rostov, however, Nikolai Tolstoy was lenient with his serfs. Leo remembered with pride that, with one exception, he never heard of corporal punishment on the estate when he was a child.

Education was not taken very seriously by landowners on the social level of Nikolai Tolstoy; landowners below his level were often illiterate. He had no fondness for pure science, but he read widely in the French classics and in political science and natural history. Like young Rostov again, he endeavored to build up a library, and he made a rule—the pious hope of many a collector of books—never to buy a new volume until he had read the old ones. His son found it hard to believe that his father obeyed this self-imposed rule with reference to the many-volumed *Histoires des Croisades* and *des Papes* that he found in the library at Yasnaya Polyana.

Apart from a few close hunting companions, Nikolai Tolstoy avoided the company of his neighbors. Nor did he allow himself to be drawn into the political activities of the local district. Like so many of the gentry who had taken part in the patriotic campaigns of 1812 to 1815, he was disillusioned by the later illiberal attitude of Alexander I and deeply disappointed by the reactionary rule of his successor. The result was an aloofness from all government service and an implied if not uttered condemnation of both the foreign and the domestic policy of his country.

Of course his son at that time did not understand the significance of this attitude, but he did fully realize that his father never humbled himself before anyone and never changed his debonair, gay, and often ironical tone. And this sense of personal dignity increased the boy's admiration of his father. The son was to possess this same consciousness of his own worth and the same unwillingness to humble himself before anyone, least of all before government officials.

Tolstoy pleasantly recalled the bright, happy demeanor of his father when he was alone with the family. His jests and yarns at mealtime kept grandmother, aunts, and children constantly amused. He would draw pictures for the youngsters which they thought the height of perfection. Just before bedtime the children would take their father's study by storm. As he smoked and read, they swarmed over the back of his huge leather divan to receive his good-night blessing. Sometimes they found him in the drawing room, where he had gone to lay out Grandmother's game of patience; he was always tender and submissive to her. While she placed her cards and took a pinch from her gold snuff-box, one of the aunts would read aloud.

> I remember once [Tolstoy wrote in his *Recollections*], in the middle of a game of patience and of the reading, my father interrupts my aunt, points to a looking-glass and whispers something. We all look in the same direction. It was the footman Tikhon who (knowing that my father was in the drawing room) was going into the study to take some tobacco from a big leather folding tobacco-pouch. My father sees him in the looking-glass and notices his figure stepping carefully on tiptoe. My aunts laugh. Grandmamma for a long time does not understand, but when she does she too smiles cheerfully. I am enchanted by my father's kindness, and on taking leave of him kiss his white muscular hands with special tenderness.

3

Tolstoy's mother had been the center of a household that radiated possessive feminine love for her five children. After her early death the other women in the family circle drew closer to the motherless youngsters. And they occupy an important place in Tolstoy's childhood.

Tolstoy described his grandmother, Pelageya Nikolayevna Tolstoy, as a woman of small intellect who had been consistently spoiled by her father and then by both her husband and son. Although he suspected that she was jealous of his mother, she deeply loved her son and his children. All sought to please her as the chief person of the household, with the natural result that she grew capricious and often behaved to family and servants with little consideration.

With that arbitrary selectivity of memory functioning over a long stretch of years, Tolstoy's mind fixed on the picture of Grandmother in her white cap and dressing jacket, smiling with satisfaction at the children's delight over the large and wonderful bubbles that arose from her old white hands as she washed them with a special kind of soap. Another picture etched in his memory represented Grandmother in a yellow cabriolet placed in a clump of hazel bushes, the branches of which footmen bent down so that she could pluck the ripe nuts without leaving her seat. The children filled their own pockets, and Grandmother took the youngsters into the cabriolet with her and praised them. Grandmother, the nut glade, the pungent scent of the leaves, the footmen, the yellow cabriolet, and the hot sun all merged in his mind into one joyful impression of childhood.

Perhaps Tolstoy's most vivid recollection of his grandmother concerned the night he passed in her bedroom with Stepanich, the old blind storyteller, whose remarkable memory enabled him to repeat word for word stories that were read to him. His hearing was so acute that he could indicate exactly the direction a mouse had taken by the sound it made in running across the floor. Tolstoy's sister related that the sightless Stepanich once interrupted a tale to remark that a mouse had just got into the oil that Grandmother used for her icon lamp. He often had his supper in Grandmother's room and recited one of his stories while she undressed and went to bed.

On one such occasion it was little Leo's turn to spend the night with his grandmother. He remembered her in the dim light of the icon lamp, propped up against the huge pillows, and dressed all in white and covered with white bedclothes. From the window seat came the tranquil voice of blind Stepanich droning the story of Prince Camaralzaman. Tolstoy could recall nothing of the tale, only the mysterious appearance of his white grandmother, her wavering shadow on the wall, and old Stepanich with his white, unseeing eyes.

Aunt Alexandra Ilyinichna Osten-Saken, the grandmother's oldest daughter, was the most unusual member of the Tolstoy family circle. Tragedy had wrecked her marriage. They had not lived together very long when her husband, a wealthy Baltic Count, showed signs of mental derangement. In a fit of insanity he shot her, almost fatally. While she was recovering, being pregnant at the time, he succumbed to another mad notion that she would betray him to his enemies, and he tried to cut her tongue out. Attendants rescued her, and Count Osten-Saken was shut up in an asylum. As a consequence of these terrible experiences, she gave birth to a stillborn girl, and friends, fearing to tell her of this new catastrophe, substituted the recently born child of a servant. She eventually returned to her parents' house, but after her father's death she and her ward, Pashenka, went to live with her newly married brother at Yasnaya Polyana.

Aunt Alexandra's misfortunes no doubt helped to deepen the Christian faith of a nature already intensely religious. Her favorite occupations were reading *The Lives of Saints* and playing devoted hostess to the numerous monks and nuns and half-crazy religious pilgrims who constantly visited Yasnaya Polyana. Tolstoy's religious mother also had a fondness for these holy people, who were familiar figures on large estates or any place where they could obtain alms. Her favorite among them, and the godmother of her daughter, was Marya Gerasimovna, who for some unknown reason masqueraded as a monk and assumed the name Ivanushka. Aunt Alexandra took her under her own protection after the death of Tolstoy's mother.

There was nothing insincere in Aunt Alexandra's religious zeal. She led a truly Christian life, avoiding luxury, dressing in the simplest fashion, accepting no service that she could perform herself, and giving away her money to the needy. She carried her disregard of worldly niceties so far that she neglected to keep clean, and Tolstoy uncharitably recalled the acrid smell that always seemed to enter the room with her.

In his old age, when Tolstoy looked back upon the people who had been close to him during his childhood, the one he singled out as having the "greatest influence" on his life was Auntie Tatyana Alexandrovna Yergolski. She was not a real aunt and he could never remember the exact relationship—she was his father's second cousin. When she and her sister were left poor orphans, Tolstoy's grandmother, after praying before the icon, drew lots with another relative for possession of the girls. Tatyana fell to her and she brought her up as one of her own children. She turned out to be an unusual child, resolute, resourceful, and devoted to her benefactress. Her courage once challenged by her playmates, she promptly placed a red-hot ruler on her arm, apparently inspired to make this particular kind of test by the dubious example of Mucius Scaevola. She was in love with the son of her benefactress, like Sonya, who was modeled on her, in *War and Peace,* but appears to have given up Nikolai Tolstoy with less regret than Sonya surrendered Nikolai Rostov: their claims were sacrificed to wealthy brides. Six years after the death of his wife, Tolstoy's father asked his childhood sweetheart to marry him and act as a mother to his children. She rejected the first part of his proposal and gladly accepted the second: for the rest of her life she took the place of a mother to the Tolstoy sons and daughter.

Auntie Tatyana was about forty when she first impressed herself on the mind of the young Tolstoy. He remembered her then with her enormous plait of crisp, black, curly hair, jet-black eyes, and vivacious expression. And from the very beginning he loved her. When he was almost five, he recalls, he squeezed in behind her on the divan, and as she caressed him he caught her dusky broad little hand with its energetic cross-vein and began to kiss it and to cry from tender love of her. He never remembered one word of reproach from her, and her whole existence seemed to be devoted to service to others. She loved others not so much for the good they did her as for the good she did them. Love, Tolstoy remarked, was her chief characteristic, and her influence "consisted first of all in teaching me from childhood the spiritual delight of love. She did not teach me that by words, but by her whole being she filled me with love. I saw and felt how she enjoyed loving, and I understood the joy of love. That was the first thing. And the second was that she taught me the charm of an unhurried, tranquil life."

4

Such were the people who surrounded Tolstoy in his infancy. The atmosphere, properly enough, was a feminine one, for he was still confined to the nursery upstairs and to the constant companionship of his younger sister. Dim recollections of being bathed and swaddled and of the secure feeling of boundless love, especially from his Auntie Tatyana, are all that he remembered before the age of five. But the world downstairs with his older brothers and their German tutor, Fyodor Ivanovich Rössel, the great world of men beyond the nursery with his father and the clever coachmen, with horses and dogs and hunting—all this awaited him. And many years later he recalled the change and resurrected all the poignant mixed feelings that attended this solemn event in his young life.

"When I was moved downstairs to Fyodor Ivanovich and the boys," he wrote, "for the first time in my life, and therefore more strongly than at any time since, I experienced that feeling which is called a sense of duty, a consciousness of the cross that every man is called upon to bear. I was sorry to leave what I had been accustomed to (accustomed to from the very beginning), and it was sad, poetically sad, to part not so much with people, with my sister, nurse, and Auntie, but with my crib and its canopy and pillows, and this new life into which I was entering seemed fearful. I tried to find a happy side to this new life that awaited me; I tried to believe the kind words with which Fyodor Ivanovich lured me to him; I tried not to see the scorn with which the boys received me—the youngest; I tried to think that it was shameful for a big boy to live with girls, and that there was nothing good in the life upstairs with nurse; but at heart I was terribly sad, and I knew that I had irrevocably lost my innocence and happiness, and only a feeling of my own worth and the consciousness that I was fulfilling my duty sustained me. Many times since I have experienced similar moments at the crossroads of life when entering upon a fresh course. I experienced quiet grief at the irreparability of my loss. I was unable to believe that it would really happen, although I had been told that they would move me downstairs to the boys. But I remember the dressing gown with the cord sewn to its back which they put on me, and it seemed to cut me off forever from upstairs. And I noticed then for the first time not all those with whom I had lived upstairs, but the principal person with whom I lived and whom I had not remembered previously. This was Auntie Tatyana Alexandrovna. I recall her—short, stout, black-haired, kind, tender, and compassionate. She put the dressing gown on me, and, embracing and kissing me, she tied it around me; and I saw that she felt as I did: that it was sad, terribly sad, but that it had to be. For the first time I felt that life was not a game but a serious matter."

III

The Green Stick

THAT LIFE IS a "serious matter" may well be a rational conviction for the adult; for the child, it is a transitory impression inspired by changes that reality thrusts into his little world of make-believe. All the burden and the mystery that troubled the thoughts of five-year-old Lyovochka quickly vanished when he found his new life downstairs a glorious game indeed.

The happy irrecoverable days of childhood stretch out before him like some illimitable terrain, mysteriously beckoning him to explore its sunny valleys and cool forests. After each day's wanderings he returns home, pleasantly weary and very hungry. The cup of milk and sugar finished, he curls up cozily in an easy chair, and healthy childish sleep weighs down his eyelids. He feels the gentle fingers of Auntie Tatyana running through his hair and hears her soft familiar voice, as though far away, tenderly urging him to bed. Her kiss on his forehead rouses him and his lips search for her hand. Soon he is tucked under the quilt, and he presses to him in a corner of the soft down pillow a favorite china toy—a hare or a dog—and hopes the morrow will be fine for an outing. Then he smilingly falls asleep, whispering a prayer to God to make everybody happy.

Once out of the nursery, Lyovochka discovered the world of nature—grass, leaves, flowers, trees, birds, and animals—in the picturesque surroundings of Yasnaya Polyana, and in his impressionable mind a lasting love for God's handiwork was born. Yasnaya Polyana, where he was to spend some seventy of his eighty-two years, was an ideal playground for a boy. Visitors entered the grounds of the estate through a gateway between whitewashed brick towers that look like two strangely shaped mushrooms topped by Chinese roofs. Grandfather Volkonski is said to have stationed guards in these towers.[1]

The way to the house led through a lane bordered with birch trees, their clean bark gleaming white where the sun struck it through the leafy shade. In front of the old manor house with its forty-two rooms was a flower garden, and behind extended a large park with ancient lime-tree alleys and several small ponds. On the edge of the estate the thick Zakaz woods were cut by the Voronka River. From the house, running through a clearing studded with springtime forget-me-nots, was the "bathing-trail" to the family bath-house on the bank of the river. Across the undulating countryside in the distance stretched from east to west a long ribbon of imperial domain known as the Zaseka forest. It bounded on one side the extensive fields beyond the gates of the estate. From the road at harvest time one could see, where a strip of thick high rye had already been cut, a peasant woman reaping with even rhythm or bending over the cradle of her child that had been placed in the shade of the tall grain. In the cleared spaces the bright yellow field was full of sheaves, which black-bearded peasants loaded on their stubby carts.

But harvest time was also hunting time, and little Lyovochka was soon initiated into the traditions of the chase, sacred among Russian landowners. He remembered the young borzois following his father out into the field and growing excited as the high grass whipped and tickled their bellies. With their tense tails raised sickle-wise, they leaped gracefully over the stubble behind the horses' feet. Milka, the high-spirited, piebald favorite dog of his father, ran in front with expectant head raised, waiting for the quarry. The peasants' voices, the tramp of horses and creaking of carts, the merry whistle of quail, the mingled odors of wormwood, straw, and horses' sweat, the dark blue of the distant forest, the light lilac clouds, and the white cobwebs that floated in the air or stretched across the stubble—all these sights, sounds, and smells lingered in his memory when years later he described the first hunting experience of his childhood.

Then there was his recollection of the big gray wolf that

[1] After Tolstoy had become master of the estate, the humble, low-born Chekhov, on his first visit to Yasnaya Polyana, lost courage when he came in sight of the aristocratic towers and ordered his puzzled driver to turn back.

the hunters caught alive and brought home in triumph. All stood around in awe as the trussed-up beast was unloaded from the cart. They held the wolf down with pitchforks, and it gnawed savagely at the cords while being untied. At a given signal the beast was released, and in a flash dogs, hunters, and horsemen flew after it downhill and across the fields. Much to the disgust of Lyovochka's father, the wolf escaped, only to appear again many years later in the famous hunting scene in *War and Peace,* but on that occasion the wolf did not escape.

2

Closer association with his brothers was of first importance in the new existence of the recent graduate from the nursery. They soon initiated Lyovochka into those exciting mysteries that are the peculiar possession of the world of childhood.

Curiously enough, black-eyed Dmitri (Mitenka) left little impression on Lyovochka during this period, although Dmitri was closest to him in age (only a year and a half older) and played with him more than the other brothers. He was a capricious, difficult child, and Tolstoy remembered only his excessive merriment and the fact that they got along well enough together.

The handsome, proud, yet sincere Sergei (Seryozha), however, Lyovochka admired to the point of hero worship. He was two and a half years older. Lyovochka, self-conscious and painfully aware of what others thought of him, was impressed by Seryozha's spontaneity of egotism and tried to imitate it. In fact, he imitated nearly everything Seryozha did: his keeping chickens, his colored drawings of them, and the original way he fed his flock in the winter by poking long slivers of bread through the keyhole. The ease and sureness with which Seryozha got things done baffled his brother and at the same time aroused his adoration. Throughout his life Seryozha remained for Tolstoy an inscrutable, mysterious, and endlessly fascinating personality.

Nikolai (Nikolenka, Koko), who was more than five and a half years older than Lyovochka, was naturally the moving spirit among the brothers in all their childhood enterprises. Not only the fact that he was the oldest, but rare qualities of mind and spirit justified his leadership. Lyovochka deeply loved Nikolai, whose influence over him was enduring and important. Tolstoy believed that Nikolai resembled his mother in his indifference to what others thought about him, in his unusual modesty despite superior mental, moral, and spiritual endowments, and in his firm refusal to judge others. Turgenev used to say of him that he lacked only certain faults to be a great writer. Tolstoy added that he lacked the writer's principal fault of vanity but possessed to a high degree a fine artistic sense, a gay, light fund of humor, an amazing imagination, and a highly moral view of life. He related how Nikolai would invent folk tales, ghost stories, or shilling-shockers for hours together, and so vividly did he realize characters and scenes that one forgot that they were all products of his imagination.

Nikolai's imagination and power of invention, perhaps inspired in this instance by his reading about freemasons and religious sects—he was a wide reader—created an exciting childhood fantasy that absorbed much of the attention and thought of the Tolstoy brothers for a brief period. (They ranged between the ages of five and eleven at this time.) Nikolai solemnly announced to them one day that he possessed a wonderful secret that could make all men happy. If it became generally known, a kind of Golden Age would exist on earth: there would be no more disease, no human misery, and no anger. All would love one another and become "Ant Brothers."[2] The children adopted the idea with enthusiasm and even organized a game of Ant Brothers. Boxes and chairs were covered with shawls, and they all cuddled together in the dark within the shelter.

Nikolai had disclosed the Ant Brotherhood to them but not the chief secret—the means by which all men would become everlastingly happy. He had written this secret, he said, on a green stick buried by the road at the edge of a ravine in the Zakaz forest. Apart from the green stick, there was also a certain Fanfaronov Hill, and he agreed to lead them up it if they would fulfill all the necessary conditions. The first was to stand in a corner and not think of a white bear. The second condition was to walk along a crack in the floor without wavering; and the third was to keep from seeing a hare, alive or dead or cooked, for a whole year. Of course, Nikolai strictly warned his brothers not to reveal these conditions to anyone. If they fulfilled them, and others

[2] *Moravskiye bratya*—"Moravian Brothers"—of whom young Nikolai had no doubt read, was probably mistakenly transformed by the boys into *Muraveinye bratya*—"Ant Brothers."

that he promised to communicate later, then they would have one wish that would come true. And they had to tell Nikolai their wishes beforehand. Seryozha wished to be able to model a horse and a hen out of wax; Mitenka wished to be able to draw everything in life size, like a real artist; and the five-year-old Lyovochka, clearly puzzled, lamely wished to be able to draw things in miniature.

The children soon forgot about Fanfaronov Hill and the green stick. Tolstoy, however, traced to the Ant Brotherhood under the shawl-covered chairs his first childhood experience of love, not love of some one person, but love of love. Huddled together under the chairs, the Ant Brothers felt a particular tenderness for each other, and they talked of what was necessary for happiness and how they would love everybody. When he was over seventy, he recalled the incident in his *Recollections:*—

> The ideal of Ant Brothers clinging lovingly to one another, only not under two armchairs curtained by shawls, but of all the people of the world under the wide dome of heaven, has remained unaltered for me. As I then believed that there was a little green stick whereon was written something which would destroy all evil in men and give them great blessings, so I now believe that such truth exists among people and will be revealed to them and will give them what it promises.

Two years before his death, Tolstoy dictated to his secretary, N. N. Gusev, the following: "Although it is a trifling matter, yet I wish to say something that I should like done after my death. Even though it is a trifle of trifles: let no ceremonies be performed in putting my body into the earth. A wooden coffin, and whoever wishes, carry it or cart it to Zakaz, opposite the ravine at the place of the 'green stick.' At least, there's a reason for selecting that and no other place." When he mentioned the green stick, Gusev observed, tears filled his eyes.

3

If Lyovochka found anything serious in his new life downstairs, it was the irksome hours of study under the guidance of his first tutor, the German Fyodor Ivanovich Rössel. Children of the Russian gentry ordinarily learned languages from foreign tutors, although such instructors were often ex-tailors, cooks, or soldiers, who had found their way into

Russia and exploited their language as a means of livelihood. Fyodor Ivanovich had been a shoemaker, a soldier, a rope-maker, and a bit of a Don Juan, if the story of his life that Tolstoy tells so effectively in *Boyhood* is authentic.

As a tutor, certainly, he had little to recommend him, except his unfailing kindness and affection for the Tolstoy children. His intellectual interests appear to have been discouragingly limited to the repeated reading of three works: a German pamphlet on the manuring of cabbage plots, one volume of a *History of the Seven Years' War,* and a treatise on hydrostatics. For good measure, he supplemented this learned feast with odd copies of the Russian periodical, *Northern Bee.*

Seated in an easy chair and arrayed in his quilted dressing gown and red-tasseled skullcap, Fyodor Ivanovich heard with an air of pedagogical pomposity endless recitations from a German dialogue book: "*Wo kommen Sie her?*" he would ask in his Saxon accent. And the pat answer would be droned back: "*Ich komme vom Kaffeehause.*" Failure to know the answer of the exercise book entailed the risk of being sent to kneel in the corner. Sadly Tolstoy recalls that corner of shame in *Childhood.* Vexed with aching back and knees, he picked plaster off the wall and then grew frightened that the noise of a particularly large piece falling to the floor might attract the attention of his absent-minded tutor. But Fyodor Ivanovich heard nothing, for he was once again deep in his treatise on hydrostatics. The kindly, sentimental tutor, however, was no tyrant. Perhaps more important than his German lessons were the virtuous precepts he encouraged of generous tolerance and loving-kindness towards all the poor and unfortunate of life, among whom he included himself.

Except for German, in which Lyovochka acquired considerable expertness, little else appears to have been within the teaching competence of good Fyodor Ivanovich. He may have fostered what seems to have been an attempt at a magazine on the part of his young pupils. In the vast collection of Tolstoy manuscripts in Moscow, two pages of note paper, neatly ruled in childish fashion in pencil, have recently turned up. They are headed "Children's Amusements," with an indication that the contributions will be written by the four brothers. Beneath this is a subheading: "First Part. Natural History. Written by C.L.N.To, 1835," that is, by Count Leo Nikolayevich Tolstoy. Seven brief accounts follow, the first of which is entitled "The Eagle." It reads: "The eagle is the king of birds. They say about it that a certain boy began to tease it; it grew angry and pecked at him." Similar descriptions follow of the hawk, owl, parrot, peacock, hummingbird, and cock. This is the first manuscript of Tolstoy in existence, and it was probably written when he was seven years of age.

Among the gentry, French was an indispensable subject in the education of any child. No doubt Auntie Tatyana, who knew the language better than her own, was the teacher in this instance. She apparently laid a good foundation, for in later years Tolstoy's knowledge of French was perfect. He began his study of the language at a very early age, for when he was five he was given the task of teaching little Dunechka her letters in French. Dunechka was the illegitimate daughter of a distant relative of the Tolstoys, A. A. Temyashyov, a wealthy bachelor. He begged Tolstoy's father, to whom he was devoted, to bring up Dunechka in his household. In return, he offered to hand over a rich property, Pirogovo, if Tolstoy's father would set aside a dowry for the girl. So the quiet, broad-faced child became a member of the family and played with the brothers.

Once, Tolstoy recalls, she and Dmitri started a game of spitting a small chain into each other's mouth, but she spat it so hard and he opened his mouth so wide that he swallowed the chain. There was much wailing until the doctor came and calmed all concerned. Indeed, Dunechka gave way to tears as easily as her young teacher, whose propensity in this direction earned him the family nickname of *Lyova Ryova,* "Cry-baby Leo." On one occasion she grew weary with his efforts and stubbornly called incorrectly the French letters that he pointed out to her. The five-year-old pedagogue persisted and Dunechka burst into tears. So did Cry-baby Leo, and when the mystified grownups arrived on the scene, the desperate sobs of both master and pupil prevented them from uttering a word of explanation.

Up to the age of nine Lyovochka's formal education was neither systematic nor thorough. His own inclination, however, and the example of his elders over this period, unquestionably encouraged that informal but valuable kind of instruction obtained from reading good books. There is no actual record of such efforts, except his own story of being asked, when he was about eight, to read Pushkin to his father. He selected from the volume his favorite pieces that he had learned by heart, such as "To the Sea" and "Napoleon":—

> *The wondrous fate has been fulfilled,*
> *The great man is no more.*

"He was evidently struck by the pathos with which I spoke those verses," Tolstoy writes, "and having listened to me, exchanged significant looks with Yazykov [Tolstoy's godfather], who was present. I understood that he saw something good in that reading of mine and I was very happy about it." Not merely the effectiveness of his son's reading, but the choice of poems must have struck the father as unusual. For the poems mentioned, among Pushkin's best shorter pieces, are extremely advanced for an eight-year-old boy, and their selection at least suggests a degree of artistic taste and understanding even at this age.

4

A few of the thirty or more serf domestics of the Tolstoys were distinct personalities and important individuals in the household during Lyovochka's childhood. Their absolute dependence on master and mistress, true of servants among the gentry before the emancipation of the serfs, often engendered a nearness and devotion to the family quite uncommon in such a relationship.

There was toothless nurse Anna Ivanovna, a relic of grandfather Volkonski's boyhood, whose extreme age and witchlike appearance frightened the Tolstoy children. She was assisted by the much younger Tatyana Filippovna, who lived long enough with the family to become the nurse of Tolstoy's eldest son. The whole life of this simple peasant centered in her foster children, and she freely gave away to her wheedling husband and son all the money that she earned. With little Dunechka had come her own nurse, Evpraksiya, an ancient woman with a pendulous jowl like a turkey cock's, in which a ball moved around. As a special treat she would allow the Tolstoy youngsters to feel this growth in her neck. The deep-voiced, genial Nikolai, brother of Tatyana Filippovna, who always had about him the pleasant smell of the stables, was the family coachman. The children loved him and were much in awe of his skill with horses. The kindly butler Vasili Trubetskoi used to carry Lyovochka up and down the pantry on his tray, and the boy also sought to keep in the good graces of the footman, Tikhon, a former flutist in the serf orchestra of grandfather Volkonski and a comedian of some ability, and of the two handsome brothers, Petrushka and Matyushka, strong and skillful huntsmen.

Of all the domestics of his childhood, the one whom Tolstoy recalled with deepest affection was the housekeeper, Praskovya Isayevna. She too had served the family since the time of his grandfather. Lyovochka would go up to her little room and have long talks with her about all those matters of supreme importance in the life of a child. She would answer his eager questions concerning the military exploits of grandfather Volkonski, and no doubt she told him a great deal about his mother, whom she loved. His only unpleasant memories of her concern the time she struck him with a wet napkin for a boyish prank and the enema she administered to him by mistake—the operation apparently had been intended for one of his brothers. She was a rare character, however, and Tolstoy frankly admits her fine influence on the development of his sensibility. So instinctive were her love and kindness that it never occurred to him until after she had died to value them for their true worth. Only then did he realize what a wonderful being she had been.

On holidays the house serfs often mingled with members of the family in the festivities. This was especially true of the celebrations at Christmas time. All would dress in outlandish mummers' costumes—a bear, a goat, a Tatar, a Turk, or a robber. Sometimes neighbors would come, such as Islenev[3] with his three sons and three daughters, weirdly made up to represent a dressing table, a boot, a cardboard buffoon, and other oddities. Bustling Auntie Tatyana quickly disguised the excited Tolstoy children. Little Masha was particularly attractive as a Turkish girl, and her brother Lyovochka thought himself very handsome as a Turkish man. He studied his burnt-cork mustache and exaggerated eyebrows in the mirror, and the expression of a majestic Turk that he tried to assume vanished in the smile of pleasure that came over his face. Music and country dances followed, and then the mummers, both serfs and gentry, formed a large circle and played traditional Christmas games. When the festivities ended, all the partici-

[3] He was the grandfather of Tolstoy's future wife and is represented as the father of the Irtenev children in *Childhood*.

pants were treated to a variety of holiday dainties.

Suffering and misfortune always puzzled little Lyovochka. When returning for a walk with his tutor, they met the fat steward Andrei, followed by squinting Kuzma, the coachman's assistant, who was on his way to the stable to be flogged. Lyovochka was horrified, although floggings (rare at Yasnaya Polyana) were the common fate of serfs. And he was doubly grieved when Auntie Tatyana, who hated corporal punishment, told him—what he did not know then—that he could have prevented the beating. He was equally shocked and bewildered when he heard Temyashyov casually relate how he had sent his man cook to serve as a soldier—a terrible calamity for a serf at that time—simply because he had taken it into his head to eat meat during a fast. And when the butler, Vasili Trubetskoi, who used to carry him around on his tray, was transferred to another estate, Lyovochka grew fearful over the instability of life and experienced a still deeper sense of love and pity for Vasili. Even his kind tutor aroused his antipathy when he condemned his own dog to be hanged because her leg had been broken. The boy felt that something was terribly wrong if poor Bertha had to be hanged merely because she was suffering and ill.

The positive side of Lyovochka's sensibility was expressed in spontaneous outpourings of love and in eager attempts to win affection. With the unwavering faith of a child he believed that love for people was a natural disposition of the soul, or rather the accepted relationship among all peoples. Its absence, whenever pointedly evident, always troubled him. To the animate and inanimate world he imparted all the happiness of his own warm and loving imagination. On a summer picnic at Grumond, a charming little village about a mile and a half from Yasnaya Polyana, he recalls his joyous feelings evoked by the event: "The coachmen stand in the shade of the trees. The light and shadow speckle their faces, kind, jolly, happy faces. Matryona the cowherd runs up in her shabby dress and says that she has waited long for us, and she is glad that we have arrived. I not only believe, but cannot help believing, that all the world is happy. Auntie is happy while asking Matryona with concern about her daughters, the dogs are happy . . . the hens, the roosters, the peasant children are happy, the horses are happy, and the calves, the fish in the pond, and the birds in the trees are happy."

On another occasion, Lyovochka's father calls upon him to make up a charade for the company (he was unusually adept at charades). He promptly obliged by combining a letter of the alphabet with those of the word for a bird, which together spell out a "small house."[4] "While I am speaking they look and smile at me, and I know, I feel, that these smiles do not mean that there is something ridiculous in me or in my speech; they mean that while looking at me they love me. I feel this, and there is ecstatic joy in my soul."

Despite his uncommon sensibility, hair-trigger emotions, and a certain shyness, Lyovochka did not shirk the rough-and-tumble world of his three older brothers. "Lyovochka the bubble"—so they called him because of his stoutness as a child—took part in all their games and fought pillow fights with gusto. Indeed, it was his endless high spirits and intense enjoyment of life that seemed to set him apart as a child. He was like a ray of light, his sister Marya said. He would dash into a room with a happy smile, as if he wished to tell everyone about a new discovery he had just made. And she related that he was fond of jests, always tender, kind, yielding, and never rude. If he were petted, tears of joy would come into his eyes.

[4] He joins the Russian letter *b* to the word for "duck" (*utka*), which results in *budka,* "a booth" or "small house."

IV

"The Desert of My Boyhood"

On a fine January day in 1837, the family *brichka* and calash stood at the front door of the manor house at Yasnaya Polyana. The commotion attendant upon preparations for a long journey reigned throughout the house. Servants ran hither and thither, angrily shouting directions to each other, lugging boxes and portmanteaus and piling them on the vehicles. A motley group of barefoot children and peasant women, with striped kerchiefs on their heads and babies in their arms, stood around the porch and watched the packing with vagrant curiosity. Coachmen greased the *brichka* and hungry dogs furtively licked the smears on the wheel hubs. Finally, all was ready. Members of the family and domestics assembled in the large living room for the traditional minute of silence before departure. Father Tolstoy, Grandmother, Aunt Alexandra, Auntie Tatyana, and all the children filed through rows of servants to receive their tearful farewells and customary kisses on the shoulder. Then with much crowding they arranged themselves in the vehicles. Little Lyovochka, with tears in his eyes, tenderly kissed the muzzle of his favorite dog, Milka, and got into the calash with his father. The coachman cracked his whip and they were off, down through the birch-tree avenue, past the whitewashed brick towers, and out on the open road to Moscow.

The oldest son, Nikolai, was now fourteen, and the time had come to think of preparing him for the university. This required special tutoring that could be obtained only in the city. Besides, the other brothers were rapidly nearing an age when the elementary instruction of Fyodor Ivanovich would not be sufficient for their proper educational training.

For the irrepressible Lyovochka this first venture into the great world beyond the towered gates was a memorable event. The road was a child's story book of scenes and people foreign to his sheltered existence. Stolid-faced pilgrims with knapsacks of birch bark on their backs, legs swathed in dirty bands, and heavy bast shoes on their feet trudged by, their staffs swinging in a rhythmical up-and-down movement. They scarcely looked at him, and he wondered where they were going and why. A carefree postboy riding past and drawling a song suddenly convinced him that a postboy's life must be the height of happiness. The red scarified stump of a beggar's outstretched arm frightened him; and he was puzzled by the contemptuous look of a carter who whipped his shuffling horse past the calash. The family put up at inns and villages on the way, and no one paid the slightest attention to them. All this strange indifference worried Lyovochka. At last they approached Moscow with the golden cupolas of its forty times forty churches gleaming in the distance, and his father proudly pointed out to him the famous buildings of the city.

The sudden awareness in the life of a child that his family was really not the center of the universe now for the first time came to Lyovochka. The villages and towns through which he had passed teemed with people who did not even know that he existed. Peasants failed to smile and bow, as at Yasnaya Polyana, and often they did not even bother to notice him. He began to wonder what could possibly interest all these people if they did not care about him and his father, grandmother, and aunts. This thought led him to speculate on how these strange people lived. Who taught their children? And how were they punished? The walls of his own childhood world at Yasnaya Polyana had finally crumbled and new horizons loomed in the distance.

2

The family rented a large and expensive house in Moscow. Lyovochka now saw very little of his father, but he took long interesting walks about the unfamiliar streets with Fyodor Ivanovich. On one of these strolls the children wandered into a beautiful private garden. With its formal flower beds, pond, and fountains, it seemed like a veritable fairyland. The owner, who chanced to encounter the youngsters in their unsuspecting trespass, was so pleased with their enthusiasm that he guided them around and then invited them to come again. On their second visit, however, they were met by a caretaker who brusquely ordered them away. Tolstoy recalled the incident as one that aroused in his young mind a sense of the injustice and cruelty of people with authority.

In the summer father Tolstoy went to Tula on business. On the way to visit his friend Temyashyov, he suddenly fell dead in the street. The theft of papers and money on his person led to the suspicion that he had been murdered by the handsome Petrushka and Matyushka, the two servants who had accompanied him on the trip. (A mysterious beggar subsequently restored the papers to the family in Moscow.) At that time it was not an unheard-of thing for serfs to kill and rob their masters. In the midst of family grief and distraction these suspicions were never pursued and the body was removed to Yasnaya Polyana for burial.

Nine-year-old Lyovochka's thoughts were strangely confused. Only after his father's death did he begin to realize how much he had loved him, and the event awoke in his sensitive mind a feeling of religious horror before the eternal questions of life and death. For some time, perhaps because he had not seen him dead, he refused to believe that his father no longer existed. While walking in the Moscow streets, he hoped for a long time that the next man he met would be his father. When he grew sad over his loss, it was largely in imitation of the grief of the grownups; and this sadness also seemed to endow him with a special importance that he valued. He rather enjoyed hearing people say of him that he was now a poor and unfortunate orphan.

Grandmother Tolstoy continually mourned the death of her son. Excessive grief unhinged her mind at times, and she imagined that she saw him in a neighboring room and held long conversations with him. Her health was undermined and she fell dangerously ill. Lyovochka and his brothers and sister were led into Grandmother's room to take their farewell of her. She lay on a high white bed, clothed all in white, and he felt only repulsion when he kissed her still white hand, so swollen that it looked like a pillow.

Grandmother's serious illness did not act as a damper on the fun-loving Tolstoy children. One day, some eleven months after the death of their father, the brothers were in high spirits over the visit of their comrade Volodenka Milyutin. In honor of the guest, Lyovochka, Dmitri, and Sergei invented a curious kind of entertainment. They collected a lot of paper and proceeded to burn it, with noisy merriment, in the chamber pots. When the conflagration was at its height, their tutor dashed into the room, his face pale and his lower lip trembling. Instead of the expected scolding, he solemnly announced to the crestfallen boys: "Your grandmother is dead!"

This second loss in the family in less than a year awakened in Lyovochka a depressing fear of death. Grandmother's corpse reminded him vividly and unpleasantly of the fact that he too must die some day. But the sad sight of her in the coffin, with her stern face and aquiline nose, and the grief of the various mourners, were compensated somewhat in his eyes by the fine new jacket of black material braided with white that was bestowed on him for the occasion of the funeral. And it pleased him, as when his father had died, to overhear the conversation of gossiping female guests who said: "Complete orphans; their father only lately dead, and now the grandmother gone too!"

3

Death worked its swift changes on the diminishing household. Saintlike Aunt Alexandra now became legal guardian of the children. Expenses had to be cut, for the family property was placed in trust. On their walks the children were assigned the interesting task, which quickly turned into a game, of spotting "to let" signs. Lyovochka won. The apartment he discovered delighted the children, in the sense that miniatures always fascinate the young: its five small rooms seemed so cozy and intimate compared to the huge rambling houses they had lived in. And they were captivated by a mysterious machine in the courtyard driven by a horse that wearily plodded in an endless circle. Lyovochka took a more sober view of the novelty of straitened circumstances when he observed that the Tolstoy children received cheap presents at a Christmas party to which they had been invited, whereas his rich Gorchakov cousins were given expensive gifts.

Family reverses, however, did not relieve the Tolstoy

brothers of the onerous burden of education. Shortly after their arrival in Moscow a rather foppish Frenchman, Prosper Saint-Thomas, was engaged as their new tutor. He had none of the kindly, generous qualities of humble Fyodor Ivanovich. Lyovochka was soon keenly aware of the difference and his relations with the new tutor left a very unpleasant and ineffaceable impression on him. As a pedagogue, Saint-Thomas was rather well-informed and fulfilled his duties conscientiously. As an individual, he possessed exactly those traits—frivolous egotism, vanity, insolence, and ignorant self-confidence—that were calculated to arouse his pupil's antipathy. Lyovochka at once recognized in the handsome young Frenchman a hidden contempt for these "barbaric" Russians on whom he was obliged to waste his polished manners and cultural superiority.

Saint-Thomas failed utterly to understand the kind, loving, but essentially proud character of the boy. A climax was quickly reached in their relations over the tutor's threat to whip him. It was not fear that aroused Lyovochka's fury. Firmly rooted in him, even as a child, was the conviction that physical violence terribly humiliates one's human dignity and pride. He rebelled against the very thought of corporal punishment. How deeply this not uncommon childhood experience burned itself into his memory and affected his sensibilities may be gauged by his remarks about it almost seventy years later: "I now do not remember the reason for it, but I thought that it was a most undeserved punishment for Saint-Thomas, first to lock me up in a room, and then to threaten me with the rod. I experienced a terrible feeling of indignation, revolt, and aversion not only to Saint-Thomas, but towards that violence which he wished to exercise on me. This occasion was perhaps one reason for that horror and aversion for every kind of violence which I have felt throughout my whole life."

There has been a tendency to magnify the importance of this episode, as though as a child Tolstoy suffered a psychological hurt that left a permanent scar on his psyche. Nevertheless, not only had he been humiliated and his pride injured, but as he sat in the dark behind locked doors and listened to the merrymaking of his brothers downstairs, he was overwhelmed by the thought that he was an outcast whom nobody in the whole world loved. It was a terrifying thought for a boy of his loving nature.

4

Lyovochka's student existence at this time fortunately did not degenerate into that of the well-birched English schoolboy. Saint-Thomas, if not his pupil, learned a lesson from this first threat which was never repeated. Henceforth he buttered the self-esteem that always lurked beneath the apparent indifference of Lyovochka. He flattered his "*petit Léon*" with having a fine head, with being a "*petit Molière*"; and at the proper moments he could not restrain a "*quel homme il sera!*" And Léon's studied contempt gradually waned; he began to think that this French dandy, despite his faults, was not such a bad fellow after all. Here the little devil of vanity that he was to fight all his life raised its head.

It was the custom to supplement a tutor's efforts with lessons from professors or university students in special subjects, such as history and mathematics. One of these student teachers summed up the capacities of three of the brothers for learning and Tolstoy commented on the judgment: "Sergei both wishes to and can, Dmitri wishes to but can't (that was not true), and Leo neither wishes to nor can (that I think was perfectly correct)." More modesty than truth is implicit in his agreement with the judgment on himself. The genius likes to fancy himself as unsuited to conventional education. Tolstoy was a poor student only when he elected to be, which was most of the time during his boyhood and youth. His assimilative powers were prodigious, but one aspect of his knotty originality was his refusal to assimilate unless his intellectual curiosity were aroused. Conventional educational methods failed to stimulate him as a boy, and this fact had a direct bearing on his remarkable experiments in education later.

Certainly the combined efforts of various teachers seem to have made little impression on Lyovochka from the age of eight to thirteen. The reading that influenced him most over this period, which he has listed, could hardly be regarded as choice pabulum for a child prodigy. It consists of the story of Joseph from the Bible, "The Forty Thieves" and "Prince Camaralzaman" from *The Thousand and One Nights,* certain Russian folk poems, Pogorelski's popular story "The Black Hen," Russian folk tales, and Pushkin's poetry, especially "Napoleon."

Some of his schoolboy exercises have been salvaged and published recently in Russia. Two of them are fables of Krylov that he appears to have written down from memory immediately after they had been read to him. The results reveal an excellent memory and something of that preference, so striking in his later literary work, for the simplest mode of expression. Then there are those eternal boyhood compositions on "Day," "Night," "Autumn," and "Spring"; they never reveal anything except clichés of observation and mistakes in spelling which, in this instance, not even his teachers seemed competent enough to detect. Several descriptive and historical exercises are more interesting. "The Kremlin" and "Love of the Fatherland" (in French) betray the mawkish patriotism—so repugnant to him later—that was part of the educational pattern in those days.

Lyovochka's earliest attempt at poetry, "To My Dear Auntie," written when he was twelve in honor of Auntie Tatyana's name-day, is among these rescued exercises.[1] This poem has no merit as verse, but is perhaps worth translating because it provides further evidence of his unusually deep feeling for this important person in his life:—

The joyous wished-for day has come,
And I can prove to you with glee,
That I was not a silent child,
When mother used to fondle me.

And now I clearly understand:
All that you've done I've kept in mind;
You sacrificed yourself for us
With heart and soul so good and kind.

I understand now all the joy
Of which this day for us is part;
That God may bless you for your deeds,
I wish it now with all my heart.

Perhaps to look upon us here
Fortune may once again be sent,
Then joys of former days will come,
And we shall live in sweet content.

I as a pledge of happy days
Accept this day with rapture dear;
For you I wish your stream of life
May always be both bright and clear.

[1] The account of Nikolai's poetical efforts in *Childhood* in honor of Grandmother's name-day is no doubt based on Tolstoy's memory of his labors over this poem for Auntie Tatyana.

5

The kind of activity that went on in Lyovochka's mind while he was doing poorly in his dull lessons would have astonished his uninspired teachers. It is no secret that children stumble upon the eternal contradictions that lie at the basis of mature philosophies. The average child, however, asks his wondering questions about man's destiny, the soul, the future life, or ultimate happiness and goes on his cheerful way, satisfied or dissatisfied with the labored answers of harassed parents. Lyovochka did not follow this customary procedure. His original mind obliged him to work out his own solutions to abstract problems, and more striking still, to attempt to put his solutions into practice.[2]

The idea occurred to Lyovochka that happiness depends solely upon our relation to external causes. It follows naturally that, if man can accustom himself to endure suffering, he can never be unhappy. No sooner was the conclusion reached than the budding philosopher attempted to practice it. In order to inure himself to severe pain, he would hold a large dictionary at arm's length for five minutes at a time, or go into the storeroom and lash his bare back so painfully that tears came to his eyes.

As might be expected, this Spartan treatment soon lost its charm, but meanwhile the incorrigible sage had adopted another theory that was a positive pleasure to subscribe to in practice. He suddenly remembered that death awaited him at any moment, and he wondered why people had not realized the obvious fact that they can be happy simply by enjoying the present and not thinking of the future. So for three whole days he completely forgot his hated lessons and did nothing but lie on his bed, reading a thrilling novel and munching gingerbread made with honey, on which he had spent his last kopek.

Lyovochka's abstract propositions were not always so easily resolved or their resolution so delightful to practice. The question of symmetry led him by a swift but illogical transition to a contemplation of eternity. He reasoned that there must be something to balance eternity after death. His conclusion was that man must have existed somewhere before life was given to him, only he has lost all recollection of this previous existence. As he gazed out of the window,

[2] In *Boyhood*, Tolstoy's account of the meditation of young Nikolai is largely autobiographical.

trying to collect his thoughts on this novel idea before expounding it on paper, he caught sight of a horse in the courtyard. At once a tangential question popped into his head: What animal or man would the horse's soul enter into after it died? An older brother coming into the room at that point and smiling at his frowning concentration was sufficient to convince him that he was thinking nonsense.

This measure of humility did not prevent Lyovochka from becoming at times a stuffy little pundit. He grew vain over his philosophical powers and often imagined himself on the road to fame, pointing out new truths for the benefit of humanity. It is a curious but understandable psychological fact, however, that the more he flattered his self-esteem in this respect, the more shy he grew about parading his worth before less favored mortals. In the end, the young philosopher blushed, stammered, and became ashamed of his simplest words and ideas in the presence of others.

Religion, that indispensable subject of young and old philosophers, and one that was to play such a significant part in Tolstoy's mature thinking, was accorded little notice in his boyhood meditations. Lyovochka had been brought up in an atmosphere of female devotion to Russian Orthodoxy and dutifully said his prayers morning and night. But the seeds of faith do not appear to have been planted deeply. At best, he accepted religion perfunctorily as a kind of family tradition, the explanation of which had long since been lost. When Saint-Thomas had locked him up in the storeroom, his anguished thoughts dwelt upon God, but then only to question the justice of His Providence.

Years later, in his famous *Confession,* he recalled that at this time—he was about nine or ten—the boyhood friend of the Tolstoy brothers, Volodenka Milyutin, burst in one Sunday to announce that he had discovered a great secret in the *Gymnasium* where he studied. The secret was that God did not exist, and that everything taught about Him was a mere fiction. The older brothers took counsel with their young philosopher Lyovochka over this astounding bit of news, and they came to the conclusion that it was most interesting and very likely correct.

6

Things of the mind and spirit did not lessen Lyovochka's capacity for boyish fun and adventure, although failure to adjust himself to the changed conditions of his life over this period often soured his enjoyment. The new world of long pants and shoulder straps had to be explored; new acquaintances had to be tried by the exacting tests of boyhood friendship; and now some mysterious addition to his sensibilities obliged him to look hard at little girls, especially if they were pretty.

That inevitable indication of developing glands began to manifest itself: Lyovochka now grew very self-conscious about his appearance, which probably contributed greatly to his natural shyness. His broad nose, thick lips, small gray eyes, and tufted hair convinced him, and with some justice, that he was positively ugly. There were moments, he admitted to himself as a boy, when he would have given anything in the world for a handsome face. He sucked some small comfort out of a long-remembered compliment that he had a "clever face and a pleasant smile." None the less, he prayed for divine interposition in his misery, but God worked no miracles for him. Meanwhile, he was forced to compete with his more attractive comrades for the coy smiles of their mutual girl acquaintances.

The sexual impulse in Lyovochka awoke early; in a few more years it would rage lustily, to his alternate delight and disgust. He was only nine when he pushed down the stairs at Yasnaya Polyana Alexander Islenev's daughter (his future mother-in-law), because this favored girl was not paying sufficient attention to him.

Pretty house serfs were often both the innocent and the guilty initiators of Russian boys into the higher mysteries of love. And Lyovochka indulged in peeping-Tom activities directed against the women's servant quarters. But when he was asked, as an old man, about his early "loves," his first and most intense love, he said, was for little Sonya Koloshin. He told in *Childhood* how Nikolai (Lyovochka) went to bed after a children's party and saw in the dark his charming Sonya with her large, lustrous eyes and shapely mouth, and he conversed with her in his imagination, using to his indescribable pleasure the intimate *thou* that he had been unable to say, despite her request, in talking to her that day. Unwilling to keep his secret, he woke his brother to tell him of his love, only to make the joyful discovery that he too loved Sonya (he wished all to love her).

But when the older brother translated his affection into terms of a desire to kiss Sonya's little fingers, eyes, lips, nose, feet, and all of her, Nikolai was deeply wounded. The pure white poetic image was distorted by this realistic fleshly touch, and he wept from sheer mortification. With this incident of boyhood love still green in his memory, Tolstoy jotted down in his diary, at the age of sixty-two: "I have been thinking of writing a novel of love—chaste love as with S. Koloshin—, in which a transition to sensuality is impossible and which serves as the best protection against sensuality." Unfortunately, this projected novel was never written.

7

Lyovochka's earnest desire for love and friendship met with little success among his playmates. Shyness and an unattractive appearance were not the only reasons. As the youngest of four brothers, he was continually placed in a position of inferiority. Always the "baby" to them and their playmates, an equality of friendship was denied him. They became heroes, not friends, when the need to love demanded expression.

On the whole, Lyovochka's boyhood was a lonely one, singularly lacking in attachments. Proud as he was, erratic, impulsive, conscious of his own worth, and already inclined to a discriminating analysis of people, his affectionate nature was turned in upon itself. He grew introspective, and much of the time he lived in a heroic world of his own creation.

Often, as he gazed out of the window during the study hour, ambitious fancies crowded his imagination. Most of them involved an abrupt change that would separate him from his family. Lessons in fencing and horseback riding, and playing at soldiers, turned his thoughts to the army. He would be a hussar. Generals would see how brave he was and lavish decorations on him. While sitting in the dark storeroom, awaiting the threatened whipping from his tutor, he saw himself free and in the colorful uniform of a hussar. He slashed away endlessly at the enemy with his saber, and finally, shouting "Victory!" he fell exhausted from his wounds. The scene quickly shifted. With his arm in a black silk sling, he strutted along the fashionable Tverskoi Boulevard in Moscow. The Emperor saw him and asked his aide about this remarkable-looking young man. When he learned of his deeds, the Emperor thanked him personally and offered him his favor. Leaning on his saber, the young hero protested his willingness to die for the fatherland on any occasion, and he demanded only one reward for his services: the privilege of slaughtering his tutor. The request was graciously granted, and he seized the hapless wretch. *"À genoux!"* he cried, only to be brought back to reality by the thought that at any moment his tutor might be in with the rod.

When the Emperor actually visited Moscow to lay the foundation stone of the Cathedral of Our Saviour, for two days Lyovochka was in a state of dizzying excitement. He flatly refused to study. Admonishments and threats were useless. Somehow, he felt, the radical change in his life was about to take place. He rushed along with the mobs to the Kremlin, and in the press had his foot run over by a carriage. But he continued to push and shout "Hurrah!" And when the monarch bowed to the crowds, Lyovochka happily felt that the salutation had been directed at him.[3] No less was he stirred by the sound of the galloping fire engines. He desired to dash out of the house and save someone heroically, and thus elevate himself in the eyes of all and change his whole life.

Some of Lyovochka's bizarre boyhood actions were no doubt a form of compensatory exhibitionism, for oddities of behavior often find their inspiration in an imaginary heroic existence. Original he certainly was, but when he entered a drawing room and carefully made his bow backwards, saluting each of the company in turn, we have the kind of originality that is prompted by the desire to center attention upon one's self. On the same order is his shaving off his eyebrows, although in this instance he was being quite rational. The hero of a novel he admired had bushy eyebrows, and Lyovochka hoped that his would grow in thick after the shaving. So they did. Another shaving incident lacked any rationale. While the horses were being changed on a journey, he disappeared from the carriage. When all was in readiness, they called for him. He stuck his head out of the station window and shouted that he would be right along. To his aunt's astonishment and chagrin, his head was half shaved.

Lyovochka's most striking bid for attention, however, almost ended fatally for him. While members of the family

[3] Tolstoy perhaps drew upon this experience in describing young Petya Rostov's attempt to see the Emperor in *War and Peace.*

in the dining room below were wondering what kept him from dinner, he was poised on the window sill of the study room upstairs. He was deeply concerned at this time with man's ability to fly, but mechanical means or the law of gravity had somehow been left out of his calculations. For he was convinced that he could fly by sitting down on his heels, clasping his arms firmly around his knees, and jumping off into space.[4] He took off, fell to the courtyard some eighteen feet below, and was picked up unconscious, fortunately suffering only a slight concussion. After a long sleep, he woke up as healthy as ever.

8

All of Lyovochka's boyhood years between 1837 and 1841 were not spent in Moscow. With the exception of 1837, the family moved to Yasnaya Polyana for the summer months. And after Grandmother's death in 1838, the children were separated for reasons of economy: the two older brothers, Nikolai and Sergei, remained at their more advanced studies in Moscow under the care of Aunt Alexandra; Dmitri, Lyovochka, and Masha stayed with Auntie Tatyana in the country, where their education was continued by transient tutors and seminarists. In the autumn and winter of 1840–1841, however, the whole family was reunited in Moscow. Financial difficulties were increased by the famine of 1840. A small property had to be sold in order to buy wheat to feed their own serfs. The children, feeling sorry for their lean ponies, stole oats from the peasants without the slightest notion that they were doing wrong.

The family had again assembled at Yasnaya Polyana for the summer of 1841. In August came the shocking news that their beloved and deeply religious Aunt Alexandra had died at the famous Kaluga hermitage founded by the fourteenth-century robber chief Optin. Auntie Tatyana at once set out for the hermitage, and the children were left in charge of their old tutor Fyodor Ivanovich and the half-mad religious fanatic, Marya Gerasimovna. They amused themselves with building a lofty throne for their dog. But the animal objected to this signal honor, jumped off its throne, and hurt its paw. The children accompanied the howling of the dog with their own wailing, and all the

[4] Tolstoy puts exactly the same notion of flying into Natasha's mind in *War and Peace,* only she does not actually jump.

while Marya Gerasimovna in the next room monotonously intoned psalms in honor of the dead. This strange scene fixed itself in Lyovochka's memory in connection with the news of his aunt's death, for whom, as the family poet, he wrote an epitaph:—

An unknown road hast thou traveled
In leaving this earth and its strife;
An envied quiet hast thou found
In the cloisters of heavenly life.
With hope of a future meeting
In that bourne beyond the grave,
Thy nephews honor thine ashes
And thy sacred memory save.

After the death of Aunt Alexandra, the guardianship of the children fell upon her younger sister, Aunt Pelageya Ilyinichna Yushkov, who lived in Kazan. She hastened to Moscow and heard the plea of the older brother, Nikolai, who was now in the first year of the university, not to desert them. Aunt Pelageya shed ready tears over the orphans and declared her willingness to "sacrifice herself." Her immediate decision was that they should all go to Kazan.

PART TWO

"In the Service

of Ambition, Vanity,

and, Above All, of Lust'

V

University Years

WHEN Aunt Pelageya finished appropriating "necessities" for the journey and the future existence of the Tolstoy children at Kazan, Yasnaya Polyana looked as though the Golden Horde had ravaged it. An immense amount of household equipment, and carpenters, tailors, mechanics, cooks, and upholsterers from among the skilled serfs were sent on ahead. The "complete orphans" with their various attendants and staples for the road set out accompanied by a long train of carriages and carts. The brothers grieved at parting with Auntie Tatyana. Their "second mother's" love and long service gave her a stronger moral claim to the children than that of their legal guardian, who always treated her with polite hostility. Aunt Pelageya could never forget that Auntie Tatyana, in her youth, had received a proposal from her husband, who still spoke with enthusiasm of *"Toinette,"* and indiscreetly recalled before his wife how *"elle était charmante!"* Auntie Tatyana's love for her nurslings, however, never wavered in the face of this meanness or of the long separation from them.

For the children the trip to Kazan in September 1841 was a prolonged picnic. They halted frequently in the woods and fields on the way, gathered mushrooms, and bathed in the streams and ponds. On one occasion Lyovochka's urge to be original got the better of him again. When the coachman stopped to adjust the harness, he leaped out of the carriage and dashed ahead at full speed. Every time they attempted to catch up with him, he strained himself to the utmost, and the carriage overtook him only when he was a thoroughly exhausted youngster.

The happy travelers finally reached Kazan and were all lodged in the spacious Yushkov house. Kazan, a thriving old river port, mellowed with an ancient history of fierce Tatar-Russian strife, was at that time a town of less than a hundred thousand inhabitants. Mongol influences still waged an equal battle with Slavic, and a typically small-town society tried desperately to assume metropolitan airs and culture.[1] Here Lyovochka was to spend the next five and a half years of his life.

Through their connections with the Yushkovs, the Tolstoy brothers had a clear title to membership in the ultra-aristocratic society of Kazan. Aunt Pelageya's vanity, dearth of brains, and excessive sentimentality were somewhat compensated for by kindness and a deep but conventional religious feeling that eventually led her to retire to a nunnery. There was nothing religious about her husband, a well-to-do landowner. His dignified black mustache, whiskers, and spectacles gave an air of respectability to the satyr-like traits of his nature, but his weakness for the fair sex ultimately brought about a separation from his wife.

As she was the daughter of a former governor of the province, even though his memory was not exactly venerated by the local citizenry, Aunt Pelageya's house was one of the social centers of the town, and she cultivated only the "very best" people. With such an experienced preceptress, the Tolstoy boys were soon much in demand in the beau monde, quite a new experience for them.

The immediate problem was the brothers' future education, one of the reasons for coming to Kazan. The town boasted an excellent university, not on a par with those of Petersburg and Moscow, but sufficiently reputable to attract scholars from Western Europe. Nikolai had failed promotion at the end of his second year at Moscow University, and he transferred to the Philosophy Faculty at Kazan. Two years later (1843), Sergei and Dmitri matriculated in the same field.

Meanwhile Lyovochka, too young to enter the university, had plenty of leisure to contemplate a career. His slight experience with formal education did not whet his appetite for more. Conventional book knowledge seemed an unnecessary obstacle to his grandiose schemes for the future. Aunt Pelageya, who sincerely wished his happiness, offered him a variety of advice. He ought to plan his career, she

[1] Kazan is now the principal city of the Tatar Autonomous Socialist Soviet Republic, and has a population of about 180,000.

said, so as to become an aide-de-camp, and preferably an aide-de-camp to the Emperor.

Her greatest joy, however, would be to see him married to an heiress and the owner of as many serfs as possible. Soon this religiously minded but worldly lady, herself the purest of beings, Tolstoy declared, strongly urged him to have relations with a married woman, on the principle that "nothing so forms a young man as an intimacy with a woman of good breeding."

Not all of this well-intentioned counsel was wasted, but still the university inevitably loomed up before Lyovochka, like some desert through which he must pass in order to reach green fields beyond. For he accepted his aunt's final advice to enter the university with the notion of preparing for a diplomatic career. Perhaps his decision was partly influenced by the fact that he would have to attend the Faculty of Oriental Languages, one of the most difficult and distinguished fields in the university.

Lyovochka busily set to work, under the general supervision of Saint-Thomas, who had come to Kazan with the family, to prepare himself for the entrance examinations. Special teachers were employed, and he studied Arabic and Turko-Tatar languages in the Kazan Gymnasium. Finally, in 1844, he was ready for the eventful May 29, when he would take his first test to prove his fitness to enter the university.

2

Saint-Thomas accompanied his tutee to the examination hall. They drove up in a phaeton behind a smart trotter, as befitted the occasion. The sixteen-year-old Lyovochka, arrayed in dazzling white linen and a dress coat that he wore for the first time, was a model of sartorial perfection. As he glanced around at the comparatively shabby appearance of most of his fellow candidates, he grew self-conscious and ashamed of his conspicuous attire, and quickly took refuge in a feeling of superiority.

The first examination was in religion. That very morning he had walked along the shore of the lake, alternately reading his catechism for this examination and praying to God to help him pass it. And the thought had suddenly flashed through his mind that everything in the catechism was a lie. Fortunately, the good Archimandrite Gabriel who questioned him knew nothing of this momentary apostasy. Besides, he had a reputation as an easy examiner, and Lyovochka experienced no difficulty in receiving a strong "four."[2] The next day's tests, however, jarred his self-confidence badly. His average in universal and Russian history was a flat "one," but then history had always seemed a "most boresome and laborious subject" to the future writer of historical fiction. Nor did the "one" he earned in geography and statistics appear very auspicious in the light of his projected career. The future diplomat, when asked to name the ports of France, could not think of a single city. Yet in such difficult subjects as Arabic and Turko-Tatar he did brilliantly, and in French he distinguished himself with a "five plus." In German also, perhaps thanks to the persistent efforts of kind Fyodor Ivanovich, he obtained a "five," and in English a "four." But his dismal work in history, geography, and statistics, along with a wretched "two" in Latin, proved to be fatal; the dreaded "refused" appeared on his final report.

Lyovochka did not allow failure to discourage him on this occasion, for a hankering after the special privileges and gay social life of the university student had taken possession of him. He applied for re-examination in the flunked subjects, and a little application enabled him to pass them. In the autumn of 1844 he matriculated at Kazan University.

At last a "man," no longer under the thumb of a tutor, Leo Tolstoy eagerly looked forward to joining the great and noble company of scholars. With a feeling of elation he dressed in his new student uniform, with its glittering gilt buttons, cocked hat, and a sword on his left hip; he received his own allowance and a trap with a spirited brown trotter for his private use. He also took up smoking, which was then the height of fashion for a young dandy. With money in his pocket and joy in his heart, he drove to his first class, hoping to meet a policeman on the way who would honor him with the customary salute to a student.

Tolstoy's initial enthusiasm for the university quickly diminished as his interest in the social aspects of student life increased. Often he failed to attend lectures, and at the midterm examinations he did so badly that permission to return was denied him. This failure was more of a shock than he

[2] Grading was on the basis of five to one, and would correspond roughly to our system of A to E: A = 5; B = 4; C = 3; D = 2; E = 1.

cared to admit. The glamour of his new uniform had not worn off. Nikolai had graduated in 1844, and Sergei and Dmitri, although not brilliant, had been advanced to the third year. At the moment he wished to emulate his brothers. A happy alternative was suggested: he could forget his diplomatic career and transfer to the Faculty of Jurisprudence. Had not all his lazy aristocratic acquaintances entered this field? It was notoriously easy; "a man must be a fool who cannot be a jurist" was the way the students dismissed it. At the beginning of the next academic year (1845), Tolstoy was safely established in the Faculty of Jurisprudence.

This faculty was the scandal of the university and an ancient object of student ridicule. Its professors were mostly crotchety German pedants who mangled the Russian language and achieved that pitiful kind of academic individualism acquired by practicing all manner of eccentricities. Students from various faculties went to their lectures simply to be amused by their queer behavior. They would uproariously applaud funny Professor Kambeck, who would begin his course every year by shouting in atrocious Russian: "Roman Law! A capital *R*! A capital *L*! And also a period!"

Despite the prevailing atmosphere of levity in his new faculty, Tolstoy began, for the first time, to take a serious interest in his studies. A few of the subjects, especially criminal law, inspired him to make some effort, and he attended with regularity the lectures of one or two of the most brilliant professors. Although he did poorly in the midyear examinations, he acquitted himself very well in the finals and was advanced to the second year. For one with his intellectual interests, however, the third-rate Faculty of Jurisprudence offered little mental stimulation, nor could it compete with his passion for social activity.

3

The aristocratic set that Tolstoy frequented in Kazan society was fabulous for its hospitality. Invitations were unnecessary in this closed circle. Friends visited each other freely, remained for dinner, chatted, and went home for a brief rest. In the evening they would be off to a ball, theater, or concert, at the conclusion of which a Lucullan-like feast was sure to be served at someone's house. Guests rarely left before five or six in the morning, slept till noon, and began the whole procedure over again.

As an eligible, titled young bachelor, with the best of connections, Tolstoy was much sought after in this society. The three brothers (Nikolai had entered the army in 1844) had by now taken an apartment of their own and lived in style. Each had a serving boy, a luxury that Aunt Pelageya had foolishly insisted upon. With characteristic aplomb, Tolstoy had already classified society and determined his exact relation to each division. People fell into two broad classes: *comme il faut* and *comme il ne faut pas.* Inherent snobbery dictated the classification and his own preference. Like Sergei, he wished to belong to those who were *comme il faut,* for they spoke excellent French, always had clean nails, and knew how to bow, dance, and converse with ease. What he most admired in this social class was its indifference to everything and its constant expression of elegant and contemptuous ennui. All others were merely boors, common, and besides, they wore untidy boots, a fault he could not abide.[8]

Although to be *comme il faut* seemed to him the height of human perfection, young Tolstoy had a positive incapacity for it. His failure caused him endless grief at this time. Much of the effort that should have been expended on studies was devoted to acquiring those graces which would enable him to shine at the dinner parties and balls of Kazan aristocracy. One look in the mirror would upset all his hopes. The face of a simple peasant stared back at him, and his big hands and feet seemed downright shameful. His muscular physique (he was practicing gymnastics daily in the hope of becoming the strongest man in the world) was not well-proportioned, and clothes somehow never set him off as neatly as they did Sergei.

Tolstoy tried to make a virtue of such handicaps, and when this failed, he took refuge in queer and original behavior, the customary retreat of the social misfit. To be outstanding was his aim; if he could not gain attention by natural graces, he would do it by calculated rudeness. When all talked, he was haughtily silent. If he elected to speak, he eschewed the usual empty compliments of fine society and endeavored to impress people by a certain impolite frankness. "Old inhabitants of Kazan," writes one of them,

[8] Tolstoy devotes Chapter XXXI of Youth to his adolescent fervor to be *comme il faut.*

"remember him at all the balls, evening parties, and gatherings of fashionable society, invited everywhere, always dancing, but not in the least pleasing to these worldly ladies as were his rivals among the aristocratic students; they always observed in him a stiffness and self-consciousness." One of his rivals remarked: "We called him the 'bear,' the 'philosopher' Lyovochka, awkward and always embarrassed."

The "bear" was a highly sensitive young animal, however, and his failure to achieve social success pained him deeply. As a participant in fashionable spectacles, where some talent rather than *politesse* was in demand, Tolstoy appears to have done well. The local newspaper records that he and Sergei acted in amateur theatricals staged at the vice-governor's on behalf of the orphaned children of Kazan.

On another charitable occasion, at the university auditorium, with all the town's notables present, Tolstoy took an important part in one of a series of *tableaux vivants,* entitled "The Suitor's Proposal." With the usual fondness of the small-town newspaper for unnecessary detail, the reporter describes the scene:—

> The old fisherman caught the young man in his net and presented him to his daughter. The sturdy simpleton (Count L. N. Tolstoy) respectfully stood erect, placing his hands behind his back. He posed. . . . The father chucked him under the chin, and with a naïvely cunning smile exchanged glances with his daughter, who in confusion lowered her eyes. The effect of this picture was extraordinary,—three times the audience demanded its repetition, and for a long time they thundered with applause. Best of all in the tableau was A. A. de Plani (lecturer in French); extremely unaffected was also the suitor, Count L. N. Tolstoy.

4

Success with fashionable ladies was one of the requisites of being truly *comme il faut.* Here again Tolstoy bungled. Marriageable girls in Kazan high society found him a rather boring cavalier and a poor dancer. One of them, Zinaida Molostvov, especially caught his fancy, but he had courage to admire her only from across the room. His shyness, alternating with moments of boorish behavior and bursts of conversation that was intended to be strikingly original, bewildered and even frightened these young things.

If he were inclined to put into practice his aunt's advice to form a liaison with a fashionable married woman, he would have been unable to survive the preliminaries of introduction. He ogled the ladies of quality from a safe distance, fell in love, and imagined scenes of delightful intimacies with them. But even the offer of an introduction to one of these intended victims terrified him, as though he were convinced that by mere acquaintance she would at once become aware of all his shameful thoughts. To his inordinately shy mind these fine ladies seemed clothed in impregnable triple bronze. How he wished to be like that Lovelace of a brother, Sergei, who seemed able to take with an easy grace all the good things that life offered him.

Yet Tolstoy's passions in his youth, as always, ran high. And the morals of young men of the gentry were, by prescription, singularly unconstrained. Wild oats were to be sown early under the common delusion that they would not have to be sown again. If Tolstoy's unattractive appearance and gauche manners could not win him success among Kazan's marriageable girls or women of quality, then he would take the other way.

Not much is known about Tolstoy's relations with loose women during his Kazan existence, but bitter references to them later suggest that his experiences made a deep impression on him. In dividing the years of his life for biographical purposes, he described the first period of "innocent, joyous, poetic childhood up to fourteen; then the terrible twenty years that followed—a period of coarse dissoluteness, employed in the service of ambition, vanity, and, above all, of lust."

When Tolstoy was only fourteen, Masha, a servant maid in Aunt Pelageya's house, aroused desires of which he was ashamed. Shortly after this he appears to have overcome his timidity. For Gusev once heard from Tolstoy's close friend, Marya Alexandrovna Schmidt, an interesting account of his first sexual experience. When he was writing *Resurrection,* his wife sharply criticized him for the chapter in which he described the seduction of Katyusha. "As an old man," she scolded, "aren't you ashamed to write such nastiness?" Tolstoy made no reply, but when his wife had left the room, he turned to M. A. Schmidt and said, almost in tears: "See how she attacks me, but when my brothers took me for the first time to a brothel and I accomplished this act, I then stood by the woman's bed and wept." In the 1880's he even confessed to a former inhabitant of Kazan that it was in the Kizicheski Monastery[4] of the city that "I had my first downfall."

Fleshly desires were at once alluring and repulsive to the young Tolstoy, but his strong moral repugnance received no encouragement from the dissolute Kazan society that he frequented. Smoking, drinking, gambling, and debauchery were the dress and loose ornament of his dandified comrades, and he admits that much of his waywardness was in imitation of the corrupt behavior he found on every side. Apparently he paid dearly for it, and not merely in moral suffering. For his first diary[5] in 1847 opens: "It is six days since I entered the clinic . . . I've had *gonorrhoea,* had it from that source whence it is customarily obtained."

Immorality is a necessary test of the moral fiber, for the plain distinction between right and wrong has nothing but a theoretical validity unless put to the proof by actual experience. Young as he was, Tolstoy had a highly developed moral sense, and every violation of it caused him infinite heart searching. In his youthful meditations he had already dwelt upon the question of love, as though seeking some idealistic conception that would purify his debauched thoughts. With the pedantic precision of a young philosopher, he neatly divided love into three kinds: beautiful love, self-denying love, and active love.[6] His own ideal for the moment partook of the best qualities of all three, and it gained substance in his dream of an imaginary woman. She had a bit of Sonya Koloshin in her, a dash of the chambermaid Masha as he had seen her washing the linen, and the external charms of a lady with pearls round her white neck whom he had noticed long ago in a box at the theater.

The beautiful vision anchored in his mind and created an inexpressible longing. He sought *her* everywhere, and ex-

[4] The discrepancy in the locale of the act is puzzling. One cannot suppose that the Kizicheski Monastery and the brothel he mentions were one and the same place, despite the amazing stories that have come out of Russia about the debauchery in monasteries. Apparently Tolstoy has confused several experiences of this nature in his youth.

[5] With some interruptions, Tolstoy continued the practice of keeping a diary, as well as various notebooks containing observations, plans, projects, etc., throughout the remainder of his life. This material, of immense biographical importance, is so extensive that it will fill thirteen volumes (with notes) of the Soviet Jubilee Edition of Tolstoy's entire works.

[6] These meditations on love are discussed in Chapter XXIV of *Youth.*

pectancy constantly titillated his hopes. But *she* appeared only in his imagination, usually when the mysterious light of the moon exalted him with a sense of beauty and a feeling of incomplete happiness. Then *she* stood before him, always sad and lovely, with her long plait of hair, full bosom, and beautiful bare arms, waiting for his embrace. As the moon rose higher and the shadows grew darker, something seemed to say to him that *she* was not the whole of happiness. The vision faded, leaving him with the ecstatic feeling that true happiness was nearer to Him, the source of all beauty and bliss. And tears of unsatisfied but agitating joy rose in his eyes.

5

The shyness that made him uneasy in the company of women also stood in the way of friendship with his fellow students. Tolstoy carried his stuffy notions of *comme il faut* from the ballroom into the classroom. *Gymnasium* graduates and poor scholarship students he scorned. In his pride and affected indifference, he always refused to bow first. When the student who sat next to him evinced a tendency to become too familiar, Tolstoy would suddenly freeze the growing intimacy with an icy remark. Yet he really wanted this gay company to like him. He longed to take part in their escapades, and probably felt a secret admiration for the madcap prince from Siberia who held the whole street in a state of siege by indiscriminately shooting at passers-by from his attic window with an air rifle.

When Tolstoy made friends, and there were a few in this Kazan period, they always belonged to his aristocratic set. The best of them was Dmitri Alekseyevich Dyakov, a youth several years older than himself. Unusually fervent attachments among young people of the same sex are a common enough experience, but in such friendships Tolstoy's intense emotional nature brought him to the dangerous edge of unnatural relationship. This was strikingly true of his youthful affection for Dyakov, which may properly be described as love. The fact takes on an added interest in the light of his wife's foolish charge against him, when he was a very old man, of homosexual relations.

Some four years after this period (November 1851), in a remarkably revelatory passage in a loose leaf of Tolstoy's diary, he writes: "I was very often in love with men. . . Of all these people I continue to love only Dyakov. For me the chief indication of love is the fear to offend or not to be liked by the person loved. It is simply fear. I was in love with men before I had any notion of the possibility of *pederasty;* but having learned about it, the thought of the possibility of such a physical union never entered my head. . . . Beauty always had much influence on my choice; however, there is the example of Dyakov. I never will forget the night, when we left Pirogovo (?), and, diving under the sleigh rug, I wanted to kiss him and weep. There was voluptuousness in this feeling, but why it occurred here it is impossible to decide, for my imagination did not paint lubricious pictures. On the contrary, I had a great aversion to them."

Utter frankness was the first condition of this friendship, and each vowed to tell the other his every thought, no matter how unpleasant. They were mutually responsive and their minds were tuned to the same philosophical key. Both worshiped an ideal of virtue and were convinced that man's mission in life was to perfect himself. The two perfectionists tried out their theory on a pretty girl whom they chanced to meet in Kazan. Her story of seduction moved them. Tolstoy offered to finance her until she got a job and could earn an honest living. She joyfully agreed and began to thank him. "Not at all," he magnanimously interrupted; "misfortune may happen to every one of us, and we must all help each other." When they met their attractive subject for reform a few days later, she freely confessed herself unable to lead any other existence than the sinful one she had grown used to. "So I could not convince her to return to an honest life," the worshiper of virtue concluded.

Thus virtue went unrewarded, but the perfectionists believed virtue was its own reward, and they serenely continued their theorizing. They would remain awake until almost dawn, arguing about abstract conceptions until words refused to yield their meaning and meaning ran all out of words.

These hours spent with Dyakov were among Tolstoy's happiest in Kazan. Their friendship brought out the finest qualities of his nature, and it is little wonder that the bond between them remained unbroken until Dyakov's death in 1891.

6

Long before the end of his second year in the Faculty of Jurisprudence Tolstoy had lost what little interest he had in the professors and their lectures. What would be termed a "gentlemanly C" in our colleges today satisfied him perfectly as a grade. Although he had deliberately selected this faculty as a "snap," his intellectual honesty and developing critical powers would not allow him to tolerate for long a situation that seemed profitless and a waste of time. It was not that he lacked interest in Roman and criminal law, psychology, logic, and the several languages and literatures in his curriculum, but he felt that they were being presented in a dull, unoriginal, and stultifying manner.

One day a fellow student and Tolstoy were late for a lecture in history. The punishment for tardiness would have done credit to army discipline: the culprits were locked up in a lecture room for the night. Such treatment was no anodyne for Tolstoy's growing hostility towards the university. His anger at first took the form of an arraignment of all poetry, apropos of a discussion of Lermontov's *Demon*. Then observing his fellow prisoner's copy of Karamzin's *History of Russia,* he at once fulminated: "History is nothing other than a collection of fables and useless trifles messed up with a mass of unnecessary dates and proper names. The death of Igor, the serpent, the stinging of Oleg[7]—are these not folk tales? Why should any one have to know that the second marriage of Ivan the Terrible to the daughter of Temryuk took place on August 21, 1562, or that the fourth to Anna Alekseyevna Koltovski happened in 1572? Yet they demand that I learn all this by heart, and if I do not know it, they give me a 'one.' And how is history written? All adjust themselves to a measure invented by the historians. The terrible tsar, about whom Professor Ivanov lectures at present, suddenly in 1560 is transformed from a virtuous and wise man into a senseless, ferocious tyrant. How and why this takes place you do not ask."[8]

His student companion and sole audience had no defense against such logic. He had heard of Tolstoy as a "queer fellow" and a "philosopher" and now he had no doubt of

[7] Tolstoy refers here to traditional stories in ancient Russian history.

[8] In this tirade may be seen the relentless future critic of conventional history books in *War and Peace.*

it, but at the same time he felt a vague sense of something remarkable, exceptional, and inexplicable about this caustic youth. Before they went to sleep on the hard school benches, Tolstoy indulged his spleen in another outburst, declaiming sarcastically about the "benefits" of this "Temple of Science" and ridiculing its professors so effectively that in spite of himself his companion was obliged to laugh. "Nevertheless," Tolstoy concluded, "we have a right to expect that we shall go out of this Temple useful and informed people. But what do we get out of the university? Consider and answer conscientiously. What do we get out of this sanctuary to return home with to the country? Of what use will it be and for whom is it necessary?"

Tolstoy was only one of many great men who questioned in their youth the values of a traditional university education. Not merely chronic contradictoriness, of which he had his full share, accounts for his criticism of Kazan University, or his negative attitude, mentioned in a previous chapter, towards any learning that failed to stir his intellectual curiosity. To these must now be added his growing tendency to question all manner of accepted institutions and conventions. The man-made ordering of civilization was not something to accept on faith. There must be for him a constant reference to cause and effect, an endless asking of the why, how, and wherefore of constituted society. No compromise would do. He must be convinced.

7

In his brief university career, Tolstoy experienced the deadening impact of stereotyped factual knowledge on a mind searching for ideas, first causes, and an understanding of life. He knew that factual knowledge was the beginning of wisdom, but he was being taught that factual knowledge was an end in itself. One of his discriminating professors, D. I. Meier, who recognized the superior mind of his indifferent student, tried to arouse his intellectual interests by setting him the task of writing a comparison of Montesquieu's *Esprit des lois* and Catherine the Great's *Nakaz*.[9]

[9] Note *Nakaz*, or "Injunction," was written by Catherine in 1766 as a guide to her Commission appointed to draw up a Code of Laws. In it she expounded her personal views on the rights of the State and on civil and criminal law. The *Nakaz* was heavily indebted to Montesquieu's *Esprit des lois* and to C. B. Beccaria's *Dei Delitti e delle Pene* (*On Crime and Punishment*).

His enthusiasm caught fire at once, for the task demanded the kind of independent effort for which he had hitherto found no outlet in his university studies.

Tolstoy read everything he could obtain on the subject. In the diary he set down the results of his analysis of Catherine's *Nakaz*. Each chapter is carefully summarized, occasional comparisons are made to the *Esprit des lois,* and frequently Tolstoy offers his own interpretations and comments. His critical remarks are often unusually penetrating and independent for a youth of eighteen. But no suggestion of his future firm opposition to every form of governmental coercion is apparent in the analysis. He accepts the autocratic framework of the Russian State and the legal system that supports it. What is more surprising, he actually asserts that "positive law, to be perfect, should be identical with moral law," a statement at utter variance with his ultimate position. Only in the matter of condemning capital punishment does he display consistency with his later views. At the end of the analysis, however, he delivers a thwacking indictment of the *Nakaz*. For he points out that Catherine is really making an unsuccessful attempt to justify her own conception of despotism by appealing to the republican ideas of Montesquieu, and that her "petty vanity" in this respect has resulted in deductions wholly illogical. The *Nakaz,* he concludes, "confers upon Catherine more fame than advantages to Russia." For the most part, his tone towards the Empress is highly respectful, but many years later, in his *Restoration of Hell,* he called her "a stupid, illiterate, and lewd wench."

In the end, this independent bit of scholarly investigation did nothing to soften Tolstoy's mounting antipathy to the university. On the contrary, he gave it as the reason for leaving. "The university with its demands not only did not assist in such a task," he wrote, "but actually hindered it." The professors, he paradoxically maintained, obstructed his thirst for knowledge. The analysis of the *Nakaz* led him into reading an endless quantity of books, but all in one direction. "This reading," he wrote, "revealed to me limitless horizons. . . . I gave up the university precisely because I wished to occupy myself in this fashion. There I was obliged to work at and study things that did not interest me and were unnecessary."

Of course, such reasoning is an oversimplification. A variety of reasons contributed to Tolstoy's decision. He had done badly in the mid-term examinations of the second year, and now with a string of unsuccessful performances behind him, he could not look forward to the final tests with equanimity. Sergei and Dmitri would finish their studies at Kazan that year (1847), and two more years in the university without their company did not appeal to him. Then in this same year a division of property among the brothers had taken place. Leo had received as his share Yasnaya Polyana and several smaller estates, amounting to about 5400 acres, along with 350 male serfs and their families. And at this time he began to express a real or imaginary sense of responsibility for all these human beings under his direct control.

On April 12, 1847, before the final examinations of the second year in the Faculty of Jurisprudence, he petitioned to be allowed to leave the university because of "ill-health and domestic circumstances." Two days later his petition was granted. The only memento that the most distinguished alumnus of Kazan University left behind him was his name scratched on a bench in one of the lecture halls.

8

In place of a grade in Russian history on Tolstoy's mid-term examination that last year, his professor had written "extremely lazy," which was undoubtedly true in that much despised subject. In general, he was anything but lazy. Intense intellectual activity was part of his nature, and he read a great deal during this Kazan period, principally in the summer vacation months which he spent at Yasnaya Polyana. Most of this reading, apart from what he had done for his analysis of Catherine's *Nakaz,* had little relation to the prescribed work of his university courses.

He gobbled a quantity of French novels by Sue, Dumas, and Paul de Kock. Their fictions seemed entirely real to him, and he discovered in himself a likeness to their characters, both heroes and villains. Less adventurous fiction and some poetry—Sterne's *Sentimental Journey,* Dickens's *David Copperfield,* Gogol's *Dead Souls* and *Tales,* Turgenev's *Sportsman's Notebook,* Druzhinin's *Polinka Saks,* Grigorovich's *Anton Goremyka,* Lermontov's *Hero of Our Times,* Pushkin's *Eugene Onegin,* and Schiller's *The Robbers*—he admitted had a marked influence on his artistic sensibilities. There was much else in belles-lettres, but his questing mind favored sterner stuff—the New Testament, philosophy, and political science. He plunged into Hegel, who was then all the rage among the illuminati, and, like most youths of the time, he read Voltaire, whose skepticism, perhaps because it lacked high seriousness, had no pronounced effect on him.

The author who stirred Tolstoy most at this time and had a permanent influence on his thought was Rousseau, whose complete works he read. He worshiped him, he said, and in place of the cross which good Orthodox believers wear round their necks, he wore a medallion portrait of Rousseau. So similar was Rousseau's thoughts to his own that it seemed as though he had been the author of many of Tolstoy's pages. Tolstoy frankly admitted that the *Confession* had a "very great" influence on him and the *Nouvelle Héloïse* and *Émile* an "enormous" influence. He could be severely critical of Rousseau, however, and the fundamental difference between them he himself pointed out later: Rousseau repudiated all civilization, whereas he simply repudiated pseudo-Christianity.

In his summers at Yasnaya Polyana Tolstoy appropriated some of the more garish aspects of Rousseau's back-to-nature teaching in a youthful attempt to live as befitted a practicing philosopher. With perhaps a feeling of relief he discarded in the country the social strait jacket of *comme il faut*. He rigged up for daily wear a loose canvas garment, which had the added advantage that it could be used as a nightshirt, and he went about in it in slippers and bare legs. His favorite occupation was communing with nature or lying down under a bush in the garden with a thick lexicon for a pillow. He allowed nothing and no one to interfere with his philosophical musings or routine. A group of young ladies unexpectedly arrived for a visit, and the philosopher was hastily summoned from his retreat in the garden. He made his appearance in the living room in his Diogenes canvas robe, slippers, and bare legs. When Auntie Tatyana remonstrated, he replied with some heat that conventional propriety should not be confused with the comfortable manner in which he was dressed.

Clothes may make the man, but Tolstoy knew well enough that a dearth of them does not make the philosopher. Behind his posing was much real intellectual effort. Apart from his intensive reading, he was also thinking and writing, all of which he regarded as a kind of extracurricular activity. Several fragmentary compositions of this time reflect the fearless quality of his mind, already indicated in his boyhood, in ranging over philosophical and abstract notions.[1] In "Philosophical Notes on Rousseau" he expatiates on the powerful influence of women for good in society and on the demoralizing effect of luxury on morality. In another piece, without a title, the young philosopher attempts to formulate rules for living and to define his own nature. On the margin are scribbled notes for future discussion: "From the very beginning I abandoned all prejudices, since I found nothing satisfactory in them." A longer article, rather expansively entitled "On the Purpose of Philosophy," concludes that the purpose is to show man how he should instruct himself, and, since he lives in society, how he ought to define his relations to people.

No doubt other compositions of this period have not survived, including one on symmetry which was lying on Tolstoy's desk when a student friend of his brother, pockets loaded with bottles for a carouse, descended on their apartment. He proceeded to read the article which seemed so brilliant that the friend was convinced it had been copied from some famed authority. When Tolstoy came in, he asked him for the name of the author. Tolstoy blushingly admitted that the article was his, whereupon the student laughed his disbelief.

9

Shortly before Tolstoy had entered the university, perhaps somewhat inspired by the singular devoutness of his brother Dmitri, he suddenly developed an enthusiasm for the picturesque ritual of the Russian Orthodox Church. He prayed, went to confession, took communion, and reveled in the thought that never had there been a young man with a soul as beautiful as his. This religiosity did not last long in the midst of the unholy pleasures of Kazan society. By the time he was sixteen he had ceased to believe the religious precepts taught him as a child. He did not deny the existence of God, but what sort of God, he could not say; he did not deny Christ and His teachings, but the substance of these teachings was not entirely clear to him. In short, while still quite young he had drifted into the familiar position of

[1] These interesting compositions, probably written when he was eighteen or nineteen, have been published in complete form for the first time in the Soviet Jubilee Edition of Tolstoy.

educated people with regard to dogmatic religion: he refused to accept the Church, but all his reason and senses obliged him to believe in God. It is necessary to remember this attitude of his youth, for his religious development, which was highly significant later, starts from this point.

The only faith that gave impulse to Tolstoy's being at nineteen was a belief in self-perfection. All his awakening moral and intellectual powers were concentrated on this ideal of life. By perfecting himself morally, mentally, and physically, he would achieve happiness. With that perennial faith of youth in the efficacy of "rules of life" to transform our human failings into inhuman perfections, he earnestly drew them up, quantities of them. The first series, in January 1847, is not very promising: "(1) To get up at five, go to bed at nine or ten, and perhaps sleep two hours during the day. (2) To eat moderately, nothing sweet. (3) To walk for an hour. (4) To fulfill all my written injunctions. (5) To [have] one woman only, and then only once or twice a month. (6) To do everything possible for myself."

These elementary rules were soon developed into an elaborate design for living, almost metaphysical in their complexity and discouragingly inclusive in scope. He set down rules for the development of the will, with various subdivisions, rules for the development of the memory, of bodily and intellectual activity, of talents, of judgment, and so on. There were rules to scorn wealth, honors, and the opinion of society not based on reason; to love all to whom he could be useful; to care nothing for the praise of people whom he did not know or disliked; and each day to express his love for all kinds and degrees of humanity in some manner or other.

Tolstoy's rules of conduct far outstripped his observance of them. Nor did he ever fail to remind himself of the fact. In his diary he jotted down: "It is easier to write ten volumes of philosophy than to put a single precept into practice." He did not realize then that his soul must be entirely cleansed of sin and temptation if he were to achieve self-perfection. Man may develop but he does not change. What he is in his youth so will he be in his old age. Tolstoy recognized this. If he sinned, it was because he did not know himself.

But even as a youth he heard the divine voices in him urging him to perfection. He wanted everybody to know and to love him, and he cherished the hope of some unusual good fortune that would make him famous. Often, however, he did not hear the voice during this period of his youth, because he did not always believe in himself. He believed in the people round him, who fostered his animal instincts, his pride and worldly ambitions, and frustrated his desire for self-perfection. With his life in Kazan partly in mind, he wrote in *Confession:* "With all my soul I wished to be good; but I was young, passionate, and alone when I sought goodness. Every time I tried to express my most sincere desire, which was to be morally good, I met with contempt and ridicule; but as soon as I yielded to nasty passions, I was praised and encouraged." This was a phase of the dualism that waged its mighty battle in the heart of the youthful Tolstoy, and the struggle cast a shadow over his whole life.

10

The thought of leaving Kazan caused Tolstoy no regret. His experience there had been disillusioning and the moral fabric of his nature had been stretched to the utmost. He now intended to spend two years in the country, and in contrast to the existence he had been leading in Kazan, this new period was to provide him with a purpose and aim in life. He wrote in his diary: "I would be the unhappiest of mortals if I could not find a purpose in life—a common and useful purpose, useful because my immortal soul by virtue of its development will pass naturally into an existence superior and more suitable to it."

If we may judge from the program of work that he outlined for himself a few days before leaving for Yasnaya Polyana, then he must have regarded his departure from the "Temple of Science" as a real opportunity to learn something. He intended, he wrote, "to study (1) the whole course of jurisprudence necessary to pass the final examinations at the university. (2) To study practical medicine, and to some extent its theory. (3) To study French, Russian, German, English, Italian, and Latin. (4) To study agriculture, theoretical and practical. (5) To study history, geography, and *statistics*. (6) To study mathematics, the *Gymnasium* course. (7) To write a dissertation. (8) To reach a reasonable degree of perfection in music and painting. (9) To write down rules [for conduct]. (10) To obtain some knowledge in the natural sciences. (11) To compose essays on all the subjects that I shall study." His intention to take the final examinations in the Faculty of Jurisprudence was no doubt prompted by the desire for a diploma, which would secure him certain privileges in the civil service.

Tolstoy seemed to relish the notion of abandoning the gay society of Kazan for the solitude of the country. For shortly before he set out, he wrote in his diary that the disorderly life that fashionable people accept as a consequence of youth is really nothing other than the consequence of early spiritual corruption. "Solitude," he maintained, "is equally beneficial for the man living in society, as society is for the man not living in it. Let a man but withdraw from society and retire into himself and his reason will soon strip off the spectacles through which he has hitherto seen everything in a corrupt light. . . ."

This longing to escape the corrupting influence of society, however, did not spoil the pleasure of a very liquid farewell that his aristocratic comrades tendered him. They accompanied him out of the town with many embraces sealed by potations deep.

VI

Man About Town

UNLIKE Horace on his Sabine farm, young Tolstoy could not sit contentedly among his Yasnaya Polyana cabbage patches. For there were those everlasting "rules of conduct" to observe and his vast "program of work" to fulfill. After all, he had not abandoned the city for the country merely to exchange the pleasures of worldly society for those of rustic simplicity. The incessant worm of perfectibility gnawed continually at his conscience.

In a separate "Journal of Daily Occupations" that Tolstoy kept at this time, he obliged himself to list his tasks for each day and opposite them his rate of performance. A typical day's planning, the third after his arrival at Yasnaya Polyana, reveals this debit-and-credit system of human endeavor in all its pathetic failure:—

5 to 6, practical agriculture 6 to 9, letters 9 to 10, drink tea 10 to 11, set copybooks in order 11 to 1, book-keeping 1 to 1:30, lunch 1:30 to 3, Italian 3 to 5, English 6 to 8, Russian history.	Nothing done

Day after day debits piled up against similar good intentions. He observes plaintively in his diary that it is difficult for a man under the influence of what is bad to develop into what is good. If only he could cease to be dependent upon extraneous circumstances, then the spirit would take precedence over matter and he could achieve his proper destiny. "Extraneous circumstances" appeared in the form of a visit from Dunechka (his childhood companion) and her husband. They "robbed me of feeling contented with myself by the impression they produced on me." For the loving couple poignantly brought home to him all the zest for life that he was denying himself in the country for the sake of his "purpose." Perhaps with the bitterness of envy he jotted down in his diary the next day the following new rule: "Regard feminine society as a necessary evil of social existence, and as such, to be avoided as much as possible. In fact, from whom do we learn voluptuousness, effeminacy in everything, and many other vices if not from women?"

2

Only a genius would formulate such a rule, but certainly no genius ever violated self-made rules of conduct with more regularity than Tolstoy. After two months of rustic seclusion, all his good intentions seemed like so much precipitated nonsense. Yet he did not surrender without a final struggle the ideals that had helped to inspire this country retreat.

In leaving the university for Yasnaya Polyana, part of Tolstoy's plan was to devote much of his effort to the affairs of the estate and the well-being of the several hundred serfs over whom he was now absolute master. His aristocratic notions of social classes permitted him to regard the enslaved position of the peasantry in the traditional manner —as something ordained by God. Many changes would take place in his intellectual and spiritual life before he began to think that peasants were the equals or even the superiors of his own noble class. Now, as their new master, he accepted his serfs as a responsibility, and he had simply a humanitarian desire to improve their lot. With the effort to perfect himself mentally in abeyance, he turned with enthusiasm to his new "purpose in life"—to do good for the peasantry. In this, he was sure, he would find real happiness.

Little direct information exists of Tolstoy's first attempt to reform his fellow men. In 1852, however, he planned a large work, "The Novel of a Russian Landowner," in which he intended to depict the relations between a master and his serfs. He attached much social significance to the proposed novel, the purpose of which he described as follows: "The hero searches for the realization of an ideal of happiness and justice in a country existence. Not finding it, he becomes disillusioned and wishes to search for his ideal in family life. His friend introduces him to the thought that happiness does not consist of an ideal but may be found in continual vital work that has for its purpose the happiness of others." Only the first part of this novel, "A Landowner's Morning," was finished, and for the material Tolstoy drew heavily upon his experiences with the peasants of Yasnaya Polyana in 1847–1848.

The autobiographical aspects are clearly discernible. The nineteen-year-old hero of the story writes his aunt to inform her of his decision to leave the university in order to devote all his efforts to his estate and the welfare of his serfs. Her answer amounts to an acute piece of self-criticism on Tolstoy's part. One does not believe in arguments and rules but only in experience, she writes, and experience tells her that his plans are childish. "You always wished to appear original," she declares, "but your originality is really nothing but excessive self-esteem." The hero is not deterred by his aunt's practical advice, for he refuses to regard the poverty of his peasants as an unavoidable evil. He abolishes corporal punishment and provides schooling and medical aid for them. Like a ministering angel, he visits their wretched, filthy hovels, and in simple-hearted fashion pours out his willingness to devote his life to their happiness.

The hero's first fine rapture does not last long. Despite all his efforts, the peasants remain poor, shirk education, and do not improve morally. Somehow his plans all come to nothing. The serfs are suspicious and regard his offers of aid as just another trick on the part of the master to get more work out of them. Helplessness, deception, and trickery beset him on every side. Perplexed in the extreme and sadly disillusioned, he finally abandons his experiment.

This is no doubt a fair description of Tolstoy's own initial attempt to understand and help his peasants. All his life the disparity between experience and theorizing confounded him. He was like so many of the young men among the gentry at that time. Their characteristic traits are brilliantly described in the heroes of nineteenth-century Russian poetry and fiction, such as Eugene Onegin, Oblomov, or the "superfluous men" of Turgenev. They grew up on country estates, completely insulated from the real business of life. The profits of serfdom took care of their financial needs, and politics, the organization of society, or the concerns of the outside world played little active part in their youthful existence, although they were quite capable of talking and theorizing endlessly about them. Even the traditional civil or military careers were regarded as mere gentlemanly formalities that customarily preceded an early retirement to the pleasant dead calm of rural seclusion.

This way of life played an important part in Tolstoy's development. His comparative isolation and severance from practical concerns intensified a natural bent for introspection. His own soul and state of mind became of much more importance to him than anything else in life. He pushed far ahead into the realm of abstract thinking and theorizing but lagged far behind in those everyday lessons that experience knocks into one in the daily struggle for economic security. His thoughts concentrated with extraordinary understanding on personal duty as revealed by the workings of his conscience and intellect, but often quite apart from any thorough comprehension of the practical affairs of the society of which he was a part. This dichotomy has obvious disadvantages, but it also lies behind his unique power to perceive the ills of society and devise a way of life that would circumvent if not solve them.

Tolstoy's lack of experience prevented him from realizing that centuries of slavery had rendered serfs incapable of believing in the sincerity of a master who desired to help them. Masters had always tricked, abused, and cheated them, and the very fact that he was their master made it impossible for them to have any faith in him. His failure troubled his conscience, depressed and saddened him, as though he were being tormented by a reminder of centuries of crime committed and unatoned for by members of his own social class. In the depths of his soul he began to feel that only by ceasing to be the master of these serfs could he win their belief in him.

3

At this time Tolstoy resembled both the town mouse and the country mouse of the ancient fable, for he liked both places. Rather, he could not be contented with one while away from the other. Now that he was in the country, all the glittering prospects of the city—fame, love, social pleasures, adventure—drew him like a magnet. The lofty purpose of his rural isolation was soon shoved aside, and his failure with the peasants quickened a desire to escape. So urgently did he feel the need to get away that he galloped after the carriage of his future brother-in-law, who was off to Siberia to clear up his affairs before marrying Marya. Only the fact that he had forgotten his hat prevented him from going along.

Shortly after this episode (October 1848), Tolstoy was on his way to Moscow. The moral walls in which he had recently immured himself were lightly vaulted, and he plunged into the mad egoism of unfettered pleasures. The Kazan period of social activity was lived all over again, only now he had the larger and more fashionable world of Moscow to play in, and in the meantime he had acquired some poise and self-assurance.

The twenty-year-old Tolstoy needed no introduction to the upper levels of Moscow society. The drawing rooms of the best homes were open to a bright youth of good family and comfortable income, and he could aspire, he said, to any damsel he chose. Numerous relatives of high social standing supported his claims to attention.

Tolstoy stayed at first with distant relatives, the Perfilyevs,[1] and then moved to quarters of his own. His first letters to Auntie Tatyana dealt largely with money matters and requests for articles that he had forgotten to take with him, again including his hat. Soon he adopted for his aunt's benefit the bored air of the youth who thinks he has arrived socially. He described his many visits to the homes of people of consequence and complained that his daily occupations were constantly upset by callers. Before a month was up his tone changed somewhat. "There is nothing either good or bad to tell you about myself," he wrote. "My existence is neither too worldly nor too retired; I'm neither amused nor bored. . . ." Another month and the familiar note of moral despair crept into his saga. "I've grown quite debauched in this social existence," he wrote. "Everything bores me frightfully; I'm dreaming again about life in the country, and I intend to return to it soon."

The beginning of the next year (1849), however, found Tolstoy in Petersburg instead of the country. He had had a second thought. It was comforting to contemplate the quiet of Yasnaya Polyana amid the noisy pleasures of the city, but then he had never sampled the pleasures of the capital

[1] V. S. Perfilyev served as the prototype, in certain features, for Stiva Oblonski in *Anna Karenina*.

of All the Russias. They apparently took him by storm. "I intend to remain here forever," he wrote enthusiastically to his brother Sergei at his Pirogovo estate. Proudly he announced that he was with his comrades Ozerov and Fyorzov, and that he had already visited the Laptevs, Obolenski, Musin-Pushkin, Milyutin, and the Islavins. "And many others have been introduced to me and I to many. In brief, it has turned out that there are many more acquaintances here than in Moscow; and they are of a *much higher quality,*" he underlined, with a resurgence of the *comme il faut* of his Kazan days. The letter has all the earmarks of having been written with glass in hand amid the promptings of jolly companions. One of them, K. A. Islavin, a rakish friend of the Tolstoy brothers, scribbled a postscript to Sergei: "Hello Pirogovo landlord! Hello terrible possessor of 313 Pirogovo slaves! What are you doing? Are you still sighing over your beloved Masha?"

With its manifold possibilities for a career, Petersburg seemed to Tolstoy a veritable Eldorado. He decided to turn over a new leaf. This city "has a great and good influence over me," he wrote to Sergei in the same letter. Here everyone was busy and it was impossible to lead the aimless life of Moscow. Although he was sure that his brother would not believe him, he insisted that he had already changed. "You will say: 'For the twentieth time now you have changed, but nothing comes of you, the emptiest of fellows.' " This time the transformation was real, he told Sergei, for he had at last convinced himself "that one cannot live by speculation and philosophy. One must live positively, i.e. be a practical man." And this newest discovery would be utilized at once, for he declared his intention of taking the examinations for the Faculty of Jurisprudence so that he might obtain his degree and enter into government service. Renewed determination rather than progress was reflected in this old ambition.

Sergei had had abundant experience with these sudden shifts in his brother's enthusiasms. He jocosely wrote back his disbelief in the announced "change," and then took the occasion to warn Lyovochka against the card sharps of Petersburg. "With your scorn for money," he cautioned, "you may well lose a large amount." The advice went unheeded and Tolstoy rapidly accumulated gambling debts. Letters to Sergei over the next few months were filled with urgent requests to sell his woodlot and his horses in order to raise money. Cards became a passion with him. Like Dostoyevsky, he imagined it possible to contrive a rational system that would assure success, and he actually drew up an elaborate series of "Rules for Card-Playing." As might be expected, the rules proved futile in the face of bad luck, and their principal precept of moderation was always forgotten in the excitement of play. In the course of the next few years his gambling habit was to bring him to the verge of financial ruin.

The fact that neither in his letters nor in his diary did Tolstoy show the slightest flicker of awareness of the absorbing political and literary activity of Petersburg's brilliant intellectuals at this time betrayed as nothing else could the nature of the company he kept and his single-minded preoccupation with himself. The February Revolution of 1848 in France had inspired in oppressed Russians the hope of reform in the viciously bureaucratic and reactionary regime of Nicholas I. The great literary critic Belinski and his followers in Petersburg had advocated a Russia modeled on the more advanced civilization of Western Europe. Revolutionary murmurings were in the air and repression was brutal. At the very time that Tolstoy was concerned solely with making a place for himself in the city's high society, the Tsar's police rounded up a group of radicals known as the Petrashevski Circle. Among them was the young Dostoyevsky, who had already won some literary fame. Dostoyevsky was on his way to a Siberian prison as a convicted revolutionist before Tolstoy grew weary of his loose Petersburg life.

Meanwhile, Tolstoy, on his own admission, had become a "practical man," and something had to be done about it. There were the university examinations to test his new resolution. Although he confessed that he knew absolutely nothing about the first two subjects—criminal and civil law—he put off his preparations until a week before the examinations. Then he plunged into study, working day and night, and passed both tests well.

Hardly had he accomplished this feat, however, when a pleading letter (May 1, 1849) was dispatched to Sergei: "I believe you are already saying that I'm the *emptiest of fellows;* and you are saying the truth. God knows what I have done! For no reason I came to Petersburg and have achieved nothing decent here, except squander money and run up debts. It is stupid. Insufferably stupid!" He had a large debt of honor to meet, and he begged Sergei to arrange for the sale of one of his smaller properties. Failure to pay would mean the loss of his reputation. Such a price, he complained, for freedom and philosophizing.

In the future, however, all would be different, if only the present mess could be straightened out. He was going to give up the university once and for all and become a cadet in the Horse Guards. The Guards would soon leave for Vienna to help the Austrians quell the Hungarian rebellion. (The moralist had no thought now for the injustice of this cause.) With luck, he might get a commission before the usual two years if he saw action. So please, he asked Sergei, send on my birth certificate, but before all else, raise the necessary funds to pay off my cursed debts.

Before two weeks had elapsed, the wind of events had shifted the young weathercock in Petersburg to a different direction. He replied to Sergei's offer of aid, coupled with a mild brotherly remonstrance, with regrets for the "various stupidities" of his previous letter, the chief of which, he remarked, was his intention of joining the Horse Guards. He reaffirmed his purpose of entering the university, and he would enlist in the army only if he failed the remaining examinations and if the war took a serious turn.

Even before his brother could answer, Tolstoy had shifted his ground again. A furtive letter to Auntie Tatyana pleaded for a few rubles, if only enough to take him back to Yasnaya Polyana. He baited the request with a promise to study for the civil service examinations that would enable him to obtain a post at Tula. This course would make it possible for him to spend the winter at Yasnaya Polyana and thus cut down his expenses. Years later he explained his sudden decision to leave Petersburg differently, and the simple reason carries conviction. "Spring arrived," he said, "and the charm of rural life again attracted me to my estate." In June he returned to Yasnaya Polyana with a talented but drunken German musician by the name of Rudolf.

4

After a summer at Yasnaya Polyana, where music, under the direction of the amiable Rudolf, occupied much of Tolstoy's time, he obtained a post in the Chancellery of the Tula Assembly of Nobles in November. This first practical endeavor proved to be no steadying influence. Such positions were purely nominal and he had almost as much leisure as at Moscow and Petersburg. He wasted it in gambling, drinking bouts, visits to gypsy haunts, and in the gay entertainments of the provincial society of Tula. Infrequent letters to Auntie Tatyana that winter revealed the emptiness of his existence. The only serious note in them was his concern over the impending birth of his sister's child.[2] "Bring forth! dear friend Mashenka," he cheeringly interpolated in one letter. "You cannot imagine how boring it is for a future uncle to be kept waiting."

Tolstoy's stay at Tula was occasionally broken by visits to the estates of his sister and brother Sergei, and to Auntie Tatyana at Yasnaya Polyana. In the company of his kind foster-mother he always regained a sense of security and a feeling of contentment with himself and life. She watched over his material welfare, mildly scolded him for gambling excessively, and continually feared that he would make a bad marriage. At times he chafed over her limited understanding of the broader aspects of morality, but in her unselfish devotion to all whom she loved he saw a beautiful life of self-sacrifice.

He would arrive at Yasnaya Polyana, feeling ashamed and morally unclean after a prolonged period of carousing at Tula. Auntie Tatyana would greet him lovingly. By old custom, he would kiss her soft, energetic little hand and she his "dirty and depraved one," and then they would converse in French. Her gentle kindness and affection never changed. He would sit in an armchair through the long winter evenings and read while she played old maid, or he would hear her soft, childlike laughter as she chatted with the housekeeper. At such moments, he said, his finest thoughts came to him, the noblest responses of his soul.

During the summer of 1850 Tolstoy again stayed at Yasnaya Polyana. For a brief period in June he resumed his diary; he felt it a valuable exercise in self-judgment. From it we learn that he threw himself zealously into the study of music, practiced faithfully on the piano, and even began to write a treatise, "The Fundamental Principles of Music and Rules for Its Study." The subject so absorbed him, he remarked, that he experienced "the happiness of the artist, although in a very incomplete way." For a time, he actually contemplated dedicating his life to music.

[2] She had married V. P. Tolstoy, a distant relative, in 1847.

The diary and "rules" always went together; a fresh crop of the latter, led off by a long series demanding gymnastic exercises, was now assiduously cultivated. Development of the body had become almost a fetish with Tolstoy and was to remain so for the rest of his life. The fine physique he acquired through constant exercise stood him in good stead in several serious illnesses. Sad experience had impressed upon him his inability to abide by moral rules. He now approached the subject with unintentionally amusing candor. Moral rules that "never change," he would eschew; only "resolutions temporal and local" that could be altered if the occasion demanded would be set down for observance. Even these simple day-by-day injunctions often proved too much for his willing spirit but weak flesh. "Yesterday," he wrote, "in addition to leaving undone what I had set for myself, I betrayed my rule. But I shall not betray this one anymore—not *to have* a single woman in the country—, except on certain occasions which I shall not seek out but will not avoid."

Within three days after this entry, the transgressor let his diary lapse again. Five months later Tolstoy was in Moscow. He had obtained a leave of absence from his Tula post, to which he was destined never to return. Provincial society, country solitude, and homemade moral rules had apparently once more been sacrificed to a desire for the pleasures of the metropolis.

In Moscow while taking an inventory of the quiet existence he had led in the country, he announced in the diary that rural life had effected "a great revolution" in him. At last he had ceased "to frame castles in Spain and plans which no human capacity could execute!" He would no longer despise the convictions of others and dismiss as unworthy of notice the ordinary concerns of mankind. There was no glory in profligacy, he reasoned, when inferior beings could surpass him in this respect. "I've come to Moscow with three aims," he candidly admitted to himself: "(1) to gamble; (2) to marry; (3) to obtain a post."

With an unexpected degree of persistency, Tolstoy now devoted himself to what he was later to despise most—worldly success. He wrote out his own "Rules for Society." Among them are such precepts as: always to seek associations with men higher in the world than himself; to ask for dances at balls only with the most important ladies; never to express his feelings; never to allow anyone to offer him the smallest insult or sarcasm without paying double for it.

In the approved manner of the fashionable fop, Tolstoy's letters to Auntie Tatyana were now filled with drawing-room chitchat and the latest society scandals. He belonged to the exclusive English and Nobles Clubs, paid court to important dignitaries, and dined and wined with this or that prince and princess. And like any typical gallant, he flirted with his hostess or fell a little in love with her. Occasionally he forgot his manners and succumbed to a genuine passion for her, as he did with the young wives of at least two of his hosts. He even began to go to church again for what seemed to be fashionable rather than sincerely religious reasons. Then there were the purely bachelor amusements of the young man in society. Gambling, riding, fencing, gymnastics, and wrestling with the local strong man helped to fill out his day. At night, carouses with his set at exclusive restaurants were usually followed by visits to brothels or breakneck rides to shady establishments on the outskirts of the city, where they listened until dawn to the haunting melodies of gypsy choruses and made love to exotic gypsy girls.

Practical affairs were not forgotten. They were intended to be a vital feature of this new dispensation that banished castles in Spain. But his success in this respect was as fugitive as ever. Once again, and now for the last time, he resurrected that pale corpse of a university degree. He suddenly felt the need to demonstrate his will power and settled upon the determination to finish his studies in the Faculty of Jurisprudence as an appropriate test case. A single reference in the diary to reading his old friend Nevolin's *Encyclopaedia of Law* is the first and last shred of evidence concerning this new effort in a dead cause. He also disinterred his former ambition for a post in the government service, and at this time he was not above seeking the support of influential officials. Another possibility, however, soon took its place—renting a posting station on one of the imperial mail routes. After a few practical gestures had been made, this scheme also came to nought. Meanwhile, gambling debts again rendered his situation precarious.

During the whole tenure of this demeaning bid for worldly success, Tolstoy's merciless self-criticism never ceased. In the end, it saved him from a way of life entirely inimical to his deepest hopes. Sins venial and unpardonable, trivial and deadly, he charged against himself with discouraging meticulosity. There is a suggestion of exaggeration and perverted ardor in this relentless self-castigation, but his sincerity is undeniable. Day after day even the slightest deviations from his accepted norm of perfection in character are duly itemized in the diary: meanness, boasting, haste, want of solidity, diffidence, sloth, presumption, affectation, pride, showing off, indecision, false shame, lack of stability, absent-mindedness, over-self-reliance, lying, thoughtlessness, gluttony, faintheartedness, apathy, quarrelsomeness, self-delusion, and a lack of discrimination. It would seem that there was no human weakness he did not possess, certainly none that he was unwilling to admit. At this time, inspired by the notable example of Benjamin Franklin, he also kept a "Franklin Journal,"[3] devoted solely to listing and appraising all his failings.

5

The most significant aspect of this unhappy Moscow visit was the birth of the creative artist. Tolstoy began to observe closely the life around him and to experience an irresistible urge to describe it on paper. At the fashionable balls and dinners he attended no detail escaped him. He would sit at the window of his bachelor apartment and watch all the unfolding comedy and tragedy of street life. A policeman strolled by and the observer wondered who he was and what kind of existence he led. A carriage drove past the window and he asked himself who was in it and what the rider was thinking. The house across the street served as a starting point for a guessing game about its inhabitants and all the intimate details of their inner lives. What an interesting book, he imagined, could be written about such people.

Hitherto Tolstoy had scribbled a fair amount on philosophy, music, and rules of conduct. In the meantime, the artist's urge to understand and describe life had been imperceptively growing within him. In a sense, the diary he had been keeping on and off for four years was an unconscious apprenticeship in the novelist's art of selection and analysis. Although dealing primarily with his own inner experiences, the diary reveals at this early stage one of the principal features of his process of creation: his intense in-

[3] Franklin's works were well known in Russia and highly regarded.

terest in fixing upon the semiconscious, suppressed motives of his actions. Even the unique rational approach to the study of his own nature, everywhere apparent in the diary in his love for classifications and subdivisions of all manner of human attributes, suggests his later talent for conquering the subconscious by an application of lucid understanding. Indeed, the transition from the self-analysis of the diary to his dissection of imaginary characters was an easy and natural one.

During these five months in Moscow, there is much evidence in the diary and letters of Tolstoy's new interest in literary expression. In one letter he admired the attempt at authorship of one of his young friends, and pointedly remarked that "at least, he gains his bread honestly, and more bread than 300 peasants bring"; and in the diary he noted the necessity of translating from foreign languages in order to improve his style. Finally, there was the terse promise to himself (December 8, 1850): ". . . I intend to write a story of gypsy life should I find time." Succeeding references show that he worked on such a tale, but whether he finished it is unknown. On January 18, 1851, an entry in the diary reads: "To write the history of my childhood." There is no evidence that he worked on this project during his stay in Moscow, but he pursued it later and it resulted in his first published piece of fiction, *Childhood* (1852).

In jotting down, as was his custom, his plans for the next day, Tolstoy wrote in the diary on March 25, 1851: "Rise at five and work at history of today until ten." He fulfilled this design, working over it for the next few days and returning to it later. The effort is the first known piece of Tolstoy's fiction. It is a considerable fragment of what was intended to be a long work under the title of *A History of Yesterday*.[4] In its present form the fragment embraces a detailed description of an actual evening he spent at the home of Prince and Princess Volkonski,[5] which he eventually intended to subordinate to a larger design. This fragment is a unique performance for a beginner. In its infinite detail, concerned largely with a minute analysis of his conscious and subconscious thoughts and feelings reacting to par-

[4] The work was published only after Tolstoy's death, and it has never been translated into English.

[5] Tolstoy was much attracted to the wife, Princess L. Volkonski, who served as the model for the "little princess," wife of Andrei Bolkonski, in *War and Peace*.

ticular situations, the work has the distinct flavor of Proust and Joyce. The immediate model, however, was Sterne, whose influence is clear in the frequent digressions, in the mixture of trivial observations with commonplace aphorisms, and in the transformation of all the unexpected and confused associations of thought that enter the hero's head as he falls asleep. The young Tolstoy reveled in his newly discovered powers of analysis, but this exuberant abandon never again appeared in his fiction.

6

Spring was filling the air again, always a harbinger of restlessness for Tolstoy. "Not long ago," he wrote to Auntie Tatyana, "I read in a book that the first tokens of spring affect usually the moral side of man. With the renewal of nature one also wishes to be renewed. One regrets the past, the time badly spent, and one repents weaknesses, and the future appears like a bright hope before us; one becomes better, morally better." In truth, he was morally sick of his Moscow life and felt the need of renewal. At this opportune moment, the arrival from the Caucasus of his beloved brother Nikolai, whom he had not seen for four years, settled the issue. He decided that he would keep Nikolai beside him as long as possible during his furlough and then accompany him to his battery in the Caucasus.

At the beginning of April, Tolstoy returned to Yasnaya Polyana. He had little time to enjoy the quiet pleasures of the country, for the next three weeks were filled with preparations for his trip. Visits had to be made to his sister and Sergei. The swift momentum of city life still clung to him. He tried to keep up his gymnastics, music, run the affairs of the estate, and do a little writing (he planned two pieces, a description of a dream and of a day's hunting). Nor, it seems, had he left his easy city morals behind him. "After dinner I spent the evening in prowling about and experiencing voluptuous desires." Struggle as he might, he could not put temptation, in the form of pretty peasant girls, behind him.

Two days after this entry, he wrote in his diary: "Sensuality tortures me. Not so much sensuality as the force of habit. I'm convinced that in another place I would not even look upon her who now, because I've already had her here, obliges me powerfully to struggle with passion and yet give way to her more often." The very next day, however, he confessed in his diary: "Yesterday could not forbear signalling to someone in a pink dress, who looked attractive from a distance. I opened the back door. She entered. I couldn't even bear the sight of her; foul, repellant. I even hate her for causing me to break my rule. The feeling of duty and aversion argued against it, lust spoke for it; the latter conquered. I repented terribly; never before have I felt this as now. It is a step forward."

The sincerity of Tolstoy's repentance may have been reflected in his serious preparations for the religious observance of Easter. He even wrote a homily, though, he said, a bad one.

On the whole, his four-year record since leaving the university had been a dismal one. Now almost twenty-three, he had failed to obtain a university degree, to find happiness in improving the living conditions of his serfs, or to secure a position in the civil service or army; nor had a modicum of success in high society satisfied him. All this was disillusioning for a youth keenly conscious of his high capacities. But as he set out with Nikolai for the Caucasus at the end of April, 1851, the young Tolstoy was dimly conscious that his past had been enriched by the stuff of life if not by material success.

VII

A Cadet in the Caucasus

TRAVELING together is like living together. If the enforced intimacy fails to breed contempt, it makes travelers inordinately sensitive to each other's slightest fault. On the road, Nikolai complained of his brother's cleanliness. Changing one's shirt "twelve times a day," as he put it, seemed excessive. The fastidious Leo, on the other hand, admired nearly everything about his older brother, except "his dirtiness." Several years of soldiering in the Caucasus had made Nikolai a bit forgetful about social amenities; it had also strengthened his independent nature, which now manifested itself in the itinerary that he planned.

Instead of taking the direct southern route to the Caucasus by way of Voronezh, he decided to head southeast for Saratov, in order to cover the long stretch from there to Astrakhan by boat down the Volga. A delightful prospect; and the additional attraction of a northern swing through Moscow and Kazan increased Leo's enthusiasm for the plan.

As though Tolstoy had a premonition that it would be long before he again saw his companions of civilized ease, two days in Moscow were crowded with calls on numerous friends. Nor did he omit to test his will power by gambling (he won four hundred rubles on this try) and by a visit to his favorite gypsies. With amazing frankness he dashed off a report to old maid Auntie Tatyana: "As you believe that *I'm a man who tests himself*, I went among the plebs in the gypsy tents. You can easily imagine the inward struggle I experienced there—for and against. However, I emerged victorious. That is to say, I gave nothing but my blessings to the gay descendants of the illustrious Pharaohs." After a hurried sitting with Nikolai for a daguerreotype, they were off.

A week in Kazan was passed merrily in visits to relatives and friends of his student days. There were dinners, concerts, and balls, and much champagne. Leo's snobbery vexed his simple soldier brother. A gentleman drove past them, leaning on his cane with ungloved hands.

"It's obvious that man is a scoundrel," remarked Leo.

"Why?" asked his puzzled brother.

"Because he is without gloves."

"But why is he a scoundrel if he doesn't wear gloves?" Nikolai demanded with an ironical smile. Leo was stumped, for he suddenly realized that any explanation would sound foolish.

The memory of a girl's face may have contributed to Tolstoy's willingness to go by way of Kazan. She was the same Zinaida Molostvov whom he had known and liked in his university days. Then, timidity on both sides had rendered dumb a mutual attraction. Five years had changed Zinaida, but had hardly made Tolstoy any less shy in the presence of a virtuous young woman. She was not a beauty, but the qualities of her mind that he now discovered, her wit, humor, and warm heart, rekindled his interest. He fell in love, and in that brief week no opportunity was missed to be in Zinaida's company. She obviously reciprocated, but for both of them love was apparently a secret thing, expansive only in hidden ways. He recalled how they stood in the side path of the archbishop's garden. It was on the tip of his tongue to declare himself, and she too almost hinted. Nothing was said, for at that moment words would have spoiled their felicity. He explained later that he had desired to perpetuate by silence "this pure yearning of two souls for one another."

Tolstoy left Kazan with this undeclared love buried in his heart. It sprouted poetry on the way. "I'm so intoxicated with Zinaida," he wrote to his sister, "that I've even had the hardihood to compose some verses:—

While towards Syzran I lingered,
And my own wound I fingered . . .

Syzran," he pedantically adds in a footnote, "is a village in the Simbirsk government." Then he concluded: "Just now Alyosha entered with tea and broke the thread of my thoughts." Like Coleridge's man from Porlock, the servant cost us the remainder of this only known love poem of Tolstoy, but perhaps without any loss to immortal verse.

It did not strike Tolstoy as paradoxical that the wings of love were bearing him swiftly away from the young lady of his heart. Soon all thoughts of Zinaida were forgotten in the attractions of the constantly shifting panorama of the strange country through which he was passing. The brothers reached Saratov, loaded their carriage on a boat, and with the aid of sails and oars made their way down the Volga to Astrakhan. From there they set out in the carriage again for their destination.

The trip made a lasting impression on Tolstoy. He described these days as the best of his life, and he once remarked that he could have written a whole book about the journey. For Russians at that time, the wild, spectacular Caucasus was a land fabled in song and story. Its mountains, precipices, and rushing torrents, its beautiful Circassian women and fierce, untamed tribesmen, had been the rich inspiration for exotic tales and poems of Marlinski, Pushkin, and Lermontov.

On the way, Tolstoy had plenty of leisure for thought. As he left civilization farther and farther behind, his consciousness of past mistakes was also left behind in the hope of a new life in which there would be no mistakes, no remorse, nothing but happiness. All that he had cared for most in the gay society of the city seemed trivial now as new and ever newer beauties of nature unfolded. Then one morning, for the first time, he saw the mountains—pure white gigantic masses with delicate contours, the clear fantastic outlines of their summits showing sharply against the far-off sky. He felt all the infinitude of their beauty, and with it a sense of complete freedom from his past. On the thirtieth of May, after about a month on the road, the brothers arrived at the Cossack village of Starogladkovskaya, where Nikolai's battery was stationed. The spell of strange places was quickly broken and, somewhat disillusioned, he asked himself in his diary how he had got there and with what purpose.

2

Starogladkovskaya nestled in a hollow on the left bank of the Terek River, which served as a border between the Grebensk Cossacks and hostile Mohammedan hill tribes. Here Tolstoy spent the next two and a half years, although he made frequent trips to surrounding villages, forts, and watering places. The banks of the river were thickly wooded and well stocked with deer, wolves, wild boar, hares, and pheasants. To the north stretched the Nogai steppes, and to the south, beyond the Terek, were the Great Chechnya River, the Kochkalov range, and in the distance the snow-capped peaks of the Caucasian Mountains.

The village consisted of a single street of reed-thatched huts, adorned with carved gables and high porches. Surrounding them were kitchen gardens, dark green poplars, and acacias with their delicate pale verdure and scented white blossoms. The inhabitants, a Cossack sect of Old Believers,[1] were a proud, independent people. They retained the Russian language and their ancient faith in all its purity, although they had intermarried with the native Chechenians and adopted their manners and customs. Plundering and war were their chief characteristics and swaggering bravery a cult. They acknowledge none but Cossacks as human beings and despised everybody else, especially Russian peasant soldiers. Drunkenness they regarded as a rite, the non-practice of which was considered apostasy. The Cossack women were in nominal subjection to the men and did most of the heavy farm work, but they were endowed with a peculiarly emancipated masculine character. A combination of the purest Circassian type of face with the broad powerful build of northern women gave them a strikingly handsome appearance in their colorful, semi-Oriental dress. In their relations with men they enjoyed complete freedom, especially the unmarried girls.

The native setting interested Tolstoy more than the battery of Russian soldiers quartered in the village. Ever since the successes of Ivan the Terrible in the sixteenth century, the Tatars had been gradually pushed back to the south until the Russians came in contact with the hard-fighting hill tribes on the northern slopes of the Caucasian Mountains. After Georgia, situated to the south of the Caucasus, had been brought into the Russian Empire in 1801, it became highly desirable to conquer the territory lying between the Terek and the newly acquired country. The Russians had constructed a whole string of Cossack outposts along the northern banks of the Terek and the Kuban, and from these they carried on their warfare against the natives. This prolonged border fighting had reached a criti-

[1] Old Believer is a general name for the sects that separated from the Russo-Greek Church in the seventeenth century.

cal stage at the time Tolstoy visited the Caucasus, for the Chechenians were ably led by the aggressive Shamil, who had skillfully organized resistance. Not until after the Crimean War was this romantic chieftain finally subdued.

Tolstoy was well received by the officers of the battery, and all the more so as the brother of Lieutenant Nikolai Tolstoy who was admired by his comrades in arms. They were a typical group of soldiers of the line, brave, hard-drinking, incessant gamblers, and for the most part, poorly educated. The commander, N. P. Alekseyev, was an exceptional individual and a general favorite with both officers and soldiers. He presented an unusual appearance, for one of his ears had been bitten off by a horse. Extremely pious, he spent whole hours in prayer, kneeling and bowing to the ground, and his dislike of vodka frequently led him to lecture the young officers, in a kindly spirit, on the evils of strong liquor. Tolstoy thought him vain, and often amused himself at dinner by pretending to drink, in order to provoke the commander to deliver his temperance sermon that always ended with an offer of sweets instead of vodka. Many of these officers had come to the Caucasus as to a promised land, in order to repair their fortunes after reverses of one sort or another back home. A few of them became the heroes and villains of Tolstoy's Caucasian tales.

3

Several days after his arrival, Tolstoy followed his brother to the near-by fortified camp of Stary Yurt, which served as a protection for Goryachevodsk. Here many invalids availed themselves of the excellent mineral springs. A few weeks later he wrote a letter to Auntie Tatyana in which he described the camp and his new life. His tent looked out on a magnificent view of the mountain. Enormous rock structures were intersected by torrents of hot water that gave off a white vapor covering the whole upper part of the mountain in the morning. The water was so hot that one could boil an egg in it in three minutes. He spent hours gazing on the savage beauty of the place and idly watching the handsome Tatar women wash clothes by stamping them with their feet in adjacent pools. The ferruginous baths, he added, helped his rheumatism.

A passage in the diary at this time belies this picture of contentment. An inexplicable despondency, he wrote, filled his soul and saddened him. While he nurtured a feeling of love for all that was beautiful, for mankind and nature, and yearned to express it, he encountered only coldness and ridicule. The cause of his despondency, he reasoned, was an application to the serious things of life too early. He took refuge in an indifference to life. There was nothing to look forward to save death—a gratifying thought. Yet how could he explain to himself, he asked, that "I can recall with pleasure the fact that I've ordered a saddle on which I shall ride in my Circassian costume, and that I shall run after Cossack women, and fall into despair because the left side of my moustache is worse than the right, and that I shall spend two hours trying to rectify the matter before a mirror?"

Perhaps something of this disillusion grew out of Tolstoy's confused feelings for Zinaida Molostvov, for his thoughts returned to the girl he had left behind in Kazan. He confessed in the diary that he was ignorant of what men call love. Was it like religion—a pure and lofty sentiment? He doubted now that he had any such feeling for Zinaida. And then he began to suspect his very doubts. "Shall I never see her again?" he wrote. "Shall I one day learn that she is married to a Beketov? [2] Worse still, shall I then see her in her gay cap, with the same clear, frank, merry, love-filled eyes as of old? Not yet abandoned are my schemes of journeying back to marry her; I'm in love, although I'm not entirely convinced that she would constitute happiness for me."

Tolstoy did nothing to demonstrate his affection. He might easily have settled the matter by a letter, but he avoided this, significantly contented to transmit his timid regards through the medium of a Kazan correspondent. "If you do not think it improper," he wrote, "you had better say to Zinaida Molostvov, *que je me rappelle à souvenir.*"

In the meantime, he forgot love while wooing God and fighting the devil. It was night at Stary Yurt, a week after Tolstoy's arrival. He sat on a drum in the tent, writing his diary. The candlelight outlined sharply the shapes of pistols, Circassian sabers, poniards, and trousers hanging along the canvas walls. The evening noises of challenging sentries, of a soldier coughing in his sleep, and the distant baying of a dog disturbed his thoughts. He was searching for a certain frame of mind, a view of things, a form of life which

[2] A. N. Beketov. Tolstoy was jealous of his attentions to Zinaida.

he was unable to define. He began to pray to God. "It is impossible to convey the blissful feeling I experienced in prayer . . ." he jotted down in his diary. "Yet, if prayer be defined as a petition or thanksgiving, I was not praying. Rather, I was yearning for something lofty and good. What that something was I cannot explain, although I clearly recognized what I desired. I wanted to become fused with the All-Embracing Substance. I besought It to pardon my sins. . . . I could not separate the feelings of faith, hope and love from my general feeling. No, the feeling I experienced last night was love for God, uniting in itself all that is good and renouncing what is bad."

This sudden religious rapture under the impact of new scenes plainly anticipated the direction Tolstoy took many years later in his dramatic search for the meaning of life. Now, the irrepressible urges of youth tripped him up in his sincere yearning after the lofty and good. "Not an hour had passed," continued his record, "before I almost consciously heard the voice of vice, vanity, of the empty side of life. I knew whence this voice came; I knew that it had destroyed my state of blessedness. I struggled but yielded to it, and I fell asleep, dreaming of fame and women. But it was not my fault; I couldn't help it."

The day after (June 13), Tolstoy congratulated himself in the diary upon exorcising the devils of vice, especially that of gambling. The very next entry (July 3), however, reads: "I wrote the above on June 13, and I have entirely wasted my time since then, for on the same day I was so carried away that I lost at cards 200 rubles of my own, 150 of Nikolinka's [his brother], and got into debt for 500 more—total 850.[3] Now I shall restrain myself and live prudently. I went to Chervlyonnaya, got drunk there, and slept with a woman. All this is very bad and troubles me deeply. Indeed, never have I spent more than two months well or so that I was satisfied with myself. Last night I lusted again. It is good that she would not give herself. Loathsome! But I write this as a punishment for myself."

The excitement of a raid on the Chechenians took Tolstoy's mind off his personal failings. He gladly accepted an offer to volunteer. The raid, led by Major General A. I. Baryatinski, commander of the left flank of the Caucasian army, had for its objective a Chechenian village up in the hills. Such actions were simple enough. The enemy invari-

[3] Approximately $450.

ably gave way slowly before the advancing Russians, and the village was taken and sacked. When the raiding party withdrew, the Chechenians, like American Indians in frontier warfare, kept up a deadly sniping from behind rocks and trees.

Tolstoy's only comment in the diary on his baptism of fire was a modest one: "Recently I took part in a raid. I didn't act well; was even unconsciously afraid of Baryatinski." The general, however, took a different view of his conduct. Shortly after the raid, he was presented to Baryatinski by Ilya Tolstoy, a distant relative, who was traveling in the Caucasus. At the meeting, Baryatinski praised Tolstoy for his courageous bearing under fire in the face of mortal danger, and advised him to hand in his petition to enter the service as soon as possible.

4

Tolstoy thought the general's advice worth considering, and his brother Nikolai seconded it. Maybe it would put an end to his ceaseless indecision. He wrote to Auntie Tatyana: "I've finally decided to serve in the Caucasus. I have not yet determined whether it will be the military or civil service under Prince Vorontsov.[4] My trip to Tiflis will decide the matter."

He sat at the open window of his hut at night and gazed out on the starry vault of heaven. It was pleasant at least to contemplate the notion of a settled occupation. A light breeze brought a scent of freshness. Frogs and crickets croaked and chirruped their monotonous noises. Memories of Katya, a Tula gypsy, banished his errant thoughts about a career. Seated on his knee one night, she had sung "Tell Me Why," and declared that she loved only him, and allowed to no one but him the liberties that required concealment behind the curtain of modesty. He had believed her artful gypsy chatter with all his soul, and under the spell of this charming memory, he burst into the melody of "Tell Me Why." The night air was filled with his animated singing, but the spell was suddenly broken by someone under his window inquiring if he were wailing a Calmuck song.

Four months passed before Tolstoy could make up his mind about the army. New companions, the beauties of nature, hunting, literary activities, Cossack women, and per-

[4] M. S. Vorontsov, Viceroy of the Caucasus.

haps a rooted dislike for the responsibilities of a settled occupation, postponed his decision. In restless activity he shuttled back and forth between Groznaya, another fortified post, Stary Yurt, and Starogladkovskaya. Sado, a "peaceful" young Chechenets, who used to gamble with the officers, became his *kunak* (sworn friend). Since he could not write or count, he was regularly cheated until Tolstoy won his endless gratitude by offering to play for him. A present of Nikolai's old silver watch sealed the friendship. Henceforth, no test of devotion was too great or dangerous for Sado. If Tolstoy needed a horse, Sado cheerfully offered his and was deeply hurt if the gift was refused. He learned that Tolstoy's brother Sergei was a lover of good horses, and he at once suggested going up into the hills to steal the finest mount for the brother of his friend. Although the son of a well-to-do father, Sado lived by such thievery. He was a *dzhigit* (a daring fellow), who considered it his prescriptive right to steal from the enemies of Russia, even at the risk of his life. And he often risked his life for a theft that would bring him a few rubles.

A more epic figure was Tolstoy's extraordinary friend Epishka Sekhin, whom he faithfully described as Eroshka in *The Cossacks*. Epishka was an ancient Cossack in whose hut Tolstoy and Nikolai were quartered. For many years he had been a notorious character in the surrounding country. Of gigantic size, unusually well-proportioned, and still very strong and lively despite his eighty years, Epishka made a striking figure in his bushy beard dyed red and ragged hunting clothes. He described himself as "a *dzhigit,* a thief, and a swindler." As a youth, he had distinguished himself as a most skillful horsethief and slayer of Chechenians. Nor had he always been too particular about whose horses he stole or what "enemies" he killed; the Russians had also been his victims, and he had twice spent time in Russian prisons. In his old age, he contented himself with hunting, drinking, spinning yarns, and singing native songs.[5]

Tolstoy spent much time with Epishka and learned a great deal from him about woodcraft and hunting. He was no doubt at this time peculiarly responsive to the old man's simple earthy philosophy, which offered a soothing solution

[5] In 1908, the great-nephew of Epishka visited Tolstoy at Yasnaya Polyana, and at his request, Tolstoy presented his portrait to the people of Starogladkovskaya.

for his own inner struggle between the good and bad impulses of his nature. God, Epishka firmly believed, made everything for the joy of man. There was no sin in any of it. Man was like an animal, declared Epishka. Wherever it went, there was its home; whatever God gave it, that it ate. It was a fraud to teach man that he would lick red-hot plates in hell for enjoying the things of this earth. For when man died, said Epishka, the grass would grow on his grave, and that was all. Undeniably this was a comforting way of life in that wild country, and despite the unrelenting prick of conscience, much of Tolstoy's stay in the Caucasus was influenced by the ancient Cossack's forthright hedonism.

In his youth Epishka had prided himself on his prowess with the girls, and he had an eye for them even in his old age. The hero of *The Cossacks* rebuked Eroshka (Epishka) for this senile propensity, calling it a sin. "A sin?" roared Eroshka. "Where's the sin? A sin to look at a fine girl? A sin to have some fun with her? Or is it a sin to love her? Is that so in your parts? No, my dear fellow, it is not a sin, it's a salvation."

Under the strong influence of these wholly natural people, Tolstoy wanted to cease thinking, to forget the puzzle of his existence. He wished to turn his back on the civilization of sophisticated society, with its artificial etiquette, its obligatory chatter, and its modish dandies and damsels with pomatum-greased hair eked out with false curls. He yearned to live like nature, as these Cossacks lived. They fought, ate, drank, rejoiced, and died, without any restrictions, other than those that nature placed on the sun, the animals, and trees. To him they seemed beautiful, strong, and free, and the sight of them made him feel ashamed of himself.

The cloak of civilization could not be sloughed off so easily. By the time his twenty-third birthday had arrived, Tolstoy and his new hopes reverted to type. He noted in the diary that from August 28 (his birthday) he would try to live in conformity with the aim he had set himself. Future occupations must again be listed, and a revised Franklin journal kept. The old rules were resurrected, and his determination set down to work on a novel, to sketch, study the Tatar language, and read. Just one week after the celebration of the birthday that was to begin his reformation, he sadly recorded in the diary: "Unfortunately I remain always the same: in the course of several days I've done all the things I disapproved of. Abrupt changes are impossible. I had a woman, showed myself weak on several occasions—in simple relations with people, in dangers, in gambling, and I'm still held back by false shame. I've told many lies. . . . I've been very lazy; and even now I cannot *collect my thoughts, and I write, but do not wish to write*." The bubble of buying a hut, marrying a Cossack girl, and settling down in the Caucasus had been pricked by the knife of conscience. The law of his being had to be fulfilled.

After jotting down a Chechenian song that he had heard, Tolstoy broke off his diary for 1851, and some seven weeks after this last entry, he left with his brother for Tiflis to take an examination for entrance into the army.

5

Most of the two months Tolstoy spent at Tiflis turned out to be a period of enforced quietude. To Auntie Tatyana he circumspectly explained that he had fallen ill with a "kind of hot fever"; to Nikolai, who had to leave shortly after their arrival, he frankly wrote: "Perhaps you think I'm entirely well. Unfortunately, I feel very badly. The venereal sickness is cured, but the after-effects of the mercury have caused me untold suffering."

The penance for his carelessness was much leisure that Tolstoy employed constructively enough. He lodged in the German quarter of the Georgian city, in a house surrounded with a garden and vines. This opportunity to brush up on his German pleased him, and to Auntie Tatyana he wrote: "You recall the advice you once gave me: to write novels. Well, I've followed it, and my endeavors, about which I shall speak to you presently, are literary. I don't know whether what I write will ever see the light of day; but it is work that amuses me, and I have persevered too long now to abandon it." Indeed, he completed the first part of *Childhood* during this period of convalescence.

On January 3, 1852, Tolstoy had easily passed the examinations to qualify as a cadet, a noncommissioned officer of artillery, but with his usual forgetfulness about personal documents, which in Russia were man's official passport from the cradle to the grave, his appointment was held up. When the papers finally arrived, an essential one—his honorable discharge from the Tula civil service—was lacking. Here was another delay, and he feared very much that he would lose an opportunity to participate in the coming winter campaign. He relieved the boredom of waiting by taking up billiards, at which game he quickly lost much more money than he could afford. Once again his financial plight grew desperate, for a gambling debt he had contracted several months before was about to fall due. The note was held by an officer and friend of Nikolai, F. G. Knorring, whom Tolstoy heartily disliked. In despair he prayed to God for aid. He was convinced that his prayer had been answered, for the next morning he received a letter from Nikolai, who wrote that Sado, Tolstoy's devoted Chechenian *kunak*, had won the note from Knorring and insisted on presenting it to his friend. Overjoyed by this "divine intervention" in a gambling debt, Tolstoy at once sent home for a revolver and a music box, which he knew would delight the generous Sado.

Worn-out with waiting for the documents that would assure him an appointment, Tolstoy used all possible influence in high army circles of Tiflis. His efforts finally succeeded to the extent of his being assigned to the 4th Battery (his brother's) of the 20th Artillery Brigade as a non-commissioned officer of the 4th class, but he was advised that his appointment would not be officially recorded until the arrival of his discharge from the Tula civil service. "You will not believe how this pleases me," he wrote Auntie Tatyana. "It will seem strange to you, that I do not desire to be free. I've been free too long in everything; and it seems to me now that this excess of freedom has been the principal cause of my faults, and that it is even an evil." The future hater of war expressed his pleasure more bluntly to his brother Sergei: "With all my strength I will assist with the aid of a cannon in destroying the predatory and turbulent Asiatics."

A definite and realizable purpose in life raised Tolstoy's spirits to a pitch of enthusiasm. On the way to rejoin the battery he wrote Auntie Tatyana that he had already undergone a moral change. Religion and experience, he said, had taught him that life was a test. For him it was more than a test; it was the expiation of his faults. This trip to the Caucasus, he now assured her, had been an inspiration from above. He would see it through. And then, in his expansive mood, he portrayed the future as he would have it.

It is interesting that this imaginary picture anticipates the ideal family happiness that he came to love. After experiencing all the adventure that life might send him, he told how he would return to Yasnaya Polyana for good. There he would live the peaceful country life that his father had enjoyed before him. He would marry and have children, who would call the aging Auntie Tatyana "grandmother." Everything would remain in the household as it had been when he was a child. Around the table at night he would tell of his life in the Caucasus, and Auntie Tatyana would recall her precious memories of his parents, over whom they would weep together tender tears of gladness. His brother would visit. Nikolai, good and noble as always and still a bachelor, would invent tales for Leo's children, who would kiss his hand in gratitude. And Leo's wife would make Nikolai's favorite dishes for him. Then they would all talk, and Auntie Tatyana would call them "Lyovochka" and "Nikolenka," as in their childhood, and she would gently scold him for eating with his hands, and Nikolenka because his hands were not clean. If he had a choice, he said, between being made Emperor of Russia or of realizing this dream, he would choose the latter. "You know me too well," he concluded, "and you know that perhaps my only good quality is sensibility. It is that quality to which I am obliged for the happiest moments of my life." Curiously enough, this ideal of happiness did come true, and with more realization of its charming details than anyone has a right to expect in daydreaming.

6

At last Tolstoy was off to the wars, a soldier in uniform, though still lacking an official appointment. The Viceroy of the Caucasus, Prince Vorontsov, had received an imperial order to put an end to the long resistance of the Chechenians. Two Russian columns moved from opposite directions to effect a junction and thus trap the enemy. Tolstoy was with the main column and on the seventeenth and eighteenth of February he saw some fierce fighting in which the Russians were victorious. With the wanton destruction common in frontier fighting, everything was put to fire and sword. Despite a mature sense of the horror of war, Tolstoy frankly admitted that he also retained a childish feeling of bravado. He was oblivious of the flying bullets and made a point, with death all around him, of trying to present an attitude of smiling indifference. When an enemy shell struck the wheel of the gun he was aiming, he escaped death by a miracle. In the diary, however, he remarked about his behavior under fire: "My state at the time of danger opened my eyes. I loved to imagine myself entirely cold-blooded and calm in danger. But in the affair of the 17th and 18th I was not so." During this campaign, he was cited twice for the coveted Cross of St. George, but once again the fact that his discharge papers from Tula had not yet arrived prevented the award's being made.[6]

After the campaign, Tolstoy's battery returned to its base at Starogladkovskaya. Here he remained for the next four months, except for brief visits to the neighboring towns of Kizlyar and Oreshyovka, a trip to the Caspian shore, and a longer journey to Pyatigorsk to receive treatment for dysentery. He was also bothered by severe toothaches and rheumatism. The diary over this period is unusually detailed. It reveals clearly that he compensated for his restricted physical activity, due to ill health, by an intense concern with his own thoughts and with reading and writing.

Contemplation of his life in the Caucasus up to this point filled Tolstoy with regrets. Gambling, sensuality, and vanity, he asserted, were the three evil passions that he had most to contend with. He was proud of the fact that of late he had avoided all occasions to gamble, without any consciousness of deprivation. Sensuality was a more difficult matter. The demands of the body, intensified by a vivid imagination, could be overcome only by strength of will and prayer to God. Even as he thought these thoughts he was trying hard to resist the attractions of his pretty landlady at Pyatigorsk.

Vanity, he despaired of banishing. "It's like syphilis," he noted. "When driven out of one part, it reappears, with added force, in another." At times he wondered if the pride that comes from vanity did not poison his capacity for friendship. With a touch of snobbish rationalization, he wrote to Auntie Tatyana: "I try to make the fewest acquaintances possible and to avoid intimacy with those that I already have. They grow accustomed to my manner and

[6] Although he had received his official appointment as a noncommissioned officer on February 13, 1852, this seems finally to have been made without benefit of his Tula discharge papers. For he was cited for the St. George Cross on February 17; the presentations were made on March 19, and he says in a letter: "Twice I had an opportunity to be presented with the Cross of St. George and have not been able to receive it because of a few days' delay in this damned paper." The discharge papers arrived one day late, March 20.

no longer importune me, and I am certain they say that I am a *queer fellow* and a *proud man.* I do not behave so because of pride, but because I am made that way. There is too great a difference in education, sentiments and manners between those I meet here and myself for me to take any pleasure in them." Yet he observed with some chagrin that Nikolai was friendly with all and loved by all.

Tolstoy was not entirely satisfied with his explanation. He agreed when his Cossack friend Epishka once told him that he was a man who could not be loved. A naturally warm heart and sympathetic nature, however, stood in the way of the snobbery that he had practiced since his university days. In a striking passage in the diary at this precise time (March 29, 1852), he suggested another explanation. "There is something in me," he wrote, "that obliges me to believe that I was not born to be what other men are. But whence does this proceed? From a lack of agreement, an absence of harmony among my faculties, or from the fact that I really stand on a higher level than ordinary people? I'm older, and the time of development is passed or is passing; and I'm tortured with a thirst, not for fame—I have no desire for fame and despise it—, but for acquiring great influence for the happiness and benefit of society. Shall I die with this wish a hopeless one?" He was perfectly sincere. From boyhood he had treasured the conviction that he was different; genius had whispered softly in his ear. But the prevailing feeling over these years had been one of defeat and unfulfilled hopes.

Tolstoy's commonplace existence at Pyatigorsk, to which he went in May, was certainly not flecked with the promise of future fame. The town had little to recommend itself. It seemed to him like a Caucasian Tula. Society consisted of landowners—the inflated term for all visitors coming to drink the mineral waters—who looked down upon the local citizens. Then there were the army officers, who regarded the native entertainment as the height of bliss. They pretended that they had come for treatment only, and hence they limped about on crutches, wore slings and bandages, caroused, and told stories of hair-raising adventures with Chechenians. Concerts, the theater, and promenading along the boulevard were the chief amusements. Ironically, Tolstoy called the life "purely Parisian," and he was vastly annoyed at having to salute these officers in epaulets, blue pantaloons, tightly drawn belts, and boots with enormous spurs. He faithfully followed his doctor's orders, bathed in the mineral waters and drank from the springs.

In June Tolstoy heard the news that Zinaida was going to marry. Strangely enough this sudden termination of a romance that he had run away from caused him little concern.[7] "The fact vexes me," was his only comment, "the more so because I have felt so little perturbed."

7

On July 3, 1852, Tolstoy wrote to N. A. Nekrasov, distinguished poet and editor of the *Contemporary,* Russia's leading progressive magazine: "My request will cost you such little effort that I am sure you will not refuse to grant it. Look over this manuscript, and if it is not suitable for printing, return it to me. If you appraise it otherwise, tell me what it is worth in your opinion and print it in your magazine. I agree in advance to any cutting that you may find necessary, but I desire that it be printed without any additions or changes in the text." He then went on to say that the manuscript was the first part of a novel under the general title of "Four Epochs of Growth," and that the appearance of the later parts would depend upon the success of the first. The letter concluded on a flattering note, prompted by his own anxiety over the worth and soundness of his first sustained effort to write fiction: "I am convinced that an experienced and well-intentioned editor, especially in Russia, by virtue of his position as a constant intermediary between author and reader, can always indicate in advance the success of a work and the public reaction. Therefore, I await your answer with impatience. It will either encourage me to continue a favorite occupation or oblige me to cease at the very beginning."

With the letter Tolstoy sent the manuscript of *Childhood.* For over a year now, very early in the morning, or late at night after hunting, carousing, or a day of activity with the battery, he had worked away at his novel. Sometimes in his enthusiasm over a particular chapter, he would read it to the critical and talented Nikolai or to a friend who dropped in, but he nearly always regretted these premature hearings. His periods of enthusiasm were very rare in the

[7] Tolstoy, however, never forgot Zinaida. Almost fifty years later, when she had long been dead, her nephew visited him, and Tolstoy questioned him about his aunt with obvious feeling.

process of creation. More often he expressed acute dissatisfaction. Three separate drafts were written out, and a fourth, done by a copyist, also received Tolstoy's corrections. Notations in the diary on the progress of the work reveal the stern demands he made on himself artistically at the very outset of his literary career. Time and again he noted that the writing went badly, the rewriting worse. "Without regret, I must destroy all unclear places, prolix, irrelevant, in a word, everything unsatisfactory, even though they be fine in themselves." Unswervingly he adhered to his own rule that no addition, however talented, could improve a work as much as a deletion. He fluctuated between satisfaction and utter dislike, and on occasion contemplated abandoning the work. At times he began to doubt that he possessed any ability. "Have I talent comparable to that of recent Russian writers?" he asked himself in the diary and answered, "Positively no." Later speculation on this subject, however, left him undecided. Then there were rare and wonderful moments when he read over a particularly successful passage and felt that genius must have guided his pen. "I reread the chapter 'Sorrow,' and while so doing wept from my very heart." He believed, like Gogol, that any work, in order to be good, should come singing from the author's soul. This can truly be said about *Childhood,* despite all Tolstoy's misgivings.

Almost two months passed before Tolstoy received Nekrasov's reply. It "drove me silly with joy," he noted in the diary. The famous editor agreed to print *Childhood* in his periodical, and added: "Not knowing the continuation, I cannot say definitely, but it seems to me that the author has talent. In any case, the author's bent and the simplicity and realism of the contents constitute the unquestionable worth of this production." He concluded with a request for the continuation and a plea that Tolstoy reveal his name. (He had signed the manuscript with the initials of his first name and patronymic—"L.N."—and only Auntie Tatyana and Nikolai were aware of his efforts to publish.)

A further exchange of letters followed, in which Tolstoy asked for payment, and Nekrasov replied that it was a custom for the best periodicals not to offer an honorarium for the initial work of an author, but that he would pay him the best rates for any succeeding contributions. And he softened this disappointment by saying that he had now read the work in proof, that he found it still better, and that he had absolutely no doubt about the author's talent.

At the end of October, Tolstoy read the published *Childhood,* but the mutilations of the censor and editor robbed him of some of the beginner's rapture at seeing his first work in print. He sat down and wrote a blistering letter, which on second thought he failed to send to Nekrasov; but a more tempered effort later was vehement enough. First he scolded the editor for altering the title to the *Story of My Childhood.* Of what concern to anybody, he asked, was the story of his childhood? Then he went on to ridicule the changes that had been made, asserting that in reading the printed version, he experienced the feeling of a father who saw his child's hair mutilated by an inexperienced barber. He ended on a pleasant note, however, agreeing to accept the fine financial offer of Nekrasov for future works (fifty kopeks a printed sheet, or about half a cent a word), and saying that he would send him something when he had it ready, but warning him once again never to tamper with his productions.

Tolstoy's vexation at the disfiguring of his brain child was soon dissipated by the news of its enthusiastic reception. *Childhood* won praise on all sides, and the public was curious to learn the new author's name. Shortly after reading his novel in print, Tolstoy went to a neighboring post to hunt with some fellow officers. In a hut he came across an issue of *National Notes* in which he found a highly laudatory review of *Childhood.* He lay on a cot and read the account, dwelling greedily on every sentence of praise. The last one must have made his heart jump: "If this is the first production of L.N., then one ought to congratulate Russian literature on the appearance of a new and remarkable talent." Tears of joy came to his eyes, and he obtained a special thrill of pleasure from the thought that the comrades sitting around him did not realize that it was he who was being praised in such lofty terms.

To fatten the young author's self-esteem came letters from Sergei and Auntie Tatyana, telling him that everybody was reading and raving about *Childhood.* Panayev, co-editor of the *Contemporary,* was avoided by his friends because he insisted upon cornering them on the street and reading extracts from the new work. Turgenev, who was under the impression that Nikolai, Tolstoy's brother, was the author, wrote to Nekrasov to tell him to encourage the author, and to convey his interest, greetings, and praise to him. In far-off Siberia the exiled Dostoyevsky wrote to a friend to ask him who was the mysterious L.N. whose recent story had so excited him. Tolstoy, like Turgenev and Dostoyevsky, had caught the public eye and that of the critics with his first published work and at once revealed himself as a coming new force in Russian literature.

There can be no question of Sterne's influence on *Childhood.* (It had already been evident in "A History of Yesterday.") Throughout this period Tolstoy read the *Sentimental Journey,* translated a part of it, and in the diary are warm appreciations of Sterne. Sterne's lively but refined humor, brilliant wit, love of humanity, and acute sensibilities, as well as his various tricks of style, attracted Tolstoy. In the several drafts of *Childhood,* however, one can observe the care with which he tried to eliminate obvious traces of this influence, but the final version still owes much to Sterne. And several succeeding works are also indebted to him. Töpfer's[8] influence is of less consequence and is mostly limited to the possibility that Tolstoy was inspired to write about childhood by the treatment of it in the *Bibliothèque de mon oncle.*

Childhood is a highly original work. What particularly impresses the reader is Tolstoy's skill in evoking childhood memories and associations that all have forgotten or only dimly remembered, but which, when recalled with feeling, seem infallibly true and delightful. At this time Tolstoy criticized Pushkin's historical romance, *The Captain's Daughter,* because the interest in events predominates over the interest in details of feeling. It was precisely the feelings of his characters that Tolstoy was primarily interested in, and in the psychological reasons why they felt thus or thus. In the Introduction to *Childhood,* he warns his readers that they must be understanding in order to appreciate the book, for he writes it from the heart, not from the head. More than that of any other major novelist, Tolstoy's fiction is autobiographical. This is no reflection on his imagination or power of invention, but the life he transposed into art was largely his own life of recorded experience and observation, rendered effective by penetrating analysis and by his subtle choice of significant psychological and real detail.

[8] R. Töpfer was a Swiss writer, whose *Bibliothèque de mon oncle* appeared in 1832 and was translated into Russian in 1848.

The convincing realism of his fiction is rooted in autobiography. Although *Childhood* draws heavily upon his own experiences, there is a great deal of sheer invention in the work. Many of the characteristic qualities of his mature art are already apparent in this first extensive effort. The customary initial period of imitation and immature attempts was avoided in his artistic development. With little faltering and no false moves, he mounted at the first try the immortal steed of great art.

Lack of money, as well as the natural urge to write, kept Tolstoy working on two other pieces during this same year (1852). He sent off to the *Contemporary* his long short story, "The Raid," the first of several works that grew directly out of his Caucasian experiences. The central incident is the action he took part in as a volunteer the year before, and several of the leading figures are modeled on officers he knew well. The tale has more substance than a mere narration of an exciting military exploit. He deliberately set out to treat realistically the themes of war and Caucasian life, which had been romantically handled in the exotic tales of his predecessors, Marlinski, Pushkin, and Lermontov. He had still not divested himself entirely of the poetry of war, but he questioned its justifiability in "The Raid." Of course, the government censor saw to it that only the "poetry" remained, and Tolstoy complained to his brother that all the good in the story had been struck out or mutilated. A recently published unexpurgated edition showing passages deleted from the original draft reveals Tolstoy as well on the way towards that opposition to war which eventually resulted in his utter condemnation of it. In his artistic treatment of the theme of war at this time and later, he was much influenced by Stendhal. Like Stendhal, he suggested the evil, crass egoism and vanity of the pseudo-heroic by a ruthless analysis of conventional thinking about military glory. But in "The Raid" he was not blind to the heroism of the simple unambitious plain soldier or officer, and his narration of incidents in this connection provides the main charm of the tale.[9]

[9] During this year he also worked on "The Novel of a Russian Landowner." And he began *The Cossacks,* a masterpiece that he did not finish until ten years later.

8

After completing *Childhood* in July, Tolstoy spent most of the remaining months of 1852 in doctoring himself. Despite his powerful physique, he was subject to a variety of illnesses that he endeavored to regard as a moral good for which he ought to thank God. While he was still at Pyatigorsk, his physician ordered him to neighboring Zheleznovodsk to try the healing powers of the mineral springs there. He left with the consolation that Pyatigorsk had been the first town in which he had committed no follies, and hence, he remarked, it was unnecessary to carry away with him any repentance. His stay lasted only three weeks, and he set out for Starogladkovskaya. Soon, poor health again forced him to go for a week's treatment to Kizlyar, after which he rejoined his battery.

Difficulties at home did not add to Tolstoy's peace of mind. With the aggravating indifference in practical matters of one "not born to be what other men are," he fully assumed that the troublesome affairs of his estate at Yasnaya Polyana would be conscientiously supervised by Auntie Tatyana, or by Sergei or his brother-in-law. To complicate matters, he was everlastingly sending home orders to sell this or that bit of property to raise money for his mounting debts. These commissions were not always carried out to his liking, which fact contributed to his present indecision with regard to terminating his army service. The freedom that he had so lightly signed away, in order to destroy "the predatory and turbulent Asiatics," seemed all the more desirable now that military life in the Caucasus had lost its novelty. The routine of Starogladkovskaya, he remarked, might even cause one to become something of a fool. Drill, maneuvers, and firing off cannons, he said, disturbed the regularity of his life. Rather caustically he noted in the diary that drill was necessary to maintain the discipline essential for the existence of a military class. And the drill habit, he declared, brought men to a state of mechanical obedience by means of petty threats, an obedience which not even the most cruel punishment could produce. Such thoughts were to reappear many years later in his denunciation of militarism. Meanwhile, he discovered that he had a maximum of two more years to serve before he could hope for a raise in rank, and he earnestly desired this promotion before he left the service.

Tolstoy's intellectual concerns, which often discouraged the friendly advances of unintellectual officers, were a welcome refuge during these months of illness. Apart from writing, he read anything he could get his hands on in this frontier town, and he also sent home for books. There was not much to be had in fiction, but he read Pushkin, Lermontov, and Grigorovich, Rousseau, Dumas, and Sue, and Sterne and Dickens. The last two especially delighted him. "What a charm has *David Copperfield*," he wrote in his diary. Dickens became his favorite English author. He generously admitted to his "tremendous influence"[1] and called him the most Christian of all English novelists. Dickens's affection for ordinary people and his constant concern for the betterment of his readers won Tolstoy's admiration.[2]

Tolstoy read with pen in hand, jotting down his reactions in the diary. His thoughts at this time about literature, and his own relation to it in the light of his dawning career, seemed to fluctuate with the uncertain state of his health. "Literature is rubbish," he wrote, "and I should like to set down here rules and a plan of estate-management." Sometime later, he observed that "the most agreeable books are those in which the author seems, as it were, to try to hide his personal opinion yet remains true to it wherever it is revealed. The most insipid books are those in which the author's point of view changes so often that it gets quite lost." Contemporary literature was declining, he decided, because authors were producing too many light books for the sake of commercial gain. In order to write well, he told himself, one must know not what to write, but what not to write. "Better with conviction and absorption to write something good and useful. One will never grow weary of such a work." For "in some people," he noted in the diary, "the fire of inspiration changes into a candle to work by. Literary success that satisfies one's own self is obtained only by working at every aspect of a subject. But the subject must be a lofty one if the labor is always to be pleasant."

In view of Tolstoy's contemptuous regard for history

[1] A good case can be made out for the influence of *David Copperfield* on *Childhood*.

[2] In a letter in 1904, he paid the following tribute in English: "I think that Charles Dickens is the greatest novel writer of the 19th century, and that his works, impressed with the true Christian spirit, have done and will continue to do a great deal of good to mankind."

during his university days, it is quite surprising to find him confessing now, in a letter to Auntie Tatyana, that he had finally accepted her wise advice and was reading history and liking it. He read Hume, Thiers, Michaud, and later Karamzin. As usual, his critical sense was uppermost, and in that alarming spirit of grandiosity with which youth plans, he dashed off in the diary: "Must compose a true and just history of Europe of the present century. There I have an aim for my whole life. Few epochs in history are so instructive as this one, or so little debated—debated without prejudice and truthfully, as we now debate the history of Egypt and Rome. Wealth, freshness of sources, and historical impartiality are a perfection unknown to us." His reading of Plato's *Politics* and Rousseau's *Contrat Social* suggested a vaster task: "Will devote the rest of my life to drawing up a plan for an aristocratic, selective union with a monarchical administration on the basis of existing elections. Here I have an aim for a virtuous life. I thank Thee, O Lord. Grant me strength." This huge plan went the way of the other, but he was beginning to feel his way towards an entirely different union of mankind, conceived in the spirit of God and founded on brotherly love.

Thoughts about reading and literature in the diary are few in comparison with those about God and immortality, about good and evil. The effort to make clear to himself the object and meaning of his life integrates all the separate periods of Tolstoy's spiritual and intellectual development. His effort now, filled with the same doubt and uncertainty as before, resulted in thoughts that were unusual for a youth barely twenty-four. Many of them anticipated his mature religious conception of life.

Simplicity, Tolstoy remarked, is the first condition of moral beauty, and clarity the best token of truth, but conscience is man's most reliable guide. "That man whose purpose is his own happiness is bad; he whose purpose is the opinion of others is weak; he whose purpose is the happiness of others is virtuous; he whose purpose is God is great." But does a man whose purpose is God find happiness? Rather, man finds happiness in doing good, and the voice of conscience is that which distinguishes good from evil. "Both inclination and fate," he concluded, "point out the road that we must choose; but always must we labor with the aim of attaining goodness."

In the Caucasus Tolstoy's thoughts turned to God and

religion with a sincerity that he had never before experienced. He prayed every morning and found a new efficacy in prayer, because it "was not harmful and was moral solitude." Several moving prayers he set down in his diary over this period. Doubts, however, always lurked in the corners of his mind. He could never succeed, he said, in deriving an idea of God as clearly as the idea of virtue. For "the idea of God comes of man's recognition of his own weakness." By the end of his second year in the Caucasus, he had arrived at a perfectly honest and conventional creed which he wrote down in the diary: "I believe in the one, incomprehensible, and good God, in the immortality of the soul, and in the eternal reward for our deeds; I do not understand the mysteries of the trinity and the birth of the Son of God, but I honor and do not reject the faith of my fathers."

The fundamental rule of behavior that lay at the base of his whole future religious philosophy Tolstoy recognized clearly at this time: "To live in the present, i.e. to act in the best possible fashion in the present, this is wisdom." He already knew, as he was to preach many years later, that happiness depended not upon circumstances, but upon oneself. His entry in the diary on his birthday was almost as severe as that of the preceding year, except that he added a note of hope for the future: "I'm now 24; yet I have done nothing. I feel that not in vain have I been struggling for 8 years with doubt and passions. For what am I destined? This the future will reveal. Killed 3 woodcocks."

9

The beginning of 1853 brought war again. Cadet Tolstoy prepared for action. Mars banished the muses, and in the excitement, contemplation gave way to martial fervor. The hill tribes were gathering, ten thousand of them, and the wily old warrior Shamil was prepared to prevent the attempt of a large Russian force to cut down the forests from Khobi-Shavdonski heights to the Argunskoye gorge in an effort to kill off the Chechenians in this territory or drive them into the Black Mountains. Fierce fighting ensued. On February 17 Tolstoy distinguished himself in a major attack in which his battery silenced the guns of the enemy. The campaign broke the back of Shamil's resistance.[3]

[3] Tolstoy's short story, "The Woodfelling," is based on this action.

The campaign also ended Tolstoy's brief period of moral resistance. In camp, drinking, cards, and wenching were the order of the day between attacks. He complained sadly of Nikolai's fondness for vodka, then got drunk himself, picked a fight with Ensign Yanovich for trying to break his fingers, and threatened to challenge him to a duel. He imagined how he would magnanimously give the ensign the first shot and then hold his own fire. The affair ended with mutual apologies, but Tolstoy earned the scowls of the officers for his tactless behavior.

Tolstoy's bravery in the attack of the 17th once again won him a recommendation for the St. George Cross. There was nothing he wanted so much as this little silver testimony of courageous conduct under fire. He stayed up so late over a game of chess that he failed to appear on duty the morning the award was to be made. Instead of presenting him with a medal, the commander of the brigade had him clapped in the guardhouse. From his prison he heard the drums beat and the band play while the awards were conferred, and he yielded to utter despair. On still a third occasion, sometime later, he was again scheduled to receive this coveted prize, a St. George Cross allotted to his battery, but upon a hint from his colonel, he gave way to an old soldier of the line for whom the reward meant a pension for life.

When the battery got back to Starogladkovskaya at the end of March, Tolstoy continued to live as he had on the campaign, like a gambler who fears to count how much he owes. His wild Chechenian *kunaks,* Sado and Balta, were always at hand to lead him into some adventure or other. He was still quartered in Epishka's hut, and the ancient Cossack, with his roaring basso, quaint language, and inexhaustible supply of yarns, provided endless entertainment. They would sit up until dawn drinking *chikhir* (native wine), while Epishka related unbelievable stories of his prowess as a hunter, of the souls he had "released" from the bodies of his enemies, of the Chechenets he snared with his lasso at the very edge of his village, and of his mighty success in stealing horses and the hearts of Cossack maidens.

In this latter competition, Tolstoy had again entered the lists. Running through the diary at this time are frank references to Solomonida, Oksana, Kasatka, Fedosya, Teodorina, Aksinya, and others. "Everything young acts strongly on me," he confessed; "every woman's bare leg seems to me to belong to a beauty." In vain he tried to abide by his rule of exhausting himself with hard physical labor when he felt the ache of strong desire, and to no purpose did he tell himself over and over again that the pleasure was brief and the remorse great. He followed a girl to the public baths, and at night reckoned up his expenses for the day: "25 rubles for the horse; 1 ruble, 30 kopeks for the girl; 1 ruble for the cab; 70 kopeks for trifles; 58 rubles remain." As on previous occasions, the cost of his promiscuity could not always be tallied in rubles and kopeks. "Kasatka," he wrote, "rewarded me with some mercury, which made me very sad." He feared, without cause, that he had contracted syphilis, but finally decided that even this misfortune might be a mixed blessing: "Yesterday, at the thought that my nose might fall in, I imagined what an immense and beneficial impulse this would give me in the direction of moral development."

At Starogladkovskaya a very noticeable change now took place in Tolstoy's relations with his fellow officers. With simple folk, such as Epishka, soldiers in the ranks, or peasants on the road, he was unusually successful in winning their confidence by his firm, straightforward, uncondescending manner. He felt that these common people were far above his own class by virtue of the work they accomplished and the privation they endured. "There is evil in them," he remarked, "but it is better to say of them (as of the dead) only what is good." With his officer friends, his equals, or those who pretended to be his equals, he was standoffish, always afraid that they would underestimate him. He did not feel at ease with them, because he was convinced that they could never sympathize with his interests. His own standards were beyond their understanding. "Once for all," he wrote in the diary, "I must become accustomed to the thought that I am an exception, and that either I am ahead of my age or am one of those incompatible, unadaptable natures that are never satisfied. . . . I have not yet met a single man who was morally as good as I, and who believed that I do not remember in my life an occasion when I was not attracted by what is good, was not ready to sacrifice everything for it." But his natural conviviality and the desire to be liked by all, which had been strong within him from his boyhood days, finally reasserted themselves. His hut became a common meeting place for the officers. They dropped in at any hour for a drink of vodka or to chat. Some of them he even impressed into service to copy his manuscripts. When he could curb his sharp tongue and hypercritical nature, they enjoyed his jollity, humor, and superb storytelling ability.

One day Tolstoy and Sado were in a convoy of stores from Fort Vozdvizhenskaya to Fort Groznaya. Although regulations strictly forbade anyone detaching himself from the convoy, because of the danger of being cut off by roving mountaineers, he, Sado, and three mounted officers, impatient with the slow pace of the infantry, rode on ahead. Tolstoy and Sado ascended a ridge to see if any of the enemy were in sight. A large band of them suddenly appeared a short distance away. Shouting a warning to their three comrades below, Tolstoy and Sado galloped for the fort, less than three miles away. The Chechenian band divided, seven of them taking up the pursuit of Tolstoy and Sado and the rest dashing after the other officers. These men had been slow to take the warning, and two of them were severely wounded before reaching the convoy. Meanwhile, Tolstoy, who had been trying out Sado's spirited new horse and might easily have escaped, refused to desert his friend, who was mounted on Tolstoy's slow ambler. The Chechenians drew nearer and nearer, while Sado tried to keep them at a distance by threatening them with an unloaded gun. The enemy could have shot them down, but apparently they desired to take them alive, especially the renegade Sado, whom they no doubt wished to torture. Fortunately, a Cossack guard at the post saw their plight. A rescue party at once galloped out and the Chechenians fled.[4] "I was almost taken prisoner," was Tolstoy's only mention of his narrow escape in the diary, "but on this occasion behaved well, though I was too sentimental."

In July, Tolstoy went to Pyatigorsk to see his sister, who had come with her husband for medical treatment. After some two years of separation, he was delighted to set eyes on Marya, but soon after their meeting he wrote home to Sergei to complain feelingly of the fact that neither she nor her husband had given the slightest evidence of any love for him. He was becoming peculiarly sensitive over his

[4] Tolstoy used this incident in his tale, *"A Prisoner of the Caucasus."*

failure to inspire in people the deep devotion of which he himself was capable. Two days before this letter, he wrote in his diary: "Why does nobody love me? I'm not a fool, not deformed, not a bad man, not a dolt. It is incomprehensible."

For the next four months Tolstoy wandered in aimless fashion from town to town in the neighborhood of Pyatigorsk, restless, uneasy in his mind, and not always well. He took up spiritualism and held seances around a table in a sidewalk café. His principal diversions, however, were women and gambling. In August he lost at cards the large sum of three thousand rubles, although in an effort to pay up his outstanding debts he was trying to live on ten rubles a month.

Tolstoy's restlessness and depression were largely induced by the uncertainty about his immediate future. He had not intended to enter the army when he came to the Caucasus, but once having joined he was ambitious for advancement and tangible rewards. He had had a reasonable expectancy of promotion after six months of acceptable service. But two years had passed and he was still a cadet. His brave behavior at the action of this year (1853) had resulted in a recommendation for a commission. Again, the lack of necessary documents was delaying this promotion, although the usual red tape of the military was also partly responsible. He had written to Aunt Pelageya to use her influence, and in July he had sent an angry letter to his commander, Baryatinski, complaining vehemently of the shabby treatment he was receiving from the man who had strongly urged him to enter the army. Finally, his patience worn out, and against the advice of Auntie Tatyana and Sergei, he sent in his request for a discharge. And when the lack of documents delayed this also, he asked for a furlough.

In the meantime, Russia had declared war against Turkey, and retirement was forbidden until the end of hostilities. Tolstoy had to reconsider his desire to leave the army. His hopes centered on the possibility of obtaining both his promotion and a furlough, and finally a transfer to the army in action against the Turks on the Danube. On October 6, he wrote to his relative, Prince M. D. Gorchakov, head of the General Staff and commander of the Danubian armies, for a transfer. Weighing the possibilities of success, he returned to Starogladkovskaya to await an answer.

10

During 1853 literary activity was an effective counterirritant for "moral deterioration." "Only work can afford me pleasure and profit," he jotted down in the diary. Initial success drove him on. A rigid schedule of work was laid out. Every spare moment he had his pen in hand. Excited over a piece, his "heart fails," and he "trembles" on taking up his copybook. He read an article on the literary characteristics of genius, which awoke in him "the conviction that I am a remarkable man for my capacity and my eagerness to work." Fame seemed within his grasp.

Tolstoy at first worked hard on *Boyhood,* the continuation of *Childhood,* but lost interest before he finished. In this work there are fewer autobiographical elements and more fiction, but it is too much overlaid with sentiment that borders on sentimentality. For a literary composition to be attractive, he felt that it should be directed by a consistent thought and penetrated by a consistent feeling. These conditions were lacking in *Boyhood*. The wonderful evocative atmosphere of *Childhood* is thinner in the sequel, perhaps because of the greater emphasis he placed upon analysis. Yet this analysis is uncannily convincing, responsive to all the evasive simplicity of a boy's inmost feelings. Some of the descriptive passages, such as the beautiful chapter on the storm, which with his own stern judgment he pronounced "excellent," foreshadow similar passages in later works. He kept the manuscript by him for further correction until after he left the Caucasus.

Tolstoy's moral dissatisfaction with himself at this time no doubt hindered the free functioning of the introspective process so necessary for a sustained effort on *Boyhood*. But this same dissatisfaction he turned to excellent use in a short story, "Notes of a Billiard-Marker," which he wrote with rapt concentration and enthusiasm in four days. He informed Nekrasov when he sent him the manuscript (September 17) that he valued this tale more than *Childhood* or "The Raid." The story has a scant autobiographical framework in the external facts of gambling with the billiard marker and the hero's first sexual experience, but Tolstoy also drew upon his own inner sufferings in his powerful analysis of the hero's moral disintegration. The tale has unquestioned autobiographical significance as a revelation of Tolstoy's spiritual distress at this time.

In 1853 Tolstoy also wrote "Christmas Eve," an unfinished short story of a young man's dissipation in Moscow; he continued "The Novel of a Russian Landowner" and *The Cossacks;* and he began "Caucasian Reminiscences," and "The Woodfelling." This represents a considerable amount of literary activity for a single year that was broken up by an extensive military campaign. And all he wrote was done with extreme care. Of *Boyhood* alone, the length of a short novel, there were three full versions.

It is interesting to observe that at this time Tolstoy began to evince a concern for the absence in contemporary literature of what he thought should be its one aim—morality. He even went so far as to say that "it would really not be a bad thing in every literary work (as in a fable) to write a moral—stating its aim." This conviction gave him an idea: "to edit a periodical, the sole aim of which would be the dissemination of works morally useful, for which contributions would be accepted only on the condition that they were accompanied by a moral, the printing or non-printing of which would depend on the author's wish." Nothing came of this strange idea, nor did he see fit to subscribe to it in his own fiction. Although his tales and novels nearly always possess a strong moral content, it never obtrudes upon the essential artistic unity of the work. But after 1880, he was to return to this idea of his youth, and it influenced his aesthetic theory and practice.

11

Back at Starogladkovskaya Tolstoy marked time, waiting for an answer to his request for a transfer. The remote and quiet life of Yasnaya Polyana beckoned to him once again. He agreed with Schiller that no genius can develop in solitude, but he was willing to take this risk if only he could get away from the Caucasus. Nikolai had already resigned from the service, and he felt lonely without him. Much of his leisure was spent in his favorite sport of hunting, which was no anodyne, however, to the depression he felt over the futility of his present existence. So strong was the desire to reform that he tried to do a good deed every day, once giving away his horse to a passing Cossack for lack of a less expensive opportunity to appease his conscience.

On January 12, 1854, Tolstoy received the welcome news that he had been transferred to the 5th Battery of the 12th

Artillery Brigade in active service on the Danube, and his request for a furlough was also granted. A week later, he joyfully set out on the long trip to Yasnaya Polyana.

Tolstoy's two and a half years in the Caucasus were a momentous period in his life. They provided a severe moral and physical test from which he emerged a maturer and more highly developed man. In his efforts towards self-perfection, he was inclined to magnify his moral failings. The remarkable fact is that he had any moral scruples left, when one considers the customary loose living of frontier soldiers and the easy morals of the natives. The sternly subjective picture of himself reflected in his diary and letters must be corrected by the objective appraisal of his friends and associates over this period. The natives held him in high esteem. They admired his simplicity, honesty, and generosity, his expert horsemanship and unquestioned bravery, which won for him their highest commendation, the title of *dzhigit*. And once he learned not to demand too much from the officers, he gained their respect and even their admiration. When he left Starogladkovskaya, his friends Zhukevich and Alekseyev, his colonel, who had borne much from him, wept sincere tears of regret. On the road home, his thoughts dwelt upon these comrades of the last two years for whom he formerly had no respect, and he admitted to himself that in the end he had become fond of them, because he had finally learned not to pick people out, but to see what was good even in the bad ones.

Although Tolstoy had repeatedly expressed dislike for his Caucasian existence, with that common perversity of man he was able to look back on it as one of the best periods of his life. Only a few months after he left, he remarked that he had begun to love the Caucasus with a posthumous but strong affection. He never attempted, however, to rationalize his loneliness and unhappiness there, or the fact that life had seemed to lose all sense for him then. Rather, he regarded it as a crucible in which his finest qualities had been severely tested. It was both "a grievous and splendid" time when he had scaled the heights of thought and enjoyed the first, unforgettable rapture of the author who has succeeded.

Tolstoy's trip home was uneventful, save for an unusually fierce blizzard that inspired his short story, "The Snowstorm." He arrived at Yasnaya Polyana on February 2, 1854.

VIII

My Hero Is Truth

At Yasnaya Polyana the cadet from the Caucasus received a hearty welcome. Tolstoy found the affairs of his estate in good order, and himself "out of date, amended and aged." The chief defect and peculiarity of his character, he presently decided, was that he had remained morally young too long, and that only now, at the age of twenty-five, had he acquired an independent, masculine view of things. He tested it that same day on a certain Mavrikiya, a pretty girl who distracted him at his prayers in chapel.

After a hurried visit to his sister's estate at Pokrovskoye, Tolstoy returned to find his three brothers awaiting him. Their reunion was joyous. Infinite talk amid infinite tobacco smoke lasted far into the night; then all four made up a bed on the floor and continued their chatter. Only Dmitri worried Tolstoy. Always strange and unconventional, Dmitri's deeply religious and chaste nature had lately succumbed to worldly temptation. His morbid conscience, like that of some character out of Dostoyevsky, had compelled him to pay for the release of his first prostitute from a brothel and make her his common-law wife. Moral and physical doom seemed already stamped upon his face and mind.[1]

A few days after their meeting, the brothers went to Moscow together. Tolstoy lavished money on military equipment, for news of his promotion to the rank of ensign had reached him. He next made his way to Dmitri's estate in the Kursk district, and from there, having first taken the

[1] Certain traits of Dmitri have perhaps entered into the characterizations of Prince Nekhlyudov in *Boyhood* and Nikolai Levin in *Anna Karenina.*

precaution to write his will, he set out for the active Army of the Danube on March 3.

Nine days later Tolstoy, almost sick with fatigue, arrived at Bucharest; he had traveled some fourteen hundred miles by way of Poltava and Kishinyov, and most of it in rickety conveyances. Instead of the atmosphere of war he expected to be plunged into, he found the city disappointingly peaceful.

Russia's gratuitous guardianship of the Holy Places of Jerusalem and her pretended concern for the fate of Orthodox Christians in Turkey had been the ostensible reasons for a break with that country. In reality, Nicholas I wished to distract the minds of his oppressed people from the annoying subject of reforms; then, he also had an interest in establishing his influence over Turkey in order to control sea traffic in the eastern Mediterranean. In July 1853, Russia had mobilized her armies and occupied Moldavia and Walachia in order to force Turkey's compliance with the Tsar's demands.

Turkey, however, was in no hurry to comply, for she had received unofficial assurances from the British of full support, despite that government's seemingly official support of Russia. With this uncertainty on both sides, hostilities progressed with caution. About the time Tolstoy reached Bucharest, the war had taken a new turn. In the preceding January, Britain, France, Austria, and Prussia had met to declare their concern over Russia's invasion of the Ottoman Empire. The principal, though unspoken, factor behind this opposition was England's determination to keep the Russians out of the eastern Mediterranean, for the Suez Canal had already been projected and England wanted no threat to these new lines to the east. France supported England, because Napoleon III had been offended by the snobbish Tsar; also, a successful war would help to prop up his insecure throne. Accordingly, England and France broke off relations with Russia in March 1854, and shortly after this, while Tolstoy was in Bucharest, the Russian armies crossed the Danube and laid siege to Silistria.

Auntie Tatyana had hopes that her darling would obtain the rather safe sinecure of adjutant to his relative, Prince M. D. Gorchakov, Commander-in-Chief of the Danubian forces. Tolstoy quickly paid his respects to the prince, and although he was kindly received, pride prevented him from making any direct overtures to the general. Since no one seemed anxious to use his services immediately, he was quite content to amuse himself with the ample pleasures afforded by Bucharest, the first European city he had seen. In the company of the prince's two nephews—"fine lads," he called them—he enjoyed his fill of Italian opera, the French theater, and less cultured entertainment.

This tourist existence came to a sudden end on March 22, when Tolstoy was assigned to the 3rd Battery of the 11th Artillery Brigade, stationed at Oltenitza, not far from Bucharest. For the moment he regarded philosophically enough the fact that he had not been taken on the General Staff as an adjutant. In May, he was able to write to Auntie Tatyana: "I have a fit of conscience when I think that you believe me exposed to every danger, while I've still not smelt Turkish powder and live here tranquilly at Bucharest promenading about, occupied with music, and eating ice cream." He remained at Oltenitza only a couple of weeks, quarreled with his battery commander, and finally obtained a post on the staff of Lieutenant General A. O. Serzhputovski, Commander of Artillery of the Army of the Danube. At first he admired the general and found the officers on the staff "for the most part, men *comme il faut.*" After fulfilling several commissions that took him about the countryside, he returned to Bucharest for medical treatment.

Towards the end of May, Tolstoy rejoined General Serzhputovski's staff which was with the army before besieged Silistria. This time he got a smell of Turkish powder. At first he had eyes only for the beautiful poetic dress that so often adorns the ugly body of war. The Russian camp was pitched on the lofty right bank of the Danube, amid the superb gardens of the city's governor. From this elevated position Tolstoy took delight in gazing out over the smoothly flowing river, dotted with green islets; and beneath him he saw, as though they were in the palm of his hand, the clear outlines of Silistria with its network of fortifications. It was a queer sort of pleasure, he remarked, to look at people killing each other; for hours he would watch in the distance bloody skirmishes between Russian and Turkish soldiers. Day and night the cannonading thundered. The first night the furious firing frightened him; he thought an assault was taking place. But he soon grew accustomed to it and amused himself by counting, watch in hand, the frequency of the explosions, reckoning one hundred and ten to the minute. The dangerous business of carrying dispatches robbed the scene of its poetic charm. On one such occasion the familiar practical joker of the army, wishing to test the young count's courage, led Tolstoy along a very exposed terrain with maddening slowness. Tolstoy showed no apparent concern over the flying bullets, but inwardly, he admitted later, he was sick with fear.

At this siege Tolstoy had an opportunity to observe the fine leadership of Prince Gorchakov. In a letter to Auntie Tatyana he described the old general's fearlessness under fire, his endless care for all the details of the action, and his sympathy for the sufferings of common soldiers and civilians. The prince became a hero in his eyes, and he now wished that his aunt's hope would come true, for he could imagine no service more worthy than that of adjutant to such a noble warrior. In this same letter Tolstoy told of the soldierly control of Gorchakov in a moment of bitter disappointment. With the utmost care he had planned the assault on Silistria, and the Russian forces had every hope of success. Shortly before the attack was to take place, an order came through to cancel it (the reason was the fear of Austria in the Russian rear). With not a word of criticism, Gorchakov cheerfully commanded a retreat, and on June 10 the Russian Army of the Danube began an orderly withdrawal to its own frontier.

2

When the army reached Bucharest, Tolstoy requested General Gorchakov for a transfer to any place where the service was more active. Operations for fistulas, however, kept him in Bucharest for more than a month. When not ill, he indulged himself in the loose living that his conscience abhorred. With tiresome iteration he repeated in the diary: "I'm firmly resolved to dedicate my life to the service of my neighbors. For the last time I tell myself: 'If three days pass without my having done anything of service to people, I will kill myself.'" Although he continued to live—not very tranquilly, to be sure—it is difficult to discover any concrete examples of service to his neighbors over this period. On the contrary, in fits of anger he beat his servant and made himself obnoxious to many of his fellow officers.

By now Tolstoy had become almost a professional self-critic; such persistent preoccupation with his faults left little time for the practice of virtues. Yet, the "masculine view of things" that he had formulated upon his return from the Caucasus began to temper these endless moral eviscerations. Instead of always reaching for the moon and falling on his belly, he tried to achieve the practical limits beyond which moral virtue ceased to be anything other than an unattainable ideal.

As soon as he was alone, Tolstoy involuntarily returned to his former ideal of perfecting himself; but now he at last realized that all along he had been confusing perfecting himself with perfection. "One must first understand oneself and one's defects well and try to correct them," he wrote, "and not set oneself the task of being perfect, which is not only impossible to achieve from the low point at which I stand, but which, when once perceived, one even loses hope of the possibility of achieving perfection. . . . One must take oneself as one is and try to correct the incorrigible faults. A fine nature will lead me to what is good without a *notebook,* which for so long has been a nightmare. My character desires, seeks, and is ready for all that is fine, and for that very reason it is incapable of being consistently good."

One is tempted to shout: Eureka! In all his voluminous self-criticism, this was Tolstoy's first clear recognition of the limitations of his own nature and of the reasonable possibilities of improving it. And with the same insight, he now admitted that he loved fame more than goodness, and that his frequent inability to make friends arose from an inclination to show his superiority. Indeed, he quickly observed that when he curbed his tendency to appear majestic and infallible, his relations with people were pleasanter and easier. Lack of character, irritability, and laziness he set down in the diary as his three chief defects, and he repeated them at the end of his daily entries so that he would not forget.

The pleasures of Bucharest, like those of Moscow and Petersburg, sorely tempted Tolstoy, and the gay young blades among his army comrades beguiled him into gambling and "gadding about," a euphemism in the diary for pursuing loose women. Some of his abandonment was temporarily checked by unexpectedly meeting his commanding officer at a brothel. An occasional romantic interlude, such as his attraction for the landlady's pretty daughter, varied this dissipation. He furtively watched her from his window at night as she leaned out of hers. A barrel organ in the street played a familiar waltz, and as the sounds faded in the distance, the girl sighed deeply, and moved away from the window. "I grew so sadly pleasant," one reads in the diary, "that I involuntarily smiled, and long continued to gaze at my street lamp, the light of which was sometimes concealed by the branches of a tree swaying in the breeze, at the tree itself, at the wooden fence, and at the heavens, which all seemed better than before." The poetry vanished with a very unromantic concluding observation: "Ate beet soup while I have diarrhea that keeps getting worse."

Despite romance, diarrhea, dissipation, and other distractions, Tolstoy made a serious effort to continue his literary work at Bucharest. His reading was considerable, including both native and foreign authors, especially Goethe and Schiller. Like Mark Twain, however, he found "something ridiculous in the German language." He also read, in a German translation, *Uncle Tom's Cabin,* which had aroused much interest in Europe. The book impressed him, not for its literary merit, but for the feeling it conveyed. The question of the emancipation of the serfs was in the air. He commented in the diary on a long discussion of Russian serfdom with one of his friends, and his reaction indicates that he had not progressed much beyond the youthful ideas in the early experiment with his own peasants at Yasnaya Polyana. "It's true," he wrote, "that slavery is an evil thing, but ours is a very benevolent evil." Nicholas I might have said the same thing at this time.

Nekrasov had written Tolstoy a very flattering letter about *Boyhood,* which had been accepted by the *Contemporary.* As usual, such praise encouraged him and he began to work hard on two other stories. This effort was cut short by an order to leave Bucharest with the staff of General Serzhputovski for the Russian frontier. He reached Kishinyov on September 9, and there he learned that he had been promoted to the rank of sublieutenant.

3

Nicholas I had displayed some of the humility of common sense in ordering a withdrawal of his army from the Danubian provinces after Britain and France had broken with him in March. Some kind of peace should have been patched up at that point, but the dogs of war had been unleashed and a few territorial or diplomatic bones had to be thrown to them before their masters could call them off. Accordingly, the British and French had started the quite needless campaign of the Crimea.

As the allies sailed up the Black Sea coast, English officers in their flagship took off their hats and bowed ceremoniously to the helpless Russians who gazed at them from the shore. This expeditionary force landed at Eupatoria on September 2, the only resistance being a plaintive plea of the Russian governor that the disembarking enemy consider itself in strict quarantine.

The day before Tolstoy's arrival in Kishinyov, a battle had been fought on the Alma River in the Crimea. The British went up the slope in the face of the enemy's fire as though they were marching at Hyde Park; their French allies, innocent of any prearranged plan of attack, fought a separate action by their side. As for the Russians under Menshikov, no one received any orders and every man did what he thought best. A victory for the allies was the result of the general mismanagement. A quiver of patriotism ran through the vast Russian Empire at the thought of the native land invaded for the first time since Napoleon. On September 11, the allies started their advance on Sevastopol, about thirty miles away, the only Russian naval base on the Black Sea.

The seriousness of their country's plight did not quickly dawn on Tolstoy and the young officers of Serzhputovski's staff. They found the lively, cosmopolitan society of Kishinyov highly diverting, and the war atmosphere only served to intensify the gaiety. Tolstoy did not lag behind his comrades in their carousing; his precious rules, though never forgotten, were broken with impunity in the excitement. The spice of royalty was added to the general liveliness by the arrival of the two young Grand Dukes, Nikolai Nikolayevich and Mikhail Nikolayevich, who were on their way to the front to bolster morale. To Tolstoy they seemed "to have the air of excessively good children and were very fine lads, both of them."

Rumors from the Crimea filled the air. When they were bad, gloom hung over the staff; a good report called for a celebration with champagne. Such was the news of the battle of Balaklava. The comedy of tragic errors of this ghastly campaign had already begun. After Alma, the allies, slowly moving on Sevastopol, were hindered by a lack of maps of the region, and those in the possession of the Russians were so inaccurate that a regiment, having marched all day away from the city, found itself back at Sevastopol by nightfall. Instead of attempting to take at once the poorly defended city from the north, as the Russians expected, the British and French marched leisurely around Sevastopol and set up their bases to the south. All this maneuvering gave the brilliant Russian engineer Totleben plenty of time to surround the city with a formidable system of defense works. The allies finally got around to bombarding Sevastopol on October 5, but failed to follow up with an assault. A week later a Russian force, under General P. P. Liprandi, attempted to relieve the fortress by a sudden attack on the English right and rear, aimed at their base at Balaklava. A fierce charge by the Heavy Cavalry Brigade checked the Russian onset, but the more famous charge of the Light Cavalry Brigade in the wrong direction did not help the British cause. In the end, the advantage was with the Russians who had cut the only road between the British and their base.

The news electrified Tolstoy and his army friends. A group of them, chafing under their enforced inaction, had decided to form a society to educate the common soldier. In a few days this idea had changed into a plan to edit a popular army magazine to help maintain a good spirit among the troops. In simple language it would carry courageous exploits, descriptions of battles, and the biographies and obituaries of worthy, and especially of obscure, men. Soldiers' songs also would be printed. After some hesitation, Tolstoy backed the plan with enthusiasm and was chosen editor. He drew up a prospectus, taking care not to offend the traditional conservatism of the military authorities, and sent it to Prince Gorchakov for approval. The prince was pleased and submitted the prospectus with a sample number of the magazine to the Emperor. Tolstoy feared that the articles he and a friend contributed to the sample number were not quite orthodox enough. In order to raise money for the project, he sent home an order to sell the large house in which he had been born, a most painful decision for him.[2] The group of young altruists waited impatiently for an answer from the Emperor.

[2] This was the central structure built by grandfather Volkonski. When it was sold and removed, the wings remained. Eventually the present main structure at Yasnaya Polyana was erected in place of the original building.

Several weeks later came the sorrowful report of the battle of Inkerman (October 24). A Russian force, superior in number, had been repulsed with a loss of more than ten thousand killed and wounded. Although rumors of treachery filled the air, the truth was that the obstinate courage, outmoded muskets, and poor marksmanship of the Russians were no match for the tough, stolid English and volatile, brave French with their modern Minié rifles. Like a slow, angry tide, the Russian forces ebbed back to Sevastopol. Both sides settled down to a winter of siege warfare.

Tolstoy's patriotism, like that of most Russians at the time, was tremendously aroused by tales of the heroic defense of Sevastopol. Fierce indignation stirred in him over the ugly rumors of betrayal and faulty leadership connected with Inkerman. In his diary he gave way to sentiments that would have shocked him years later. "Horrible slaughter!" he wrote. "It will weigh on the souls of many! Lord, forgive them! The news of this affair [Inkerman] has produced an impression. I met old men who wept aloud, and young ones who swore to kill Danenberg [commander of the Russian forces at Inkerman]. Great is the moral strength of the Russian people. Many political truths will come out and develop in these days of difficulty for Russia. The feeling of passionate love for the fatherland that is arising and flowing from the misfortunes of Russia will long leave its trace in her."

Tolstoy could not continue to remain at Kishinyov while his countrymen were dying behind the earthworks of Sevastopol. He felt ashamed of his very security when he heard that I. K. Komstadius, a young friend on the staff of the projected army magazine, had been killed at Inkerman. A request for a transfer to Sevastopol was finally granted. He left Kishinyov with a group of officers, and because of the blockade traveled by way of Odessa, Kherson, and Oleshko. At the latter place he was detained, he wrote in the diary, "by a pretty and intelligent Ukrainian girl whom I kissed and caressed through the window. At night she came to me. . . . My remembrance would have been better," he ruefully concluded, "if I had remained at the window." Meanwhile his friends had left him far behind. Would he be late for the storming of Sevastopol that was threatened? He hurried on and reached the city November 7.

4

The storming turned out to be just another rumor. Tolstoy had demanded a transfer to the besieged city, he told his brother Sergei, partly because he wanted to see the war, partly to get away from General Serzhputovski's staff which he had come to dislike, but mostly because of the feeling of patriotism that now strongly influenced him. When he saw the appalling conditions of Sevastopol and the spirit of the defenders, he was filled with an ardent desire for victory. Enthusiastically he wrote to Sergei: "The spirit among the troops is beyond any description. In the time of ancient Greece there was not so much heroism. Kornilov,[3] making the rounds of his troops, instead of hailing them with: 'Good health to you, lads!' says: 'If you must die, lads, will you die?' And the soldiers shout: 'We will die, Your Excellency! Hurrah!' And they do not say it for effect," continued Tolstoy, "for in every face one saw not jesting, but earnestness, and 22,000 men have already fulfilled that promise."

Russian soldiers have never been deficient in courage, but an inspired bravery took possession of the defenders of Sevastopol, especially in the early days of the siege when their strength was fresh and hopes high. In this same letter to Sergei, Tolstoy proudly described how soldiers nearly mutinied when ordered to withdraw from batteries where they had been exposed to shellfire for thirty days; how they snatched the burning fuses from fallen bombs; how priests fearlessly read prayers under fire at the bastions; and how women from the town were wounded and killed while carrying water to the troops. They were wonderful days, he declared, and thanked God that he had been spared to see such people live in this glorious time. He admired the French and British prisoners he talked with. They appeared morally and physically finer than the Russian soldiers, who seemed "small, lousy, and shriveled up" in comparison. But he promised Sergei to tell of the brave deeds of these lousy, shriveled heroes who would not be convinced that the enemy could take the city.

Shortly after reaching Sevastopol, Tolstoy received an

[3] Vice-Admiral V. A. Kornilov, who played a most distinguished role in the first days of the siege and was fatally wounded at the initial bombardment.

answer to his petition to edit a popular army magazine. The Emperor's reply was "No." Ironically Tolstoy wrote to Nekrasov: "On my project the Emperor most graciously gave his permission to print our articles in *The Gazette*," the dull official publication of the Ministry of War. Tolstoy suspected that people in the capital, who feared the competition of his proposed magazine, had used their influence against it; another guess was that his plan did not accord with the government's views. Such reactions indicate his political naïveté, a kind of ignorance not uncommon among young men of his class. No one with even the slightest awareness of the black reactionary and bureaucratic nature of Nicholas I would have ventured to hope for his approval of a popular army magazine, the purpose of which was to educate and brighten, no matter how harmlessly, the lives of his millions of ignorant peasant soldiers.

Tolstoy's stay in Sevastopol on this occasion lasted only eight days. He was transferred again to another artillery brigade, and his battery was ordered to take up a position near Simferopol, a few miles from the besieged city. Five days after his arrival at his new post (November 20), he inserted in the diary a brief poem, among the very few verses that he wrote in his lifetime:—

When, tell me when I at last may start
This aimless, passionless life to forsake?
When cease to feel the wound deep in my heart,
While still not knowing how to soothe its ache?

The wound that's pained me from life's dawn,
This only God alone can know about;
Of future nothingness the bitter pawn,
Of sadness that wearies and wearying doubt.

5

For more than a month Tolstoy remained with his battery at the little Tatar village of Eski-Orda near Simferopol. The comparative quiet of this bucolic setting was a striking contrast to the thunder and slaughter of Sevastopol. Hunting, dancing, music, reading, and philosophical disputes with the officers took the place of warlike activities. Of late, however, the art of war had been much on Tolstoy's mind. Whatever his deficiencies as a soldier, and they were many, he was a keen observer of army detail. Like most intellectuals in such circumstances, he had a certain contempt for the professional military mind, and the tragic consequences of its inefficiency aroused his anger. By now sober reality had dulled the fine edge of his patriotism, and he began to see clearly that things were going badly for the Russians, and that they must completely reorganize themselves or fall. On a visit to Sevastopol on December 5 to obtain guns, he noted with satisfaction the improved order that had been introduced in the defense by the new commander of the city's garrison, Baron D. E. Osten-Saken. Such a hopeful turn of affairs perhaps emboldened Tolstoy to offer some suggestions of his own for improvements. On his next trip to Sevastopol (January 15), he visited the vital Fourth Bastion, talked with Totleben, and then presented to Osten-Saken a project for the reorganization of batteries. He also worked on another plan for the formation of rifle brigades as a means of overcoming the fatal inferiority of the Russians in small-arms equipment.[4]

How these innovations were received is not known. Perhaps they were placed in the same category as the suggestion of Tolstoy's friend, Prince S. S. Urusov, a brave officer and brilliant chess player. He proposed to Osten-Saken that a challenge be sent to the English to play a game of chess for the foremost trench in front of the Fifth Bastion, a trench that had already changed hands several times at the cost of hundreds of lives. At any rate, it is unlikely that the fresh views of a mere sublieutenant would be taken seriously in a military bureaucracy noted for impregnable traditionalism. That he got a hearing at all may be attributed to certain privileges he enjoyed as a relative of Prince Gorchakov, who had recently been appointed Commander-in-Chief of all the Russian forces in the Crimea.

The seriousness of the situation, however, deeply impressed Tolstoy and drove him on to a bolder attempt at reform, to which has been given the title "A Memorandum on the Negative Aspects of the Russian Soldier and Officer." This document is a bitter arraignment of the inhuman conditions, the graft and mismanagement, in the Russian army. "By virtue of my oath," he wrote, "and still more because of my feeling for humanity, I cannot be silent about an evil that openly exists and obviously involves the destruction of millions of people and of forces of worth and of honor to the fatherland." With dogged factualness he described in

[4] The drafts of these projects have been lost.

turn the position of soldiers, lower officers, generals, and the commander-in-chief. A soldier is beaten if he smokes a pipe with a long stem, if he wishes to marry, or if he dares to notice how his superior steals from him. How many Russian officers, Tolstoy asked, are shot by Russian bullets? Our soldiers are brave, he said, because death for them is a blessing. "The majority of officers have one aim—to steal their fortunes out of the service, and they retire once they have achieved this end. . . . We have not an army," he concluded, "but a crowd of oppressed, disciplined slaves, confessed plunderers and hirelings."

There are a great many more forceful home truths of this sort in the memorandum, and Tolstoy ended it with an earnest appeal for reform. His original intention was to send the document to one of the Grand Dukes. Fortunately, he abandoned this idea and wisely kept his plan of reform out of circulation. The thought and indignation behind it, however, soon found another outlet in a purely literary work.

6

Another transfer in the middle of January moved Tolstoy to a new battery stationed on the Belbek River, about seven miles from Sevastopol. It was an unfortunate change. The chief interest of his captain, a huge, awkward brute, was in lining his pockets with the battery's surplus funds. He was "the dirtiest creature imaginable," complained Tolstoy, "and the senior officer a nasty, mean, little Pole. And I'm bound to, and even depend on, these people." It was cold in the earth huts; there was not a single book to read and no one to talk to. In his disgust and boredom he sought relief in gambling. Just at this low point he received the five thousand rubles for the sale of his house, money that he had requested for the now abandoned plan of the army magazine. In two days and nights of steady playing, he lost it all and even went into debt. The fever gripped him; he continued to gamble in the vain hope of recouping his losses. His situation grew desperate. He thought of obtaining a leave, of procuring a transfer to Kishinyov, or of entering the Military Academy. Although he flattered himself that he played "scientifically" on the basis of the elaborate system he had worked out, his reputation as an unlucky gambler became a byword. A few of the officers tried to protect him by refusing to play with him.

Tolstoy's only solace during this unhappy time was his friendship with a shadowy young officer, A. A. Bronevski. "I have never encountered a better heart," he wrote of him to Auntie Tatyana, "or a character as noble as that of this man . . ." Probably out of a discussion with Bronevski emerged a most significant thought. For Tolstoy entered in his diary on March 4: "Yesterday a conversation about divinity and faith suggested to me a great, a stupendous idea to the realization of which I feel capable of dedicating my whole life. This is the idea—the founding of a new religion corresponding to the development of mankind: the religion of Christ, but purged of all dogma and mysteriousness, a practical religion, not promising future bliss but realizing bliss on earth. I understand that to bring this idea to fulfillment the conscientious labor of generations towards this end will be necessary. One generation will bequeath the idea to the next, and some day fanaticism or reason will achieve it. *Consciously* to contribute to the union of man and religion is the basic idea which I hope will improve me." The Ant Brotherhood's green stick on which was written the mysterious message of childhood days seems to have taken root.

At this time of deep personal discouragement amid the surroundings of war Tolstoy was suddenly illuminated by the spiritual incandescence that would brighten the road of the last thirty years of his life. But this seed of a new religion had been planted in him very early. For years, however, his quest for fame and selfish personal happiness left the seed unnourished in the dark earth of his soul; and when it broke through at last the flower that grew was born of this same seed that bloomed prematurely for a passing moment in his rough soldier's camp on the Belbek.

For some eight months, since leaving Bucharest, Tolstoy had shirked his writing. In his present frame of mind, he was inclined to blame the army for his lapse. "A military career," he noted in the diary, "is not for me, and the sooner I get out of it and devote myself entirely to literature the better." A letter from his sister dispelled this gloomy thought. She told of her acquaintance with Turgenev (he eventually fell a bit in love with Marya), who lived not far from her estate, and of the famous author's lavish praise of her brother's ability. And his inertia entirely vanished after reading a very flattering review of "Notes of a Billiard-Marker," which had appeared in the January *Contemporary*.

"This is pleasant," he observed, "and useful in that it inflames my vanity and incites me to activity." He at once got to work on *Youth,* the sequel to *Boyhood.* Sometime before, he had written to Nekrasov to offer him the material that he and his friends had intended for the stillborn army magazine. Nekrasov now wrote of his eagerness to publish such material, which Tolstoy had neglected to say was almost nonexistent at that moment. This encouraging answer, however, inspired him to work on his own contribution, and he began the first of his three celebrated Sevastopol sketches.

Events interrupted Tolstoy's writing but also provided him with the opportunity for invaluable material. On February 18 Nicholas I had died, but his successor, Alexander II, decided to continue the war. Tolstoy heralded the new reign in his diary with the following observation: "Immense changes await Russia. One must work and be strong in order to take part in the great moments in the life of Russia." His own immediate part was to be a very dangerous one. On March 28 the allies began a terrific bombardment of Sevastopol. For ten terrible days the smoke-filled city cowered under a hail of cannon shot and exploding bombs from some two thousand guns. An assault was expected and Tolstoy's battery, along with many others, was ordered to Sevastopol.

7

The Fourth Bastion,[5] most southern end exposed point in the labyrinthine Sevastopol earthworks constructed by Totleben, was under almost continual fire, and many men had died in its defense. Here Tolstoy was placed in charge of a battery of guns and served on a schedule of four days on and eight days off from April 3 to May 15.

Life at the Fourth Bastion, with the enemy lines scarcely two hundred yards away, was rendered bearable only by the rough tenderness of comradeship that often exists in circumstances of constant danger. In this early example of modern trench warfare, heroism was a matter of retaining one's humanity under the slow, disintegrating agony of ever-present death. The chief thing was not to think. Under

[5] This fortification was called the Flagstaff Bastion by the English.

these trying conditions, Tolstoy's nature expanded and exulted. He got on excellently with everyone. "What a fine spirit there is among the sailors!" [6] he wrote in the diary. . . . "My little soldiers are also grand, and I'm happy when with them." The next day: "The same Fourth Bastion, which I'm beginning to like very much. . . . The constant charm of danger, observing the soldiers with whom I'm living, the sailors, and the methods of warfare, are so agreeable that I do not wish to leave here, all the more so since I should like to be present at the assault, if there is to be one."

When not directing the fire of his battery, Tolstoy worked feverishly away at his manuscripts of *Youth* or the first Sevastopol sketch in the bombproof dugout, an oblong hole in the rocky ground covered with oak beams. The dull boom of cannon fire could be heard overhead, or the more distinct sound of a rat scratching among the stones. By the light of a candle a group of soldiers crouched in the corner and played "noses." Tolstoy wrote away undisturbed by their laughter when the winner smacked the loser's nose with the pack of cards. He took particular note of their rough humor. A soldier tumbled into the dugout and one of the group cried out:—

"Hullo, brother! Why not stay outside? Don't the girlies play merrily enough out there?"

"They're playing such fine tunes as we never heard in our village," the newcomer retorted good-naturedly.

Or some one of the group would leave the dugout, followed by a laughing shout:—

"Look out, or you'll be getting your discharge in full before tonight!"

Here was rich ore for an author, and Tolstoy mined it assiduously at the Fourth Bastion. By the end of April he sent to Nekrasov his first sketch, *Sevastopol in December*. It was published in the June number of the *Contemporary* and aroused much favorable comment. Alexander II read it with emotion, had it translated into French, and is reported to have dispatched an order to "guard well the life of that young man."

Tolstoy's service at the dangerous Fourth Bastion revived in him the exalted patriotism that thrilled everyone during the early days of the siege. His first Sevastopol sketch

[6] Many sailors from the sunken and bottled-up Russian warships in Sevastopol Harbor valiantly aided in the defense of the city.

described that time in brilliant genre pictures of the city and of individuals among its inhabitants and defenders. Nothing could have been better calculated to raise the flagging hopes of a nation sick with the carnage and suffering of Sevastopol. Tolstoy frankly and most effectively appealed to the patriotism of the Russian people by telling them of the noble spirit and simple, self-sacrificing heroism of the city's brave defenders.

Towards the end of his period of duty at the Fourth Bastion, Tolstoy's own spirits wavered. Was he good for nothing, he wondered, save cannon fodder? The wretched existence undermined his health, and daily exposure to mortal danger from the thudding cannon shots, bursting bombs, and whistling rifle bullets was reflected in his prayer in the diary at this time: "O Lord! I thank Thee for Thy constant protection. How surely Thou leadest me to goodness. And what an insignificant creature I should be if Thou shouldst abandon me. Do not desert me, O Lord! Help me, not for the satisfaction of my insignificant aims, but to achieve the eternal, great, and unseen aim of existence of which I am conscious."

He believed the soldiers' spirits were failing; their former stubborn conviction that Sevastopol would never fall had vanished. Deeply disturbed, he drafted a report to General Gorchakov (probably never sent), in which he predicted in burning words the capitulation of Sevastopol, unless something were done at once to recapture its defenders' indomitable spirit and enthusiasm.

Tolstoy had had his fill of the Fourth Bastion, and a letter at this point from his influential Aunt Pelageya to her relative General Gorchakov gave him some hope of realizing his ambition of an appointment as adjutant to the Commander-in-Chief. Instead, he was not entirely dissatisfied to receive charge, on May 15, of a battery of mountain guns stationed on the Belbek River, and without any regrets he soon left the Fourth Bastion to take up his new post.[7]

[7] It has been argued that this transfer was made at the command of the Tsar, who wished to protect Tolstoy's life after reading *Sevastopol in December*. However, he could hardly have read the sketch before May 15, the date of the transfer. It is more likely that Aunt Pelageya's letter was the principal factor in the transfer. That is, Prince Gorchakov did not see fit to grant her request to make Tolstoy an adjutant, but he did remove him from a perilous post, and gave him what was in effect a promotion.

8

While in charge of the battery, Tolstoy hardly acquitted himself with distinction. Although he loathed corporal punishment, he beat his soldiers in fits of temper. The swearing of officers at their troops disgusted him and he invented a meaningless "cuss word" to replace the most obscene of these oaths. Yet, when he left the service, his troops told his successor that never had they known such a swearer as Count Tolstoy. His defiance of army tradition irritated his equals, and on one occasion earned him a severe reprimand from his chief.

In budgeting for a battery, the government permitted a surplus over fixed charges, with the intention that it should be used for miscellaneous items. It became an accepted practice for commanders to pocket as much of this surplus as possible; in fact, they actually came to believe that the government connived in this "harmless" form of peculation. Of course, various "economies" were introduced in the matter of soldiers' supplies, in order to assure a surplus worth taking.

So settled was this tradition that Tolstoy, upon becoming commander of a battery, deliberately planned to use funds from the surplus to pay off some of his debts. His moral sense, however, convinced him that this would be stealing. When other battery commanders learned that he intended to turn back any surplus, they saw to it that he was summoned before General N. A. Kryzhanovski, Artillery Chief of Staff. The general roundly scolded him for prejudicing the legitimate "earnings" of the other commanders. Tolstoy stood his ground; he answered that the money was not his, and hence he would return it to the government.

In most respects, however, Tolstoy was well liked by his fellow officers. The more modest, manly, and understanding attitude he had fostered towards the end of his service in the Caucasus was continued in the Crimea. A few warm friendships sprang up. No one could ignore his straight, well-formed figure and the striking if not handsome face, set off by wonderfully thoughtful and penetrating eyes. His conviviality, the masterful way in which he told a tale, his fine sense of honor in all relations, and his brave bearing and generosity were commented on by his fellow officers. They marveled at his strength, for he would lie down and lift from the floor two heavy men standing one each on his outstretched hands.

"Tolstoy inspired all of us," wrote one of his Sevastopol comrades, "during the trying times of the campaign, by his anecdotes and couplets deftly struck off. He was really the soul of the battery. When Tolstoy was with us, we never noticed how the time flew, and there was no end to the general gaiety. . . . When the count had vanished, driving off to Simferopol, then everyone had a long face. One day passes, then a second, and a third. . . . At last, he would return, like the prodigal son, gloomy, worn out, and dissatisfied with himself. . . . He would take me aside, quite apart, and begin his confession. He would tell all—how he had caroused, gambled, where he had spent his days and nights; and he would condemn himself and suffer as though he were a real criminal. He was so distressed that it was pitiful to see him. That's the kind of a man he was. In short, a queer fellow, and to tell the truth, one not entirely understood by me; on the other hand he was a rare comrade, the most honorable soul, and a man one never forgot."

9

For the next two and a half months after taking charge of his battery, Tolstoy avoided reasonably well the excesses into which inactivity usually led him. He read Goethe, Thackeray, and Balzac, translated a poem of Heine, and finished the third and last version of "The Woodfelling," which appeared in the *Contemporary* in September. Feeling that he had been influenced by Turgenev in this tale,[8] he asked permission to dedicate it to him. Turgenev was flattered and readily agreed.

On the day Tolstoy dispatched the story, he began work on another Sevastopol sketch. The writing absorbed him. He had taken an entirely new point of view, and when he sent *Sevastopol in May* to his publisher on July 4, he accompanied it with a letter, in which he wrote: "Although I'm convinced that it is incomparably better than the first, I'm certain that it will not be liked."

Tolstoy was right. The editors feared the sketch could not be published. They managed to get it past the censor with a few changes, but it was hastily recalled in proof. The

[8] At most, the influence is very slight.

President of the Censor's Committee, expressing surprise and anger that the editors had ever entertained the idea of printing such a piece, banned it because of the "ridicule of our brave officers, the brave defenders of Sevastopol." He ultimately reconsidered and passed the sketch, after making numerous deletions and changes. So completely altered were the whole narrative, tone, and intention, that Panayev decided not to publish. The President of the Censor's Committee, aware that he had virtually transformed the sketch into a propaganda document for the government, now insisted that it be printed. Panayev had to comply, but he refused to place Tolstoy's name to *Sevastopol in May* when it appeared in the *Contemporary* in September.

Tolstoy's first patriotic Sevastopol sketch had contributed greatly to his reputation, and he fully realized the fact. He wrote in his diary at this time: "Have only now reached a period of real temptation through vanity. I could gain much in life if I wished to write without conviction." *Sevastopol in May* is emphatic proof of the resolute manner in which he turned his back on this temptation. The idealizing patriotism of the first sketch has vanished. Longer service and broader experience had finally convinced him to take a stand that had always been his. War with all its cruelty, stupidity, and mock heroism was exposed. Boldly he declared at the end of this second sketch: "There, I have said what I wished to say. . . . The hero of my tale, whom I love with all the power of my soul, whom I have tried to portray in all his beauty, who has always been, is, and will be beautiful—is truth."

Under the uncompromising, dazzling light of truth, Tolstoy revealed the folly, hypocrisy, and utter futility of all this slaughter. The questions the diplomats had not settled, he remarked, still remained unsettled by powder and blood. All was vanity, vanity on the very brink of the grave. Officers were eager to climb on the shoulders of fallen comrades in order to reach the promotions their deaths had made possible. Every one of them was a little Napoleon, a petty monster ready to kill men to get an extra medal or one-third additional pay.

War became for Tolstoy the greatest of crimes, the antithesis of every Christian belief. With feeling he described the raising of flags of truce to enable the Russians and French to gather the mangled corpses that lay in the flowery valley between the opposing lines of trenches. The air was filled with the smell of decaying flesh. While the bodies were piled on carts, French and Russian soldiers fraternized, borrowed tobacco, and laughed and joked in friendly fashion over their efforts to make themselves understood. At last, the grisly business of burying the dead was finished; the fraternizing ceased. "The white flags are lowered," wrote Tolstoy, "the engines of death and suffering are sounding again, innocent blood is flowing and the air is filled with moans and curses."

The Tsar's censor, of course, could not permit such truths to reach the great gray masses that were dying by the thousands at the earthworks of Sevastopol. When Tolstoy received the news that his sketch had been mutilated and printed, he wrote in his diary: "It seems that I'm under the strict observation of the Blues [the police] for my article. I wish, however, that Russia will always have such moral writers; but I can never be a sugary one, nor can I ever write from the empty into the void, without ideas, and above all without aim. Despite a first moment of anger in which I promised myself never again to take my pen in hand, my sole and chief occupation, dominating all other inclinations and activities, must be literature. My aim is literary fame, the good that I can accomplish by my writings."

Tolstoy's bitterness over the censor's arbitrary distortion of his sketch was somewhat assuaged by the indignation and praise of Nekrasov, who wrote: "The shocking disfiguring of your article has quite upset me. Even now I cannot think of it without regret and rage. Your work, of course, will not be lost . . . it will always remain as proof of a strength that was able to speak such profound and sober truth in circumstances amid which few men would have retained it. It is exactly what Russian society now needs: the truth—the truth, of which, since Gogol's death, so little has remained in Russian literature. You are right to value that side of your gifts most of all. Truth—in the form you have introduced it into our literature—is something entirely new among us. I do not know another writer of today who so compels the reader to love him and sympathize heartily with him as he to whom I now write. And I only fear lest time, the nastiness of life, and the deafness and dumbness that surround us, should do to you what it has done to most of us, and kill the energy without which there can be no writer—none at least such as Russia needs."

Nekrasov's fear was groundless; the last thing his budding author would do would be to turn his back on truth.

10

Literature could not overcome Tolstoy's feeling of boredom with the war as he remained inactive with his battery of mountain guns on the Belbek. He tried to amuse himself by visiting Bakhchisarai, the former capital of the Crimean khans, and by hunting wild goats on the Chatyrdag. "My service here in Russia," he noted, "begins to madden me just as it did in the Caucasus."

Others were also beginning to grow bored with the war. The horror, misery, and suffering of the past winter left the conviction on both sides that the siege could not go into another year. Thousands rotted from disease; hospital facilities for the wounded were totally inadequate; and so bad were conditions in Russia that two thirds of the recruits sent from the interior died by the wayside of sickness and starvation. Alexander II ordered his army chiefs to take decisive action. On August 4 they attacked the allies on the Chernaya River, and before the day's fighting was over, the Russians were driven back with terrible losses. When Tolstoy's battery, which was moved up, was not called upon to fire, he volunteered for other activities. Much of the responsibility for the slaughter must be attributed to the muddling of the Russian generals. Around the campfire a collective effort by Tolstoy and his fellow officers to compose an army song on the event failed. Tolstoy tried alone, and the next day he offered to his friends a rollicking song that pilloried the generals. Soon the verses went singing through the army, and any peasant soldier would hum you:—

On the fourth or thereabout,
The devil sent us out
To take that hill,

or the still more popular stanza:—

So they all in council met,
Each stiff-shirt and epaulet,
Even copper Bek-kok.[9]

[9] Major General A. P. Plats-bek-Kokum, chief of the military police of the Southern Army.

The authorship of the song was generally known, and Tolstoy's jibes at the High Command were probably part of the reason why he did not easily win promotion.

This defeat on the Chernaya River pretty much sealed the fate of the defenders of Sevastopol. On August 24, the sixth and last bombardment began. After three days of constant blasting, the city was reduced to ruins. At noon on the twenty-seventh a general assault took place. Tolstoy happened to be in Sevastopol at that time and aided in the defense. The Russians repulsed the allies at all points save one, the highly strategic Malakhov Redoubt, which was captured by the French. With this key point lost, further resistance was useless, and the Russians prepared an immediate withdrawal.

Tolstoy wrote home to Auntie Tatyana: "For the second time in my life, my birthday, the 28th, has been a memorable and sad day for me: the first was 18 years ago at the death of Aunt Alexandra, and now it is the loss of Sevastopol. I wept when I saw the city in flames and the French standards on our Bastions; in many ways it was a very sad day." He also requested her advice on his desire to leave the army. For after the fall of Sevastopol, subsequent inaction on both sides dwindled into peace.[1]

A short time before the fall of the city, Tolstoy had mentioned in his diary that he had suddenly rediscovered his former view of life, "the aim of which is welfare and the ideal is virtue." He blamed military society for his lapses, and now contemplated his reform with pleasure. The gesture in this direction was a plan to accumulate sufficient money to free his estate from debt and liberate his serfs. Further, the idea occurred to him to expose all the wretchedness of serfdom in his "Novel of a Russian Landowner," and to point out the means of correcting it. At about this time he jotted down in his notebook[2] the following thought: "With the widespread use of the machine the number of people released for intellectual work necessary for the good of society will increase. The evil of the machine will become

[1] The most mismanaged campaign in modern history came to an end with everybody forgetting just why it had begun. At any rate, the only tangible result of the treaty was the exclusion of Russian warships from the Black Sea, a nearly irrelevant but costly gain that ceased to be enforced in a few years.

[2] Tolstoy's notebooks, not to be confused with his diaries, were records that he kept of thoughts, plans, literary projects, and miscellaneous reminders.

apparent when the people released by it remain unsuited and too undeveloped for intellectual work." His social as well as moral consciousness had come to life.

All these good intentions were forgotten in the atmosphere of defeat that swept along with the retreating troops. Tangible results he obtained only in his literary aim: he continued to work on *Youth* and had started a new Sevastopol sketch based on the events of August. In truth, all his aims were literature, and in the diary he indicated that he was beginning to recognize the fact: "My career is literary. Write and write!"

Now he realized more than ever that military service was a serious hindrance. He eagerly accepted General Kryzhanovski's request that he collate the various reports of artillery action on the day Sevastopol fell, and draw up a comprehensive account that he would take, as a courier, to the military authorities in Petersburg. His study of the reports of these artillery commanders increased his contempt for military history. Years later he regretted that he had not kept copies of them as examples of the naïve and unavoidable falsehoods out of which military descriptions are compiled. And he imagined that his former comrades would have a good laugh on reading the incredible statements they made at the orders of their commanders, without knowing anything of what they wrote.

Tolstoy reached Petersburg on November 21, and he soon sent in his resignation. Sevastopol and its heroic dead were behind him at last, but he never forgot them. Like any old soldier who survives a famous battle, he could not conceal a feeling of pleasure at having been a participant. Nevertheless, his experiences at Sevastopol dated the end of his career as a militarist and the beginning of that of pacifist. Not that he at once began preaching the beating of bayonets into plowshares. But at Sevastopol his mind had been stored with a wealth of argument and his heart with a feeling of implacable hatred for war. Arguments and feeling emerged in 1889 in a preface he was asked to contribute to A. I. Ershov's *Recollections of Sevastopol*. There, in brief form, he condemned the terrible bloodshed of the siege and pointed out its utter futility. What was more frightful than the suffering, mutilation, and death of man's body, he maintained, was the mutilation and death that war brings to man's soul.

Before Tolstoy's resignation went through, he was promoted to the rank of lieutenant for "distinguished bravery and courage" in the battle at the Chernaya River. Many years later he jocularly remarked of his military career: "I did not become a general in the army, but I became one in literature."

IX

Return of the Hero

LATE ON a December morning in 1855 the poet A. A. Fet, then an army officer on a furlough to Petersburg, called upon his friend Turgenev for a glass of tea and a chat. Noticing in the hallway a short saber hanging on the wall, he asked the dignified Zakhar to whom it belonged. The servant answered in a low voice that it was Count Tolstoy's, a guest of his master. For an hour Fet and Turgenev conversed in whispers in the latter's study for fear of waking the sleeping count in the next room. "He's like this all the time," Turgenev smilingly explained. "He has come from his battery at Sevastopol, is staying with me, and has gone off on a tangent. Sprees, gypsies, and cards every night; then he sleeps like the dead until two o'clock in the day. I tried to restrain him, but I've given it up now." Tolstoy finally sauntered in and was introduced. In his reminiscences Fet remarks: "From the first moment I noticed in young Tolstoy an involuntary opposition to all commonly accepted opinion."

The Petersburg literary group was curious about the mysterious "L.N.T." and eager to welcome him as one of them. On the road he had received a letter from the excited Turgenev, who offered to go as far as Tula to meet him. Tolstoy accepted his generous invitation to stay at his apartment in the capital. If not exactly a military hero, he returned to Petersburg to find himself a literary hero. At first he reveled in the new experience.

With such a sponsor as Turgenev, the leader of the capital's literary world, Tolstoy was soon presented to all the important writers. In the 1850's the Petersburg literary set consisted of a group of self-indulgent men, whose concern for their own immortality did not prevent them from being interested in the social and political problems of the day. A relatively small and provincial group, it moved in a Masonic-lodge atmosphere of half-mystery and jealous devotion to literary ritual and comradeship. Their favorite publication was the *Contemporary,* and its editors, Nekrasov and the less talented I. I. Panayev, were the artful instigators of frequent literary gatherings in the interests of their magazine. On such occasions the hostess was Panayev's wife, the beautiful black-eyed Avdotya. Gossip had it that the co-editors were also co-husbands.

Nekrasov and Panayev had been followers of Belinski, radical critic and leader of the Westerners, and they had turned the *Contemporary*[1] into the most living literary review in Russia and the rallying ground of all progressives. With the accession of Alexander II the hope of reform filled the air, and writers of the *Contemporary* helped to spread the liberal virus. There were, however, sharp degrees of liberalism among them, and a "civil war" had already broken out. Led by Chernyshevski and Dobrolyubov, the young radical contributors who had sprung from the people were beginning to attack the tired liberalism of Turgenev and the older aristocratic writers.

The sublieutenant fresh from Sevastopol took the *Contemporary* adherents by storm at the end of 1855. Tolstoy was perhaps too conscious of the fact that he was the lion of the moment; soon some of his admirers set him down as a cub, and nearly all of them eventually felt his claws. The day after his arrival he dined with Nekrasov. It was their first meeting, although they had been corresponding for three years. Nekrasov, the hard-living, democratic poet, clever gambler, and astute publisher, was much impressed by his young aristocratic author. He promptly wrote to V. P. Botkin, a rare critic and later a good friend of Tolstoy: "L.N.T., i.e., Tolstoy, has come. . . . What a fine fellow he is, and what an intelligent one! . . . A dear, energetic, generous young hawk! and, perhaps, an eagle!" At the dinner was A. V. Druzhinin, critic and author, and into his

[1] They had bought this magazine, founded by Pushkin and Pletnyov, in 1846, by which time it had become an antique mouthpiece of aristocratic writers.

diary that night went an account of his meeting with Tolstoy.[2]

The next evening Turgenev did the honors.[3] A few days later the poet Ya. P. Polonski wrote in his diary (diary writing was epidemic in those days) of meeting Tolstoy at the Chess Club amid a notable company of literary luminaries. Evening gatherings and introductions continued during December. At some of them he read parts of *Youth* or the recently finished *Sevastopol in August.* Next day the diaries and letters of his listeners registered enthusiasm. Magazines competed for his favor, and he promised contributions indiscriminately. The new *Russian Messenger* advertised "L.N.T., one of the most remarkable of our writers," as a future contributor; and *The Library for Reading* made a similar announcement.

Turgenev was delighted with his guest. He wrote to the elegant critic P. V. Annenkov, who in a review of "Notes of a Billiard-Marker" had already included Tolstoy among the immortals: "Imagine, for more than two weeks now Tolstoy has been living with me, and what I would not give to see you both together! You cannot picture to yourself what a dear and remarkable man he is, although I have nicknamed him the 'troglodyte,' because of his savage ardor and buffalo-like obstinacy. I have grown to love him with a strange feeling that is almost parental." The troglodyte, however, would creep into the cave of his own mind and roar at the parental Turgenev who, although only ten years older, insisted upon watching over his guest "like an old nurse," as he expressed it.

At first Tolstoy was pleased and flattered with all this attention. At the Hôtel Napoléon he held an evening of his own for the *Contemporary* set and introduced some gay gypsy entertainers to take the minds of these literary pundits off shop talk. In his immaculate uniform, and faultlessly groomed, he conducted himself with severe decorum, as though he were acting according to a studied course of behavior. With individuals he sometimes showed the temper

[2] Author of the highly successful novel *Polinka Saks,* Druzhinin was also a deep student of English literature and an unusually good translator. He rendered several of Shakespeare's plays, and among his finest criticism are articles on Dr. Johnson, Boswell, Crabbe, and Scott.

[3] Among those present were A. I. Goncharov, who would soon write his famous novel *Oblomov,* the novelist and dramatist, A. F. Pisemski, the poet, A. N. Maikov, and the journalist, A. V. Nikitenko.

of his mind, but in large groups he usually remained silent and observant. He was taking the measure of his admiring literary colleagues.

2

Still in the army, Tolstoy had been detailed as an inspector in a Petersburg munitions factory. After a month he obtained a brief leave to go to Moscow, for there another literary group was eager to honor him. The stern Moscow Slavophiles, with their deeply rooted nationalist convictions, detested the Petersburg Westerners and the progressive views of the *Contemporary* set. Tolstoy was entertained by S. T. Aksakov,[4] distinguished writer and fervent Slavophile. The sons of Aksakov were introduced and the novelist and wit D. V. Grigorovich.[5] These sober, almost fanatical guardians of undefiled Russianism liked him. When old Aksakov wrote to Turgenev of the visit, he described Tolstoy as "wise and serious," "capable of understanding strict thought," and a man from whose future literary development he hoped much. And Tolstoy rather liked them. However, their "convictions"—a fashion word among intellectuals in Russia then—irritated him, as did the "convictions" of the Petersburg Westerners. He thought that both sets were tilting at windmills.

The serious illness of his brother Dmitri cut short Tolstoy's pleasant visit in Moscow. He hurried to Oryol and found Dmitri dying from consumption. The appearance of his childhood playmate shocked him—Dmitri's enormous hands hung to the two bones of his arms, and his wasted face seemed all eyes, the same beautiful, serious eyes as of old, but now fixed on him with a continually questioning look. His pockmarked Masha, the girl he had taken from a brothel, tenderly watched over him. All the evil thoughts Tolstoy used to have about Dmitri crumbled to dust, and he felt terribly depressed. He stayed only two days and returned to Petersburg by way of Moscow. There he learned that Dmitri had died on January 21. A naked reference to the fact is all that appears in the diary. Many years later he censured his behavior:—

[4] He wrote the well-known books *Family Chronicle, Years of Childhood,* and *Recollections,* which have been translated into English.

[5] Later Tolstoy met the high priest of Slavophilism, A. S. Khomyakov, and his acolytes, the Kireyevski brothers.

> I was particularly detestable at that time . . . I pitied Dmitri, but not very much. . . . It really seems to me now that his death troubled me chiefly because it prevented me from taking part in a Court spectacle that was then being arranged and to which I had been invited.

The details of that pathetic scene in Oryol, however, were not lost on Tolstoy the artist. They reappeared in the description of the death of Nikolai Levin in *Anna Karenina,* and even the pockmarked Masha lived again in Nikolai Levin's faithful, pockmarked Marya Nikolayevna.

3

Back in the capital the lion began to show his claws. By now he had a clear comprehension of the civil war that raged among the *Contemporary* circle. He saw that each side hailed his talent and hoped for his allegiance, and that both were afraid and jealous of him. The aristocratic liberals were sure of him; after all, he was a count, and they expected him to share their hate for Chernyshevski and Dobrolyubov, the snake and rattlesnake, as Turgenev dubbed them. Tolstoy called a plague on both their houses, and did not hesitate to roar at either.

Tolstoy first directed his fire at the liberal aristocrats, and most of all at their leader, Turgenev. Both he and Turgenev were well-born and novelists. On the surface, at least, they appeared to have a sincere appreciation of each other's ability. But Turgenev's "disinterested love for utter truth" annoyed Tolstoy. It was merely a phrase, he believed, coming from a flabby nature. This giant of a man, with his huge shoulders, striking features, and shock of hair, prematurely graying, failed to impress discerning people like Tolstoy. They found in him a lack of spirituality; he seemed capable of experiencing only physical feelings.

With persistent and deadly effect Tolstoy began nagging Turgenev on his political convictions. At an evening gathering at Nekrasov's the familiar argument began all over again.

"I cannot agree that the things you've said are your convictions," Tolstoy declared to Turgenev. "I stand with a dagger or a saber at a door and say: 'While I live, no one shall enter here!' That is conviction. But you people try to conceal from each other the essence of your thoughts and you call that conviction."

"Then why do you come here?" Turgenev screamed, almost choking, his voice ascending to a thin falsetto that he could not avoid in warm arguments. "Your standard is not here! Be off to your princesses!"

"Why should I ask you where I ought to go!" Tolstoy coolly retorted. "Besides, idle talk will not become conviction simply by virtue of my going."

Tolstoy's point was that these men were being hypocritical when they flaunted their convictions. Convictions were invented by the intelligentsia so that they would have something to talk about. As for himself, Tolstoy would have asserted that he lived by instinct. The "rules" that he composed to guide his existence were suggested not by conviction, but by moral instinct. And moral instinct he could trust, but only his own. Here was the quintessence of individualism.

What Fet had described as Tolstoy's involuntary opposition to all commonly accepted opinion contributed to his antagonism on this and on similar occasions. In literary no less than political and social questions, he strove always for originality in discussion. Even Shakespeare was sacrificed to this passion. "How sorry I am that you are late," Panayev declared to a friend who called on him just as Tolstoy left. "What marvels you would have heard! You would have learned that Shakespeare is an ordinary writer, and that our astonishment and delight over Shakespeare are nothing more than a desire to keep up with others and the habit of repeating foreign opinions. . . . Yes, how curious! The man simply does not wish to know any traditions, either theoretical or historical."

The war was on. Tolstoy harried Turgenev, nor were other members of his group spared. He was invited to a dinner for the staff of the *Contemporary* at Nekrasov's. When someone praised George Sand's new novel, he abruptly blurted out his hatred for this favorite French author. And he shocked all present by declaring that if such women as George Sand's heroines really existed, then they ought to be bound to the hangman's cart and driven through the streets of Petersburg for the general edification. Avdotya Panayev, the hostess, whose worship of George Sand was common knowledge, preserved a pained silence. In an instant the room was in an uproar. But Tolstoy had ideas about George Sand and he maintained his point. Her love of sheer animalism in man, disguised with a cloak of poetry and aesthetic feeling, disgusted him.

The offended host Nekrasov hurried off a letter to Botkin: "But what nonsense, brother, he [Tolstoy] poured out yesterday after dinner! The devil knows what's in his head! He says much that is stupid and even nasty." And a day later Botkin received another letter on the same theme from the wounded Turgenev. "I've almost broken off with Tolstoy," he wrote. "He uttered so much nonsense and crudity on the subject of George Sand that it is impossible to pass it on. The dispute went far—in a word he angered everyone and showed himself in a most disadvantageous light."

Turgenev struck back, not very cleverly or successfully. He was no match for Tolstoy in an argument. With an ironical expression on his face, Tolstoy would listen to his opponent, piercing him with his penetrating glance, his lips pressed together in an expression of concentration that suggested he was thinking up some devastating epigram or an answer that would perplex by its unexpectedness. Turgenev complained that his young rival never believed in people's sincerity or spirituality, and he confessed that nothing was more disconcerting than Tolstoy's inquisitorial look which, when accompanied by a few biting words, goaded a man to fury. If we can believe Avdotya Panayev, who thought Tolstoy carried himself with an "affected jauntiness," Turgenev was not above evincing a most unparental spleen and literary envy behind his troglodyte's back. At Nekrasov's once, when Tolstoy was not present, Turgenev said of him: "Not one word, not one movement of his is natural! He is eternally posing before us, and I find it difficult to explain in a clever man this impoverished count's arrogance."

The boiling-over point was reached in a quarrel that Grigorovich humorously described to Fet. Again, the unfortunate Nekrasov's quarters were the locus. "You cannot imagine what a scene it was," said Grigorovich. "Ach, my God! Turgenev squeaked and squeaked, holding his hand to his throat, and with the eyes of a dying gazelle, he whispered: 'I can stand no more! I have bronchitis!' and with huge strides he began pacing back and forth through three rooms. 'Bronchitis?' Tolstoy growls after him. 'Bronchitis is a metal!' Of course, Nekrasov's heart sank: he feared to lose either Turgenev or Tolstoy in whom the *Contemporary* found excellent support, and hence began to beat to windward. We were all agitated and did not know what to say. Tolstoy in the middle room lay sulking on a morocco divan, while Turgenev, spreading the tails of his short coat by placing his hands in his pockets, continued to go back and forth through all three rooms. To avert a catastrophe, I went up to the divan and said: 'My dear Tolstoy, don't agitate yourself! You don't know how he esteems and loves you!' 'I'll not permit him to do anything evil to me!' exclaimed Tolstoy with dilated nostrils. 'Look how he keeps marching past me on purpose, wagging his democratic haunches!' "

Not only the democratic haunches of the *Contemporary's* liberal aristocrats bothered Tolstoy: so did the radical haunches of Chernyshevski and his followers. He tolerated them for a brief time, but he soon turned on them also and their exiled oracle Herzen, who in distant London had highly praised *Childhood*. At the house of a well-known sculptor, Tolstoy listened patiently while Herzen's latest work was being read aloud. After the reading, he boldly attacked this author's revolutionary writings, and was so convincing that he persuaded the host to abandon his enthusiasm for Herzen.

Despite his own proneness to anger in debate, Tolstoy severely criticized the splenetic and indignant attitude of the progressives in preaching their reforms. Only a loving man, he maintained, could see things clearly and do good. He jotted down his own definition of liberalism in his notebook: "There are two liberalisms—one that desires all people to be my equals, so that they should be as good as I am; the other wants all to be as bad as I am. The first is based on a moral Christian feeling, a desire for the happiness and good of my neighbor; the other is based on a desire for the unhappiness of my neighbor." These liberals were advocating equality and reforms when he knew that many of them were devoted to swilling, gambling, and immorality. The fact nauseated him. His own private life was far from exemplary, but he was willing to admit the fact and did not try to reform others.

Within a few months after his arrival in Petersburg from Sevastopol, Tolstoy had won for himself in the *Contemporary* circle the reputation of being a "savage" young man. At a card party one evening a letter arrived for Nekrasov from M. N. Longinov, a genial but not too reputable historian of literature and contributor to the *Contemporary*. Busy with his hand, Nekrasov requested Tolstoy to read the letter. Unfortunately it contained an aspersion on Tolstoy's liberalism. He read through to the end, said nothing, but went home and sent a challenge to Longinov. Nekrasov learned of the matter and pleaded with Tolstoy to withdraw his challenge or he would have to shoot it out with him, for Nekrasov insisted on assuming full responsibility for the mess. Tolstoy remained adamant. Longinov settled the matter happily by the simply unorthodox procedure of not answering the challenge. Three months later, in the peaceful seclusion of Yasnaya Polyana, it suddenly occurred to Tolstoy how offensive his behavior had been. He at once wrote to Nekrasov to ask his pardon and promised to do the same with Longinov.

The diaries and correspondence of the *Contemporary* circle in 1856 indicate that their final judgment on Tolstoy was a mixed one of bewilderment over his views and conduct and admiration for his talent. They perceived in him an enormous literary and moral force, and the several groups trying to influence opinion on the magazine were willing to overlook his prickly and independent nature if they could gain his support. For a time he allowed himself to be swayed by the most conservative faction, principally by Druzhinin, and somewhat by Botkin and Annenkov. Eventually these willing survivors began to savor of the partisanship and the "force-of-convictions" school that Tolstoy abominated. His growing displeasure was reflected in the diary: "In the evening with Druzhinin and Annenkov; the former rather irksome." His entry the next day described the whole editorial staff of the *Contemporary* as "disgusting." And a few days later he jotted down: "Goncharov, Annenkov—all disgust me; especially Druzhinin, and they disgust me because I want affection, friendship, but they are not capable of it."

Of the whole Petersburg group at this time, only Fet retained Tolstoy's lasting friendship. And perhaps it is significant that Fet was the least "literary" of the circle, and the most conservative. Tolstoy's inability to get along was not merely a case of bad manners or of his irritating contradictory nature, of which he was entirely conscious. Konstantin Aksakov in a letter to Turgenev came close to the real reason why he antagonized his fellow writers: "Count Tolstoy was in Moscow. . . . A strange person! Why does he act so immaturely? Why so unsettled? . . . It seems as though there is still no center in him."

This was true. Tolstoy had no moral or spiritual center as yet; he was in the process of finding one. But this was a search he must conduct himself. He was not being reactionary in turning his back on the *Contemporary's* progressives, for he really shared some of their advanced views. Now, however, as later, his individualism would not permit him to subordinate his views. All must come from within himself. It was both an aesthetic and an intellectual pride. The thinker, like the artist, insisted upon originality.

4

The literary group did not monopolize Tolstoy's time, for his stay of six months in Petersburg was a repetition of his hectic social life of some four years before. He had acquired more poise and worldliness, and his fame as an author had widened the circle of his acquaintances and made him a much desired guest in the homes of prominent families where he occasionally read his stories. His capacity for light entertainment was undiminished; nor had the stern conscience that censured his indulgence lapsed. There are frequent clipped references to the city's grisettes, particularly to an Alexandra Petrovna and an Alexandra Zhukov. The diary, that faithful chronicle of his sins, venial and unpardonable, records for April 21: "Gadded about the Nevski and ended up at a bath.[6] Terrible! But absolutely the last time. This is no longer temperament, but simply habitual lechery." Apparently as a precaution for the future, he set himself the rule not to drink more than half a glass of vodka at a time, one glass of strong wine, and one tumbler of light wine. A few weeks later an entry relates how he and a friend went with two girls to an amusement park. "Disgusting!" he wrote. "Wenches, stupid music, wenches, an artificial nightingale, heat, cigarette smoke, wenches, vodka, cheese, wild shrieks, wenches, wenches, wenches!" And the next day he underlined: *"I make myself this rule forever: never to enter a pub or a single brothel!"* Before the day was over, another lapse obliged him that night to repeat in a postscript to this entry: "My foot will never, never enter a public place, except a concert or theatre."

Among Tolstoy's new friends in the Petersburg social world, perhaps the one who remained closest to him and

[6] Some of the public bathhouses at the time were little better than houses of ill-fame.

influenced him most in later life was his "aunt" (actually a first cousin once removed), Countess Alexandra Andreyevna Tolstoy, eleven years his senior. She was a Maid of Honor and governess in the family of Grand Duchess Marie, daughter of Nicholas I. A woman of remarkable tact and unusual gifts of heart and brain, she occupied a position of consequence in the political and literary world of the capital. Their affection for each other deepened over the years, and her strong intellect and love of truth inspired a trust and confidence in her judgment that Tolstoy rarely accorded to other people. In his old age, after reading over their extensive and notable correspondence, he remarked: "When I look back on my long dark life, my remembrances of Alexandra will always be a bright gleam, like a light that shines from under a door in a dark corridor."

She recalled his frequent and welcome visits: "I see him quite clearly as he returned from Sevastopol, a young artillery officer, and I remember what a fine impression he produced on all of us. At that time he was already a public figure. All were enraptured with his charming creations, and we were a bit proud of the talent of our kinsman, although we did not foresee his future renown."

5

A reviewer had lyrically advised Tolstoy in print not to write better but more. He improved upon the advice and wrote both more and better during this brief period. Direct contact with literary admirers gave him a sense of great things expected of him. With not a little pride he mentioned in the diary and repeated in a letter to his brother Sergei that the Emperor read *Childhood* to his wife and wept. He had no doubts about his future career now, and the praise of friends and rivals had banished uncertainty about his talents. Subjects for stories filled his mind, and living material on the Petersburg streets—a constable settling an altercation or the character of a Russian crowd listening to an orator—were jotted down for future reference.

In December 1855, Tolstoy finished *Sevastopol in August,* the first of his works to appear under his full name.[7] The inspired war correspondent of the two previous

[7] It was published in the January *Contemporary,* 1856.

Sevastopol sketches has disappeared; in the third he is the storyteller transposing the stuff of life into art. The didactic element and lyricism are absent. Living characters, especially the Kozeltsov brothers, lend a touch of unity to a loosely constructed story. In its leisurely, panoramic method of narration, in the manner in which plot is sacrificed to accumulating detail, and in the studied objectivity, one can detect the certain influence of Thackeray, whom Tolstoy had been eagerly reading and deeply admiring over this period. The three Sevastopol pieces are clearly efforts in the direction of *War and Peace*.

An entirely different matter is "The Storm."[8] The theme was suggested by the fearful night Tolstoy spent on the steppes in a blizzard on his return from the Caucasus in 1854. Such an experience was a commonplace in Russia and not infrequently ended fatally. There is no plot; the theme is the storm, but it is realized so vividly that it takes on the human attributes of an intensely imagined character. With some justice early reviewers compared "The Storm" to a poem in tonal quality and structure. The effectively repeated motifs of the snow and wind amount almost to the incremental repetition of a folk ballad. So acute is the sensuous perception of bitter cold and driving snow that the reader imaginatively experiences the effect of the elements.

The following month in the *Contemporary* appeared Tolstoy's next piece, a novelette entitled *Two Hussars*. It is unlike anything he had done previously and he never returned to this type of subject. The story falls into two parts. In the first is portrayed Count Fyodor Turbin,[9] a typical officer in a hussar regiment at the beginning of the nineteenth century. He is a handsome, fire-eating young aristocrat, who appears for one night in a provincial town and throws its society into a turmoil by his drinking and wild escapades, and before leaving he seduces a pretty widow. Yet no one is shocked by his behavior, for his daring, generosity, and noble nature win the admiration of all. In the second part—about twenty years later—his son is described (it is mentioned that the father had been

[8] It appeared in the March number of the *Contemporary*, 1856.

[9] The model was very likely a distant relative, Count F. I. Tolstoy, "The American" (so called because of some time spent in America), a famed duelist and adventurer whom Tolstoy had known from childhood.

killed in a duel). The contrast is pointed, for the son is a member of contemporary society, a calculating, materialistic prig. Chance brings him to the same provincial town. As an officer he is quartered in the house of the widow his father had seduced, and he tries unsuccessfully to seduce her pretty daughter. His petty, self-conscious nature has none of the natural, lovable quality of his scapegrace of a father, and he leaves behind him a definitely unpleasant impression.

In the diary Tolstoy noted a friend's remark that the second hussar was described without love. This is the key to the story. At this time Tolstoy entered a significant literary observation in his notebook: "The first condition of an author's popularity, i.e., the way to make himself loved, is the love with which he treats all his characters. That is why Dickens' characters are the friends of all mankind; they serve as a bond between humanity in America and in Petersburg; but Thackeray and Gogol, though faithful to life and artistic, are pitiless and not at all loving." In *Two Hussars* the father is in a sense a Dickensian character, and the son has the evil aspects common in the delineation of Thackeray's men. Thackeray's influence is evident in the introduction to the tale and in the manner in which the family relationship is used to join both parts, a method Tolstoy employed later in *War and Peace*.[1] The real theme of *Two Hussars* is the opposition of two generations; Tolstoy's preference for the older generation and his condemnation of the modern are patent. His attitude may have been a reflection of his dislike for the *Contemporary* writers, and they appeared to recognize the fact by receiving the tale with marked reservations.

To fulfill his promises to editors, Tolstoy published in 1856 two short stories, "Meeting a Moscow Acquaintance in the Detachment,"[2] and *A Landlord's Morning*.[3] The material for the first is drawn from his Caucasian experiences and concerns the unfortunate history of a nobleman condemned to serve in the ranks as a common soldier; the second is the

[1] The influence of English novelists played a very important part in the development of Tolstoy's art. Russian critics have devoted some attention to the subject, but a comprehensive study has still to be made.

[2] This long and awkward title was forced on him by the censor who was suspicious of the original short *Razhalovanny*—"A Man Reduced to the Ranks."

[3] The first story was published in *The Library for Reading*, and the second in *National Notes*.

considerable fragment of the unfinished "Novel of a Russian Landowner."

Youth, the last work of this period[4] was the final part of *Childhood and Boyhood.*[5] The keen critic Druzhinin, who read the manuscript, wrote Tolstoy that no other author of the time could have so seized and sketched the agitated and turbulent period of youth, and that he ought "to spit in the face" of anyone who claimed that the work was inferior to the preceding parts.

> Do not fear your reflections [he wrote], they are all clever and original. You have an inclination towards extremely fine-spun analysis that may become a great defect. You are sometimes on the point of saying that so-and-so's thigh indicated that he wished to travel in India! You must restrain this tendency, but do not squelch it for anything in the world. All your work over your own talent has to be of such a nature. Each of your defects has its share of strength and beauty, and almost each of your merits bears in it the seed of a defect.

Tolstoy's popularity suggested the feasibility of publishing his collected works in book form even at this early stage. In September 1856, his *Army Tales*[6] appeared, and the next month *Childhood* and *Boyhood.* They received little notice and sold poorly. This first literary disappointment was a new experience and disturbed him. The failure was perhaps partly owing to the fact that the stories had already appeared in the *Contemporary.* Something of the cool reception, however, must be attributed to the changing attitude of the liberal Petersburg critics whom he had offended. They were demanding works of political and social significance to meet the progressive spirit of the age. But Tolstoy was not a writer to fall into an accepted groove; he had to carve his own. He wanted to try his hand at new forms and subjects. Over this period he worked on at least four separate plans for dramas. And in the diary he expressed his desire to strike out on new literary paths: "How I long to have done with magazines in order to write in the way I'm now beginning to think about art: awfully lofty and pure."

[4] Published in the January number of the *Contemporary,* 1857.

[5] During this brief period Tolstoy also worked on *The Cossacks;* and a number of fragmentary plays, stories, articles, and projects have come down to us. These may be found in Volumes V and VII of the Jubilee Edition.

[6] The book consisted of "The Raid," "The Woodfelling," and "Sevastopol Sketches."

6

Turgenev pointed out in a letter to Druzhinin that *A Landlord's Morning,* which had just been published, conveyed the unpleasant impression that all efforts of landowners to enlighten or improve the conditions of the peasantry led to nothing. The real moral of the work, however, is that so long as serfdom exists the master will be unable to better the lot of his peasants, despite the most disinterested endeavor to do so. Tolstoy had not accepted such a position when at Yasnaya Polyana he had conducted the experiment with his serfs that provided material for this fragment of a novel. Since then his ideas on serfdom had changed. He had seen peasants undergo the horrors of war with endurance and courage; he had watched them die on the bastions with the calm resignation and simple humility of men who had a compact with God. Now he was prepared to put into practice some of the theories that serf-owning progressives of the *Contemporary* circle were still talking about.

On March of this year, the young Alexander II had made a historic address before the assembled nobles of Moscow. He warned them that the time would soon come when Russia's serfs must be freed, and he concluded with the famous statement that it would "therefore be much better for it to come from above than from below." While the government prepared its own program for abolishing serfdom, the way was left open for individual owners to take action.

Tolstoy decided to take such action. Towards the end of April, while still in Petersburg, he wrote in the diary that his relations with his serfs was beginning to trouble him and that he felt the need of "learning, learning, learning." For advice he sought out his friend, K. D. Kavelin, a writer and authority on the question of emancipation. Kavelin's practical wisdom encouraged him. Tolstoy felt "bright, hopeful, and happy," and planned to go back to the country with a written project. For further information he canvassed the opinions of high liberal government officials. When at last the project was drafted, he took it for the necessary approval to A. I. Lyovshin, Assistant Minister of the Interior, who received him "drily." Tolstoy acidly commented in the diary on the old men in government service who were unfitted for the work of change. Although his plan was not immediately accepted, he decided to go to Yasnaya Polyana and place it before his serfs.

Tolstoy stopped off at Moscow, and there ten days bright with love and excitement banished temporarily all thoughts of his serfs. Among his numerous visits was one to the parents of D. A. Dyakov, the close comrade of his student days at Kazan. There he met Alexandra Obolenski, Dyakov's married sister. He left the house "passionately in love" with her, as he mentioned in the diary. The feeling took complete possession of him, and he acted like a shy schoolboy with this married woman. He avidly followed her every movement and searched her face for the slightest sign that she recognized his secret passion. Now he could not make up his mind to stay or to leave Moscow. He contrived to be at evening gatherings where she was a guest and yet hardly dared converse with her. "No," he told himself in the diary, "I'm not being carried away in saying that she is the sweetest woman I've ever known. She has the most refined, artistic, and at the same time moral, nature." If he did not respect her husband so much, he decided, it would have been painful for him to imagine his intimate relations with his own wife. When she remarked in his presence that she had no lovers at the time of her betrothal, he hopefully took this as a hint that she had not been in love with her husband then. After a visit she gave him her hand at parting and it made him "terribly happy." Then, recalling his childhood love for Sonya Koloshin, he wrote: "Since Sonechka's days, I have positively not experienced such a pure, strong, and good feeling. I say 'good,' because though it is hopeless, I rejoice in arousing it."

It was difficult for Tolstoy to accept his sudden love as "hopeless." The day before he left Moscow, he paid a final visit to Alexandra Obolenski and came to the conclusion "that she knows my feelings and that she is pleased. I'm terribly happy." He almost decided to remain another day in order to see her once more, but he feared to tempt fate.[7] Just before he left Moscow, he went with Konstantin Islavin, the son of an old neighbor at Yasnaya Polyana, to visit the country house of Islavin's married sister, Lyubov Bers. There he met her happy family of children, and he noted

[7] There is a brief fragment, apparently the beginning of a short story, in which Tolstoy writes of his love for Alexandra Obolenski. It has recently been published in Volume V of the Jubilee Edition.

in the diary: "What dear, merry little girls! We walked and played leap-frog."

7

A year of war had altered Tolstoy's opinions; the man who had scorned the organized liberalism of the *Contemporary* circle now observed in the diary: "In comparison with my former Yasnaya recollections of myself, I feel how much I've changed in the liberal sense. Even T.A. [Auntie Tatyana] displeases me. In a 100 years you couldn't knock into her head the injustice of serfdom." That very day of his arrival at Yasnaya Polyana he decided to call his peasants together to explain his startling plan to free them.

Tolstoy had prepared his project with care and a practical business sense rarely attributed to him. He spoke to a meeting of his 309 male serfs in simple, measured words: "The Lord God has put into my mind the thought to set all of you free. If it were possible to go to a court of justice now and free you by legal decree, I would do it. But I have taken counsel with wise and old men about this matter, and they have explained to me that it is impossible to do this at once and why it is impossible and how the matter must be arranged." Then he went on to explain his plan. He told them that his estate was mortgaged, and until the debt was paid he had no right to give them their freedom, and even if he could, liberty for them without land would be disastrous. Therefore, he offered to allow each household four and a half *desyatins* (about twelve acres) of land. Half a *desyatin* would be given outright, and for the remainder they would pay five rubles a *desyatin* for thirty years. Of this sum, one ruble would go to pay off the mortgage, and the other four would purchase for them the rest of the allotment of land. At the end of the thirty years they would be free of all obligations to him. He concluded his speech with the following advice: "Think about this matter, talk it over among yourselves, take counsel with your elders, and in three days come back and tell me what you have decided, whether or not you agree. If you find in it anything that seems unjust or not according to law, then show me and I will correct and change it."

Tolstoy was well pleased with this first meeting and he felt that the peasants believed in him. Once again, he had failed to take into consideration the innate hostility for the master that centuries of serfdom had deeply rooted in the peasantry. He kept a record, *The Diary of a Landowner,*[8] of the meetings with his serfs and individual peasants. This account clearly reveals their traditional fear of change and their inborn suspicion of a master bearing "gifts" to them. In the end, they refused to agree to the plan, and they justified their refusal by seizing upon a wild rumor—widely believed by the peasants—that at the approaching coronation the young Tsar would free the serfs and give them all the land, and hence their master was scheming to forestall this blessing by obligating them to a prior contract.

The failure of his project was a keen disappointment. At their request Tolstoy tried to remedy the immediate condition of his serfs by releasing some of them from obligatory labor by substituting a fixed yearly payment, not an unusual arrangement. Rather bitterly he told himself that the peasants did not want their freedom, and in the diary he well summed up the relationship between him and his serfs: "Two powerful men are joined with a sharp chain; it hurts both of them, and when one of them moves, he involuntarily cuts the other, and neither has room to work."

The behavior of the peasants in this whole matter alarmed Tolstoy, and he drafted an extraordinary letter of warning to his Petersburg friend Count D. N. Bludov, influential President of the Department of Laws.[9] He related the outcome of his project and then went on to add: "The despotism of the landowners has already engendered despotism in the peasants. When they told me at the meeting that I should give them all the land outright, and I said that I should be left without my shirt, they laughed, and it was impossible to blame them." For the landowner, he continued, it was now a question of land or life, and he confessed, contrary to the view he had expressed in his speech to the peasants, that he could not understand why all the serfs were not freed without the land. If it meant the growth of a huge proletariat, what then? Western Europe had its proletariat and had survived. Whatever historical phenomena the proletariat produced, while producing the revolution and Napoleon, it had not yet said its last word, and we could not judge of it as a completed historical phenomenon. (The Lord knows, might it not be the foundation

[8] Published for the first time in 1931 in the Jubilee Edition.
[9] This letter, it appears, was never sent.

for a renascence of the world towards peace and freedom?) He concluded: "If within 6 months the serfs are not freed, there will be a conflagration. Everything is ready for it. Treasonable hands are not lacking to light the fire of revolt, and then the conflagration will spread everywhere."

Tolstoy's prophecy of a revolution was right, but his chronology was off by some sixty years, and his conjecture of the future world mission of the proletariat is still one of the great question marks of history. The emancipation of the serfs took place five years after his letter and without any serious disturbances. But the letter reveals Tolstoy in a confused state of mind, pulled this way and that by both liberal and conservative tendencies. Essentially, his approach to the peasant question was a moral one: he felt a moral, not a political, duty to give them their freedom. And his lack of success at Yasnaya Polyana did not change his point of view in this respect. The letter to Bludov shows him attempting to serve two ends: to acquit himself of a moral duty by freeing the serfs, and, in a bourgeois fashion, to protect himself economically by keeping his land, without which the peasants would starve. Nor did he ever completely find his way out of this dilemma, despite the moral absolutism of his later years.

8

After the collapse of his plan to free the serfs, Tolstoy remained at Yasnaya Polyana for the next five months. The leisurely existence of a country gentleman was occasionally interrupted by serious efforts at reading and writing.[1] The calm of village life was hardly ruffled by the drowning of a peasant in the Yasnaya Polyana pond, and the discovery of a young soldier hanging in the woods. A description of the suicide in the diary showed Tolstoy's uncanny gift for realistic details—"The soldier looked as though he were standing, his trousers tucked into his boots, a dirty shirt, cap turned inside out, overcoat thrown aside, legs strangely bent," and the corpse's clothing "was thickly covered with little yellow worms."

A severe illness was not allowed to interfere with Tol-

[1] He read with much admiration the poems and biography of Pushkin, Gogol's *Dead Souls,* Goethe's *Sorrows of Young Werther, The Newcomes, Little Dorrit,* and *Pickwick Papers;* and he finished writing *Youth* and began several stories and plays.

stoy's gymnastics or his passion for hunting, and he made several visits to his sister, to Sergei, and to Turgenev's estate at Spasskoye Lutovinovo.[2] Turgenev had gone abroad before Tolstoy left Petersburg and had written two letters which had helped to improve their relations.

On one of their walks together they stopped before an old broken-down horse and Tolstoy, stroking it, began to tell what he imagined the horse was thinking and feeling. So realistically did he project himself into the animal's consciousness that he astonished and delighted Turgenev declared that Tolstoy must at one time have been a horse.

These visits, however, did little to warm the two hypersensitive writers to each other. Tolstoy decided that Turgenev's whole life was a pretense of simplicity. Sharp discussions ensued and Tolstoy concluded that Turgenev was uncongenial. After one of their meetings, Turgenev wrote Tolstoy: "I can assure you I never thought that you were evil, never suspected literary envy in you. I (pardon the expression) surmised much in you that was fatuous, but never anything bad. But you are too penetrating not to know that if one of us comes to envy the other, then surely it is not for you to envy me." The strange magnet that attracted Turgenev to Tolstoy never lost its power.

Flagrant village immorality intensified Tolstoy's emotional instability at this time. His debauched surroundings suggested a play, "Free Love,"[3] that would involve—he noted in the diary—the perverted relations of a "proprietress with her footman, a brother with his sister, and a father's natural son with the father's wife, etc." On his own part, the Petersburg grisettes who had tempted him were now displaced by willing village girls, nor did the wives and daughters of his neighbors escape his attention. "I'm insufferably abhorrent in my irresistible inclination towards vice," he complained. "Vice itself would be better."

Marriage as a remedy had already suggested itself to Tolstoy. His continual emotional excitement, he felt, was bad. After all, he was twenty-six, and it was time to settle down. He wanted to love and be loved. "Everything seemed to grow bright," he wrote in the diary, after receiving affectionate notes from two of his friends. "Yes, the best way to obtain true happiness in life is, without any rules, to throw

[2] About seventy miles from Yasnaya Polyana and sixteen from Pokrovskoye, the estate of Tolstoy's sister.

[3] Only the beginning of this play exists.

out from oneself on all sides, like a spider, an adhesive web of love to catch in it all that come: an old woman, a child, a girl, or a policeman." While in Petersburg he had written to Aunt Pelageya that he was thinking about marriage and would regard every eligible young lady he met from this point of view.

It is not surprising, then, that Tolstoy should meekly agree when his old friend Dyakov, who visited Yasnaya Polyana in June, advised him to marry Valerya Vladimirovna Arsenev. "After listening to him," he wrote in the diary, "it also seems to me the best thing I can do." The Arsenevs lived five miles away at Sudakovo. In the family were an aunt, three daughters, a son, and a French governess, Vergani. As an old friend, Tolstoy had been appointed the son's guardian and hence had easy access to the family.

Up to this point Tolstoy had paid little attention to Valerya, who was the oldest daughter, a pretty girl of twenty. Now, urged on by Dyakov, he rode over to Sudakovo to investigate. Valerya, if we may judge from the diary, did not stand his first inspection very well: "It is unfortunate that she is without backbone and fire—like vermicelli—but kind. And her smile is painfully submissive. Returned home and sent for the soldier's wife." The last cryptic sentence refers to a peasant soldier's wife with whom he had illicit relations. Not a very auspicious beginning for Valerya, but then his curiosity was aroused and he had plenty of time on his hands.

Over the next four months there were frequent exchanges of visits, and Valerya was submitted to the searching observation of a man who seemed more concerned with the idea of marriage than with marriage itself. The diary was the repository of Tolstoy's fluctuating impressions. Because Valerya chattered about clothes and the coronation, to which she was going, he decided that she was "frivolous" and his "passion" a fleeting thing. A few days later he saw her in a white dress and thought her "very charming." This same day at Sudakovo was one of the pleasantest in his life, and it prompted him to wonder whether he could love her seriously. On his next visit, however, he discovered that she was badly educated, "and ignorant if not stupid." Two days later the Arsenevs visited him, and he wrote: "Valerya is a splendid girl but she certainly does not please me. Yet, if we meet so often, I may suddenly marry her." Then he decided that her bare arms were unshapely and upset him, and he disliked her showy morning gown.

The Sudakovo household had smelled a suitor, a difficult one to snare they quickly perceived, but a highly desirable one in name, ability, and in a large estate. Valerya deserved much of the criticism Tolstoy aimed at her, and she soon became painfully aware of his faultfinding. Although she obviously hoped to marry him, she was quite capable of showing her resentment of his parental attitude. She had capacities, but apparently not the kind to inspire lasting love where it did not first exist.

After a few weeks of this querulous courting, Tolstoy reached a point where Valerya's frivolity and absence of care seemed hopeless. He was afraid, he noted, that hers was a nature that could not love even a child. Finally, he wrote in the diary: "I fear marriage as well as baseness, i.e., of amusing myself with her. But to marry, much would have to be changed, and I have still a great deal of work to do on myself."

Suddenly, something happened to soften Tolstoy's attitude. It may have been Valerya's imminent departure for the coronation or simply a new effort on her part to please him. For he now noted that she wore her hair behind her ears because he liked it so, that she dressed less gaudily, and worked hard over his favorite piano pieces. He thought she had grown "ten times nicer" and "above all more natural." Valerya appealed to him for the first time as a woman, he wrote, and he could now look at her bare arms without disgust. He even talked to her about marriage and concluded that she was "not stupid and remarkably kind."

Valerya left to attend the coronation of Alexander II at Moscow in the middle of August. A few days later Tolstoy confided to himself: "I've been thinking more and more of little Valerya these days." He began to miss her and could not refrain from writing her. Valerya's failure to answer grieved him. At last a letter arrived from her to Auntie Tatyana. In this letter, which he read, she described in great detail the coronation ceremonies, the parties, festivities, and the clothes she wore to them, and the aides-de-camp who flattered her with their attention. Tolstoy was vastly irritated and promptly dispatched a scolding letter to the girl he was seriously thinking of making his bride. The letter was a cold piece of irony, fitfully garnished with morsels of playful sarcasm. He had written his first, he said, while trying to check his affection; in this one he must try to check the "calm hatred," the sadness and disappointment, that reading her letter to his aunt had aroused in him. He twitted her about her fondness for fine clothes and aides-de-camp. "To love high society," he wrote, "and not man is dishonest, and even dangerous, because in it trashy people are to be met with more frequently than in any other society, and for you it is even not suitable, for you are not in high society yourself, and therefore your relations, based on a pretty little face and a red-currant dress, would not be at all pleasant or dignified. As for the aides-de-camp, I believe there are forty of them in all, and I know positively that only two are not scoundrels or fools—consequently there's also no joy in this."

It was the letter of an unreasonable and perhaps jealous man. Valerya did not deign to answer it. Anxiety banished his anger. He wrote again, begging her forgiveness and "two words" in reply to tell him she was not angry. Only after her return at the end of September was he restored to favor, and then her chatter about Moscow and high society raised his doubts again. Worse still, she admitted to having fallen in love with her Moscow music teacher, Mortier de Fontaine, a well-known French composer and pianist. Tolstoy was deeply offended, felt ashamed for himself and for her, yet he confessed on this occasion that for the first time he experienced something like feeling for her. Two days later he made a significant entry in his diary: "I'm not in love, but this bond will always play a great role in my life. If I have not yet known love, then, judging by the small beginning that I feel now, I shall experience it with terrible force, and God forbid that it should be for Valerya. She is completely empty, without principle, and cold as ice, so that she is continually being carried away."

For the next month Tolstoy tried to assure himself that he cared nothing for Valerya. But he kept on seeing her. And the realization that her family frankly considered him as good as engaged determined him to have an explanation. Like a man who fears his ultimate offer of love will be rejected, he had invented a humorous character for himself and one for Valerya whenever he wished to talk to her about marriage and family life. He became Mr. Khrapovitski (Mr. Snorer) and she, Miss Dembitski. As Khrapovitski he told the governess his true position and she relayed the story to Valerya. This secondhand apology made little impression on her, and he regretted it.

Tolstoy was acting like a man who was too proud to fall in love. In the absence of a spontaneous affection, he unconsciously strove to stifle his growing feeling for Valerya by an avid analysis of it. Feeling, however, would not be denied. After his "explanation," he attended a ball with Valerya at Tula and his feeling again eclipsed his reason: "Valerya was charming. I'm almost in love with her"; and when he showed her this page in his diary, she promptly tore it out for herself. Alarmed over the mounting tumult in him, he suddenly decided to go to Moscow in the hope that separation would give them both a clearer perspective on the possibilities of the future.

9

On the way to Moscow, Tolstoy thought only of Valerya, and upon his arrival he wrote her. In a parable of the silly man and the good man—his emotional, feeling self and his rational self—he explained to her that the silly man, whom she preferred, loved her for the sake of his own happiness, but the good man, his own favorite, loved her for the sake of her happiness. He argued for the good man, who had advised him to depart "for our mutual happiness." "I already love in you your beauty," he wrote, "but I'm only beginning to love in you that which is eternal and ever precious—your heart, your soul." They must not indulge themselves in a momentary passion; they must be sure their love would be lasting. Then he fell into his exasperatingly parental mood: "Please *go* for a walk every day whatever the weather may be. This is excellent, as any doctor will tell you, and wear a corset and put on your stockings yourself, and generally make various improvements of that kind in yourself. Do not despair of becoming perfect." And he concluded by holding up his own practice as a model, urging her to plan the occupations of the day and check them in the evening, and be able to go to bed at night with the conviction that she had done some good to someone.

In the correspondence that ensued between Tolstoy and Valerya[4] over the next three months, he hardly varied this attitude of the self-appointed preceptor. In one of his notebooks at this precise time, he observed: "Everything I've

[4] Her letters, unfortunately, have not been preserved.

loved—a dog, a horse, a woman—I've always compared it with an ideal of perfection for that particular species. . . ." He sought for nothing less than perfection in a woman, without realizing that a man in love takes perfection for granted. Not really being in love with Valerya, he could afford to indulge in the pleasure and risk of trying to make her perfect—the ideal wife who would enable him to realize his ideal of family happiness.

Tolstoy remained but a short time in Moscow, staying with his sister Marya who was having difficulties with her husband. He dined with Botkin and the famous dramatist Ostrovski, whom he dispatched in the diary as "a dirty but kind man, though a cold egoist." The Sudakovo miss, however, was on his mind, and he made an ungracious notation on her: "I tried to think of Valerya and thought about brothels; this hurt me."

Tolstoy went on to Petersburg, where he arrived November 7. The next day he sent a scorching letter to Valerya. He had learned that her affair with the music teacher was common gossip in Moscow. Stung by this knowledge, he asserted that her nature was cold, incapable of love, and that her feeling for him would soon vanish. All this arose, he pointed out, from her light nature, and he begged her to reform, concluding with the advice that she should be utterly frank with him if they were going to remain friends and love each other.

Repenting his harshness, he hastened the following day to send another and kinder letter that strikingly revealed his own thought at this time. If he had erred in his last, he hopefully explained, it was because one must err boldly and resolutely in order to come nearer the truth. Her trouble was that she had not learned to suffer. "Ach, if you could only understand and feel through suffering, as I have, the conviction that the only possible, entirely true, enduring and highest happiness is obtained by three things: work, self-renunciation, and love." Two persons united in this conviction could be completely happy. To salve the sting of his previous letter, and perhaps because he really believed it at the moment, he told her that she had an extraordinarily lovely nature, and that in all his disappointments the fact that "there is a girl back there" was the most comforting thing he knew. He begged her to write him, and he ended with an unusually frank statement that very accurately summed up his whole relationship with Valerya. "You see," he wrote, "I so strongly wish to love you that I teach you how to make me love you. Indeed, my real feeling for you is not yet love, but a passionate desire to love you with all my might."

Love, however, is not teachable; its devotees learn by instinct not by rote. Valerya's instincts were better than Tolstoy's. He insisted upon playing the pedagogue simply because he could not trust the instincts of his heart. Still not hearing from her, he wrote an amusing letter in which, after confessing that he loved her terribly, he pictured their life together as the Khrapovitskis, Mr. Khrapovitski despising society and adoring a peaceful family life in the country, his wife dreaming of social life in Petersburg. On their united income, he pointed out the impossibility of living the whole year or even part of it in the city in an expensive manner. They must compromise and reside seven months in the country and five in Petersburg in a sixth-floor flat, with books, music, pictures, concerts, and quartets at home. There would be no luxury, balls, and high society. He broke off at this point, and not receiving a letter from Valerya the next day, he added an angry note to tell her of his complete indifference.

In a few days two delayed letters from Valerya arrived. His immediate answer was filled with affection. He doubted the whole universe, he wrote, save that good was good, and it was this alone that kept him going. And he knew that she could be good if she would only try. Another letter from her sent him into an ecstasy of devotion. It was clear that she loved him; she even completed his unfinished sketch of the Khrapovitskis' married life. In answer he poured out details on his writing, telling her that he valued his literary reputation almost as much as a certain young lady. In his ardor the Khrapovitskis got down to the fifth floor, then the fourth. The best society, that is the educated, cultured, and talented, would come to their modest home. "God help you, my darling," he exclaimed, "go ahead, love, love not me alone, but all God's world, nature, music, poetry, and all that is charming in it, and develop your mind so as to understand the things that are worthy of love on earth." Then he interrupted this frenzy to preach that the chief destiny of woman is motherhood, and he ended, aggravatingly enough, with a lecture on taste in clothes.

This letter marked the high point of Tolstoy's regard for Valerya. His expression of feeling for her in the remainder of the correspondence swiftly subsided; in the end, only rationalizations for his lack of feeling remained. Thus, in his next letter, he resurrected the music teacher in what seemed to be a deliberate attempt to pick a quarrel. He had learned that she still corresponded with him, and he wanted her to summon him to Sudakovo and tell him flatly that she was through with him. Her religious nature prompted from him an unusual statement that had a strangely prophetic ring in the light of his future difficulties with the woman he did marry. "Whatever our future relations are," he wrote, *"let us never speak about religion and all that refers to it.* You know that I am a believer, but it may very well be that my faith differs from yours, and this question must never be touched, especially by people who want to love each other."

Tolstoy's growing coldness soon became apparent to Valerya. She took him to task for it and complained of his habit of lecturing her. His reply was an attempt to exaggerate his "nasty, suspicious, changeable nature" in an obvious effort to discourage her, and he finally fell into the last resort of a man trying to justify a love grown cold: the plea that love and marriage would bring unhappiness to them both and therefore they should try to remain friends. Her answer was a letter forbidding him to write to her. But he replied, offering the customary explanations in such a situation.

During the whole period of this correspondence, Tolstoy led his usual intense social existence in Petersburg. Much of his time was spent in the company of his literary friends,[5] who eventually began to bore him extremely; he heard a great deal of music; and often he had recourse to loose women. He seemed to feel no urge to keep himself pure and chaste for the girl who might have become his wife. At a masquerade, a "sweet mouth" approached him. "I solicited it for a long time," he wrote in the diary. "It came with me, and at home was very reluctant to unmask. As like

[5] With some of these friends, especially Druzhinin who originated the idea, he drew up a project to establish a Society for the Aid of Needy Authors and Learned Men. The money was raised and the Society functioned very satisfactorily. Dostoyevsky was one of its early beneficiaries.

A.D.[6] as two peas, only older and the features coarser. I took her home, and the whole night and the next day I recovered my happiness."

On November 28 he received his long-awaited discharge from the army, and he decided to gratify a wish that had been with him for some time: to go abroad. He left Petersburg on January 12, and after stops in Moscow and Warsaw, he arrived in Paris February 9.

Tolstoy had not entirely forgotten Valerya. Several letters to Auntie Tatyana, who had very much favored the match, made a sincere effort to explain his conduct. "I never loved her," he wrote, "with a real love. I was carried away by the reprehensible desire to inspire love. This gave me a delight I had never before experienced. But the time spent away from her proved to me that I did not even have the desire to see her, still less to marry her. It was terrible for me to think of the obligations I should have to perform towards her without loving her; so I decided to come away sooner than I had intended. I have behaved very badly; I have asked God to pardon me, and I ask the same of all whom I have grieved, but to mend this matter is impossible, and nothing in the world can renew it now."

The feeling persisted that he had played a shabby part in the affair. Just after he wrote what he thought was to be his last letter to Valerya, he had a strange dream in which he saw slaughter on the floor and a naked brown woman on his chest stooping down and whispering something to him. He felt a need to justify his behavior and purge his mind of the whole episode. This he later attempted in his short novel *Family Happiness* (1858–1859). He re-created the situation and tried to prove that if he and Valerya had been married, their different views of what made for happiness in such a relationship would have led to unhappiness for both.

Family Happiness does not justify Tolstoy's actions, but it admirably explains the reasons and feelings behind them. Psychologically he was not yet ready for marriage, but he wanted to realize his ideal of family happiness. Just before he left Moscow for abroad, he met a thrice-married lady, Baroness E. I. Mengden. He was impressed by her culture and intellect, and could not resist drawing a comparison between her and the provincial little Valerya. In the diary

[6] Possibly Alexandra Dyakov (Obolenski).

he noted that Baroness Mengden was charming and that he might have very happy relations with her. Then he concludes: "Perhaps the whole delight consists in standing on the threshold of love." And this statement may also be accepted as the real explanation of his behavior towards Valerya.

X

The Grand Tour

CULTURED RUSSIANS, like the English, regarded a grand tour through the countries of Western Europe as a fitting climax to a young man's education. Tolstoy was a bit old for such a finishing touch; he had come to Paris not so much with the desire to learn from foreign travel as to escape—to escape from Valerya, from the Petersburg literary circle, and from one of his periodic attacks of dissatisfaction with the lack of purpose in his life.

Paris was more than a haven for the fugitive; it was a veritable Isle of the Blessed—for a time at least. All the pleasures of the city were open to Tolstoy, without the foreigner's usual lonely introduction to them. For here solicitous "old nurse" Turgenev eagerly greeted his troglodyte and found a suitable *pension,* where French sociability and conversation, interspersed with jests and puns in a babel of languages, cheered him at once. At the typical *pension* table he found a philosopher, a Spanish countess spangled with romantic adventures, an opinionated American doctor, an Italian abbé who declaimed the *Divine Comedy,* a playwright with long hair, and a female pianist who had composed the best polka in the world. After dinner, chairs and tables were pushed back for dancing on the dusty carpet, and in the dark hallway furtive flirting went on.

Aristocratic Russian families settled in the city gladly opened their doors to Tolstoy, and touring cousins were happy to dine with him. At the *salon* of his distant relatives, the Trubetskois, he met a weird assortment of people, from Jesuits to unsuccessful revolutionists. Nor was he indifferent to the Trubetskois' daughter, whose marriage soon took place and wrung from him a confession of sadness and envy. He was also welcome at the Lvovs', until the jealous husband began to suspect his attentions to his wife. Tolstoy was really interested in their niece, attractive Princess Ekaterina Lvov. Interest blossomed into affection. He noted in the diary that he was a fool not to try to marry her. Later, when away from Paris, he even wrote Turgenev for his frank opinion of whether or not a proposal to the princess would be acceptable. Nothing came of the matter; he was still unready to cross the threshold of love. There were numerous dinners and dances; and his rakish cousin, N. M. Gorchakov, took him to public balls and initiated him into the city's demimonde. Here was God's plenty, and a society in which he felt completely at home.

Tolstoy was tireless in his activities. An Italian and an English teacher were engaged to give him lessons. Stock tourist places were visited—the museums, the bourse, Fontainebleau, and Versaille. He attended the theater diligently and enjoyed nearly all of it. Of the French plays he saw, he had harsh words only for one type: "Racine's drama and the like are Europe's poetic wound. Thank God we've not got it and shall not have it." The opera, always a bastard art to Tolstoy, he enjoyed in Paris almost against his will, but the concerts threw him into ecstasies. After a performance of Beethoven's "Trio" (opus 70), he decided that the French played him like gods. Attending lectures of distinguished professors was more in fashion among tourists then than now, and Tolstoy went to the Sorbonne and the Collège de France to hear talks on dramatic poetry, the classics, political economy, and international law.

Quiet evenings with Russian literary friends visiting Paris varied this intensive fare, and of these Turgenev was the one most frequently visited. Turgenev could not seem to live with Tolstoy or without him. Tolstoy's opinion of his friend fluctuated. At one moment he found him "good but terribly weak," then he was "vain and shallow," and a few days later he decided that Turgenev "does not believe in anything" and "does not love, but wants to love." Upon saying farewell to him in Paris, however, Tolstoy confessed in the diary: ". . . I wept. I don't know why. I'm very fond of him. He has made and is making a different man of me."

The period was a low one in the fortunes of Turgenev. He was ill and was having difficulties with the great love of his life, the famous singer, Pauline Viardot-Garcia. Tolstoy thought that he exaggerated both complaints and was annoyed by his feminine querulousness and self-pity. After Tolstoy had been in Paris a short time, he agreed to go with Turgenev to Dijon to help him get over his "moral loneliness," his illness, and the feeling that his imaginative powers were failing. In a letter to Annenkov, Turgenev described the two of them at work in a little hotel room, almost sitting on the hot coals to keep warm. While Tolstoy industriously scribbled page after page, he looked on wistfully and lamented that he had long since sucked his own lemon dry. And with a sunset glow of artist's temperament, he ordered Annenkov either to print the last manuscript he had sent him or "consign it to a quiet end in the water-closet."

The two authors were getting along capitally together, and Tolstoy even admitted that he had misunderstood Turgenev in the past and generously granted his artistic superiority. Within five days this literary honeymoon ended. Tolstoy read the draft of the new tale to him, and Turgenev reacted coldly. He decided categorically that Turgenev had "never loved anyone." They quarreled once again, and Tolstoy left for Paris. In all their relations his esteem for Turgenev as a great artist was patent. In fact, this feeling irritated him, and he wished to free himself of it.

Back in Paris, Tolstoy once more applied himself wide-eyed to monuments and cocottes. He felt his lack of knowledge amid the culture and art of the French capital. Sergei arrived, but Tolstoy's sincere delight over the presence of his brother quickly vanished. He discovered that they had little in common. Nikolai, with his artistic soul (his charming "Hunting in the Caucasus" had just appeared in the *Contemporary*), understood him thoroughly; Sergei loved without understanding him. He soon left Paris, somewhat to Tolstoy's relief.

After almost two months of dizzy, delightful playing, Tolstoy started a letter to Botkin, in which he enthusiastically declared that he could not foresee the time when this great city would lose interest for him. He described the artistic pleasures he had enjoyed and the striking differences in French and Russian life, "especially the social freedom of which I did not even have a comprehension in Russia." Two months more at least, he reported, must be spent in this delectable place.

The next day Tolstoy completed the letter, but Paris in

the brief interval had taken on all the aspects of a Sodom. Early that morning he had gone, in the spirit of a tourist seeing the sights, to witness the execution of a certain Francis Richeux, who had killed and robbed two persons. The scene shocked Tolstoy's sensibilities.

> This spectacle made such an impression on me [he wrote to Botkin] that I shall not recover from it for a long time. I saw many horrors of war in the Caucasus and elsewhere, but if a man were torn to pieces before my eyes, it would not be so repulsive as this dextrous and elegant machine with which in a flash a powerful, fresh, and healthy person is killed. In the first instance there would be no intelligent will, but the human feeling of passion; in the other, there is a refined quiet and convenience in killing and nothing at all majestic. The insolent audacious desire to fulfil justice, the law of God. . . . The repulsive crowd, the father who explains to his little daughter the clever, convenient mechanism that does this, etc. Human law—nonsense! . . . I understand the laws of custom, of morality and religion . . . and I feel the laws of art that give happiness always; but for me, political laws are such a horrible lie that I do not see in them anything either better or worse. . . . I will never again look at such a thing, and I will never anywhere serve *any* government.

The image of the guillotine haunted Tolstoy. "A stout, white robust neck and chest," he jotted down in the diary. "He kissed the Gospels, and then—death. How senseless!" He had nightmares. The glistening knife descended on him. He awoke trembling and felt his neck for a cut. The scene would not fade from his mind. Many years later, in both *Confession* and *What Then Must We do?*, he recalled this execution and condemned it. For the arbiter of good and evil, he decided, is not what people say or do, nor is it progress, but one's own heart.

Paris became hateful to Tolstoy. He did not stop to reason that Moscow or Petersburg could present scenes of equal horror. His intensely impressionable nature revolted at any display of human cruelty. His mind was keyed to the disharmony between absolute good and man-made laws, even to the extent that he was beginning to doubt the so-called benefits of civilization. Now, he could find no further charm in this city of refinement and culture, and the day after the execution, he noted in the diary: ". . . Suddenly a simple and sensible idea occurred to me—to leave Paris." The following day he set out for Geneva.

2

The greater part of the trip to Geneva was by rail, and it bored Tolstoy. "For God's sake, travel wherever you like but only not by rail," he wrote to Turgenev, from whom he had taken a tearful farewell. "The railroad is to a journey what a brothel is to love: just as convenient, but also just as humanly mechanical and deadly monotonous." The last leg of the trip in a coach raised his spirits. An open road and a moonlit night, in which everything stood out and was suffused with love, banished the specter of the guillotine and his baleful thoughts of Sodom-Paris. "For the first time in a long period, I sincerely thanked God that I was alive."

Tolstoy's reason for selecting Geneva as a haven was the presence there of his relative, Countess Alexandra Tolstoy. She was traveling with the family of Grand Duchess Marie as the companion of her children. The day after his arrival Tolstoy called on the countess at the luxurious Villa Bocage and vehemently poured out his disgust for Paris. He had almost gone out of his mind with the things he had seen. Nineteen of the thirty-six couples in the apartment building where he had lived, he charged, were unmarried. It had revolted him. And then the execution had murdered his sleep. So he had rushed headlong to his dear relative, feeling sure that she would save him.

Happily, "Granny" (so Tolstoy humorously called the countess because he thought her too young for the usual Russian appellation of "aunt") thoroughly understood her eccentric "grandson." His impressions, she guessed, were nearly always extreme, but she was fond of him and liked his modesty, liveliness, and kindly, expressive eyes. With her sharp intellect she had already recognized in him a kindred characteristic: they were "both terrible enthusiasts and analysers, who loved goodness, but did not know how to follow it properly."

Soon they were on terms of intimate friendship and acted together like two youths off on a holiday frolic. His visits were always welcome, for both children and grownups unfailingly responded to his intense, active personality. Cultured Russian travelers in the neighborhood quickly became his friends. They made up a group for an excursion to Vevey, and after they arrived climbed to Glion. Good company, perfect weather, and lush fields of spring flowers gladdened all. They reached the hotel at the top of the mountain in a sweat and found the public room crowded with English and American tourists. Comfortable, self-centered, joyless English travelers annoyed Tolstoy. To him their inner world seemed asleep. "The English are morally naked people and go about like that without shame," he noted in the diary. Perhaps he thought their stuffiness needed a jolting, for after tea he unceremoniously sat down at the piano and called upon his friends to sing. The countess and Madam Pushchin, who had excellent voices, started with "God Save the Tsar," and soon the men chimed in. Russian and gypsy songs were rendered, anything that suggested itself to Tolstoy, who accompanied and acted the part of conductor. The open windows, the expansive view over the surrounding countryside, and the impromptu spirit of the performance enlivened the whole room, and the delighted audience called for more and more. This joyous excursion ended when the countess had to return to Geneva to the duchess. Tolstoy remained at Vevey and reproached his Granny for leaving him for the "Chimney," as he sarcastically called the Court and its royalty. Letters and telegrams reached her daily, and on one occasion even a bit of verse, to tell her of his eternal devotion or of some humorous adventure. In revenge for her desertion, he and some friends made occasional sorties across the lake to take the countess by surprise with some practical joke or other.

After two weeks of sightseeing, during which Tolstoy visited Chillon, Villeneuve, and Savoy, and all the while kept up a flirtation with an English girl named Dora, he returned to Geneva and the countess. He went on another excursion with her and her sister, this time to Salève. Her woman's intuition, supported by a penetrating and deeply sympathetic mind, attracted him. He found in her what Valerya or any other woman he had met lacked—a clear understanding of his complex, often paradoxical, feelings and thoughts. They had long discussions, with lancet in hand but always with mutual affection and respect for each other's views. The subject was often religion, in which they had no common ground, for she was a serious and devoted believer and he was altogether uncertain of what he believed. Yet his sudden attendance at church and reading the Bible at this time may have been inspired by her influence. This woman who had remained unmarried by choice, despite all her charm and high connections, came close to fulfilling his ideal of the wife whom he would love more than any woman had ever been loved. "I'm so ready to fall in love that it's terrible," he wrote in the diary. "If Alexandra were only ten years younger! A fine nature." She was young enough to be his Granny, but too old to be his wife.

3

With his base at Clarens, Tolstoy pushed out into the surrounding Swiss countryside on short sightseeing trips. In the middle of May he took a ten-day hike into the mountains with Sasha Polivanov, the eleven-year-old son of an acquaintance at Clarens. He mentioned in his notebook that he was interested in the reactions of an innocent boy. Sasha sometimes proved to be a trial, but Tolstoy loved children and could enter into their special world and win their trust and confidence. The itinerary took them through Montreux, Les Avants, Col de Jaman (to Château d'Œx) and back to Clarens by way of Interlaken, Grindelwald, and Fribourg.[1]

With knapsacks on their shoulders, man and boy trudged over the mountain roads, exchanging their impressions on the natives they met and on the natural scenery that unfolded before them. Tolstoy was unusually responsive to all manifestations of nature. He had a poet's eye, the microscopic eye of a Tennyson that lingered with rapt attention on the tiniest detail of flower and tree, on the slightest nuance of color and fragrance. Shortly before starting out he had written to Auntie Tatyana from Clarens to tell her that he spent most of his time gazing at and admiring the wonders of nature in the neighborhood of this village, where his beloved Rousseau's Julie had lived. And now, the account of his walking trip reveals a Rousseauistic quality in nature descriptions interpenetrated with feeling and sentiment.

In his *Travel Notes* Tolstoy wrote: "Surprisingly enough, I have been living at Clarens for two months, and each time in the morning, or especially just before evening after dinner, when I open the shutters on which the shadows of night are falling and look out over the lake and on the mountains, green in the foreground and blue in the

[1] His *Travel Notes in Switzerland* has recently appeared in Volume V of the Jubilee Edition.

distance, reflected in it, the beauty dazzles me and suddenly acts upon me with the power of the unexpected. At that moment I wish to love, and I even feel love for myself, and I regret the past, hope for the future, and there is joy in me at being alive. I want to live forever, and thoughts about death are filled with a childishly poetic horror. Sometimes, while sitting alone in the shade of the little garden and gazing, always gazing on the shores of the lake, I experience a kind of physical impression, as though the beauty pours through my eyes into my soul."

Such expressions of feeling before the majesty of nature are not infrequent in the *Travel Notes*. Yet it is curious that these towering mountains and clear blue lakes filled him with a nostalgia for the rolling steppes and forests of his native Russia. He blamed his spirit of contradiction for the fact that the traditionally beautiful view of the Jaman mountain left him unmoved. This was a sight for English tourists to gape at, he scornfully remarked. It was all bare and cold, foreign to his warm temperament. "I love nature," he wrote, "when it surrounds me on all sides and extends unendingly, and when I am a part of it. I love it when I am surrounded by warm air, and when that air rolls away into the measureless distance; and when those same sappy blades of grass that I crush as I sit on them form the green of the boundless meadows; when those same leaves that flutter in the wind run their shadows across my face and form the line of the distant forest; when the same air that you breathe makes the deep azure of the illimitable heavens; when you do not exult and rejoice alone in nature, but around you buzz and whirl myriads of insects; and beetles, clinging together, creep about, and all around you the birds pour forth song."

4

Shortly after returning from his walking trip, Tolstoy set out for Turin to join Botkin and Druzhinin, where they visited art galleries, monasteries, and Roman ruins. His friends accompanied him back to Clarens, walking part of the distance by way of St. Bernard. Although he worried about consumption, which ran in the family, Tolstoy's energy seemed inexhaustible.

A few days' rest in Clarens and Tolstoy was off again to

Lausanne, Berne, and Lucerne. As he came into Berne the shouts of drunken soldiers did not destroy the beauty of an enchanting moonlight night. He heard the corn crakes and the croaking frogs, and his soul responded to the beauty of nature, but with a kind of sweet suffering. At a fete he attended, every seemingly insignificant detail was etched on his memory—officers flourishing their sticks, a man with a torn coat, the hot smell of trampled grass, a proud and irate dandy, a tall Swiss adjusting his braces, a poor Russian bear, and a pretty but fatty woman.

At Lucerne a curious incident occurred. Returning to the Schweizerhof Hotel at night, he noticed a tiny man who stood outside and sang Tyrolese songs to a guitar. The balconies of the hotel were crowded with well-to-do tourists who enjoyed the singularly fine performance. When the street singer begged for money, the guests turned away in silence. He went off muttering to himself and the crowd ridiculed him. Tolstoy overtook the man and invited him back to this exclusive hotel for a drink. The guests were shocked, and the waiter and hall porter grew offensive over this breach of decorum. Tolstoy became furiously angry and scolded them all.

A few days later Granny arrived at Lucerne. The last time she had seen him was at Vevey. At the hotel there the waiter had informed her in a mysterious voice that she was wanted downstairs. She descended and was greeted by Tolstoy and two of his friends wrapped in long cloaks, with feathers in their fantastic hats. In the fashion of strolling players, they had spread music on the floor, and with sticks for instruments had set up an indescribable cacophony or cat's concert. Granny nearly died with laughter and the Grand Duchess's children were inconsolable at having missed the performance.

The countess now found Tolstoy in anything but a playful mood. He was still excited and burning with indignation over the incident of the itinerant singer. In her *Reminiscences* she remarked that the affair made such a strong impression on him that it involuntarily communicated itself to others. After he had told her of how he had ordered supper and champagne for the man, she judiciously commented: "I scarcely think the guests or even the poor musician himself quite appreciated the irony of this action." Within a few days Tolstoy called on the "Chimney" to read them "From the Diary of Prince D. Nekhlyudov" or, as it is known in English, "Lucerne." The story of the humiliated singer had received the form of enduring art.

Tolstoy remained a few more days in Lucerne, spending much of his time with the countess and amusing the Grand Duchess's children. The youngsters were diverted by his antics, and expressed wonder at the number of cherries he could eat at a sitting. He endeared himself so much to them that they begged for his company when the Grand Duchess's party moved on by boat to Küsnacht. Tolstoy was invited to go along, and he pushed on further to Zurich, Schaffhausen, and Friedrichshafen. Nothing of consequence happened on the journey; he continued to Stuttgart and Baden-Baden, where he arrived July 12.

5

A letter to Auntie Tatyana from Lucerne had mentioned an extensive itinerary for the remainder of Tolstoy's stay abroad—Holland, London, then back to Paris, Rome, Naples, and possibly a return to Russia by way of Constantinople and Odessa. This plan was gambled away at the roulette wheels of Baden-Baden. He ventured a few francs and lost. The next morning he was back and played well into the night with indifferent success. The gambling fever gripped him. The following day he lost everything, borrowed two hundred francs, and lost again. He promised himself to play no more, having already run through three thousand francs.

Penniless, Tolstoy dispatched a telegram to Nekrasov for money, and wrote letters to Sergei, Botkin, Turgenev, and Granny, who at once sent him funds. The good Turgenev, who was staying at Sinzig on the Rhine at the time, worried over his troglodyte and set out for Baden-Baden. The money that Turgenev loaned him on his arrival, however, quickly went the way of the rest, and Tolstoy cursed himself as a "pig" and a "good-for-nothing."

This final loss convinced Tolstoy of the necessity of leaving the city and returning to Russia. A letter from Sergei strengthened his decision, for he learned that their sister had finally broken with her husband because of his infidelities. Marya declared that she did not care to be the chief sultana in his harem.

Tolstoy's first stop was at Frankfurt, where he visited

Granny. Distinguished guests were present. She recalled the occasion: "I almost cried out in horror when the door opened and Leo stood there in a more than incredible costume. Neither before nor after have I seen anything like it. He was like a bandit, not a gambler who had lost all his money. Obviously displeased that he did not find me alone, he stayed a brief time and vanished." When the guests learned that this singular personage was Tolstoy, they were disappointed at not being introduced, and went into raptures over his literary talent.

Tolstoy pushed on to Dresden, visited the bookshops and the art gallery, where the Sistine Madonna moved him deeply. At Marienbad he met a group of Russians, among them the Lvovs, and his interest in the pretty princess flared up again. Later, he wrote Granny about his strangely mixed reactions on this occasion: "I was exactly in the proper mood for falling in love, for I had just lost heavily at cards, was dissatisfied with myself, and entirely idle. It is a theory of mine that love consists of the desire to forget oneself, and therefore, like sleep, it comes over a man most frequently when he is displeased with himself or unhappy. Princess Lvov is beautiful, clever, honest, and has a sweet nature. I wanted with all my strength to fall in love with her, saw her a great deal, and nothing came of it. For God's sake, what does this mean? Am I a freak of some kind? It is obvious that something is lacking in me. And this something, it seems to me, is a small dose of conceit."

Granny, wiser than he in these matters, reminded him that Providence especially reserves marriage to herself and arranges for the best, if only people do not spoil things by considerations of vanity, money, or ambition; and she good-naturedly promised that she would never let him remain a bachelor. Yet it was with some reluctance that he left the princess for Berlin. There he attended a concert, but the street debauchery disgusted him. The following day he took the boat at Stettin and arrived in Petersburg July 30.

6

In his letter to Botkin from Paris, Tolstoy had firmly declared that he was not a writer. By this he meant that he was not a writer in the sense that the Petersburg literary set understood the calling. For them, authorship was simply self-expression; Tolstoy regarded his art as a medium for moral self-protection and ultimately for the perfection of mankind. He held truth to be the most valuable possession of an author, but, contrary to Mark Twain's advice, he did not always use truth economically.

During this first tour abroad Tolstoy worked intermittently on several tales.[2] At the end of 1856 social and political questions had been much on his mind; now he was concerned with the question of art. Art, he felt, must be based upon some moral truth that would go deeper than the "convictions" of the Petersburg *Contemporary* authors. And his story "Albert" was designed to convey this belief.

The life of a talented but hopelessly drunken violinist, Kiesewetter, whom Tolstoy had met in Moscow the previous winter, provided the material for "Albert." The story is a protest against society's inability to understand and protect real art, and it was his first literary failure. There is reason to believe that he thought this tale a step in the direction of the new art, "awfully high and pure," to which he had pledged himself shortly before coming abroad. Nekrasov returned the manuscript with a broad hint that Tolstoy refrain from publishing it. He pointed out the tendentiousness and banality, and suggested that the morally sick and drunken Albert needed a doctor more than the appreciative understanding of society. Tolstoy was hurt and the criticism contributed to a growing coldness between him and Nekrasov that finally resulted in his breaking with the *Contemporary*. He reworked the story in an effort to eliminate the special pleading, but he did not entirely succeed. His lyrical description of the effects of music on a listener, inspired by his own powerful reactions, is superb, and is perhaps the only distinguished feature of the tale.

"Lucerne" actually appeared before "Albert," although written after,[3] and may be considered a variant of it. Tolstoy called it an "article," and packed into it all that the limitations of fiction prevented him from saying in "Albert." It is his first moralistic tract. Here he develops ideas of the beauty of primitive art and its blending with nature,

[2] *The Cossacks,* "Far-Away Field" (a projected novel on which he made only a beginning), a short story, "Albert," and "From the Diary of Prince D. Nekhlyudov" or "Lucerne."

[3] "Lucerne" was published in the September number of the *Contemporary,* 1857, and "Albert" in the August number, 1858.

and of the fixed opposition of nature, morality, and art to political laws, organized government, and civilization. The voice of Rousseau rings loud and clear. "Lucerne" is a slight thing in the totality of Tolstoy's vast literary creations, but it is a highly important signpost pointing the direction of much of his future thought.

7

These few months abroad coincided with an obvious step forward in the growth of Tolstoy's historic mission. His contact with the culture and civilization of Western Europe had not so much changed as accelerated a development in his thinking. Upon his arrival in Paris he had prophetically observed that this trip "must certainly mark an epoch" in his life. Doubts about the meaning of life had only timidly knocked at the door of his mind; now they boldly entered it. "Last night," he wrote in the diary, "I was suddenly tormented by doubts of *everything,* which arose in me. And now, though they do not torment me, they are still in me. Why? And what am I? It seemed to me more than once that I was solving these questions, but no, I have not fixed them in my life."

Rebellious thoughts and feelings prompted by Tolstoy's experiences in the Caucasus and at Sevastopol were now affirmed in an uncompromising and dogmatic manner. This was particularly true of his attitude towards war. He went to the Invalides to see the imposing sarcophagus of Napoleon. Angrily he commented: "This deification of a malefactor is terrible. Soldiers are animals taught to bite everybody. They ought to die of hunger. Legs torn off—serves them right." An entry in his notebook was less bitter: "Is it worthwhile to dress a man in a uniform, separate him from his family, and give him a drum to beat in order to make an animal of him?"

Much of Tolstoy's reading during this first tour bore some relation to the questioning in his mind. Fiction and poetry occupied little of his time. He read Balzac's *Honorine* and *Cousine Bette* and credited the writer with an immense talent, but he thought the introduction to the *Comédie Humaine* shallow and self-satisfied. Freytag's novel *Soll und Haben* he set down as poor, and he read Goethe's *Wilhelm Meister* and his poem *Wilkommen und Abschied.* He thought Dumas *fils* talented in *La dame aux perles* but filled with depravity.[4]

Tolstoy's interests were in sterner literature. He read the Gospels, Khomyakov's religious pamphlets, and political and historical works.[5] In his notebook he also mentioned that he read Proudhon, although he did not indicate which of the several works that the great French socialist and political writer had published by 1857. It was probably the well-known *Qu'est-ce que la propriété*. This introduction to the ideas of Proudhon was a matter of primary significance. When one remembers that Proudhon was already maintaining that private property was theft; that government of man by man in every form was oppression; and that the highest perfection of society was to be found in the union of order and anarchy, then much in the development of Tolstoy's future thought becomes clear.

It is of some importance to point out the results of this reading which are immediately apparent in Tolstoy's notebooks. For it is not generally recognized that even this early his mind began to grapple with the ideas that twenty years later were to change the whole course of his life.

Tolstoy's criticism of Proudhon, for example, was characteristic of his thought at this time. He wrote in the notebook: "While reading the logical, material Proudhon, his mistakes were as clear to me as were the mistakes of the idealists to him. How often does one see the powerlessness of one's mind—always expressing one side; but it is better to see this one side in past thinkers and workers, especially when they complement each other. From this comes love, uniting all these views into one, and this is the single, infallible law of humanity."

Such a statement looked forward to Tolstoy's notion of universal love, and he was already beginning to think about its primary obstacle—modern civilization. He asserted that there was an equal compensation in the absence of civilization, a thought that led him to make random observations in the notebook about the political organization of society.

[4] He also read E. About's *Germain* ("a silly novel"); H. C. Andersen's *Improvisatore;* F. Bremer's *The Neighbours* ("a very bright, attractive talent, but as usual with women, too sugary"); and E. Gaskell's *Life of Charlotte Brontë.*

[5] He read G. M. Sarrut's *Biographie des hommes du jour;* E. Girardin's *De la liberté de la presse et du journalisme;* Napoléon III's *Idées Napoléoniennes;* E. de las Cases's *Le Memorial de Sainte Hélène;* and A. de Tocqueville's *L'Ancien Régime et la Révolution.*

"Nationality," he declared, "is the one single bar to the growth of freedom"; and he went so far as to maintain that "the absence of laws was possible, but there must be security against violence." Finally, he was led for the first time to a contemplation of that idea which in later years covered his name with both fame and infamy. "All governments," he wrote, "are in equal measure good and evil. The best ideal is anarchy."

There was much else in the notebooks over this brief period abroad that showed a surprising advance in Tolstoy's political, social, and moral views. He condemned British imperialism and the shedding of blood for any political gain; he hazarded the guess that socialism was impossible; and he asserted that the Russian people were capable of living under a republican form of government. The twenty-nine-year-old thinker had already found the road that would lead him straight to his epoch-making revolt against the whole organization of modern civilization. But he was never satisfied with abstract thought. Ideas must be translated into action. Only thus could he perfect himself and serve others. Just before he left Europe for Russia, a modest plan of action occurred to him that would soon occupy much of his time, and with unique results. "The idea came clearly and strongly into my head to start a school in my own village for the whole district, and of general *activity* of that kind. Above all, continuous activity."

XI

Literary Crisis

A GRAY, dewy morning. The birch trees. Russia at last! Tolstoy's eyes filled at the sight of his native land. Nekrasov carried him off to his country place at Peterhof for a few days. He read "Lucerne" to the company and was pleased to note that it produced an effect. But he was anxious to get home. Affairs must be put in order and his future determined without any more nonsense. On the way he defined his new purpose in life: literary work first, then family duties, and finally estate management. As for his obligations to humanity, he decided that one good action a day would suffice.

"Delightful Yasnaya!" Tolstoy exclaimed on arriving. His feeling of pleasure, however, quickly gave way to one of loathing. What shocking sights in this fatherland of his—a gentlewoman beating her little daughter on the street with a cane, an official at the station thrashing a sickly seventy-year-old man, and his own bailiff punishing a tipsy gardener by sending him over the sharp stubble in his bare, wounded feet to watch the cattle. Were his countrymen all sadists? He could not rest until he had poured out his sentiments in a letter to Granny. "In Russia it is bad, bad, bad!" he protested. "In both Petersburg and Moscow all cry out over something, are indignant, expect something to happen, and in the village we have only patriarchal barbarism, thievery, and lawlessness. Do you believe it, upon arriving in Russia I long struggled with a feeling of repulsion for my native land, and only now do I grow accustomed to the horrors that make up the eternal conditions of our life." His only salvation, he told her, was the moral world and the world of art and poetry. He sat alone at Yasnaya Polyana. The wind howled and it was cold and dirty. With clumsy fingers he played an andante of Beethoven and wept tender tears; or he read that "wonderful *Iliad,*" or invented men and women of his own and scribbled their doings on paper; or he found a refuge in thoughts about the real people he loved.

The culture and refinement of Europe had done their work. In retrospect Paris was no longer a Sodom to Tolstoy. What difference was there between the frightfulness of the modern guillotine and the horrors of Russia's primitive conditions of life? He soon regained his perspective, but this profound disillusion hovered in the background of his existence over the next two years and was periodically intensified by unhappy personal experiences.

August and September Tolstoy spent in the country. Literature—the first objective of his new purpose in life—received little attention, but he did make a serious effort to occupy himself with the family and the estate. The poverty of his serfs troubled him, and he began a regular policy of allowing peasants to buy their freedom. He tried to increase the value of his land; he planted a large number of trees in the park of Yasnaya Polyana, and soon he ordered the building of a house to replace the one he had sold several years before.

Tolstoy visited neighbors, among them the Arsenevs. Sudakovo seemed sad and gloomy. One might begin all over again, he mentioned in the diary, but Valerya he finally dismissed as a kind but empty girl. His chief enjoyment was hunting, and for this sport he went frequently to Pirogovo, an estate owned by Marya and Sergei. He felt a new responsibility for Marya and her children since she had separated from her husband. The relations of brother and sister at this time were not always pleasant, for she was beginning to evince a strong feeling for Turgenev, who obviously fostered it but had no serious intentions.[1] Tolstoy grew apprehensive, for he knew Turgenev's moral weaknesses.

Tolstoy could not throw off the feeling of boredom and sadness that had come over him upon his return to Russia. He wished to lead an active and self-denying life, by which he meant to labor, to think, and to give himself to others. Yet a sense of futility continually gnawed at him. "The ideal is unattainable," he jotted down in the diary. "I've

[1] It is very likely that Turgenev's *Faust* was inspired by his affection for Marya, and he dedicated this work to her.

already destroyed myself. Work, a small reputation, money. What for? Material enjoyment—also what for? Soon eternal night. It always seems to me that I shall soon die." At twenty-nine the gloomy spiritual condition that tormented him in later life had already begun to manifest itself.

A scheme for encouraging tree-planting in the Tula province took Tolstoy's mind off his morbid thoughts. He wrote up the project,[2] and in the middle of October he went to Petersburg to submit his plan to the proper government authorities.

2

Cautious officials deftly shelved Tolstoy's project. A further disappointment was the discovery that his literary fame had virtually vanished among the Petersburg cognoscenti. "My reputation has fallen or hardly squeaks," he noted in the diary. "And inwardly I felt terribly grieved; but now I'm calmer. I know that I have something to say and the strength to say it powerfully; then let the public speak what it will." One solid consolation was the company of Granny, who had returned from abroad. He declared enthusiastically that he had never met a woman who even reached to her knees.

Tolstoy spent the remaining two months of 1857 in Moscow. His sister, brother, and Auntie Tatyana also arrived for the gay winter social season. Marya was a fine pianist, and frequent musical evenings at home were arranged. Nor did he miss an opportunity to take her three children to the theater, where they fell asleep, or to the zoo at which they remained wide-awake. One of these outings inspired a tale that he wrote for the amusement of his adored and adoring nephew and nieces.[3]

He saw a great deal of Nikolai, whose droll humor, brilliant conversation, and simple, lovable nature made him a general favorite. Although they had the deepest admiration and affection for each other, Nikolai, who distinguished so clearly between the real essence of life and its ephemeral aspects, often treated his brother to a gentle "riding" because of his snobbish lapses and fondness for modish clothes.

[2] It has been published in Vol. V of the Jubilee Edition.

[3] *A Tale of How Varinka Quickly Grew UP* (Jubilee Edition, Vol. V).

Indeed, Tolstoy might be seen any day strutting along the boulevard, dressed in a short winter overcoat with a stylish gray beaver collar, his well-groomed dark curly hair showing under a glossy hat cocked fashionably to one side, and jauntily swinging a cane like any lord of creation. In the homes of Moscow's best families his proud bearing, lively personality, and flashing eyes instantly commanded attention. In conversation his face became animated, and he talked loudly and clearly. There was an aggravating positiveness in his exposition, and it was obvious that he feared to be wrong in either words or deeds. Ideas and projects sprouted in his head like mushrooms, and to all who listened he gave the impression of originality and immense driving force.

Whenever Tolstoy was in the city, he insisted on regular physical exercise. At two o'clock in the afternoon, his friends knew they could locate him at Moscow's fashionable gymnasium. While a group of bald-headed businessmen and government officials with pendulous stomachs looked on with bored dissatisfaction, Tolstoy, clad in tights, dexterously leaped over the vaulting horse, without touching a cone placed on the back of the apparatus.

Nor was the science of the tender passion neglected during his stay in Moscow. Many years later a feminine admirer recalled that at this time Tolstoy "still flirted and was a swell whom all of Moscow zealously courted, for he was very much interested in women." The urge to marry was stronger than ever, but Granny's Providence gave him no aid, and he was loath now to let reason dictate where the heart had not spoken. The Valerya incident had taught him a lesson. He was thrown again with Alexandra Obolenski, and perhaps because the issue was bound to be hopeless, he felt himself "passionately in love with her." And he renewed his acquaintance with the Lvovs, who were also staying in Moscow that winter. Now he shifted his attention to the younger sister, Alexandra, but he showed even less zeal for her than he had for Ekaterina.

Two plain-appearing but intellectual girls, Olga Kireyev and Alexandra, the sister of his close friend B. N. Chicherin, obviously set their caps for him. But he did not like intellectual women, and the seventeen-year-old Olga's enthusiastic disbelief in Christ pained him extremely. There were others, prettier and less intellectual, who caught his eye. Ekaterina, a daughter of the poet Tyutchev, whose verse he greatly admired, he confessed himself "ready to marry, quietly, without love, but she would have accepted me with studious coldness." Meanwhile, Providence was arranging things to suit herself. He had taken to visiting the Bers family again. In this merry household the girls with whom he had played leapfrog the preceding year were fast growing up. The two oldest, Elizaveta and Sonya, delighted in the lively amusement he provided. He remarked to a friend: "If Sonya were sixteen and not fourteen, I would propose to her at once."

3

Tolstoy remained in Moscow until April of 1858.[4] During this time he saw much of Fet, who had become one of his closest and most valued friends, and Chicherin, a brilliant philosopher and jurist, who stimulated him intellectually and influenced him to take an interest in science. He began to read up on the subject of geology and also the curious works in natural science of Michelet—*L'Oiseau* and *L'Insecte*.[5] On the theme of religion, however, he differed emphatically with Chicherin, as he did with everyone. After a warm discussion of Christianity, he set down the following thought that he found no reason to alter during the remainder of his life: "Christ did not impose but revealed a moral law that will always remain as a standard of good and evil."

With the first breath of spring, the season that always filled Tolstoy with a joyous feeling of renewal, he was off to Yasnaya Polyana (April 9). "It's spring, Granny!" he proclaimed in a letter to Countess Alexandra Tolstoy shortly after his arrival, and continued:—

> For good people it is splendid to live in the world, and it is fine even for me. In nature, in the air, in everything

[4] With other enthusiasts, Tolstoy helped organize during this winter a Musical Society that later developed into the Moscow Conservatory, of which Nikolai Rubenstein became director.

[5] From 1857 to 1859 Tolstoy's reading was varied. Among other things, he read the Gospels, *Don Quixote,* Rabelais' works, Goethe's *Faust,* Macaulay's *History of England,* the tales of H. C. Andersen, George Eliot's *Scenes from Clerical Life* and *Adam Bede,* Gogol's *Letters* and the second part of *Dead Souls,* Goncharov's *Oblomov,* Kozlov's *Poems,* Saltykov-Shchedrin's *Death of Pazukhin,* and the *Correspondence* of P. V. Annenkov and N. V. Stankevich.

> is hope, the future, and a charming future. . . . I well know, when one reasons it out sanely, that I'm a frozen, old, rotten potato stewed in sauce, but spring acts on me so powerfully that I often catch myself in the full blaze of dreaming I'm a plant that is just about to put forth its leaves with other plants, and will go on growing simply, calmly, and happily in God's own world.

Yasnaya Polyana was Tolstoy's "fatherland." Without it, he admitted, it would be difficult for him to comprehend his relation to Russia. His housekeeper, Agafya Mikhailovna,[6] was the first on hand with a warm welcome and a list of complaints, and Vasili the bailiff waited patiently to present an account of his stewardship. For twelve years Tolstoy had been dabbling at estate management, but this spring he had decided to tackle the job in all seriousness, and to begin by doing away with the intermediaries who stood between him and direct contact with his peasants.[7]

With that curious compensatory desire of the intellectual for hard physical labor, Tolstoy plunged into farming. Writing and reading were almost entirely forgotten. He tried to become a practical squire and drove himself as hard as his peasants. Nor did he spare blows, and on one occasion he even ordered a stubborn serf to be flogged, although he at once grew conscience-stricken, asked the victim's pardon, and gave him three rubles. He tried his hand at plowing and discovered the poetry of work in guiding the colter through loamy spring earth. The blood raced through his veins, hours passed, and he went home with an appetite and a satisfying fatigue he had never before experienced.

Nikolai amusingly observed to Fet that his brother was trying to become acquainted with peasant life. He described how Tolstoy regarded his serf Ufan as an emblem of village strength and admired the way he stuck his arms out when plowing. In imitation, Tolstoy "ufanized," that is, stuck his own elbows out wide as he drove the plow. His insistence on taking a hand in all manner of work on the estate, without omitting anything, not even his gymnastics, also drew Nikolai's raillery. The bailiff, he remarked, saw things dif-

[6] This house serf spent all her life at Yasnaya Polyana, serving in various capacities. She had a unique personality and was a talented narrator of folk tales. Tolstoy portrayed her in *Childhood, Boyhood,* and in *Anna Karenina.*

[7] He announces this determination in an unfinished sketch, "Summer in the Country" (Jubilee Edition, Vol. V).

ferently. When he came to the master for orders and found him head downward, swinging by one knee from a horizontal bar, he did not know whether to listen to his orders or be astonished at him.

There were few visitors that summer at Yasnaya Polyana. Turgenev came for several days and they got along pleasantly enough in that curious state of armed neutrality that always existed between them. On a return visit to Spasskoye, however, Tolstoy found his friend unendurably ponderous. A more welcome visitor at Yasnaya Polyana was the aged mother of Countess Alexandra Tolstoy. He wrote Granny of the joy this visit had given him, and in the same letter he also described his simple country pleasures. Two nightingales sang below his window, and he noticed that they answered the sixths in a Haydn sonata that he strummed on the piano. He stopped and so did the birds, and they began their warbling again when he played. "I spent about three hours at this game," he wrote. "The balcony was open, the night warm, the frogs were about their business, and the watchman about his—splendid! Pardon me if this letter seems to come from the forest primeval. I must confess that I have gone a little off my head with the spring and the solitude. I wish you the same with all my heart. There are moments of happiness stronger, but none more harmonious than these."

Granny did understand his groping, his wonderment that Truth and Beauty, as he pointed out in another letter, can live in the same corner with Christian sentiments, like a dog and cat. She replied:—

> . . . I am never worried, whatever you say. The seed is germinating, and God placed it in too good a soil for it to be stifled. Everything standing in the way of Truth shall be cast aside one day. On my part, I see (as it were) only the mechanical working of your soul. That is the ship that is being built and has not yet left the dock. When I see it majestically sail past from the level at which I flounder, I shall cry out: "Saint Leo, pray for us!"

"Saint Leo," however, doffed his canonical robes when he left the sanctum of his study where he penned these lofty sentiments on Truth and Beauty. In the fields, woods, and bathhouse he was Squire Tolstoy, and over his serfs he claimed all the ancient prerogatives appertaining to that title. His victim at this time—apparently a very willing one

—was a pretty young married peasant girl by the name of Aksinya Bazykin. In May he noted in the diary: "Today, in the big old wood. I'm a fool, a brute. Her bronze flush and her eyes . . . I'm in love as never before in my life. Have no other thought." Something of his unusual contentment with village life this summer must be attributed to the pleasures Aksinya afforded him. The customary transient liaison of master and serf developed into a firm attachment. A son, Timofei, was born.[8] The veiled references to Aksinya in the diary suggest—as he actually admitted—that his feeling for her had become that of a husband for a wife. His conscience troubled him. A sense of guilt at times amounted literally to physical suffering, but so completely was his desire concentrated on Aksinya that at times even the voice of conscience was stilled. Three months before his death, Tolstoy told his official biographer, P. I. Biryukov, that his affair with Aksinya was one of two moral lapses in his youth that most tormented him throughout his life. This illicit union served to intensify his desire for marriage as the only hope of escape.[9]

At night, seated in his comfortable armchair in the quiet living room of Yasnaya Polyana, Tolstoy's conscience found peace in the serene companionship of Auntie Tatyana. If she had known of his affair with Aksinya, she would have suffered for him but not censured him. For she never told these children, who had been left to her care, how to arrange their lives. All her moral influence rested on the sweet, tranquil existence of unobtrusive love that she led. Although deeply religious, she did not discuss religion, and Tolstoy, after some unhappy attempts, avoided this subject with her. She seemed to have a trusting faith in everything, except the doctrine of eternal punishment, for she could not imagine how God, who was goodness itself, could ever desire man to suffer. Her charming Old World affability put all at their ease, yet she did not live in the past and tried to keep up with all the interests of her nephews and niece. The new telegraph wires along the road puzzled her.

[8] In later years Timofei served as coachman to one of Tolstoy's sons, a situation ironically reminiscent of the illegitimate coachman-son of Tolstoy's father.

[9] So strong was this attachment that Tolstoy felt impelled to make use of it several times in his fiction. It appears in *Polikushka,* "Idilliya," and in "Tikhon and Malanya"; and it is most fully described in *The Devil* in the love of Eugene for Stepanida.

When driving with Tolstoy one day, she asked him to tell her how words were sent by telegraph. He explained the process as simply as possible and she indicated that she understood. After keeping her eye on the wire for some time, she asked in a puzzled tone why she had not yet seen a single letter go along it. Years after her death, he suffered pangs of remorse at the remembrance that he had sometimes denied her money for sweets that she kept in her room, more to treat others with than to indulge herself. She often called him "Nikolai," which pleased him immensely, for he thought it showed that her conception of him and his father was mingled in her love of both.

4

Early in September Tolstoy attended an election of the Tula nobility. He appears not to have been very friendly with his fellow landowners at the meeting, but he was one of the signers, along with Turgenev and Khomyakov, of a resolution that favored emancipation of the serfs, with a just allotment of land. This document reflected the growing feeling throughout the whole country that the time for freeing the serfs had arrived.

Tolstoy returned to Yasnaya Polyana (September 20) and remained until December when he went to Moscow again. A friend, S. S. Gromeka, who was as enthusiastic as Tolstoy about hunting, invited him and Nikolai to take part in a bear hunt at Volochok, a village on the road to Petersburg. The affair was arranged in elaborate fashion, with a host of peasant beaters and a professional huntsman to direct all details.

It was known that a particularly large she-bear had so far escaped the hunters, and the next day the party set out to track it down. The bear was raised and surrounded in a patch of forest by beaters. Hunters took their positions at the approaches and the beaters set up an infernal racket to drive the bear out. Although the huntsmen had been advised to stamp down the snow at their stations in order to have complete freedom of movement, Tolstoy obstinately remained standing up to his waist in it, declaring that he was there to shoot, not box, the bear. Running from the beaters, the animal turned into an approach, saw the hunters, and quickly swerved towards Tolstoy's post. So surprised was he that the bear got to within six paces of him before he remembered to fire. The shot missed, and he fired a second time with the bear on top of him. But the bullet failed to stop the beast and Tolstoy was bowled over. The next thing he knew he felt something heavy weighing him down and his face being forced into the bear's mouth. He instinctively tried to draw his head into his shoulders in an effort to free his nose and eyes from the enormous teeth that were gnawing at him. His face felt as though it were being cut by knives. The end had come, he thought. Then suddenly the weight lifted from him, and the bear vanished. The professional hunter had immediately perceived Tolstoy's plight, and, dashing up with only a stick in his hand, had frightened the animal off. The flesh above and below Tolstoy's eye had been badly torn. He was taken to a near-by town, and after the wound was sewn up, he suffered no ill-effects. The huge bear was eventually killed and Tolstoy claimed the skin, which may still be seen at Yasnaya Polyana. He returned to Moscow, immediately wrote Auntie Tatyana about his adventure, and thanked God for his unusual escape.[1]

5

Tolstoy began 1859 with a firm declaration that "I must get married this year or never." He had passed the thirty mark, an inevitability that worried him excessively. Aksinya worried him more, and soon he confessed to himself: "Ive even become terrified at the thought of how close she is to me." Matrimony would solve everything, but it was a solution that still evaded him.

For consolation Tolstoy went to Petersburg in March to visit Granny, that unfortunately passé embodiment of his ideal woman. He spent "ten of the happiest days," and the countess noted in her diary: "Met with dear Leo. As formerly, he is a queer fellow, but also a remarkable mind and heart."

Tolstoy justified her description of "queer fellow" by suddenly departing for Moscow without troubling to take his leave of the countess. She was deeply hurt. A letter of explanation promptly arrived: everything was so good with her,

[1] Tolstoy described this incident in one of his tales for children, "The Bear-Hunt."

he wrote, and got still better day by day that if he had not left, there would never have been any reason to go. What he did not explain was that her charming company constantly reminded him of a happiness he was searching for and could not find. His peace of mind was better sustained by keeping up their friendship at a distance, and he promised to write her every week.

The gentle resentment in the countess's reply had an undercurrent of feeling that ran deeper than mere affection. Tolstoy could not fail to understand her comparison between the small dissonances of friendship and those of married life, or the reference to herself as an old woman whom he would never again find so receptive and inclined to be so infinitely sincere. She too was reminded of a happiness that she had almost ceased to search for. A difference of eleven years in their ages kept her innuendo within the bounds of infinite delicacy and refinement. And at the end of her letter, she firmly slammed the door: "Get married, my dear Leo, and without delay, while egoism has not yet had time to dry all over you. Having dispensed little of self-denial, you have much to give away—if that does not happen to be the same as almsgiving—; whosoever gives shall be enriched. Thanks for your visit. When I succeed in detaching it from your abrupt departure, I am heartily and sincerely thankful."

Tolstoy kept his promise for a time and wrote her about every week. The Easter holidays had arrived and, knowing it would please her, he announced his intentions of going to church. In another letter, however, he told her that the experiment had failed. He could pray at home and read the Gospels, but to stand in church, surrounded by a motley crowd, and listen to the unintelligible mumbling of the priest—all this was utterly impossible. To make matters worse, he twitted her on her own sincere faith, asking her to make over to him some of her holy radiance.

His levity drew a withering arraignment from the countess, all the more devastating in that she wrote out of love for him. His letter, she said, had caused her sharp pain, tears, and confused thoughts. "What pride, ignorance, and sloth in a sentiment that you probably believe to be respectable or reverent," she wrote of his attitude towards the Easter services. "It seems to me that you sometimes combine within yourself every idolatry of heathendom—while adoring God in a sunbeam, in an aspect of nature, or in one of the innumerable aspects of His glory—, but you never understand that you must rise to the source of life to be enlightened and purified." She blamed his spirit of pride for the fact that he disdained the simple worshipers and priest. Did her dear "grandson" require a service performed in a solemn or poetical manner before he could pour out his heart to God? If he did not understand the prayers in church, why not work at them? "It would be worth your while to work at them," she wrote, "even at the expense perhaps of husbandry and literature. Ignorance by design is no justification. But you must have gratuitous ecstasies, ravishments, and sudden transports leading you into a blissful state, without disturbing your idleness and with no effort of volition on your side." She concluded on a note of love for him and with a prayer that he might one day find true humility that teaches more than all our so-called sublime thoughts and craving for God.

Tolstoy was deeply moved by this deserved rebuke from a religious and wise woman. His faith was in an amorphous state, yet he felt it essential to defend his position to the countess. The result was a rather remarkable letter. He had been bad, he admitted, but was it necessary to punish him like that? A man who had won his convictions from life did not speak about them, and he assured her that she did not know his. But he would try to make his convictions on religion clear. He told her of the meaningless traditional faith of his childhood, and how even as a boy he had brushed this all aside. Then he gave an account of his spiritual struggle in the Caucasus. "I found that immortality exists, that there is love, and that you have to live for others in order to be eternally happy. These discoveries surprised me by their conformity with the Christian religion, and from this time onward I began to search for them in the Gospels instead of in myself, but I found little there. I did not find God there, or the Redeemer, or the Sacraments—nothing; and I searched with all the vigor of my soul, and I wept and tormented myself and craved for only one thing—truth."[2]

At this point in his letter the effort to explain seemed futile to Tolstoy, and he generalized by saying that he loved and esteemed religion, and that man could never be good or happy without it. At moments, he wrote, he had a gleam of

[2] He means that he did not find in the Gospels his own conception of God.

faith; but he had neither religion nor dogma. "Further," he continued, "with me religion is the outcome of life and not the reverse. Whenever I lead a good life, I feel religion near at hand and am quite ready to step into this blissful world; but when I lead a bad life, there seems to be no need for religion." This is a fair statement of Tolstoy's attitude towards religion at this time and for a number of years to come. The need of religion was great, but he could win his way to spiritual faith only through intellectual conviction.

6

Towards the end of April Tolstoy went to Yasnaya Polyana for the summer. His abysmal frame of mind was in marked contrast to the high spirits of the preceding spring. There was a worm that wanted to turn and wriggle somewhere deep down inside him, he complained to Granny. Work alone was left him. But what was work, he asked? A pitiable trifling: you shovel, make haste, and your heart keeps narrowing, shrivels, and dies. He had in mind not only his labor on the estate, but also his writing, for he had reached a severe crisis in his literary career.

Upon his return from abroad in 1857, Tolstoy's disillusion with Russia did not except the contemporary state of literature and his own contribution to it. He wrote Botkin that he could not believe, with Turgenev, that literature existed only for the man of letters, and was an end in itself. Literature should be a means towards an end, and man's chief occupation should be outside literature.

In 1858 Tolstoy conscientiously directed his activities away from literature. Turgenev wrote to Annenkov:—

> You have astonished me with your news of Tolstoy's reforestation projects. What a man! With perfect feet, he is determined to walk on his head. Not long ago he wrote Botkin a letter in which he said: "I'm very glad that I did not heed Turgenev and become a mere man of letters." In answer to this I asked: What does he want to be—an officer, a farmer, etc.? Now he tries to prove to himself that he's a timber expert. With these capers I fear only that he will throw the spine of his talent out of joint. In his Swiss tales a very pronounced curvature is already noticeable.

In truth, when "Lucerne" had appeared both critics and public were mystified, and with the publication of "Albert" in 1858, the worst fears of Nekrasov were fulfilled—it was whispered about that Tolstoy had lost his grip, that the great literary promise of his earlier fiction had come to nought. The discovery that his reputation had fallen supported Tolstoy's belief that contemporary authors, in their insistence upon themes of social and political significance, were undermining the reading public's taste for pure literature. His reaction was characteristic: Russia needed a new periodical whose writers would endeavor to correct prevailing literary tendencies. Eagerly he wrote of the project to Botkin.

> The aim of the periodical [he declared] is just this: artistic pleasure,—to weep and to laugh. The magazine will prove nothing and know nothing. Its one criterion will be cultured taste. The magazine will not desire to know either this or that line, and still more emphatically, it will not care to know the needs of the public. . . . It will not stoop to public taste but will boldly become the public's teacher in the matter of taste, but *only in the matter of taste.*

Botkin was not snared by this idealistic bait. A good novel from Tolstoy, he cannily answered, would improve public taste more than ten such magazines. Other prospective editors among his literary friends were equally discouraging. Stubbornly he tried his hand at a purely artistic piece that might have been designed as a contribution to just such a magazine as he had in mind. He called it "The Dream," and it amounts to a lyrical variant of an episode in "Albert" in which the poor musician dreams of the beautiful woman who is his ideal.[3]

At about the same time (January 1858), Tolstoy began "Three Deaths," another brief piece that was intended to exemplify the moral truth of pure art. He described the death of a noble lady, a peasant, and a tree. The lady's death is ugly and pitiable, for she fears to leave this earth and can obtain no consolation from the Christianity she has believed in. On the other hand, the peasant dies calmly, because his religion is Nature which has taught him that all things must pass away. The tree also dies quietly, honestly,

[3] In 1863 Tolstoy sent "The Dream," under a pseudonym, to I. S. Aksakov for publication in his magazine. Aksakov rejected it, and wrote, not knowing Tolstoy's authorship, that the piece was "too baffling for the public, its contents too indefinite, and perhaps entirely understood only by the author."

in beauty. There is no dissonance in this death, as in that of the lady, only harmony with creation.

In published form "Three Deaths"[4] simply fortified the growing feeling among critics that Tolstoy's powers were failing. Throughout the remainder of 1858 and the first half of the next year he worked, in a discouraged frame of mind, on *The Cossacks* and *Family Happiness.* The first had gone through a bewildering evolution in form and subject matter since he began it in the Caucasus, and now, as though conscious of its superior merit, he hesitated to hurry the completion of the story. *Family Happiness,* however, he began and swiftly carried through. His love affair with Valerya—the inspiration of this short novel—was still fresh in his memory, and his occasional meetings with her at this time no doubt fed his desire to justify in fiction the treatment he had accorded her in real life.

Before *Family Happiness* was finished, he was so uncertain of its success that he contemplated publishing the novel under a pseudonym. When he read the proof sheets of the second part, he was horrified. "A shameful abomination," he jotted down in the diary, and he hastened off a letter to Botkin, directing him to hold up the printing and burn the manuscript. But it was too late. Botkin, in whose criticism he had most faith, tried to reassure him, but Tolstoy considered himself finished as a writer. Although his attitude was extreme, he had good reason to doubt the merits of his novel. Fine descriptive passages and the sensitive handling of the heroine's feeling of love in the early parts are offset by the clouded design of the whole and by a puzzling, inconclusive ending. As Botkin pointed out, a persistent puritanism in the point of view vitiated the total effectiveness of *Family Happiness;* and the absence of any tangible social significance once again disappointed the public.

On February 4, 1859, Tolstoy was inducted into the Moscow Society of Lovers of Russian Literature, and he used the occasion to vent his wrath against contemporary literature. The tendentiousness that had entered Russian literature at the time of Gogol had by now swept all before it, and the trend continued for many years. Art was expected to indict political and social abuses or offer a progressive program of reform. Unfortunately the literary atmosphere became almost as muddled and disputatious as the political

[4] It appeared in *Library for Reading,* No. 1, 1859.

atmosphere in the nineteenth century, but such a result was inevitable in a country still struggling with political feudalism and a nascent economic capitalism.

In his brief speech before the assembled men of letters of the Moscow Society, Tolstoy declared: "The majority of the public has begun to think that the problem of all literature consists only in the denunciation of evil, in the debate and correction of it, in short, in the growth of a civic feeling in society." He did not condemn this utterly, but he pleaded for moderation and for a greater emphasis on the rich variety of approach in the world of art. "A literature of the people is its full, many-sided consciousness, in which must be equally reflected popular love for goodness and truth, as well as the popular contemplation of beauty in a given epoch of development. . . ." And he concluded: "There is another literature, reflecting eternal and universally human interests, the most precious, sincere consciousness of the people, a literature accessible to every people and to all times, a literature without which no single people, gifted with strength and richness, has ever developed."

This is the substance of what Tolstoy had been saying to Botkin, Druzhinin, and Fet over the past two years, and it describes the artistic purpose behind the last few works he had written. But the stern president of the Moscow Society, A. S. Khomyakov, coldly answered Tolstoy's speech by reminding him that, however eternal truth and beauty may be in art, the artist is a man of his own times, and that the present historical moment was one in which self-indictment acquired a special significance and an indefeasible right, and hence must manifest itself in literature.

The time would come when Tolstoy's own views on literature for the people would radically change, but at the moment he had reached a point of despair and thought of giving up writing entirely.[5] To scribble stories was stupid and shameful, he told Fet in a burst of enthusiastic confidence, when he learned that this poet was thinking of settling on an estate near him and making literature secondary to husbandry. Turgenev railed at Tolstoy's new resolution, and Druzhinin wrote him a pathetic plea not to deprive

[5] Apart from the works mentioned in this chapter, Tolstoy also wrote between 1857 and 1859 the following fragmentary pieces: "Notes of a Husband," "Easter Sunday," "How Russian Soldiers Die," and "Notes on the Nobility." These pieces are published in the Jubilee Edition (Vol. V).

Russia of his literary leadership. Tolstoy, however, could not give up literature any more than he could cease his search for truth; one was the essential medium for the expression of the other. But in his present frame of mind, he required a new outlet for his energies.

The idea of starting a village school now took hold of Tolstoy with peculiar force, for he saw in it a direct connection with his retreat from literature. For whom did Russian authors write? For themselves and the cultured few. For masses of illiterate Russian peasants, literature was useless. If they could not read his writings, then he would teach them. This was the first and essential step towards the creation of a "literature for the people." Here was a purpose that would satisfy his thirst for activity and moral influence.

XII

Europe Once More

ON A FINE morning in early autumn, 1859, some twenty peasant children waited expectantly at the manor-house door of Yasnaya Polyana. The master had announced that a school would be opened and lessons given free. All the youngsters were dressed for the occasion—clean white shirts, new bast shoes, hair glistening and plastered down with oil. Suspicious parents stood around and talked in nervous, subdued tones among themselves. What was their strange, unpredictable master up to now? Did he wish to teach their children and then hand them over to the Tsar to be soldiers? One mother kept insisting that the lessons were free. Why, Ivan Fokanov had been going to the sexton for lessons for three winters at two rubles a month, and he had still not learned a thing! It was said that the master would also take grownups free, and several parents signified their intentions of attending the school.

Suddenly a loud voice sounded from behind the door. Parents hurriedly admonished their children again to bow low and say: "I wish you health, your excellency!" Tolstoy appeared. All bared their heads and bowed to the ground.

"Good morning! Have you brought your children?" Tolstoy asked, turning to the parents.

"Just so, your excellency," they chorused with bows.

"Well, I'm very glad," he said, smiling and looking them all over. His appearance did not accord with their notions of a teacher. He was so plainly dressed, his hair as long as theirs, and his common face with its broad peasant nose was covered with a thick black beard, like that of a gypsy. With assurance he walked into the crowd of children and singled one out.

"Do you wish to learn?"

"Yes."

"What's your name?"

"Danilka."

Swiftly he questioned the others in similar fashion, a smile on his lips and merriment in his eyes. Then he led them into the house, up the stairway, and through the huge living room. Scared, wide-eyed children noticed the lofty ceiling and the floor cleaner than the tables in their wretched little thatched huts. Numerous portraits on the walls at once caught their attention. These figures looked so magnificent, holy, like the icons they saw in church. Several of the youngsters involuntarily started to cross themselves.

"Those are not gods, but people, my relatives and friends," the teacher explained.

Tolstoy shepherded them into a neighboring room that had been fitted up with benches and blackboards. This was the schoolroom, he announced. Regular lessons would begin on the morrow. Today, he would just write a few letters of the alphabet on the board and they would try to learn them. But first he questioned them a bit further about their work in the fields and their reasons for wanting to go to school. With humor, kindliness, and simplicity he tried to banish timidity and win confidence. Soon they were repeating the letters of the alphabet after him, their young voices rising to a fearless crescendo as he prompted "Louder! Louder!" In no time they were a happy, excited group working together and following the teacher with rapt attention until the lesson ended.

"Now go home and God bless you!" Tolstoy said. "Come early tomorrow. We'll have another lesson. Come. I'll be waiting."

"We left the school and said good-bye to our dear teacher, promising to come early on the morrow," recalled V. S. Morozov, one of the young pupils at the first meeting. "Our rapture was boundless. Each told the other over and over again, as though he had been the only one to notice it, how our teacher had appeared, how he questioned us, how he talked, and how he had smiled."

2

Work at the new school filled Tolstoy with an enthusiasm and energy that delighted some of his friends and annoyed others, particularly Turgenev. Everything was sacrificed to the project. Estate affairs became a bore; "pretty stories" were scorned (at most he pecked away halfheartedly at *The Cossacks*); and even his precious diary was allowed to lapse in the excitement of proving in practice that all existing methods of pedagogy were necessarily wrong.

Tolstoy kept his friends well posted on the progress of his experiment. After a couple of months of teaching, he wrote to Druzhinin and gleefully drove home the significance of his new enterprise by ordering this self-appointed gadfly of his literary ambitions to remove his name from the list of members of the Literary Fund, since he was through with writing. And to Fet, after blasting away at modern authors, he pompously declared: "We don't need to learn, we need to teach at least a little of what we know to Marfutka and Taraska."

The philosophical Chicherin required a more thoughtful letter. He had written to Tolstoy from abroad to urge him, with some condescension (he did not have a high opinion of Tolstoy's intellectual sanity), to give up his idle country existence, get married, and devote all his attention to literature. In reply, Tolstoy vigorously defended his activities and condemned Chicherin's inability to comprehend their value. "The self-delusion of so-called artists," he wrote, "which you—I flatter myself with the hope—charged me with only out of friendly consideration (while not understanding me), this delusion is only for him who submits to it; it is the most rascally meanness and falsity." Chicherin never could appreciate the moral satisfaction Tolstoy derived from "teaching the alphabet to dirty little boys," and soon their interesting correspondence lapsed, as well as the friendship that had begun with so much zeal on both sides.

With a half year of successful teaching behind him, it was almost inevitable that Tolstoy should find himself bedeviled in a maze of speculation on pedagogy and obsessed with schemes for improving national education. When he opened his school, free education for peasant children did not exist in Russia. Occasionally, a village would boast of a priest or an old ex-soldier who taught a few children at so much per head. The subjects were elementary, the method a mixture of blows and learning by heart, and the results negligible. This situation Tolstoy wished to remedy by substituting public education based on entirely original pedagogical methods.

In March 1860, Tolstoy wrote a long letter to E. P.

Kovalevski, an old friend of his Sevastopol days. More important, he was the brother of the Minister of National Education, and Tolstoy hoped to persuade him to intercede on his behalf. In the letter he described the unusual success of his school, and mentioned that he already had fifty students and that the number was growing constantly. "Wisdom in all worldly affairs, it seems to me," he continued, "consists not in recognizing what must be done but in knowing what to do first and then what comes after." He boldly questioned the value to progress in Russia of roads, the telegraph, literature, and the arts as long as only about one per cent of some seventy millions of people were literate. Such widespread ignorance represented an acute danger to the healthy functioning of a state. It was clear, he asserted, that the greatest daily need of the Russian people was public education. But if one waited for the government to remedy the lack, he maintained, the situation would never be improved. At this point he fell into his familiar paradoxical vein: "Over the dispute as to whether or not literacy is useful, one must not laugh. This is a very serious and melancholy argument, and I deliberately take the negative side. *Literacy,* the process of reading and writing, is harmful." And he justified his position by citing the unvarying practice of teachers, trained in government schools, of setting their pupils to read only religious works that produced a devastating effect on the intellectual faculties. What Tolstoy had been leading up to in all this was the utter incapacity of the government to understand the educational needs of the public and the best methods of satisfying them. As a remedy, he proposed the establishment of a Society for National Education. Among its duties would be the setting up of public schools where they were most needed; the designing of courses of instruction; the training of teachers in suitable educational methods; and the publishing of a journal devoted to the dissemination of its own pedagogical ideals.

If the government would only permit the formation of such a society, Tolstoy pledged all his time and effort to it. Since he was in the bad graces of the authorities,[1] he asked Kovalevski's aid in pushing this program. If the project were not permitted, he jokingly signified his intention of

[1] Tolstoy was convinced of this after he learned that the government had discovered the part he played in composing the unpatriotic Sevastopol soldier's song.

starting a secret Society for National Education. At any rate, he declared that he would publish a pedagogical journal and that he was engaged in writing an article on education. Rather whimsically he concluded his letter: "Whatever you may think, it is almost certain that you will answer me with: 'It is clear that you, Leo Nikolayevich, are stuck in the country and fussing again with these projects.' "

Unfortunately, Kovalevski's answer has not been preserved but it is fairly certain that neither he nor his brother gave Tolstoy any support. Fragments of pedagogical essays have survived from this time (about March 1860), and it is clear that he was trying to handle the larger abstract concepts of educational theory without a sufficient knowledge of their history. He began one of the fragments with the assertion that "For every living condition of development, there is a pedagogical expediency, and to search this out is the problem of pedagogy." His search, however, led him nowhere, and the article abruptly broke off.

Educational theory in Russia was entirely dominated by foreign influence, particularly German. Tolstoy considered going abroad again to make a firsthand study of foreign pedagogical methods. He decided to start sooner than he had expected. His brother Nikolai had already gone abroad in an effort to remedy a dangerous tuberculous condition, and Tolstoy was worried because he had not heard from him for some time. Having placed his school in charge of a teacher who had been working under his direction, he sailed from Petersburg with his sister and her three children July 2.

3

Tolstoy landed at Stettin on July 5 and proceeded without delay to Berlin. Marya and her children went to Soden, a Prussian health resort, where the sick Nikolai was staying. Having received some reassuring news from his brother, Tolstoy decided to remain in Berlin for a few days to begin his quest for knowledge in matters educational. For a time, aching teeth rendered the search heroic. He had even less faith in dentists (somewhat justified at that time) than in physicians. At any rate, he preferred to endure periodic misery from decayed molars and actually appeared to derive a certain moral satisfaction from such suffering.

Tolstoy visited the Moabit Prison, museums, and the university, and he heard lectures on history and physiology by distinguished professors. A friendly young German student took him to a meeting at a workers' club. Here he heard another lecture, and he was so much interested in the "question box" device used to stimulate discussion by the audience that he returned the following evening.

After ten very agreeable and useful days in Berlin, he left for Leipzig. He set out busily to visit schools in that city, but severe headaches and hemorrhoids put an end to all activity. Apparently his suffering was intense enough to drive him to a physician, and upon his advice he went to Kissingen for a cure. Here he quickly recovered and remained a full month, for the news from Nikolai was still encouraging. Except for a walking trip in the Hartz Mountains, Tolstoy devoted all of his stay in Kissingen to pedagogical researches. He visited the schools, and remarks in the diary reflect his disappointment: "Have been to a school. It is terrible! Prayers for the king; blows; everything by rote; terrified, beaten children." And there are similar entries after other inspections. His thoughts constantly returned to his own experiment, and he wrote anxiously to Auntie Tatyana: "Tell the teacher to send me news about the school: How many students come and whether they learn well? I shall certainly return in the autumn and intend to occupy myself more than ever with the school, so I do not wish its reputation to be lost while I am away, and I want as many students as possible from different parts." And in the diary he noted: "The idea of experimental pedagogy has agitated me. I can scarcely contain myself. . . ."

When he was not observing educational practice at first hand, Tolstoy applied himself to reading pedagogical theory. He also dipped into Montaigne, "the first to express clearly the idea of freedom in education," he wrote in the diary. "In education, once more," he concluded, "the chief things are equality and freedom." There were likewise entries at this time on his reading of Francis Bacon, "the founder of materialism," on Luther, whom he called great, and on Herzen—"a scattered intelligence, morbid pride, but breadth, cleverness and kindness; Russian refinement." One author whom Tolstoy read at this time with very emphatic but mixed reactions was Wilhelm Riehl, the remarkable German ethnographer and professor of the history of culture at the University of Munich.[2] With his growing interest in popular education and in the inherent artistic possibilities among the masses, Tolstoy found much pertinent material in Riehl's historical treatment of Germanic folk art and traditions.

In Kissingen, Tolstoy very likely discussed Riehl's works with Julius Froebel, a nephew of Friedrich Froebel, the celebrated educational reformer and founder of the kindergarten system. Tolstoy no doubt learned a great deal from him about his famous uncle's pedagogical experiments. Julius Froebel left a curious account of Tolstoy: "Progress in Russia, he told me, must come out of public education, which among us will give better results than in Germany, because the Russian masses are not yet spoiled by false education. Something better will come out of a child who has been educated correctly from the first year than from one who has been subjected to a spurious education for several years." Tolstoy went on to inform him of his own school in which learning was in no sense obligatory. "If education is good," he said, "then the need for it will manifest itself like hunger." Froebel also relates that Tolstoy spoke of the Russian masses as a "mysterious and irrational force," from which would one day spring an entirely new organization of the world, and that from the Russian artel there would develop in the future a communistic structure.

This interesting report of Froebel reflects the proud, dogmatic, almost arrogant attitude that Tolstoy adopted towards most of the European personalities he met on this second trip abroad. While sincerely seeking knowledge, he invariably made it clear that he belonged to no school of thought, had his own point of view on most questions, and that Europeans did not understand the real failings of their civilization. On the other hand, Froebel's account of Tolstoy's views on the Russian masses was no doubt colored by his own radical leanings and his knowledge of Russian radical thought (he was acquainted with Bakunin and Herzen).

While Tolstoy was still at Kissingen, Nikolai felt improved enough to pay him a visit. Nikolai's condition shocked Tolstoy. His brother seemed so intelligent and lucid

[2] The works of Riehl that Tolstoy read were *Naturgeschichte des Volks als Grundlage einer deutschen Social-politik* and *Kulturstudien aus drei Jahrhunderten.*

in his illness, filled with the desire to live, yet without a spark of vital energy. After a few days, a sudden relapse obliged him to return to Soden. Extremely worried over Nikolai, Tolstoy finally decided to join him and he arrived at Soden on August 14.

4

Tolstoy remained only three days at Soden, long enough to inspect a school. He and his brother left for Hyères on the southern coast of France; doctors had strongly advised a warmer climate for the fast-failing Nikolai. On the way they stopped at Geneva, where Tolstoy visited the college and an orphanage; a "drunken professor" and "deformed children" were his only comments in the diary.

Tolstoy's experiences at Marseille inspired one of the most striking passages in an article that he published two years later—"On Public Education." He visited the primary schools of the city and several institutions for older children. The futility of the subjects taught and the lifeless, unimaginative methods of teaching them provoked his criticism. None of the pupils appeared to be able to think or to apply the facts that they had learned. He questioned one boy on the history of France, and the boy answered well what he had got by heart, but to a question slightly off the beaten path, Tolstoy received the answer that Henry IV had been killed by Julius Caesar. Quizzing on other subjects brought similar results. Tolstoy concluded that the school system of Marseille was extremely bad and that its pupils must grow up in utter ignorance. His opinion of the people, if not of the schools, changed after he had spent some time roaming about the streets and talking to workers and children. They seemed intelligent, free thinking, and surprisingly well-informed, but with no thanks to their schooling. He discovered that they absorbed history from such thrillers as *The Three Musketeers* and *The Count of Monte Cristo,* of which novels scores of cheap editions were obtainable; and that they learned politics and much other useful knowledge from newspapers, magazines, and endless discussions in their cafés. "Here is an unconscious school undermining a compulsory school and making its contents almost of no worth [he said in an article] . . . What I saw at Marseille and in all other countries amounts to this: everywhere the principal part in educating a people is played not by schools, but by life." Here we have the kind of characteristic half-truth that Tolstoy was fond of deducing from incomplete experience, and later this conclusion became an important factor in his educational theorizing. But even half-truths that blasted away the hard shell of traditional and erroneous thinking on vital social problems had their value for him.

The brothers reached Hyères on August 25 and took comfortable quarters in a *pension*. Marya and her children also arrived and rented a place near by. Nikolai seemed to improve in the mild climate. Tolstoy sent Auntie Tatyana a letter of hope; and to Dyakov, Nikolai wrote in a similar strain, beguiled by one of those deceptive periods of improvement so common in tuberculosis. The ravages of the disease had gone too far, however, and in less than a month (September 20) after his arrival at Hyères, Nikolai died.

5

Nikolai's death profoundly affected Tolstoy. His admiration and respect for him had never wavered since those golden childhood days of the Ant Brotherhood, when young Nikolai seemed to possess the secret of universal happiness written on the green stick buried in the Zakaz woods. With some rancor but not without justice, Turgenev had remarked that Nikolai practiced in life the humility that his brother Leo preached. Druzhinin, commenting on his brilliant literary talents, thought his command of language superior to that of Leo. Despite all the urgings of admiring friends, however, Nikolai could not overcome a rooted dislike for regular composition. He was one of those men whose innate nobility of soul was always shyly concealed beneath a self-effacing modesty.

"Nikolai is dead!" sounded like a dirge in Tolstoy's letters for weeks. All his values were thrown into confusion and his natural doubts intensified. With the morbidity of grief, he dwelt with loving care on all the trifling details connected with his brother's death. It was not like Dmitri's death, he told Sergei. With Dmitri were joined only memories of childhood, but Nikolai was a positive personality whom he loved more than anyone in the world. To Fet, he wrote that Nikolai had died in his arms, and that nothing in life had ever made such an impression on him.

> It is true, as he said [continued Tolstoy], that nothing is worse than death. But when one reflects well that that is

> the end of all, then there is nothing worse than life. Why strive or try, since nothing remains of what was Nikolai Nikolayevich Tolstoy? He did not say that he felt the approach of death, but I realized that he watched every step of its approach and knew with certainty how much of life remained. Some moments before his death he drowsed off, but suddenly he awoke and whispered with horror: "What is that?" That was when he saw it—the absorption of himself into nothingness. And if he found nothing to cling to, what then will I find? Still less! . . . A thousand times I say to myself: "Let the dead bury the dead." One must use somehow the strength that remains to one. . . . But as soon as man reaches the highest degree of development, then he sees clearly that it is all nonsense and deceit, and that the truth—which he still loves better than all else—is terrible. And when you look at it well, and clearly, you awake with a start and say with terror, as my brother did: "What is that?" Of course, so long as the desire to know and speak the truth exists, one tries to know and speak. That alone remains to me of the moral world; higher than that I cannot place myself. That alone I will do, only not in the form of your art. Art is a lie, and I can no longer love a beautiful lie.

Nikolai's death had shattered Tolstoy's former complacent acceptance of immortality. For several weeks he lost interest in everything, even in his diary, and when he resumed it the first entry reads: "Nearly a month has passed since Nikolai died. This event has torn me terribly from life. Again the question: Why? Already the departure draws near. Whither? Nowhere! I try to write, I force myself, but it does not get on—because I cannot attach enough significance to the work, which it must have if I am to possess the strength and patience to work. At the very time of the funeral the idea occurred to me of writing a materialist Gospel, a Life of Christ as a materialist." Perhaps he thought that there was also a materialistic immortality, like that suggested by the peasant in "Three Deaths": he had serenely accepted his passing as a unification with deathless Nature. Nikolai too had loved nature, and in the letter to Fet, Tolstoy had expressed the dim hope that there, in nature, of which we become part in the earth, something will remain and be found.

In the course of a few weeks, however, Tolstoy began to recover some of his former faith in immortality. A boy in the neighborhood died of tuberculosis, and in the diary Tolstoy queried: "What for? The only explanation is furnished by a belief in a future life. If that does not exist, there is no justice, and justice is unnecessary, and the need for justice is a superstition."

6

Depression and a sense of futility clung to Tolstoy for some time. His only escape was in work. From the cave of grief he could tell Fet that art was a beautiful lie that he could no longer love, but what solace had he left save art? And soon he wrote Auntie Tatyana to send him his manuscript of *The Cossacks*.

Art came hard, for Tolstoy's thoughts reverted to the real purpose of his trip abroad. From Hyères he wrote Granny of his absorption in educational experiments. "I can sincerely say that this is now the sole interest that binds me to life. Unfortunately, this winter I cannot occupy myself with this matter here; I work only for the future." He had begun an article on public education, and his interest in teaching found some outlet in Marya's three children. In his sister's *pension* there also lived a Russian lady with her nine-year-old son, Sergei Plaksin, who joined the class, although he was in delicate health. Tolstoy loved walking and took the children on excursions into the country. On the way he would hold them spellbound with tales of wonders, of a golden horse and a giant tree from the top of which all the world was visible. Tender of little Sergei's weak lungs, Tolstoy would hoist him to his broad, muscular shoulders and continue his tale as they walked along.

After dinner at the *pension,* Tolstoy would organize an opera or a ballet, with himself at the piano and the children as the assisting artists. Before the bedlam reached its height, the audience, consisting of Marya and Plaksin's mother and his nurse, was more than ready to call a halt to the performance. Then came gymnastics. Lying at full length on the floor Tolstoy would get up without using his hands, a feat the youngsters found difficult to imitate. Or he would delight them by turning somersaults on a homemade apparatus. The study hour followed. He placed the children around a table and set them to writing a theme on some such subject as the difference between Russia and other countries. This was hard and not always congenial work, but they did it eagerly in anticipation of his exuberant and amusing comments on the results. If their exercises were good, he would reward them—on one occasion with water-color paints which he taught them to use. Whether on excursions, at lessons, or in settling their disputes, these children hung upon his every word and would have laid down their lives for him.

After Nikolai's death, Tolstoy had little taste for Hyères society, but eventually he took to visiting a few socially prominent Russian families at this health resort. His sister recalled how on one occasion he was to be the lion of the evening. He failed to appear at the appointed time, and as the evening wore on the guests grew more and more glum, despite the frantic efforts of host and hostess. Very late the lion arrived, garbed in a hiking costume and wearing wooden sabots. He had come directly to the party from a long walk, and because of his tardiness he had not bothered to go home and change. The party brightened and took on a new life as Tolstoy at once launched into a convincing argument on why wooden sabots were the most comfortable of footgear. The guests were charmed by his bizarre appearance and natural gaiety, and in no time he had them all singing the songs he played on the piano.

7

December and January (1861) were spent in a sightseeing tour of Italy, but the Italy that had charmed and inspired so many foreign writers left no solid impression on Tolstoy and is nowhere reflected in his works.

It was largely an educational mission that took Tolstoy to London in the middle of February; he was determined, he wrote his brother Sergei, to learn everything of significance in foreign pedagogy so that nobody in Russia would dare question his authority in this respect. He found it difficult to admire the individual Englishman, whose native temperament was so utterly unlike his own, although he shared to some degree the general continental enthusiasm for the English nation as a whole, for its just laws, its liberal thought, and democratic government. Turgenev mildly reproved him for a letter containing snap judgments on England, and the scholarly Chicherin advised him of the necessity of a thorough study of the history and social background of this country before venturing to condemn it. Tolstoy could not help contrasting the tender solicitude of Russians for convoys of prisoners on their way to Siberia with a scene he witnessed in the London streets of a crowd that threatened to tear a criminal to pieces before the police intervened.

Tolstoy did find some things to his liking in London. He daily visited the Kensington Museum and pronounced it the best institution of higher learning that he had seen in his travels. He also heard Dickens—"a genius born once in a hundred years," he declared—deliver a lecture on education. Tolstoy could hardly have got much out of this performance, for though he could read English well at the time, he had had little practice in hearing or speaking it. This difficulty must also have hindered his appreciation of a three-hour speech delivered by Palmerston in the House of Commons. Whether he understood or not, he condemned the great Prime Minister's effort as "boring and meaningless."

Tolstoy lost no time in fulfilling his real purpose in coming to London—a study of the city's educational system. Free lectures by experts at the Kensington Museum won his unstinted praise. These talks were suggested by practical questions of visitors, and hence they conformed to the criterion of utility, always a primary principle in Tolstoy's pedagogical ideals. He applied to the Council Office of the Department of Education for permission to visit schools. An official, R. R. Whings, provided him with a letter of recommendation; and it is very likely that he also used the influence of Matthew Arnold, a prominent inspector of schools at that time, whose acquaintance he seems to have made.[3]

About a year later Tolstoy wrote an account of one of his visits to a London school in an article, "Social Work in the Field of Public Education." For his benefit the English teacher endeavored to show his students' ability in an object-lesson test. The object selected was cotton, and the students answered well a series of set questions on where cotton grew, how it was manufactured, and so on. Tolstoy, guessing that they knew these answers by heart, requested permission to ask some questions of his own. He completely stumped the students with such questions as: To what class of plants does cotton belong? What kind of soil is necessary

[3] Whings's letter of recommendation has turned up among Tolstoy's papers, and in it his acquaintance with Matthew Arnold is cited as a reason for according Tolstoy the special privilege of visiting schools. (See the Jubilee Edition, VIII, 609.) It may be recalled that years later Arnold wrote a critical essay on Tolstoy.

for its growth? He concluded that the object-lesson method was wrong, because its radius was seriously limited by the knowledge preferences of the teacher, and because its ideal application would involve the teaching of an impractical number of subdivisions of the sciences.

Nor did English textbooks escape the sharp pedagogical eye of Tolstoy; he made a collection of them, as he did in several of the countries he visited. A list of over fifty English textbooks and educational journals compiled at this time exists among his papers, and apparently he read most of them, for his incisive critical notes appear beside many of the titles.

The man Tolstoy saw most frequently in London was the distinguished Russian revolutionary exile, Alexander Herzen. He had long been eager to meet Tolstoy whose *Childhood* he had praised highly in his famous contraband periodical, the *Bell*. Herzen had written Turgenev, on the occasion of Tolstoy's first visit abroad, that he would be "very, very glad" to make his acquaintance, and that he was a "sincere worshiper of his talent." Tolstoy was not too well disposed to like this man, the fount of inspiration for the Petersburg radical intelligentsia whom he distrusted, nor had his works impressed him. But their meetings in London were cordial. They had many vigorous but friendly disputes. Herzen wrote Turgenev that Tolstoy was a fine and warm-hearted man, but why, he asked, did he feel it necessary in argument to take everything by a brave assault as at Sevastopol? He found him stubborn and felt that his head had not yet been picked over and swept clean. On one occasion Herzen's young daughter, Natalya, received permission to sit quietly in the corner of the room during Tolstoy's visit. She had already read his stories and had formed her own childishly idealized impression of one of her favorite authors. Her ideal vanished when Tolstoy entered, foppishly garbed in the latest English fashion and impetuously pouring forth a description of a cockfight and a boxing match that he had attended. Many years later Tolstoy gave his own recollections of these meetings with Herzen. He pronounced him an unceremonious, sympathetic, brilliant, and interesting man. And he expressed the conviction that Herzen was immeasurably higher than any of the political thinkers whom he had known in his lifetime.

Tolstoy availed himself of Herzen's wide acquaintance with prominent European revolutionary figures by requesting letters of introduction to some of them. One he eagerly sought was to the great French socialist Proudhon, who at that time was living in exile in Brussels. Armed with the letter, he left London for Brussels on March 4.

8

At their meeting Proudhon impressed Tolstoy as a man who had the courage of his convictions. In turn, the Frenchman wrote Herzen that the faces of Russians who visited him fused in his mind, "But a Mr. Tolstoy has been calling on me over the last few days, and he is a savant who has presented to me quite a different side." Another letter to a friend is slightly more revealing:—

> A well-informed man, Mr. Tolstoy, with whom I have been talking these last few days, told me: "There you have a real emancipation. [Alexander II's decree of emancipation had appeared March 5, 1861.] We do not free our serfs with empty hands, we give them property along with their liberty!" He also said to me: "You are much read in Russia, but they do not understand the importance you attach to your Catholicism. Only after I had visited England and France did I understand how right you were. In Russia the Church amounts to zero!"

These two men, who intellectually had so much in common, talked about Proudhon's book, *La Guerre et la Paix,* which was just then going through the press. This book was translated into Russian in 1864 with the title *War and Peace.* Although Proudhon's book is a work on the principles of international law, Tolstoy was indebted to it for much more than the title. A study of *La Guerre et la Paix* reveals a good deal about the whole theory of war that Tolstoy incorporated in his novel.

Sometime after this meeting, Tolstoy began an article as follows:—

> Last year I chanced to speak with Mr. Proudhon about Russia. He was then writing his work *On the Law of War.*[4] I told him about Russia, about the freeing of serfs, and of the fact that in the upper classes a strong interest in the education of the masses was noticeable, and that this interest sometimes expressed itself comically and had

[4] Tolstoy, of course, means *La Guerre et la Paix.* Although the book was already finished, Proudhon was actually writing an introduction to it at the time of Tolstoy's visits.

> become a fashion. "Is it possible that this is really true?" he said. I answered that as much as one can judge from a distance, Russian society now showed itself conscious of the fact that without education of the masses no governmental organization can be durable. Proudhon jumped up and walked about the room. "If this is true," he said to me, as though with envy, "the future belongs to you Russians." I relate this conversation with Proudhon [concluded Tolstoy] because in my experience he was the only man who understood in our time the significance of public education and of the printing press.

Tolstoy presented a letter from Herzen to another exiled revolutionary writer in Brussels, the old and poverty-stricken Polish patriot, J. Lelewel, who had taken part in the rebellion of 1830. This sudden fondness for radicals, however, was not allowed to interfere with Tolstoy's pedagogical interests. He inspected schools in the Belgian capital; and in a letter to Sergei he wrote that upon his return to Russia he intended to publish a pedagogical periodical on the results achieved in his school at Yasnaya Polyana. And in his notebook at this time (March 16), he jotted down: "My one aim is education of the masses. My one faith, which I dimly feel, binds me to the career of education."

9

Germany next became the center of Tolstoy's pedagogical studies. He continued his travels through Eisenach to Weimar, where he stopped for a few days. Visits to Goethe's house and the court of Grand Duke Karl Alexander left him unimpressed. "The stupid ladies of the Court!" he fulminated in the diary. "The beautiful German woman of the people, who must be regarded as a fool, is wiser than them all." His thoughts were on educational problems. He engaged a young German mathematics teacher, G. F. Keller, to instruct at Yasnaya Polyana, and he was already drafting a program for his proposed pedagogical magazine and writing two articles for it, one on rules for elementary schools and the other on foreign educational methods.[5]

In Weimar and near-by Gotha, kindergarten schools had been developed along the lines laid down by Friedrich

[5] These articles—"Project for Rules of Elementary Schools" and "A Letter to an Unknown on the German Schools"—were never finished. The fragments have been published in Vol. VIII of the Jubilee Edition.

Froebel. Tolstoy visited them and talked with the teachers, a few of whom had been students of the great Froebel. Tolstoy appeared in one class, announced his purpose without any formalities in quite perfect German, and then abruptly asked the instructor what plan he observed in teaching history. The astonished teacher was able to outline his method and Tolstoy busily took notes while he talked. He then sat through a lesson on history and scribbled more notes. The next lesson was in German composition. Tolstoy expressed great interest and requested to be allowed to remain. The teacher set a subject and asked the children to write a letter on it in their copybooks. The visitor roamed among the benches and looked at the efforts of many of the young pupils. At the conclusion of the exercise, he boldly asked permission to take the copybooks home with him, as he wished to study the results of the lesson. But the teacher, justifiably exasperated by this time, refused because the students were poor and could not afford the loss of their notebooks. Tolstoy agreed, went out and bought a package of writing paper, and returned with the request that the youngsters copy what they had written on the paper he distributed. In the meantime, the harassed instructor had consulted his director and was told to show the visitor every courtesy. Accordingly, the copies were made and Tolstoy left with them in triumph.[6]

Tolstoy realized that French, English, and even Americans merely imitated German educational theory, but he was fast growing weary of theories. With the Germans, theory had come first and the children were its victims. In the kindergartens he saw nothing but "geometrical drawings and basket-work–trifling! It is impossible to determine the laws of a child's development," he continued. "These children learn by heart what is of no use to them; as for what touches them directly, they have no means of grasping it."

Tolstoy wrote Auntie Tatyana that he would return by way of Petersburg, for he wished to obtain permission to publish his pedagogical magazine. Three days at Dresden were crowded with inspections of schools, buying textbooks, visits to Russian friends, and attendance at the theater and opera, which left him with the impression that Germans

[6] As confirmation of this story, published by W. Bode ("Tolstoi in Weimar," *Der Säemann,* Leipzig, September 1905), these exercises with the teacher's notes have turned up in Tolstoy's papers.

were men of talent but tortuous. On April 9 he was in Berlin.

There Tolstoy saw in the flesh the one man in all Germany he was perhaps most eager to meet—the novelist Berthold Auerbach. Four years before he had read and admired his *Schwarzwälder Dorfgeschichten,* tales of peasant life in the Black Forest. Shortly before this second trip abroad, he had also read Auerbach's *Ein Neues Leben,* a sentimental novel of rural life, with a schoolteacher for a hero, and filled with the romanticism and philosophical reflection typical of the author. Tolstoy was under no illusions about the literary value of this novel, but he declared it to be a most remarkable book, and he asserted that it influenced him to open his school and to take an interest in public education.

The hero of *Ein Neues Leben* is Count Eugene Falkenberg. Sent to prison for his part in the 1848 revolution, he eventually escapes and plans to go to America. At this juncture he meets a village schoolteacher, Eugene Baumann, who dreams only of emigrating. They agree to exchange names and documents: the count becomes Eugene Baumann, a village teacher, and the real teacher goes to America. The remainder of the book concerns the pseudo-Baumann's experiences in conducting a rural school. It turns out that he loves this work, considers it the highest of vocations, and many pages are given over to describing his pedagogical experiments and his moral and social views on public education and peasant life. With most of the ideas that Auerbach expresses through the medium of his hero, Tolstoy found himself in complete and enthusiastic agreement. Baumann declares against all theories and systems. The teacher must devise his own methods, and his success will depend upon his natural pedagogical talents and the force of his own personality. Tolstoy must have exulted when he read of the hero's belief that this world will become a better place only when the people in it become better. The purpose of education, the hero continues, is to make prisons and coercive laws unnecessary; every man will find a law in himself, and he will live in conformity with this law just as naturally as he breathes. In the schoolroom he allows his children complete freedom to come and go as they wish, to behave as they like. Everything must be done to encourage in the student a feeling of his own worth. In this novel Tolstoy found exactly what he sought—a moral formulation of the whole problem of public education, a formulation obviously based on the moral precepts of his beloved Rousseau.

The very day of his arrival in Berlin, Tolstoy sought out his "biographer." And as though to give point to the unconscious prescience of Auerbach, Tolstoy introduced himself ecstatically as Eugene Baumann. For a moment the novelist was taken aback and actually feared that he was to be charged with blackmail or defamation of character. Tolstoy hastened to assure him that he was Eugene Baumann not in name, but in character. He then told Auerbach of his school and how much he was indebted to his inspiration. In their long conversation, Auerbach lived up to the exalted impression Tolstoy had formed of him from his books. That night he wrote in his diary with special emphasis: "Auerbach!!!!!!! A most delightful man! He has given me light." Then he related that Auerbach talked of "Christianity as the spirit of humanity than which there is nothing higher. He recites verse admirably. . . . He is forty-nine, straightforward, youthful, believing, and not troubled by negation." The next day he visited him again and decided that he was a true Christian (Auerbach had abandoned his Jewish faith). Apparently, Auerbach was equally pleased with his strange and impetuous disciple. He wrote to a friend: "Count Leo Tolstoy visited me two days ago. I experienced spiritual joy upon beholding such an exalted nature as this man's."

Tolstoy spent only three days in Berlin. In this short time, however, he did not fail to talk with several figures in the educational world, among them F. Diesterweg, the prominent director of the Teacher's Seminary. Tolstoy set him down as intelligent but cold. On April 12 he departed for Russia, which he never left again during the remaining fifty years of his life.

XIII

Yasno-Polyana School

THE LITTLE peasant children of the school shouted an affectionate welcome to Tolstoy upon his arrival. His absence had dragged heavily for them; they had not got along too well with the other teachers who on rare occasions had even punished them. The youngsters gathered around Tolstoy on the porch, plied him with eager questions, and familiarly felt of his new blouse and trousers. Some told him that he had grown old, and he jokingly agreed. Then he presented Keller, the youthful teacher he had brought from Germany. As Tolstoy gazed fondly upon these glowing, fresh young faces, he was filled with a spirit of rededication to the whole difficult problem of public education in Russia.

To be on the safe side, he now obtained formal authorization from the Tula authorities to conduct his school (previously it had been a purely private enterprise). While a new schoolhouse with three rooms was being prepared, classes were held in the garden under an apple tree. The children sat in a half-circle around the master and listened to the lesson while they nibbled grass and made lime and ash leaves pop. Soon he received permission to publish his magazine and at once plunged into the business of writing educational articles as well as teaching.

For the next year and a half Tolstoy worked with self-sacrificing zeal[1] on theoretical and practical problems of education. Few questioned his sincerity, and his contributions to the field were original, though often weakened by perverse and exasperatingly dogmatic reasoning. Truth was his sole aim. He occasionally forgot, however, that his sweeping generalizations were based on a limited experience with

[1] The school cost him about two thousand rubles a year, and the twelve issues of his magazine some three thousand rubles.

his own little school and on the efforts of unique students and a unique teacher.

Some professional educators criticized his ignorance of theory. But a thorough knowledge of his efforts abroad and a careful study of his own contributions reveal that there was little of consequence on the subject that he had not read. On the other hand, he often seemed to have read merely to confirm his own preconceived ideas. A persistent skepticism was the trade secret of his educational thinking, as well as of his thinking in nearly every other field.

Tolstoy's ideas on teaching and educational theory appeared in a series of articles and notes in *Yasnaya Polyana,*[2] to which teachers and students also contributed. After extensive reading and observation, Tolstoy reached the conviction that all education should be free and voluntary. He supported the desire of the masses for education, but he denied that the government or any other authority had the right to force it upon them. The logic of things and his study of the operation of compulsory education abroad convinced him that it was an evil. The German father, he pointed out, often objected to sending his children to school, for he needed their assistance at home, and the children reflected their parents' hostility in their active dislike of studies. Pupils should come to learn of their own accord, for if education were a good, it would be found as necessary as the air they breathed. If people were antagonistic, then the will of the people should become the guiding factor. This faith in the "will of the people," even though the people opposed the commonly accepted notions of progress, contained the seeds of Tolstoy's later anarchism and was a direct slap at the radical reformers who would uplift the masses even against their will. Had he not observed that many of these progressive liberals, worshipers of culture and civilization, in the depths of their souls scorned the masses and their dirty children whom he proposed to educate? But the people could get along without the progress

[2] Twelve numbers of this monthly magazine (the issues were often late) appeared between February 1862 and March 1863. Tolstoy's contributions consist of twelve extensive articles and a series of notes. All this material, including variants of published articles, fragments of several hitherto unpublished ones, and the "Diary of the Yasno-Polyana School," has been brought together for the first time in Vol. VIII of the Jubilee Edition. This volume is an impressive monument to Tolstoy's total accomplishment in the whole field of educational theory and practice.

of the intelligentsia. In generations of workers, he maintained, there existed more strength and a greater consciousness of truth and goodness than in all the generations of barons, bankers, and professors. He made an exception of America in his condemnation of compulsory education, for he admitted that in America it had the sanction of a democratic electorate and was therefore in a sense not forced upon the people.

Tolstoy believed that education should answer the needs of the masses, but his own conception of the people's needs had nothing in common with that of contemporary progressive thinkers. Nor did he have any patience with the widespread pedagogical conviction that education should mold the character and improve the morals of people. These were matters for family influence, he declared, and the teacher had no right to introduce his personal moral standards or social convictions into the sanctity of the home. In public education he was concerned with the peasants, the vast majority of Russia's population. But he was not concerned with elevating the peasant above his class by the power of education (a definite evil in his eyes); he was concerned with making him a better, more successful, and happier peasant.

In this position the individualistic direction of Tolstoy's thought was apparent. The assumption of civilization's progress in Macaulay, Buckle, and especially in Hegel, he firmly rejected. For some time now the opposition between the good of the individual and the good of society had been troubling him. He was already developing a philosophy hostile to the pragmatic ideal that progress could be achieved only by social education of the people through the medium of democracy. Progress was personal, he felt, and not social. Education must serve the individual and not society, for the individual's capacity to serve humanity was what gave meaning to life. Yet he did not appear to see the contradiction in his rejection of the whole modern concept of progress. He would teach the peasant child what he needed, but what he needed was often conditioned by the social system in which he lived.

Tolstoy defined education as "a human activity, having for its basis a desire for equality, and a constant tendency or urge to advance in knowledge." Education, he declared, was history and therefore had no final aim. Its only method was experience; its only criterion, freedom.

2

Tolstoy attempted to realize in practice even the extreme aspects of his educational philosophy. He regarded his own school as a pedagogical laboratory, and the teaching in it he based on experimentation that was constantly informed by a search for the fundamental laws of life. But he never believed that Yasno-Polyana School was necessarily a good model. He frankly stated that the best school for a Russian village might well be the worst possible model for a school elsewhere. This fact followed from his conviction that a school and its methods must adapt themselves to the peculiar conditions of the pupils.

Yasno-Polyana School was noncompulsory and free to all. One of the three large rooms in the renovated building boasted a museum that was open to the public on Sundays.[3] The number of pupils varied, but the average was about forty. Most of them were peasant boys of Yasnaya Polyana, but some came from villages as far as thirty miles away. Several girls were also enrolled. With the exception of three or four adults who attended irregularly, the ages of the pupils varied from seven to thirteen, and they were roughly divided into three groups. Classes ordinarily ran from eight to noon, and then from three to six, but, as Tolstoy proudly wrote Granny, they often continued an hour or more beyond closing time, "because it is impossible to send the children away from school—they beg for more." Many even lingered on till late in the evening and then passed the night in a hut in the garden.

During the morning mechanical and graded reading[4] were taught, composition, penmanship, grammar, sacred history, Russian history, drawing, music, mathematics, natural sciences, and religion; in the afternoon there were experiments in physical sciences and lessons in singing, graded reading, and composition. No consistent order was followed, however, and lessons were lengthened or omitted according to the degree of interest manifested by the students. There were three teachers besides Tolstoy. On Sundays they met to talk over the work and to lay out plans for the following

[3] The school was in a two-story brick wing of the Tolstoy manor house and exists today.

[4] "Mechanical reading" was intended simply to acquaint beginners with the process of reading freely; "graded reading" meant to read with skill and understanding.

week. But there was no obligation to adhere to any plan, and each teacher was placed entirely upon his own. For a time they kept a common diary in which were set down with merciless frankness all their failures as well as their successes.

Originality was the guiding spirit. Freedom ruled, but not to the extent of anarchy, as some critics have supposed. In his inspection of schools abroad, especially in Germany, Tolstoy had seen everywhere rigid discipline, a constant demand for silence and obedience, the refusal to allow pupils to criticize, and an utter lack of initiative. All this, he asserted, had a stupefying effect on children; teacher and pupil regarded each other as mutual enemies. A certain amount of disorder on the surface, he felt, was even useful and necessary. When the German teacher left his classroom hard at work, all remained quiet for a short time. But if he listened at the door, he would soon hear the class in an uproar, with the pupils indulging in the usual pranks performed in the absence of authority. Tolstoy often tried the same experiment in his own school. When he left the room in the middle of the lesson, however, his pupils were enjoying complete freedom. They behaved as though he were still in the room; they corrected or praised each other's work, and sometimes they grew entirely quiet. Such results were natural in a school where the pupils were not obliged to attend, to remain, or to pay attention. Tolstoy insisted that only in the absence of force and compulsion could natural relations be maintained between teacher and pupils. The limit of freedom in the classroom was defined by the teacher, by his knowledge, and by his capacity to manage. And the pupils, Tolstoy asserted, should be treated as reasoning and reasonable beings; only then would they find out that order was necessary and that self-government was the best way to preserve it. If pupils were really interested in what was being taught, he declared, disorder would rarely occur, and when it did, the interested students would oblige the disorderly ones to pay attention.

The successful functioning of such a school demanded unusual ability on the part of the teacher. Tolstoy admitted this, and just claimed for himself a certain pedagogic tact. Always in his mind was the pupil's convenience in learning and not the teacher's in teaching. He insisted that there was no best method in teaching a subject. The best method would always be that which the teacher happened to know best. A method was good which when introduced did not necessitate any increase of discipline, but that which required greater severity was bad. The method should develop out of the exigencies of a given problem in teaching, and it should fit and please the pupils instead of the teacher. In short, teaching, according to Tolstoy, could not be described as a method; it was a talent, an art. Hence, finality and perfection were never achieved in it; development and perfecting continued endlessly.

Tolstoy's own practice did not fall behind his original notions of how students should be taught. He tried to understand the inner needs of each child and to conform to them. In teaching the alphabet, he began by printing—not writing—the letters on the blackboard and by asking the children to copy them. At the same time he showed his pupils how to form words with the printed letters. The transition to writing he purposely delayed, for he was convinced that hastening this process resulted in illegible handwriting.

The common practice of quizzing an individual pupil before the whole class was discouraged at Tolstoy's school. He believed that such a procedure was most inimical to the building up of friendly relations between teacher and students. It seemed to him like a condescending and humiliating exercise of unlawful authority. His own method was to ask a question and allow all to answer at once. When nothing could be made out of the chorus of voices, he hushed the pupils and then called on one. When this one reached the end of his information, the teacher called on others until the question was fully answered. This method developed of itself, and when controlled was very successful and kept the children in a happy and highly competitive spirit.

Since experimentation was the basis of classroom instruction, Tolstoy never hesitated to change a method when it seemed inadequate. The teacher considered himself wrong and not the pupils when interest flagged. Under the spur of competition, the children themselves sometimes hit upon highly successful methods of learning. For example, despite all his efforts, progress in reading lagged until a pupil voluntarily announced that within a week he would learn how to read as well as the best student in the class, a boy who had had previous instruction. Others took up the challenge, and soon all were furiously at work. The rivalry grew so intense that many of the slower students insisted upon taking their books home at night and doing extra work. Within three weeks extraordinary progress was made.

Somewhat the same experience occurred in penmanship. The pupils grew bored with their attempts to write well, and they resisted the teacher's efforts to have them recopy exercises. Some members of the older class, however, wrote Bible stories in their copybooks. Then they desired to take them home, perhaps to read to their parents. But the originals were so crumpled and illegible that one of the boys asked for paper to rewrite his stories. This idea took hold of the others. Soon they were all demanding paper to copy out their tales, and they boasted to each other of the excellence of their handwriting.

In reading and writing, pupils found the stories of the Old Testament most acceptable. So enthusiastically did they read and retell these tales that Tolstoy concluded that the Old Testament should serve as a model for all children's primers. When he read the Bible to them, it seemed to him that a corner of the veil of knowledge was lifted and they yielded themselves to him completely. The children fell in love with the book, he declared, and with learning, and with him. The only kind of reading matter that could compare with it in popularity were folk tales, popular legends, proverbs, and verses. In teaching the Bible so successfully, Tolstoy learned a deeper appreciation of its literary and moral values.

Tolstoy had his own method of teaching drawing. He thought it useless to oblige beginners to copy complete figures or pictures, for they had no understanding of their evolution. His method was to evolve a figure on the blackboard before their eyes by drawing horizontal and vertical lines, dividing them into segments by dots, and then connecting the parts. Pupils were called upon to criticize the lines and the relation of one to the other as he drew them. Often he asked a boy to add the next line or even to invent the shape of the figure. In this way a more lively interest was aroused and the inevitable question, Why? was constantly anticipated.

Music, one of his favorite subjects, presented peculiar difficulties, and Tolstoy's efforts to devise an effective method found him drifting into the technique of Chevet, which he had seen employed among classes of Paris workmen. He used numerals instead of notes to indicate sounds, and he taught rhythm separately from pitch. On this basis his best pupils, after a few lessons, were able to write down the melodies of songs that they knew and were almost able to read music at sight. Tolstoy avoided what he called the false taste of the community and concentrated on the laws of music. Nothing so harmed musical instruction, he declared, as a superficial knowledge of the subject.

In this free atmosphere of student-dominated learning, certain subjects were resisted in a manner that led Tolstoy to doubt their ultimate usefulness or to question the desirability of teaching them to youngsters. Grammar was such a subject. Although his instruction favored analysis, the kind involved in grammar put the pupils to sleep, or they openly avoided that class. To write correctly and to correct mistakes made by others gave his pupils pleasure, but this was only true when the process was unrelated to grammar. After much experimentation with teaching this subject, he reached the conclusion that "grammar comes of itself as a mental and not unprofitable gymnastic exercise, and language—to write with skill and to read and understand—also comes of itself."

History and geography likewise provided difficulties. Tolstoy early discovered in his teaching experience that it was difficult for children to comprehend general notions; they had to begin with something tangible, something related to their own common experiences. Formal instruction in history, for example, got nowhere; pupils stubbornly refused to be interested in ancient history. Even Russian history fell flat until he hit upon the happy idea of giving his own artistic version of Napoleon's invasion of Russia, which delighted his pupils. He decided that in teaching history, it was necessary to start from the end rather than from the beginning, and that the more legendary and artistic the narrative the more interesting it was to children. With geography he had no success whatever until he aroused his pupils' curiosity about the relative geographical position of their own village, but their interest scarcely went beyond this elementary knowledge. The fact that the earth revolved on its axis and passed around the sun bored them. He was ready to believe that nothing more to the point had ever been said on the subject than the remark of the hero's mother in Fonvizin's comedy, *The Minor*. She was urged to have geography taught to her booby of a son: "Why teach him all the countries?" she demanded. "The coachman will drive him wherever he may wish to go." Both history and geography, Tolstoy finally decided, ought not to be taught until the university, and even then he was altogether unconvinced of their utility to students.

3

Over the door of Yasno-Polyana School was the inscription "Enter and Leave Freely." Perhaps he was thinking, by way of contrast, of Dante's inscription over hell, "Abandon All Hope, Ye Who Enter Here," which Tolstoy would hardly have hesitated to place above the entrances to most of the European schools he had visited. Certainly the atmosphere of his own school convinced the children that education was a precious and joyous heritage.

On a cold winter morning the bell would ring for the start of school. Children ran out into the village street. There was no lagging on the way, no urge to play the truant. Each child was eager to get there first. The pupils carried nothing in their hands, no homework books or exercises. They had not been obliged to remember for today any lesson done the day before. They brought only themselves, their receptive natures, and the certainty that it would be as jolly in school today as yesterday.

Before the teacher arrived the pupils gathered near the porch, pushing each other off the steps or sliding on the frozen crust of the road. A few would go into the classroom and read, write, or play. When the teacher came he might find on the schoolroom floor a heap of squealing children shouting:—

"The pile is too small! You're squashing me, kids! Enough; cut out pulling my hair!"

As the teacher entered the voice from the bottom of the heap would cry out: "Peter Mikhailovich! Tell them to stop!"

"Good morning, Peter Mikhailovich!" shouted the others, continuing their game.

The teacher would take the books and give them to those who had followed him to the bookcase. The boys who were sprawled on the top of the heap would ask for books without getting up. The heap would become smaller by degrees. The moment the majority had books, the rest would run to the case and shout:—

"Me too, me too! Give me yesterday's book; give me the Koltsovian book!"[5]

If there were two left who, excited from the struggle, still rolled on the floor, those who had books would cry out to them:—

"You there, don't bother us. We can't hear a thing. Cut it out!"

The excited boys would cease their wrestling. Quite out of breath, they would seize their books, and, while applying themselves, they would still keep swinging their legs for a time from unalloyed excitement. Soon the martial spirit would take flight, and the reading spirit would reign in the room.

These youngsters, sitting wherever they pleased—on benches, tables, window sills, or floor—would now attend to their reading with the same eagerness with which a moment before they had been struggling with each other. They did not whisper, giggle, or show any lack of attention once the lesson was under way.

Though in the course of a lesson the pupils preserved quiet, they did not hesitate to walk around and look at each other's copybook or show their exercises to the teacher. Often a particularly stimulating one-hour lesson would run into three hours, and still the children would call for more of the same. If some one of the older boys expressed weariness, the others scornfully ordered him to "go to the babies." On the other hand, they were free to leave whenever they wished, and often they took advantage of this if they were tired, or if the lesson was boring, or especially if there was a holiday on the morrow.

Two or three boys might suddenly rush into the room during the second or third afternoon class and hurriedly pick out their caps.

"What are you up to?" one of their comrades would ask.

"Going home."

"But studies; there's to be singing."

"The boys say they're going home," added another, slipping away with his cap.

"Who says so?" And several more youngsters would vanish.

[5] The poems of the Russian writer A. V. Koltsov, whose simple verse tales of country life were much liked by both Tolstoy and the students.

"What is this?" the perplexed teacher, who had prepared the lesson, would ask. "Wait!" But the room would quickly empty, and the mortified teacher would have to submit, his hurt feelings perhaps assuaged by the fact that such scenes gave deeper meaning to the six or seven classes that these children voluntarily attended each day.

Tolstoy, like Rousseau, was opposed to both punishments and rewards in his school, features that he condemned most vigorously in schools abroad. Since the object of education was to bring happiness, the use of violence served only to frustrate it. The principle was deeply rooted in his own childhood experiences. Yet the habit of punishment was so ingrained in the teachers that they indulged in it on several occasions, but the results only fortified his conviction that it was a grave error. He sorrowfully admitted to losing his temper once and pulling a pupil's hair because he could not solve a simple problem in arithmetic. When two boys were discovered to have pilfered books, pencils, and a Leyden jar, Tolstoy in his embarrassment submitted the case to the pupils. They suggested placing a placard with the word "thief" on the culprits. The guilty pupils were extremely mortified by this punishment. One of them, however, was not deterred from stealing again, and the same punishment was repeated. Tolstoy could not bear to witness the boy's sufferings under the jibing and mockery of his fellow students, and he tore off the "stupid label." "I convinced myself," he wrote, "that there were secrets of the soul, hidden from us, upon which only life can act, and not moral precepts and punishment. . . . Our world of children—of simple, independent people—must remain pure from self-deception and from the criminal belief in the legality of punishment, free from that belief and self-deception that the feeling of revenge becomes a just thing the moment you call it punishment."

4

The spirit of freedom and equality that reigned in Yasno-Polyana School placed the teachers on a level with their pupils without any sacrifice of respect or authority. Tolstoy had an unusual gift for this difficult kind of familiarity which is so easily abused by youngsters. He insisted upon being addressed simply as Leo Nikolayevich instead of "your excellency," and in turn he learned to call them all by their nicknames. Pupils did the ordinary chores connected with the school, and to a few of the older boys Tolstoy gave bits of land to cultivate, for he strongly believed that manual labor should be an essential part of education. In the gymnasium that he provided for the children, he behaved as one of them. With strength and agility he led them in stunts on the apparatus and urged them to engage in gymnastic competitions. Alarmed village mothers were not slow to ascribe digestive troubles of their children, especially the belly-aches that followed the customary gorging after a Lenten fast, to this new passion for violent exercise in the gymnasium.

At the end of a lesson Tolstoy would announce that it was time to eat and play, and challenging them to race him outdoors, he would leap downstairs, three or four steps at a time, followed by the pack of screaming, laughing children. Outside in the snow he would face them.

"Now, all of you at me! Bet you can't down me!"

The students would cling to him in front and behind, try to trip him, throw snowballs at him, leap on him, clamber over his back, desperately striving to pull him down. But he was too strong for them, and like a powerful ox he would cart them around on top of him. After a time, from weariness, but more often for fun, he would fall in the snow. Then their delight was indescribable! They at once began to cover him with snow and pile themselves on top of him, crying: "The heap is too small, the heap is too small!"

On one occasion Tolstoy bundled his class up and took them off to Tula to visit the circus. The gaping wonder of these little peasant lads, who had never seen such a spectacle, repaid him for his struggle with the crowds, a dispute with a policeman, and quarrels with adults who obstructed the vision of his young charges. At Shrovetide he treated the whole school to a monster feast of the usual pancakes and sour cream. And at Easter he gathered all the pupils in a classroom where tables were loaded down with presents—cloth for shirts, concertinas, pencils, and jackknives. Each child was allowed to go to the tables and select the present he desired. Then nuts and candies were distributed. At Christmas he again entertained them with a tree and gifts.

It is little wonder that the children came to love their school and the teachers, especially Tolstoy. He was like an older brother to them, and they responded to his efforts with devotion and tireless interest. Yet he was careful not to thwart their independent natures and to preserve relations that were at once free in thought and action. Their special treat was to gather around him on the terrace of his house at night after school was over. They pressed him for stories, and he told them tales of the Caucasus or of his narrow escape from the bear, and showed them the mark of the beast's teeth above his eye. In return, they related village tales of wizards and wood devils. When they asked if he believed in wizards and ghosts, he said with some firmness that he would give a hundred rubles to anyone who would show him a wizard. Sometimes these conversations became serious and he would tell of his war experiences and paint all the horror of men killing men. Once he said to the children: "I've been thinking that I'd like to throw over my estate, my life as master, and become a peasant, build a hut on the edge of the village, marry a country girl, and work as you at mowing, plowing, at every kind of labor." The youngsters solemnly debated this proposition. Tolstoy attentively listened to their thoughtful reasoning and occasionally jotted down a note in his little book.

The close, even tender, relations that existed between Tolstoy and some of the older boys of the school are beautifully reflected in one of his articles in the pedagogical journal. It was a moonless winter night. School had just let out and the younger pupils noisily coasted downhill on sleds into the village. Fedka,[6] a lad of ten, with a sensitive poetic, yet daring nature, suggested to Tolstoy that he accompany him and two of the older boys home on a roundabout way through the woods. The danger of wolves fascinated the youngsters. The four set out together and skirted the forest, the boys hopefully on the lookout for wild animals. They chatted about Caucasian robbers, of Hadji Murad, and of the brave Cossacks that Tolstoy had often told them about. Although Russian peasant children very early learned to scorn affection and were even offended by the most commonplace caresses, in the darkness of the night, at the most fearful part of a tale Tolstoy was narrating, Fedka furtively clasped two of his teacher's fingers in his little hand and held on. When the story ended the agitated Fedka and the other boys demanded more. The wind sounded through the aspens and the snow crunched under their feet. Tolstoy concluded his tale by telling how

[6] Fedka, a favorite pupil, was V. S. Morozov, who lived to an old age and left highly interesting memoirs of his school days.

a Chechenian brave, surrounded by enemies, sang his death song and threw himself on his dagger. The children were silent for a moment, and then ensued a discussion about the import of the warrior's death song. Fedka, his appetite for horror aroused, asked Tolstoy for the story of his aunt whose throat had been cut.[7]

No sooner had this tale been finished than Fedka, with one of those mysteriously swift and unconnected transitions of children, suddenly asked why they had to learn singing in school. "What is drawing for?" Tolstoy rhetorically asked, puzzled for the moment about how to explain the usefulness of art. "Yes, why draw figures?" Fedka questioned. The other boys joined in the discussion. "What is a lime tree for?" asked Syomka. Each began to speculate on these questions, and the facts emerged that not everything exists for use, but that there is also beauty, and that art is beauty, and in the end Fedka understood why the lime tree grows and what singing is for.

"It feels strange to repeat what we then said," Tolstoy remarked, "but it seems to me that we said all that can be said about utility, and plastic and moral beauty." They continued on their way to the village and the boys reluctantly left Tolstoy for their miserable thatched huts and poverty-stricken parents. Fedka was the last to go. He still clung to Tolstoy's hand out of gratitude it seemed, and as he entered his hut, in which his father and the drunken village tailor were gambling, he said pathetically; "Good-bye! Let us always have walks like this!"[8]

Such experiences led Tolstoy to meditate on the age-old question of the moral and practical utility of educating the masses. The cultured, he said, would remonstrate: Why give these poor peasant children the knowledge that will make them dissatisfied with their class and their lot in life? We cannot all be thinkers and artists, for someone must labor. But moral questions and doubts troubled Fedka, countered Tolstoy, and you could not put him off with three rubles, a catechism, and the necessity of hard labor. "He needs," concluded Tolstoy, addressing the cultured upper class, "what your life of ten generations unoppressed by labor has brought to you. You had the leisure to search, to think, to

[7] A distant relative of Tolstoy had recently been murdered in this fashion by her cook.

[8] Tolstoy reprinted the account of this incident at the beginning of his famous treatise, *What Is Art?*

suffer—then give him that for which you suffered; this is what he needs. You, like the Egyptian priest, conceal your selves from him by a mysterious cloak, you bury in the earth the talent given to you by history. Do not fear: nothing human is harmful to man. Do you doubt yourselves? Surrender to the feeling and it will not deceive you. Trust in his [the peasant boy's] nature, and you will be convinced that he will take only that which history commanded you to give him, that which you have earned by suffering."

5

The question of art and its relation to his young peasant pupils interested Tolstoy. He discussed the subject in one of his most remarkable articles,[9] inspired by an unusual experience in composition in his school. Themes on the customary subjects, such as descriptions of a forest, a pig, or a table, drove the children to tears. He then suggested that they write a story on peasant life to illustrate a proverb. The pupils found this difficult too, but one boy proposed that Tolstoy write the story himself in competition with them. He composed several pages and was interrupted by Fedka, who climbed on the back of his chair and read over his shoulder. Tolstoy explained the plot of the story and the boys immediately became interested. They criticized what he had done and suggested different ways of continuing. Fedka took the leading part in this discussion and surprised Tolstoy by his imagination and sense of proportion, the chief quality in every art. Tolstoy set to work to write to the dictation of his pupils. Syomka and Fedka, who angrily rejected superfluous details offered by the others, eventually took command of the situation, and the rest of the boys went home.

Tolstoy described how he and his two pupils worked feverishly from seven in the evening till eleven. Neither hunger nor weariness bothered them. In his account of their collective efforts, he gave a number of convincing examples of the artistic rightness and fitness of details, descriptions, and selection that the boys argued and insisted upon. They drew from their experience with village life and characters, and they were nearly always right. Tolstoy was tremendously excited and admitted that he had felt such a strong

[9] "Who Should Teach Whom to Write, We the Peasant Children or the Peasant Children Us?"

emotion only two or three times in his life. He was amazed over his discovery of such artistic and creative powers in two peasant lads who could scarcely read or write, and it seemed almost offensive that he, a nationally known author, was virtually unable to instruct these eleven-year-old pupils in his art. Not even the great Goethe, he ecstatically exclaimed, achieved such artistic heights.

The next and still a third day they continued the story with equal enthusiasm. Then the work was interrupted because Tolstoy had to go away for a few days. During his absence a craze for making popguns out of paper swept the school, and the unfinished manuscript of the story was unwittingly sacrificed to this childish diversion. When Tolstoy discovered the loss upon his return, he was deeply chagrined. Fedka and Syomka, aware of his keen disappointment, offered to reproduce the tale themselves. They came after school one evening at nine o'clock and locked themselves in his study. Tolstoy listened at the door and heard them laughing. Then all grew quiet, except for subdued voices discussing the story and the scratching of a pen. At midnight he knocked and was admitted. Fedka still had a few more sentences to dictate to Syomka, who stood at the large table busily writing, his lines running crookedly across the paper and his pen constantly stabbing at the inkpot. At last Tolstoy took the copybook. After a merry supper of potatoes and kvas, the boys lay down on their sheepskin coats under the writing table, and until sleep overtook them, their charming, healthy, childish laughter rang through the room.

Tolstoy read the story over and found it very similar to the original draft. Some new details had been added, but the tale contained the same feeling for beauty, truth, and measure of the first version. And he printed it with very few changes in his magazine.[1] From this unique experiment in composition he drew some interesting conclusions. He declared that nearly all contemporary art was intended for people of leisure and artificial training and was therefore useless to the masses, whose demand for art was more legitimate. He dismissed with some vexation the stale notion that in order to understand and appreciate the beautiful a certain

[1] The title is the Russian proverb, "The Spoon Feeds, but the Handle Sticks in the Eye." Other tales written by his pupils were printed in the magazine, and he declared them to be equal to anything in Russian literature.

amount of preparation was necessary. "Who said this?" he asked. "Why? What proves it? It is only a shift, a loophole to escape from the hopeless position to which the false direction of our art, produced for one class alone, has led us. Why are the beauty of the sun, of the human face, the beauty of the sounds of a folk song, and of deeds of love and self-sacrifice accessible to every one, and why do they demand no preparation?" He questioned whether Pushkin's poems or Beethoven's symphonies were as art so absolutely and universally good as popular folk songs.

Tolstoy's position was no doubt extreme, and there was also considerable exaggeration in his unqualified praise of the literary ability of his pupils, who were no doubt inspired to an extraordinary degree by his own artistic interests. Ten years later, when he reprinted one of Fedka's stories,[2] he found it necessary to rework the whole, and he cut out many of the features that he had originally found so beautiful. Yet the schoolboy efforts of his peasant pupils taught him the fundamental truth that the need to enjoy and serve art was inherent in every human being, and that this need had its right and should be satisfied.

6

Although the Society for National Education that Tolstoy fondly projected found no support among government officials, his Yasno-Polyana School was not without its influence. After the emancipation of the serfs, the government encouraged them to open their own schools. Peasants in the Tula district appealed to Tolstoy for teachers and he willingly suggested a number. In 1862 there were no less than thirteen village schools in the neighborhood of Yasnaya Polyana, and their teachers were all zealous disciples of Tolstoy's pedagogical methods. They were mostly youths who had been dismissed from the universities for their part in the radical student movement of 1862. "Each one of them arrived," he wrote to Granny, "with a manuscript of Herzen in his suitcase and revolutionary thoughts in his head, and in the course of a week each without exception burned his manuscript, discarded his revolutionary thoughts, and taught peasant children sacred history, prayers, and passed out copies of the New Testament to be read at home."

[2] "A Soldier's Life," reprinted in Tolstoy's *ABC*.

These would-be young radicals, turned rural schoolteachers, worshiped Tolstoy and caught from him the devotion and enthusiasm that transformed their difficult task into a pioneering venture. They lived like peasants, taught from seven in the morning until late at night in dirty, stuffy huts, using tables for blackboards, and they received in return for their services scarcely enough money to keep them alive. At first, like Tolstoy, they had to overcome the ignorant suspicions of peasant fathers and mothers who distrusted these new-fangled methods of teaching and were alarmed because their sons were not regularly beaten by the masters. The fact that they were entirely free to send their children to school or take them out broke down resistance, and then the happiness of the youngsters and the obvious progress they made in so short a time eventually won the parents' complete confidence.

A religious prophet and his disciples could hardly have been more devoted to each other than Tolstoy and these young teachers. He inspired them with a love for their peasant children and set them a compelling example of self-sacrificing service. When Tolstoy was obliged to be away for some time, A. P. Serdobolski, a teacher in one of the village schools, wrote him of their progress, and concluded his letter:—

> We await you with impatience; without you things are not as they should be. I confess that our common effort can proceed only under your personal direction, that it can be fired only by your warm love for it. I am not convinced that all the teachers here love this undertaking, but I am convinced that they will love it as I love it, and as Tomashevski[3] loves it, if they will only find in it that poetry, that rapture which shines forth from your own being.

7

In a brief note "To the Public" that introduced his pedagogical magazine, Tolstoy eagerly invited criticism. He even wrote a letter to Chernyshevski, now one of the most popular progressive thinkers, in which he requested a sincere review of the magazine in the pages of the *Contemporary*. The desire to publicize his educational ideas as

[3] A. K. Tomashevski, one of the most successful of the village teachers recommended by Tolstoy.

widely as possible was part of Tolstoy's larger plan, but this appeal to a radical critic was singularly misplaced in view of Tolstoy's hostility towards the *Contemporary* circle. Chernyshevski did not miss this handsome opportunity to flay the aristocrat of Yasnaya Polyana. The review was painstakingly insulting. Tolstoy was held up as an ignoramus in the field of education and advised to return to his lessons in the university. The problems of what and how to teach children that he had labored so hard over were declared by Chernyshevski to be long since solved, and he bluntly told Tolstoy that if he did not know these simple matters, then nature had deprived him of the capacity to acquire the most elementary knowledge in education.

Tolstoy was deeply offended and did not deign to reply to such contemptuous and unconstructive criticism. He might have anticipated Chernyshevski's opposition if not his severity, for in the first and succeeding numbers of his pedagogical magazine, he had lightly disposed of all the Western European and Russian educational thinkers who were most esteemed by the *Contemporary* radicals. Nor was hostile criticism lacking in formal Russian educational circles. Tolstoy was called a "pedagogical nihilist," his experiment set down as a complete overthrow of educational order and discipline, and his school was described as one in name only: a "Jewish synagogue or a gypsy encampment."

A smattering of praise for some of the less extreme aspects of Tolstoy's experiment appeared in a few Russian literary periodicals, and several teachers, weary of the slavish devotion to everything German in pedagogy, bravely encouraged him. In general, however, his efforts were received in silence, and in no instance did he inspire among educators an enthusiastic acceptance of his experiment. His essential principle of freedom for both teachers and pupils was too radical a demand for even the most progressive theorist.

Of course, Tolstoy's educational ideas had no chance of a favorable hearing in his own day. He revolted against established opinion in the name of healthy common sense. Still worse for his case, he scorned scientific exposition in his articles and used the simple and forceful prose of which he was a master. If he had elected to write treatises on experimental pedagogy in the accepted trade jargon, buttressed with elaborate footnotes and well-chosen citations from authorities, he would doubtless have gained a hearing, even if an unfavorable one. His extremely radical position—really to the left of Rousseau—represented a danger not only to the whole foundation of educational practice, but to the authority of the State. The freedom that he advocated seemed to verge on anarchy, and children educated in this spirit would hardly grow up with the proper reverence for those institutions of the tsarist government that had been hallowed by a tradition of corruption and oppression. His educational philosophy would place the human worth and well-being of the individual above the well-being of the State.

Despite this hostility during his lifetime, Tolstoy's educational ideas and practice did not fall on barren ground. In recent years there has been a marked tendency to acclaim him a brilliant innovator and one of the most significant of educational reformers. Experimental schools in America and abroad have profited from the full accounts he left of his own experiences. His method of teaching the alphabet and of reading, his insistence on self-reliance by obliging pupils to do manual labor, and his belief that the child should be allowed as much freedom as possible in the classroom—all these features of his system have had their influence in later progressive education. And one of his principal theses, that the school should always remain a kind of pedagogical laboratory in order that it might not fall behind universal progress, has found wide acceptance as an educational premise.

8

By September of 1862 there were plenty of indications that Tolstoy's zeal for his school was waning. His absorbing experiment had fulfilled its purpose: the school contributed as much to the historical development of Tolstoy as it had to the education of peasant children—it brought him back to his career of fiction writing. It was as though a kind of catharsis had been effected that once again left his mind and spirit free for artistic work.

Although Tolstoy in later years commented slightingly on his educational efforts, he never really regretted them. In 1904 he wrote of his teaching experience: "The brightest period of my life gave me not female love, but love for people, for children. This was a wonderful time, especially in contrast to the preceding gloom." And as an old man, he noted in his diary that the happiest periods of his life had been those in which he surrendered his whole existence to the service of people, and among these he listed as first the time he had spent in educational work. And to Granny he wrote: "You know what the school meant to me from the very moment that I opened it. It was all my life, it was my monastery, my church, in which I redeemed myself while being saved from all the anxieties, doubts, and temptations of life."

Tolstoy's satisfaction was shared by the teachers who worked under him, and some of the pupils seem to have enjoyed a lasting and beneficial experience from their close contact with his powerful personality. His favorite pupil Fedka, looking back over a span of fifty years, recalled his schoolboy days: "There I am a ten-year-old schoolboy, there is young, jolly Leo Nikolayevich; there I am sliding down the steep hill, romping with Leo Nikolayevich, covering him with snow, playing ball, walking in the woods and fields, and having conversations on the terrace, telling our tales about the wizards. . . . The remembrances of those happy, bright days of my life I have never lost and never will. The love for Leo Nikolayevich that burned within me then still burns brightly in my soul and illumines my life."

XIV

A Challenge to a Duel

Freeing the serfs intensified the radical movement in the 1860's. All over Russia demands for further reforms outstripped the intentions of a government which was the most liberal in the country's long history of despotism. Tolstoy remained outside this social ferment, for he involuntarily opposed external, epidemic pressures. Comment in his diary and letters was conspicuously absent at the time of the emancipation of the serfs, but he must have rejoiced inwardly, as he no doubt did over other governmental reforms.

According to the terms of the emancipation, peasants were allowed to buy small plots of land, paying their former masters in money or labor. It was anticipated that endless controversies would arise over the size and value of these parcels of land, as well as many other vexing problems connected with the new social status of the peasants. To settle such difficulties, the government created in the various districts the new post of Arbiter of the Peace.

Upon his return from abroad in May 1861, Tolstoy learned that he had been nominated for the position of Arbiter in his district. The friendly governor of the Province of Tula apparently considered him an ideal man for the task, but the noble landlords were of another mind. Tolstoy's liberal experiments with his own peasants, his generous treatment of them before and after the emancipation, and his proud, opinionative, and slightly contemptuous attitude had won him the reputation in the region of being a crank, even a dangerous person. The landlords wanted an Arbiter who would respect their traditional rights and not strain the quality of justice on behalf of the peasantry. Opposition took shape at once. The Marshal of Nobility protested that the nomination was thoroughly distasteful, but the governor refused to be persuaded. Tolstoy was fully aware of the hostility. He wrote to Granny of his candidacy: "I did not dare to refuse before my conscience in view of this terrible, uncivil, and cruel nobility that promised to devour me if I accepted the post of Arbiter."

Tolstoy took up the challenge, determined that the peasants should have fair play, and he went about it with all the buffalo-like obstinacy that Turgenev had observed in him. He demanded that landlords recompense their peasants for beatings and for detaining them in service months after the emancipation; he protested the removal of peasants from their legal homesteads on an estate to land of less value; and he uncovered swindles on the part of landlords to deprive their former serfs of land to which they were entitled under the terms of the emancipation act.

For his efforts the peasants worshiped Tolstoy and the landlords hated him. He received threatening letters from landlords. They wrote denunciations of him, planned to thrash him, and conspired to involve him in a duel. The emancipation itself had caused them grief enough, and they did not propose to make any further concessions. Tolstoy's intention was to deal fairly with both sides, but he lacked a conciliatory spirit and was incapable of softening his notion of justice with administrative tact. While displaying a militant attitude towards his equals, he was ready to wait on his inferiors upon his knees. There were stories of his endless patience with peasants, even when they vainly persisted in trying to persuade him to do what he considered unjust. On the other hand, at the Magistrates' Session, where landlords registered complaints against his decisions, he stubbornly refused to alter them, despite the fact that all the judges opposed him. On one occasion he demonstratively walked out of a meeting because those present would not agree with his opinion.

The situation went from bad to worse. A petition of complaint was circulated among the landlords and sent to high government authorities in an effort to have Tolstoy removed. His judgments were reversed by the Magistrates' Session, but often when he appealed to the Government Session, which was uninfluenced by the nobles of his district, his original decisions were upheld. Finally, in February 1862, he wrote an indignant letter to the Tula Board of Peasant Affairs. He objected that many of his rulings had been reversed without legal justification, a situation that destroyed confidence in his office and rendered useless all his efforts. A list of such reversals was enclosed, and he refused to continue the duties of Arbiter until all these cases had been investigated by the Board. Shortly before this he wrote to Botkin: "I fell into the job of Arbiter of the Peace quite unexpectedly, and despite the fact that I conduct the business most coolly, and in a scrupulous manner, I have earned the terrible indignation of the nobility. They even want to beat me and to take legal action against me, but neither one nor the other will succeed. I wait only until they have calmed down, and then I shall resign." There was no possibility that the enraged landlords would calm down, and at the end of April he sent in his resignation on the score of illness.

A sincere desire to serve his fellow men had no doubt prompted Tolstoy to accept the post of Arbiter of the Peace. He regarded it, as he did his educational work, as a kind of moral activity. But the task had nothing to do with moral absolutes or abstract justice. The accommodation of means to an end required for the satisfactory handling of any social problem was nearly always beyond him. The problem must be solved in his own way, and that had little relation to the opinions or wishes of others. His experiences as Arbiter of the Peace merely added to his growing conviction of the stupidity of civil institutions. In all of them justice and the public welfare were sacrificed to an apparent order that sanctioned the oppression of the weak and the iniquity of the strong.

2

Two of Tolstoy's friends, Fet and Turgenev, regarded his efforts to serve society as schoolmaster and Arbiter of the Peace with distrust, but for different reasons. Since he had become a gentleman farmer on an estate not far away, Fet had grown very close to Tolstoy. They exchanged visits and carried on a lively correspondence filled with their agricultural experiences, but also rich in thoughts on questions of religion, philosophy, and art. Tolstoy highly esteemed his friend's common sense and his literary talent. Indeed, Fet was quite capable of writing some of the best lyric poetry in Russia while managing a large estate with unusual success. He did not worry so much about Tolstoy's desertion of his art in order to be of service to peasants, but the impracticality of his efforts and the absence of any possibility of material gain gave him concern. Turgenev, on the other hand, imagining himself the literary midwife who had brought Tolstoy's brain children into the world, had no patience with these madcap activities that interfered with the further artistic productions of his prize pupil. Not long after Tolstoy's return to Russia, these three friends were thrown together in a meeting that ended in an epoch-making quarrel.

Turgenev returned from abroad in May and eagerly sought out Tolstoy, whom he had not seen for some time. Turgenev had just finished the manuscript of *Fathers and Sons* and perversely longed to submit it to his dangerous friend's critical eye. Tolstoy arrived at Turgenev's estate, Spasskoye, on May 26. The meeting went off cordially enough. After a fine dinner, Tolstoy was maneuvered to a large sofa in the drawing room. The precious manuscript was placed in his hands, and he was discreetly left to devour this new feast in majestic solitude. Tolstoy soon fell sound asleep, either from the effects of the large dinner and his comfortable position on the sofa, or because the novel bored him (he did decide that it was artificially constructed and the contents unimportant). He awoke, he said, with a strange sensation and with the conviction that just as he opened his eyes he saw Turgenev's broad back disappearing through the doorway.

In spite of the frayed feelings engendered by this unpleasant occurrence, the two friends set off gaily the next day to visit Fet at his new estate, Stepanovka, where they were accorded a joyous welcome by Fet. Knowing Turgenev's love for good eating, Fet had his cook prepare a magnificent dinner, topped off with champagne. After dinner they walked in the fields, lay down in the tall grass, and continued their discussion with verve and freedom. Harmony reigned. Upon retiring that evening Turgenev playfully remarked that his host and hostess would spend the night on a cloud, between heaven and earth. In a sense, this was a just observation, retorted Fet, but a position not a little inconvenient.

The next morning around the samovar, Turgenev sat on one side of his hostess and Tolstoy on the other. Madame Fet, aware of the importance Turgenev attached to the education of his natural daughter, asked him if he were satisfied with her English governess. He praised the governess and added that with English exactitude she had requested him to fix the sum his daughter might give for charitable purposes. "And now," continued Turgenev, "she requires my daughter to take in hand and mend the tattered garments of the poor."

"And you consider that good?" asked Tolstoy.

"Of course: it places the doer of charity in touch with everyday needs."

"But I consider that a well-dressed girl with dirty, ill-smelling rags on her lap is acting an insincere theatrical farce."

"I beg you not to say that!" exclaimed Turgenev, his face flushing.

"Why shouldn't I speak about what I'm convinced of?" Tolstoy replied.

"Then you consider that I educate my daughter badly?"

Tolstoy answered that he thought just that, but that what he had said did not refer to Turgenev personally but simply expressed his own notion.

Turgenev in anger cried: "If you speak in that way I'll punch you in the face."

Upon that, Turgenev jumped up from the table, clapped his hands to his head, and rushed out of the room. A moment later he returned and declared to Fet's wife: "For God's sake, excuse my improper conduct which I deeply regret!" and again left the room.[1]

The worried and unhappy Fet, knowing the fiery tempers of both his guests, endeavored at once to put distance between them. Tolstoy with difficulty was hurried off to near-by Novosyolki, the estate of Fet's brother-in-law. Pride and self-esteem, however, had received a deadly blow, and Tolstoy's first act upon arriving at Novosyolki was to write a note to Turgenev, in which his fury was barely concealed by the icy tone: "I hope your conscience has already told you that you have not behaved properly to me, especially in the eyes of Fet and his wife. Therefore, write me the kind of a letter that I could send to Fet. If, however, you find that my demand is unjust, then inform me. I shall wait at Bogoslovo."

At Bogoslovo, the post station nearest to Novosyolki, Tol-

[1] Subsequent events indicate that on this occasion Turgenev also asked Tolstoy's pardon, but not with sufficient definiteness to satisfy him.

stoy waited impatiently for an answer. It did not come. He sent for pistols, and wrote a second note to Turgenev, this time a challenge. Nor did he wish to fight, he hotly asserted, in the trivial manner of literary men who end their ridiculous duels with champagne toasts; he wanted to shoot it out in real earnest, and he hoped Turgenev would meet him in the woods on the edge of Bogoslovo.

Tolstoy waited all night without any thought of sleep. But no Turgenev. Finally, a letter arrived in answer to Tolstoy's first note. It had been delayed because Turgenev had mistakenly sent it to Novosyolki. With excessive politeness he wrote:—

> Dear sir, Leo Nikolayevich! In answer to your letter, I can only repeat what I considered it my duty to announce to you at Fet's: carried away by a feeling of involuntary enmity, the reasons for which need not be considered here, I insulted you without any definite provocation on your part and I asked your pardon. . . . What happened this morning proved clearly that attempts at intimacy between such opposite natures as yours and mine can lead to nothing good; and I the more readily fulfill my duty to you because the present letter probably terminates our relations with each other. From my soul I hope that it is satisfactory to you, and I consent in advance to your making what use you please of it. With complete esteem, I have the honor to remain, dear Sir, your most humble servant, Iv. Turgenev.

About the contents of this letter Tolstoy wrote to Fet: "I wish you well of your relations with that man, but I scorn him. I have written to him and broken off all relations, except that I hold myself ready to give him any satisfaction that he may desire. Despite all my apparent tranquillity, I was disturbed in spirit and felt I must demand a more explicit apology from Mr. Turgenev, which I did in my letter from Novosyolki. Here is his answer, which I accept as satisfactory, merely informing him that my reason for pardoning him is not the opposition of our natures but one which he may surmise."

Meanwhile, the much harassed Turgenev had received Tolstoy's note containing the challenge, and he hastened to write another letter that was a curious mixture of abjectness and fussy justification. He admitted Tolstoy's right to demand satisfaction, weapon in hand, and then added:—

> I will say without phrases that I would willingly stand your fire in order to efface my truly insane words. That I should have uttered them is so unlike the habits of my whole life that I can only attribute my action to the irritation aroused by the extreme and continued antagonism of our views. This is not an apology, I wish to say not a justification, but an explanation. And therefore at parting from you forever—for such occurrences are ineffaceable and irrevocable—I consider it my duty to repeat once again that in this affair you were in the right and I in the wrong. I add that here is no question of courage which I wish or do not wish to show, but an acknowledgment of your right to call me out to fight, in the accepted manner of course (with seconds) as well as your right to pardon me. You have chosen as you pleased, and there remains for me simply to submit to your decision.

Tolstoy could not resist a reply to this letter, in which he bluntly wrote Turgenev: "You are afraid of me, but I scorn you and do not wish to have anything to do with you." Two months passed, and an echo of the quarrel is heard in Tolstoy's diary: "Have had a remarkable wrangle with Turgenev, a final one. He is an utter villain, but I think with the passing of time I shall not be able to refrain from pardoning him." The prophecy was correct. Tolstoy's pride and sharp temper made enemies easily, but he could not treasure up grudges for long. Periodically he felt it necessary to cleanse his soul of ill-feeling towards his fellow men; at such moments it became insupportable for him to know that he had an enemy. In another two months he wrote in the diary: "Be fair about Turgenev. I was going to, but for some reason or other haven't written him a letter, in which I wished to ask his pardon."

The next day Tolstoy did write a letter which contained the frank sentence: "If I offended you, pardon me; it makes me unbearably sad to think that I have an enemy." This letter had been sent to Turgenev's Petersburg bookseller to be forwarded to him. Since Turgenev went abroad, the letter did not actually reach him until some three months later.

In the meantime, fate once again played the estranged friends a shabby trick. Tolstoy received the following letter from Turgenev who was in Paris:—

> Before my departure from Petersburg, I learned that you disseminated in Moscow a copy of your last letter to

> me, in which you call me a coward, a man not willing to fight with you, etc. It was impossible for me to return to the Province of Tula at that time, and I continued my journey. But, as I consider your *behavior after all that I have done to efface the words that slipped from me* to be offensive and dishonorable, then I warn you that I will not let this instance pass without attention; I will return to Russia in the spring and demand satisfaction from you. I consider it necessary to inform you that I have made known my intentions to my friends in Moscow in order that they may counteract your loose rumors.

Tolstoy's answer was prompt: "In your letter you call my behavior dishonorable; apart from this you personally told me that you would punch me in the face. But I ask your pardon, confess my fault, and decline the challenge." Apparently he accompanied this with another letter, for Turgenev wrote to Fet that Tolstoy had satisfactorily explained the ugly rumors as pure invention. Actually, Turgenev's challenge to fight a duel eight months hence had struck Tolstoy as a little silly.

When Tolstoy's letter of reconciliation that had been sent through the bookseller finally reached him, Turgenev felt that his own actions had been hasty. Having in mind the baffling imponderables that had complicated the whole quarrel, he wrote Fet:—

> From all this one must conclude that our [Tolstoy's and Turgenev's] constellations move through space in resolutely hostile conjunction, and that therefore we had better, as he himself proposes, avoid meeting. But you may write or tell him (if you see him) that I (without phrase or joke) love him very much *from afar,* esteem him, and watch his fate with sympathetic interest, but that in proximity all takes a different turn. What's to be done! We must live as though we inhabited different planets or different centuries.

Fet had the temerity to convey these friendly sentiments to Tolstoy. For his pains he received the following brusque note in reply: "Turgenev is a villain who ought to be beaten, which I ask you to transmit to him as accurately as you transmit to me his precious maxims, despite my repeated requests not to speak of him. I ask you not to write to me any more, for, as with Turgenev's letters, I will not open yours." Thus Fet was also placed beyond the pale for a time.

Trivial as the cause may seem, this quarrel interrupted the friendly relations of two of Russia's greatest novelists for seventeen years. Turgenev could not easily become reconciled to the fact that his troglodyte had grown up and no longer required the care of his "old nurse." Tolstoy's own capacity for friendship was considerable, but his occasional irritability, his spasms of intolerance, and especially his excessive demands resulted in his having relatively few close friends in the course of his long life. Commenting on the quarrel, Botkin justly said of Tolstoy that he had an ardently loving soul and that he wanted to love Turgenev, but his impulsive feeling encountered merely mild, good-natured indifference. This would never do with Tolstoy.

3

Tolstoy's educational activities and the demands made upon him as Arbiter of the Peace affected his health. He also felt spiritually ill, for it seemed that all his efforts towards human betterment were leading him nowhere. A cough developed and he was haunted by the specter of tuberculosis. The doctor advised a rest. In May, Tolstoy decided to go to the Bashkirs on the steppes, breathe the fresh air, drink *kumys* (soured and fermented mares' milk), and lead an animal existence.

For company on the road, Tolstoy offered to take along two of his favorite pupils, Vasya Morozov[2] and Ignat Chernov. The wide-eyed wonderment of the boys at their first sight of Moscow amused Tolstoy. They stayed in the city for a few days. Tolstoy visited the Bers family, who were on the point of leaving for their country home. So intimate had he grown with this family, and so highly did they prize his company, that they willingly put off their departure. They worried about his thinness and racking cough. In the general conversation at dinner, Tolstoy complained of his onerous duties as Arbiter of the Peace. The daughters were more interested in their visitor than in what he was saying. Spirited fifteen-year-old Tanya, the youngest, observed in a whisper to Sonya that their oldest sister Liza "sentimentalized" for Tolstoy's benefit. The smile never left her face, and she spoke in a quiet unnatural voice. For some time now Liza had been cherishing hopes. After dinner Tolstoy

[2] Vasya (V. S.) Morozov is Fedka, the pupil who distinguished himself in Tolstoy's literary experiments in his school.

presented his two little peasant pupils, and he was proud of their grown-up behavior in the presence of fashionable people.

That night in their bedroom, the observant Tanya noticed that Sonya was unusually sad and prayed for a long time. At the conclusion of her prayers, Tanya asked:—

"Sonya, tu aimes le conte?"

"Je ne sais pas," she softly answered, obviously not surprised at the question. "Ach, Tanya, his two brothers have died of consumption!"

It was long before Sonya went to sleep. Tanya heard her indistinct murmuring and saw how she wiped away her tears. The wise little Tanya understood that Sonya also had hopes, and that night she lay awake for a long time while wondering about the eventual outcome of this sisterly duel for the heart of Tolstoy.

The next day Tolstoy and his young companions resumed their journey, proceeding to Tver by rail. At the station the baggagemaster must have taken him for a country bumpkin with two sons clinging to his coattails, for he repeatedly ignored Tolstoy's request for his luggage.

"The devil! What a bothersome fellow, what an uproar!" growled the bumptious official to Tolstoy's insistent demand for service.

"Do you know to whom you speak and whom you insult?" shouted Tolstoy in a sudden burst of temper. "I'm Count Leo Tolstoy!" He stormed at the official, told him that he was an author, and threatened to write to the newspapers about him. In a moment the baggagemaster was all deference. With endless apologies he quickly produced the luggage. Tolstoy soon regained his composure and laughingly remarked to young Morozov: "How I scolded him! He kept saying all the time: 'Pardon, it's my fault,' but I ought to have asked his pardon because of my lack of restraint and my pride."

From Tver the travelers took a steamer down the Volga to Samara, and then rode horseback some ninety miles to Karalyk, where they found the nomadic encampment of the Bashkirs. Not a tree or bush could be seen on the vast, rolling steppes. In a native tent Tolstoy and his young companions lived the simple life of these Asiatic nomads for more than two months. The Bashkirs grew very fond of him. They were Mohammedans and he talked seriously with their old men about religion and God. With the youths he was a general favorite. They liked his jolly disposition and called him "Prince Tul"—that is, Prince of Tula. He participated in their athletic competitions, and none of these husky young Bashkirs could throw him in wrestling.

This life in the open steppes and the salutary properties of the large quantities of *kumys* that he drank soon improved Tolstoy's health. He wrote to Auntie Tatyana that he was growing fat, that his cough had almost disappeared, and that he had discovered and visited an old Sevastopol friend who had become Ataman of Uralsk.

One morning at tea a disturbing note was interjected into Tolstoy's peaceful, healthy existence: a letter from Auntie Tatyana was handed to him. He read it and grew pale and agitated.

"Aleksei Stepanovich!" he shouted to his servant.

"What do you wish, your excellency?"

"Such a bundle of news from Yasnaya Polyana!"

"What is it, your excellency?"

"The Lord knows what it is. The gendarmes, the police, have come to our house, conducted a search, turned everything upside down, flung around all my books and papers, and have made a regular pogrom. It is frightful, frightful! And what have they been searching for there? They have terrified Auntie, driven her from her room, and upset the whole bed. It is terrible! It's an insult! I shall not let it stand thus. I'll write to His Majesty. It is impossible to put up with this!"

After such bewildering news, Tolstoy could no longer remain away from home, and he soon took his farewell of the kindly Bashkirs. They surrounded him and begged him to return soon. In their broken Russian they said: "Fine prince, jolly, love our joke; never was such a prince." He and his young pupils waved them good-bye and promised to return the following year.

Tolstoy arrived in Moscow about July 20. He stayed long enough to visit the Bers family and to pour out to these sympathetic friends the shocking story of how his house had been ransacked by the police. Then he hurried on to Yasnaya Polyana, anxious to learn all the details. In the meantime he turned over in his mind various schemes for demanding redress for this offense against the sanctity of his home and his personal honor.

4

For some months the police had had their eye on Tolstoy, nor did they lose sight of him for the remainder of his long life. Revolutionary manifestoes had begun to appear furtively in various parts of Russia. The secret police of the Third Section of the government grew worried. Large-scale conspiracies were imagined and many harmless "enemies of the state" were relentlessly tracked down. One of Tolstoy's young teachers, a university student, was suspected of having a part in the printing and distribution of antireligious works. As a consequence the Moscow police in February (1862) sent M. I. Shipov to Tula to investigate Tolstoy and his teachers. The sleuth could hardly have expended much effort on his commission, for it appears that he spent most of his time and the government's money in the pothouses of Tula.

In May, hearing that Tolstoy had left for Petersburg,[3] Shipov also set out for that city, and upon arrival he reported to the Chief of the Third Section, General A. L. Potapov. Meanwhile, the sleuth himself had been spied upon, for the Tula police had sent in a report of his debauchery to his superiors. Shipov slipped away to Moscow when he learned of this denunciation. There he was arrested for drunkenness, and in the hope of obtaining his freedom he manufactured an extraordinary cock-and-bull story that bore all the evidence of alcoholic inspiration. He declared that Count Tolstoy was surrounded by twenty young radical university students who lacked proper resident passports, and that they possessed an illegal press on which they intended to print forbidden works.

Since this startling information did not soften the police, Shipov had another try at it, and this time his imagination soared to dizzy heights. He asserted that Count Tolstoy employed a special courier on mysterious trips to Kharkov and Moscow; that various people came to sell the count strange merchandise; that he planned to print illegal manifestoes to be sent abroad; and that his house was honeycombed with secret doors and stairways, and was guarded at night by a large force.

For some reason this last parcel of humbug impressed

[3] This undoubtedly was a false lead on the occasion of Tolstoy's departure for Samara by way of Moscow.

the Moscow police. Illegal manifestoes were always sure bait. The drunken sleuth was sent to Petersburg to Prince V. A. Dolgorukov, head of the police of the Third Section, with a report containing all his testimony. Although Shipov's unreliability was mentioned, an investigation was advised on the basis of his evidence. Accordingly, on July 6, a certain Colonel Durnovo of the Secret Police descended with his myrmidons on Yasnaya Polyana. His orders were to conduct a thorough search and to arrest the responsible persons if incriminating evidence were discovered.

The police deployed through the village like an attacking force bent upon capturing it. Auntie Tatyana and Tolstoy's sister were in charge at Yasnaya Polyana. The terrified ladies were reduced to a fainting condition by the appearance and actions of the police. Everyone was placed under guard; rooms, chests, desk drawers, and all corners of the house were ransacked for hidden documents. Even the floor of the barn was torn up, and the pond in the park, which was dragged, yielded only a few innocent fish instead of the illusive secret printing press and illegal manifestoes. The schoolhouse and Tolstoy's Kursk estate were also searched, and all persons on the property were minutely questioned.

After this formidable effort, Colonel Durnovo's full report to his superior was a disappointing confession of misdirected endeavor. Nothing incriminating was found. In some cases the resident passports of the young teachers did not seem to be in order; three of the teachers had taken part in student disturbances; one was the son of an exiled father; and another had in his possession a copy of Herzen's contraband periodical, the *Bell*.[4] The examination of various people connected with the estate or in the neighborhood elicited the information that Tolstoy was a proud man, and that in his function of Arbiter of the Peace he had made enemies among the landowners and had treated the peasants with special consideration. The report also charged that towards his own peasants he had been unduly generous, and with the pupils in his school "even friendly."

When Tolstoy received the news at Samara of this police invasion, his first impulse was to write to Granny. Flaming indignation distorted his judgment and allowed him to attribute to this friend, because of her high connections with

[4] It appears that Tolstoy's housekeeper, upon the arrival of the police, concealed in the garden his portfolio which contained letters of Herzen, his portrait, and some copies of the *Bell*.

the Court, an unconscious share in the injury inflicted on him.

> Fine friends you have! [he stormed] True, all the Potapovs, Dolgorukis, Arakcheyevs, and dungeons—all these are your friends! . . . Some one of your friends, a filthy colonel, read all my letters and diaries which I thought to entrust to the person closest to me only before my death; he read over two sets of my correspondence[5] that I wished to keep hidden from all the world at any price, and he left, admitting that he found nothing *suspicious*. It is my good fortune and that of your friend that I was not there —I would have killed him. Fine! Glorious! That is how your government makes friends for itself. If you will recall my political attitude, then you know that always, and especially since my love for the school, I have been entirely indifferent to the government, and even more indifferent to the present liberals, whom I scorn with all my soul. Now I can no longer say this. I possess bitterness and revulsion, almost hatred, for that dear government. . . .

Tolstoy concluded his angry letter with insolent disparagement of Granny's good sense: "Some days ago I wrote you that it was impossible to seek out a quiet retreat in life, but that one must strive, work, and suffer. All this is possible only if one can escape somewhere from these bandits with their preciously washed and scented hands and cheeks and their affable smirking. In truth, I shall retire, if I live long enough, to a monastery, not to pray to God—this is unnecessary in my opinion—, but in order not to see all the nastiness of worldly debauchery, of pompous self-complacency in epaulets and crinolines. The devil! How do you, an excellent person, live in Petersburg! I shall never understand this, or have you already cataracts on your eyes so that you can see nothing."

When Tolstoy finally arrived at Yasnaya Polyana and learned from Auntie Tatyana and his sister every last detail of the police's offensive behavior in his home, his initial rage gave way to black despair. It is difficult to appreciate the intensity of his feelings over this whole incident, certainly not an unusual one in Russia at this time. Injured pride and honor, the fright that those near and dear to him had

[5] One of these was undoubtedly his correspondence with Valerya Arsenev.

suffered, the knowledge of his innocence, a belief that he had been irremediably compromised in the eyes of everybody, and a feeling of the hopelessness of redress—all contributed to the solemn conviction that his life was ruined. He wrote Granny again, a long letter this time, in which he pleaded for her advice and her intercession with people of authority in the hope that some explanation or apology would be offered him. With wearisome iteration he went over the details of the search and added some new ones; patiently he rehearsed his activities of the past two years and insisted upon their innocent and purely humanitarian character. Now all the happiness he had gained from such work was ended, he lugubriously declared, never to return again. His dear Auntie Tatyana was still weeping, had fallen ill, and was growing thin daily from the shock she had received; his sister was also terribly disturbed; his enemies, the landowners, were in ecstasies; his peasants had lost confidence in him, and all regarded him as a criminal. Now, he added, he kept a pair of loaded pistols in readiness to shoot the police should they dare return. Ought he to write the Emperor about the matter, he asked Granny? "There is no other outlet for me," he asserted, "than to receive some such public satisfaction for the offense (to correct it is now impossible) or to expatriate myself, which I have firmly resolved to do."

Granny's answer to these two letters was full proof of her sincere devotion to Tolstoy and at the same time reflected the discreet part she was obliged to play as a member of the Court circle. She condemned utterly the treatment he had received and offered every expression of sympathy, but she attempted to explain, though not justify, the search of his house on the score of the widespread treason in the land. Then she advised him to write to the Emperor and also promised to use whatever influence she had to obtain redress.

Tolstoy accepted this advice. His letter was presented by one of his friends, an imperial aide-de-camp, to the Emperor. Who had ordered the search, he asked in the letter, and he requested that the guilty ones, if not punished, be informed of the abuses they had perpetrated in the Emperor's name. The head of the secret police, General Dolgorukov, sent his own report of the affair to the Emperor. He took care, however, to omit all references to an illegal printing press, manifestoes, and secret doors and stairways. The only evidence he had acted upon, he explained, was the information that the resident passports of some of the young people about Tolstoy were not in order, and this was found to be correct. The Emperor was entirely satisfied with this doctored explanation, and Dolgorukov was merely ordered to write to the Governor of Tula that the search at Yasnaya Polyana, apart from revealing that a few of the young teachers did not possess satisfactory passports, was not to be considered as having any consequence for Count Tolstoy. Here was small comfort for the proud and offended Tolstoy.

Nor was the unhappy incident of the search the full measure of the government's officious prying into Tolstoy's personal affairs at this time. In October (1862), the Minister of the Interior wrote to the Minister of National Education about the harmful aspects of Tolstoy's pedagogical magazine. He complained that its general direction and spirit perverted the fundamental values of religion and morality, and he suggested that the censor's attention should be specifically directed towards correcting this situation. Fortunately, the Minister of Education was enlightened and fair-minded. He disagreed with his colleague, insisted that there was nothing irreligious in the magazine, and maintained that Tolstoy's extreme educational ideas might be better corrected by criticism in pedagogical periodicals than by the prohibition of the censor.

In part, the fears of the Minister of the Interior were correct: Tolstoy's educational articles did call into question the whole contemporary concept of morality. The spirit of Christian anarchy that he was later to preach so openly and eloquently had already crept into his thinking. For in his educational articles he condemned the false morality of government and society, their despotism, use of force, and belief in the legality of punishment. And he frankly stated his conviction that the masses could exist without the educated classes, and hence without government, but that the educated classes could not exist without the masses.

The government had dimly begun to recognize in Tolstoy a mortal enemy. He himself was not entirely aware of the full implications of the fact, and his first encounter with hostile authorities pained him deeply and intensified his mounting dislike for organized government.

5

Tolstoy's turning to his school and pedagogical magazine was in some respects an escape from the literary art in which he thought he had failed. This decision was not taken without a struggle, nor did the struggle cease during the whole period of his educational activities. To be sure, he had little time for creative writing or even for reading belles-lettres.[6] Yet the urge to create fitfully contended with his other time-consuming efforts.

While he was abroad, engaged in inspecting schools and reading quantities of pedagogical treatises, Tolstoy began three separate works of fiction that he continued after his return to Russia. Two of these were short tales that he never finished.[7] The third work was *Polikushka,* a novelette that he completed in 1862 and published the following year. Without being tendentious, the story exposed the hard features of peasant life. The tone of refined humor that aimed to ridicule the false and insincere in art appeared for the first time in his fiction. Here he upheld the canons of truth and simplicity that dominated his future tales and novels. The amazing concentration of effects and the complete revelation of character in so brief a scope marked a distinct advance over the best of his earlier efforts and stamped *Polikushka* as a little masterpiece.

These writings do not represent the sole artistic activity of Tolstoy during these lean years. An unhappy occurrence set him to work, however begrudgingly, on a major production that he had had on the stocks for a long time. On the occasion of a visit to Moscow in January, 1862, his old gambling mania seized him. He could not resist the temptation of a game of Chinese billiards (a game something like bagatelle) and in short order he lost a thousand rubles. Not having so much money on hand, he approached the publisher Katkov, who agreed to give him the required sum as an advance on *The Cossacks.* During the ensuing months Tolstoy struggled to complete the first part of this work on which he had labored intermittently ever since his

[6] Between 1860 and 1862 there is evidence that Tolstoy read works of Homer, Plato, Goethe, Hugo, Koltsov, Tyutchev, Fet, Turgenev, and Dostoyevsky.

[7] These fragments, "Tikhon and Malanya" and "An Idyll," may be found in Vol. VII of the Jubilee Edition.

Caucasian days. But the writing dragged on until the next year.

So far as the reading public was concerned, Tolstoy's name had vanished from the literary arena. Over the years 1858 to 1860 not a single mention of him occurred in reviews or critical articles. In 1862, however, the brilliant critic, Apollon Grigoryev, devoted a whole article to Tolstoy in Dostoyevsky's magazine, *Time*. The critic remarked on the contemporary indifference to Tolstoy, then went on to show how much this was undeserved, and concluded that he possessed talents hardly equaled by any living writer in Russia or abroad.

His literary stagnation troubled Tolstoy, for he was first of all an artist. In the full tide of enthusiasm for educational work he had complained of an acute dissatisfaction with himself. His thoughts were in a chaos and he seemed to be getting nowhere. The fundamental demand of his nature was the need to search—to search for truth, for the meaning of life, for the ultimate aims of art, for family happiness, for God. Only when the search had ended—however temporary this period of certainty might be—could all his intellectual and spiritual powers combine to produce art. In a letter to Fet that has already been mentioned in connection with the Turgenev quarrel, Botkin keenly perceived this fixed relation between Tolstoy's art and his philosophical uncertainty.

> His [Tolstoy's] mind is unfortunately in a chaos [Botkin wrote], by which I mean that it has not yet reached any definite point of view on life and the business of the world. That is why his convictions change so often, and also why he is so inclined to go to extremes. . . . Without some firm ground under one's feet, it is impossible to write. And that is the reason why he *cannot* write, and this will continue to be the case until his soul finds something on which it can rest.

Tolstoy's soul very shortly found that something on which it could rest—the ideal of family happiness that had been the object of his search for years. Once this search was ended, he entered upon the greatest creative period of his life.

XV

Marriage

FROM HIS early youth Tolstoy had been searching for family happiness, not yet recognizing it as one aspect in his endless struggle between good and evil. In his old age he looked back with frank disgust on this period as one in which the selfish pursuit after personal pleasure had predominated. And with a sense of horror he severely castigated himself for his sins of the flesh. If his capacity for sensual pleasure was great, it was not abnormal. The most intimate pages of his diary reveal simply a strong, healthy, animal nature, and at the same time they record a manly struggle against excesses. Neither in his life nor in his art is there a suggestion of joyless profligacy or sniggering indecency. His moral dualism was the conflict of all mankind: a struggle between conscience and the appetites, reason and the vital impulses, order and life. Both sides were strong within him. His appetites and his capacity for enjoying them were above the average, and his craving to bring order into the chaos of life was unquenchable. He could not eliminate either, nor could he be satisfied with anything less than absolute victory. In this lies his greatness.

At this point in his career, however, Tolstoy dreamt about that still unexplored realm—family happiness—as a positive good, an ideal, the anticipation of which comforted him in penitent moments or during those periods when his search for truth and goodness led him into a blind alley of despair. Like Levin in *Anna Karenina,* marriage for Tolstoy was synonymous with the joys of family life. A wife seemed merely the indispensable instrument for achieving the ideal. On several occasions in the past he had played with the idea of marriage, but only now did there exist for him that favorable conjunction of forces that appears to determine the ascendancy of marriage in a man's life.

2

For some time now Tolstoy had been weighing in the scales every eligible girl who crossed his path, but all had been found wanting. About the latest of these, Ekaterina Tyutchev, he wrote to Granny immediately after his return from abroad in May, 1861: "The excellent girl E. is too much of a hothouse plant, too trained in 'fool-proof enjoyment' to be able to share my work or even to sympathize with it. She is occupied with the preparation of moral sweetmeats, and I have to do with soil and manure." Here, as in all other cases, he unconsciously demanded perfection to compensate for an absence of love. The passionate experience with his peasant Aksinya Bazykin, who seemed so much like a wife to him, had failed to teach him that there was no substitute for love.

Tolstoy was almost thirty-four. He envied the family happiness of his friend Fet, and it pained him to think that he might long since have had children of his own. Was he not now too old? At times this thought enabled him to dismiss the compelling urge to marry with a sense of relief. He realized that it must be soon or never. At this crucial time his attention centered on the Bers family.

The mother, Lyubov A. Bers, only two years older than Tolstoy, had been his childhood playmate. She had grown up at Krasnoye, an estate some twenty-five miles from Yasnaya Polyana. A. M. Islenev, her father, who had been a close friend of Tolstoy's father, was an unusual character. A striking example of the energetic hard-living old Russian provincial nobility, he was a passionate hunter, a lover of gypsies and of their haunting songs, and a desperate gambler. At a single sitting he was reputed to have gambled away all his money, serfs, dogs, horses, his wife's jewels, and even the home over her head.[1]

When only sixteen Lyubov married the thirty-six-year-old Dr. A. E. Bers. He first met his future wife when he was

[1] Tolstoy drew heavily upon Islenev and his family for characters in *Childhood, Boyhood,* and *Youth*. Islenev is the model for Nikolai Irtenev's father, and his second wife appears as "La belle Flamande." Mimi, the French governess in the family, and her daughter Katenka, likewise serve as models.

summoned from the Turgenev estate near by (he had had an affair with Turgenev's mother) to attend her in an illness. They settled in Moscow, where both the doctor's practice and his family flourished. His engaging manner with the ladies, and perhaps his medical skill, gained him many patients among wealthy aristocrats, and he was eventually appointed Court physician with quarters in the Kremlin. Here his five sons and three daughters grew up. Fet, whom Tolstoy introduced into the family at this time (1862), described them as follows: "I found the doctor an amiable old gentleman of courteous manner and his wife a handsome, majestic brunette, who obviously ruled the household. I refrain from describing the three young ladies, the youngest of whom possessed an admirable contralto voice. All of them, notwithstanding the watchful supervision of their mother and their irreproachable modesty, had that attractive quality which the French call *du chien* [spirited]."

There was nothing very spirited about Liza, the oldest of the three sisters, a beautiful girl of nineteen, tall, with fine features and serious, expressive eyes, but with a cold, unsociable nature. She held herself aloof in the household. Eternally with a book in her hand, she scorned the customary games and amusements of a large family and gave herself up to things of the mind.[2] Tanya, four years younger than Liza, was a striking contrast to her sister. Affectionately nicknamed "Tatyanchik the Imp," she was her father's favorite and the spoiled tyrant of the household. Her passionate, artistic nature bubbled over with enthusiasm and excitement on the slightest provocation, and although she was something of an egotistical little show-off, her warm heart was always filled with irrepressible love for everyone and everything around her.[3]

The nature of eighteen-year-old Sonya (Sofya Andreyevna), a healthy, rosy girl with great brown eyes and dark braids, was in a sense a mean between the two extremes of her older and younger sisters. Despite her lively disposition, she affected a sentimentality that easily slipped into melancholy. Sonya's father remarked that she could never be completely happy. In her happiness something always seemed to be lacking, and she once admitted to Tanya that she

[2] Many of Liza's traits appear in the characterization of Vera Rostov in *War and Peace*.

[3] Tanya was the principal model for the unforgettable heroine of *War and Peace*—Natasha Rostov.

could always find sorrow in her joy. A fondness for children and domestic tasks appeared in Sonya even as a young girl, and she early exhibited a curious miserly trait.

Liza and Sonya were educated by expensive tutors at home, and both girls passed the university examinations that qualified them for teaching. Sonya loved literature, painting, and music, but in none of them did she possess any exceptional talents. Tanya, with her fine voice and artistic ability, was destined for a musical career by her parents.

Expansive hospitality reigned in the Bers household. Guests were endless, and on holidays favorite "Anke pie"[4] was always served, a dish that later symbolized for Tolstoy the material well-being of the privileged classes. The children were constantly entertaining crowds of young people with games and music, and often they put on plays. The gelid Liza maintained a decorous deportment amid these carefree gatherings, and her stern mother always held her up to her sisters as a model of correct behavior. But Sonya and Tatyanchik the Imp secretly yearned to turn the heads of the uniformed students whom their oldest brother, a member of the cadet corps, brought home on vacations. One of them, Mitrofan Polivanov, had already turned Sonya's head. They whispered eternal devotion to each other, but Mitrofan, with the magnanimity of a boyish lover, graciously granted her complete freedom to break her plighted word should she fall in love with another. The little firebrand Tanya, who still played with her favorite doll, Mimi, shared Sonya's secrets of the heart, and in turn confessed her own romantic passion for her cousin Kuzminski.[5] Here was a merry society of Moscow girls with their ribbons, calicoes, shy coquetry, and all the poetry and stupidities of youth.

The awkward girls of a few years back had been transformed by 1862 into attractive young ladies. Liza and Sonya had finished their schooling, wore long dresses, and did up their hair in the latest coiffures. Tolstoy now grew more interested. With the bookish Liza he discussed literature, and urged her to write articles for his pedagogical magazine. Duets on the piano or a quiet game of chess delighted the sentimental Sonya. With Tatyanchik the Imp, he played the

[4] A rich pastry garnished with almond chips and named after a frequent guest of the family, Dr. N. B. Anke, who was responsible for the recipe.

[5] Traits of both Polivanov and Kuzminski appear in the characterization of Prince Boris Drubetskoi in *War and Peace*.

schoolmaster, set problems in arithmetic, obliged her to recite verses, and when success crowned her efforts, he triumphantly carried her around the room on his back.

The sisters eagerly looked forward to Tolstoy's visits. Even the numerous servants, whom he regaled with jokes and stories, loved him. The merry household grew still merrier when he was present. He would gather them all about the piano to sing gypsy songs, or he would accompany Tanya in a solo. When her performance particularly pleased him, he would laughingly call her "Madame Viardot" after the great concert singer. Sometimes he improvised subjects for brief operas and obliged the young people to make up the words (the more incomprehensible the better), which they sang to familiar motifs.

These frequent visits to a family with at least two marriageable girls soon set tongues to wagging. Gossip represented Tolstoy as the suitor of the oldest sister. His own sister, a lifelong friend of mother Bers, favored Liza. Such a solid, serious, and well-educated girl, Marya told him, would make an excellent wife. The solid Liza was indifferent at first, but the persistent gossip began to arouse her from her books. All noticed that she paid more attention to her appearance, and soon she was madly in love.

From the very first, however, the serious Liza left Tolstoy quite cold. "Liza Bers tries to tempt me," he had written in his diary in September 1861, "but nothing will come of it. Calculation alone is not enough, and there is no feeling." The spirited Imp was more to his liking, but she was still a child. On the other hand, he began to observe that Sonya grew more attractive with every passing day. Her Polivanov was away in Petersburg. She wept over him and eagerly read to her younger sister the letters this delicate lover sent. Somehow *"le comte"* as a lover had not at first dawned upon her consciousness. She had known him as a little girl when she had gone into raptures over his *Childhood* and *Boyhood,* copied pages of them into her diary, and memorized whole passages. Sonya regarded the author through a prism of poetic ecstasy. He became her shining hero. She tied ribbons to the chair on which he sat, and even wrote out from *Youth* several lines that she wore next to her heart as a precious jewel. Sonya was then a child of eleven. Now she was eighteen, and a furtive mouse of an idea crept into her mind that she was not unattractive to this man almost twice her age. His face was common, almost ugly, but there were a strange charm and spiritual power in his piercing glance. He was also a count, a famous author, and the possessor of a large estate. It was a challenge to win the love of such a man. The more her thoughts dwelt upon him, the paler grew the image of her young cadet at his military studies in Petersburg. And suddenly Sonya was almost ready to confess to herself that she was in love not with Polivanov, but with Tolstoy.

3

A few weeks after Tolstoy's return in July 1862 from Samara, a series of events threw his emotions into a turmoil. Mother Bers decided to take her three daughters on a visit to Ivitsy, the estate of their grandfather. On the way she planned to stop over at Yasnaya Polyana, some thirty-five miles from Ivitsy, in order to see her childhood friend, Marya Tolstoy. No doubt this ambitious mother also had in mind the fact that her friend's brother was being much talked of as a suitable match for her eldest daughter.

The party arrived at Yasnaya Polyana in the early evening. Tolstoy tried to conceal his agitation over all this charming feminine company by indulging in gestures of fussy hospitality. It was discovered that one bed was lacking. He suggested a huge armchair, and Sonya at once elected it for herself. With awkward, unaccustomed movements he began to spread the sheets, and these preparations filled her with a pleasant sense of intimacy. While the table was being set for supper, Sonya wandered into a small reception hall off the dining room. Venetian doors in the center wall opened onto a balcony from which one had a clear view of the countryside. She took a chair out on the balcony and sat there to admire the landscape. Forbidden thoughts, happy and serious, ran through her maiden mind. Tolstoy called her to supper, but she declined. Bits of the merry conversation floated out to her. Without finishing his meal Tolstoy finally joined Sonya. She did not remember their conversation, only that he said: "How clear and simple you are," and this pleased her. That night she fell happily asleep in the armchair, her young heart gladdened by the thought that *he* had prepared this bed for her with his own hands.

The following day Tolstoy, rid of his initial feeling of constraint with his guests, became the soul of easy hospitality. Neighbors called and a picnic was planned. He invited Sonya to accompany him on horseback while the rest of the party went in a carriage. As she cantered beside him Sonya thought she could never be happier. They all halted by a stack of fresh hay in a meadow in the Zasek woods. The meal was enlivened by his banter and merrymaking, and at its conclusion nothing would do but that they must all climb on the haystack and sing songs.

The guests continued their journey to Ivitsy the next day, promising to call again on their way home. Lively grandfather Islenev received them joyfully, pinching the fresh cheeks of his granddaughters and ordering up all manner of old-fashioned entertainment for these "Moscow ladies" as he called them. Shoals of neighbors were invited, and there were rides, picnics, and at night dances for the young people and whist for their parents.

The day after the arrival of the girls Tolstoy suddenly appeared on his big white horse. Liza blushed, accepting it as a compliment, and so did Sonya who immediately became unnaturally lively. But it was Sonya that he singled out for his special attention, and the observant Tatyanchik read in her sister's eyes: "I want to love you but I'm afraid." Polivanov and Liza, like ghosts, stood always before her.

At the dancing the following evening Tolstoy preferred to play cards or talk with the mothers and fathers. He was too old, he told Tanya and Sonya, when they teased him to dance. After supper the capricious Tanya was asked to sing. She refused, and to escape her petitioners ran into the drawing room and hid under the piano. Suddenly Tolstoy and Sonya entered. They seemed agitated. Tanya did not dare to move. Sonya wished to leave, for her stern mother had already ordered her to bed.

"Sofya Andreyevna, wait a moment," pleaded Tolstoy.

"What for?"

"Read what I'm going to write for you."

"All right," she agreed.

"But I shall write only the initial letters and you must guess what the words are."

"How so? But that's impossible! Well, write."

Tolstoy wrote with a piece of chalk on the surface of a card table the letters "Y.y.a.n.o.h.r.m.t.s.o.m.a.a.t.i.o.h."[6]

[6] The initial letters of the Russian words, of course, are different, but the following translation is an exact rendering of the Russian sentence.

Sonya read with some prompting from Tolstoy: "Your youth and need of happiness remind me too strongly of my age and the impossibility of happiness."

Her heart beat loudly, her face burned. She felt that something she had hoped for and dreamed of was about to happen, and she was both eager and afraid. All her senses were sharpened to a point of miraculous comprehension.

Then Tolstoy wrote further: "I.y.f.e.a.f.o.a.m.a.y.s.L.D.-m.w.y.s.T."

Again Sonya read with a bit of help: "In your family exists a false opinion about me and your sister Liza. Defend me with your sister Tatyanchik."

At the conclusion of the second sentence, Sonya, hearing her mother calling her to bed, ran out of the room. Before she fell asleep that night, she wrote the sentences in her diary. She fully realized that something serious and significant had taken place between her and Tolstoy, something that would not cease there. Only to Tanya, a witness to the whole scene, did Sonya confide her hopes and misgivings.[7]

Tolstoy departed the next day. Once again he saw the Bers family at Yasnaya Polyana on their return journey to Moscow. When they were saying their farewells, to the surprise of all he announced that he would drive to the city with them. His simple excuse was that it would now be boring and empty at Yasnaya Polyana. The sisters were delighted, and Sonya must have imagined that her battle was nearly won. For most of the journey he contrived to sit with her alone, somewhat to the indignation of the now jealous Liza. During the long hours of the trip he told Sonya the story of his life, of the beauties of the Caucasus, and of his adventures there. Perhaps like Othello he hoped to win this credulous girl by an account of the dangers he had been through. Unlike Desdemona, however, she fell asleep before his story ended. But until the fatigue of the journey had taken its toll, she had been a most enraptured listener to this real tale of her favorite author.

4

It was the middle of August. The affairs of his school and periodical weighed upon Tolstoy, but he could not tear himself away from Moscow. Passion gambled with reason

[7] This scene was utilized by Tolstoy in describing Levin's proposal to Kitty in *Anna Karenina*.

and his future destiny was the stake. The Bers family moved to their summer house at Pokrovskoye only eight miles from the city. Here Tolstoy was almost a daily caller, often walking the distance. His frequent visits began to embarrass him as well as the members of the household, yet he could not stay away. The parents were confused as to his intentions and began to treat him with some restraint. Sonya, tortured by his uncertainty, received him with conflicting emotions, one day gay and bright, the next sad and gloomy. Why did he not declare himself?

At Pokrovskoye there were long walks together on beautiful moonlight nights, but no romantic scenes took place. Once Sonya sat in her father's carriage, from which the horses had just been unharnessed. She called out to Tolstoy in a merry mood: "When I'm an empress, I'll be driven about in such a carriage." He impetuously seized the shafts, and with an unusual show of strength wheeled her around the yard, shouting: "This is the way my empress will ride!"

Throughout all this period of indecision, Tolstoy kept his diary, and it is a sorry record of confusion and struggle. His first entry referring to Sonya occurred on August 23, after having spent the night at the Bers home. "She's a child!" he wrote. "Just like one! Oh, if I could only place myself in a clear and honorable position. . . . I'm afraid of myself: what if this be only a desire for love and not real love? I try to see only her insufficiencies. . . ."

Several days later Tolstoy recorded some interesting observations on the manuscript of a story he had begged from Sonya. She had written it when she first sensed her attraction for him, and now she willingly let him have it, perhaps in the hope that it would allay his doubts and sting him to action. For the tale was a frank narrative of their relations, thinly disguised as fiction. Tolstoy was described as Dublitski, a middle-aged man of unattractive appearance, energetic and wise, but with unsuitable views on life. Sonya, as Elena, fell in love with him, but worried about her young suitor Smirnov (Polivanov) and her older sister, who was in love with Dublitski. In her perplexity she thought of entering a convent, but in the end arranged a marriage between her sister and Dublitski. Then Smirnov finally returned and married Elena.

Sonya gained little by this transparent hint, although Tolstoy did finally admit to her that the tale had agitated him and kept him awake all night. The reactions he concealed from her, however, appeared in his diary: "She gave me her story to read. What energy of truth and simplicity! Vagueness tortured her. I read all without anxiety, without a show of jealousy or envy, but the 'unusually unattractive appearance' and 'instability of conviction' hurt me much. I calmed myself. All this is not about me. Work, and just the satisfaction of one's needs."

His imagined calm was murdered the moment Sonya entered his thoughts, and he could not keep her out of them. Two days after this entry (his thirty-fourth birthday), he busied himself with work and visits, and refused to be disturbed. But a "bouquet of letters and flowers" from the Bers family arrived. Sonya's brief contribution to the family's collective congratulatory epistle—her first letter to him—set him off once again on the treadmill of his emotions. "If I were an empress," she wrote, recalling their recent pleasantry at Pokrovskoye, "I would send you on your birthday a most gracious mandate, but now, as a simple mortal, I *simply* congratulate you with having come into God's world, and I wish that you may look on it for a long time and if possible, forever, and with the same eyes as now." Was there some hidden meaning in this ordinary note, he wondered. He tried to draft a reply, but the words would not come. Then he sought to regain tranquillity once more by reminding himself in the diary: "Ugly mug that you are! Think no more of marriage; your calling is something other, and for that much has been given you."

Such indecision was no comfort to Sonya's titillated emotions. It appears that at this point she treated him to a wholesome dose of jealousy. A history professor of thirty-five, N. A. Popov, had evinced an interest in her charms, and to do them more homage he had hired a summer house quite near Pokrovskoye. She liked the professor with his expressive gray eyes and slow, deliberate movements, and perhaps with design she would often engage him in serious conversation in Tolstoy's presence. The diary registered his immediate alarm: "To the Bers'. Sonya with Popov. I'm not jealous," he protested. "We walked, the arbor, a melon for supper—her eyes, and the night! . . . Fool! She's not meant for you; yet I'm in love, just as with S. K. and with A.[8] No more. I spent the night with them, did not sleep, and always she. Have you not loved? she asks, and I feel so funny and happy."

[8] Sonya Koloshin and A. A. Obolenski.

This slip of a girl was swiftly and utterly taking possession of his heart. He awoke in the morning with a sweet sense of the fullness of a life of love. He visited friends and thought he heard Sonya's voice when some other girl spoke. By comparison, all other girls seemed to him "vile, dried-up things in crinoline." In vain he told himself that he was "an old devil" who ought to stick to his pedagogical articles.

September arrived and the family returned to Moscow. Tolstoy diligently continued his vigil at their house. In a moment of misplaced confidence, Sonya confessed to her mother that she expected a proposal from him. She was testily ordered to forget such nonsense and to cease imagining that everybody was in love with her. Meanwhile, father Bers began to grow angry with the ubiquitous Tolstoy for not making an offer to Liza.

On his next visit Tolstoy noticed that father Bers sat angrily in his study. The whole family was grave and stern. He knew what they were waiting for. As he looked at the cold Liza, all he could think of was what a dreadful misfortune it would be if she should become his wife. He took refuge in Sonya's blushes and obvious agitation in his presence. "Oh, Dublitski, don't dream!" he cautioned himself in the diary. "I began to work but I could not go on. Instead of work I wrote her a letter. . . . I *cannot, cannot* leave Moscow." Sleep deserted him and he felt that he was acting like a boy of sixteen.

In the letter he explained that he had never loved Liza, and, as that "unusually unattractive devil" Dublitski, he could have no pretension to Sonya, whom he regarded as he would a child he loved. Then he pathetically and perhaps hopefully concluded: "I am Dublitski, but I can never marry a woman merely because a wife is necessary. I demand the fearful, the impossible from marriage. I demand to be loved as I can love. But this is impossible." And he added a postscript that in the future he would cease to visit them.

On second thought, Tolstoy decided not to send the letter; he knew that he could not break off his visits. As the tide of his emotions rose, his capacity for positive action seemed to diminish. He wrote in his diary that he waited for the evenings to see Sonya like a schoolboy waiting for the coming of Sunday. Often now she greeted him sternly. After one such meeting on September 10, he entered in the diary: "I left discouraged again, but still more in love than before. *Au fond* sits hope. One must,—it is necessary to cut this knot. . . . Lord help me, God, teach me! Again, a sleepless, torturing night; I really feel, I who used to laugh over the sufferings of lovers. I deserve this punishment because of my ridiculing. How many plans I have formed to tell her or Tanichka, but all in vain. . . . Lord, help me, teach me! Mother of God, help me!"

Tolstoy did not trust himself to make another visit the next day. But this brief separation only added flame to his passion. "I'm in love as I never believed it possible to be in love," he wrote in the diary on September 12. "I'm a madman. . . . A Dublitski, it may be, but I'm made beautiful by my love. Yes. I will go to them tomorrow morning. There have been minutes, but I have not made use of them. I've been timid; one must simply speak. I want to return at once and say all, and before everybody. Lord, help me!"

This brave resolution deserted him on the following day. His entry reads: "Each day I think it is impossible to suffer more and at the same time remain so happy, and each day I grow more frenzied. Again I departed anguished, remorseful, but happy at heart. Tomorrow I shall go as soon as I arise and tell all or" . . . he added: "shall shoot myself," but crossed this out. "Four o'clock in the morning. I've written a letter; I'll give it to her tomorrow, i.e. today, the 14th. My God, how I fear to die. Happiness, and such a happiness, seems to me impossible. My God, help me!"

Although Tolstoy visited Sonya on each of the next two days, he did not dare to present the letter. Such lack of resolve from a man of his age and experience with women may seem puzzling, yet it was in accord with his nature and with the special circumstances of the situation. He had always been shy with women, and particularly with women of his own social standing. Then Sonya's description of Dublitski had intensified his poignant feeling about the disadvantages of his unattractive appearance and of the considerable disparity in their ages. Finally, with his pride and egoism, he no doubt feared the consequences to him of a refusal.

5

On the evening of September 16 Tolstoy called on the Bers family again. He seemed agitated. The letter he had written for Sonya three days before still nestled in his pocket.

Ill at ease, Tolstoy asked Sonya to play a duet with him

and then decided not to. They sat quietly at the piano. She gently fingered the accompaniment to the "Il Baccio" waltz that she was learning for her sister. His agitation quickly infected Sonya. Nervously she called to Tanya to sing the piece.

Tanya agreed, but she noticed that the request seemed to displease him. She was in voice that night. Standing in the center of the room, she soon forgot them both in her rapt concentration on the song. Sonya stumbled on the accompaniment and Tolstoy slipped into her place and took it up, at once giving new life to Tanya's voice and the words of the song. He promised himself that if Tanya took the final high note well, he would give Sonya the letter.[9] The little singer ended, soaring to the final high note with perfect ease.

"How you sing tonight!" he exclaimed in an excited voice.

At this moment Tanya was called from the room to help with the tea. They were alone.

"I wanted to speak with you," Tolstoy began, but he could not continue. "Here is a letter that I've been carrying around in my pocket for several days. Read it. I'll wait for your answer."

Sonya seized the letter and ran downstairs to her room and locked the door. She opened the letter with trembling hands and read:—

"This is becoming unendurable. Every day for three weeks I have been saying: today I shall tell all, and I have been going away with the same anguish, remorse, fear, and happiness in my soul. And every night, as even now, I examine the past, torment myself, and say: why have I not spoken, and I tell myself how and what I should have said. I have taken this letter with me in order to give it to you if I again find it impossible or lack the spirit to tell you all.

"*The false opinion in your family* about me, it seems, arises from the belief that I am in love with your sister Liza. *This is unfair. Your story is constantly in my mind,* and after reading it I became convinced that I am Dublitski, and therefore to dream about happiness ill suits me; that your conception of love is too romantic . . . that I have not envied and will not envy the man you may love. It seems to me that I can rejoice over you as over a child.

[9] Tolstoy often decided to act positively or negatively on the basis of such wagers with himself, a habit he also attributed to Pierre in *War and Peace*.

"At Ivitsy I wrote: *Your presence too strongly reminds me of my age and the impossibility of happiness, and just you. . . .*

"But even then and afterwards I lied to myself. Then even more so I could have given over everything and again gone into my monastery of lonely work and become absorbed with affairs. Now I can do nothing of the kind, and I feel that I have made a mess of things in your family, that having grown cold, my dear relations with you, as with another honest person, are ended. But I cannot take my leave, and I do not dare remain. You, an honest person, and with hand on heart—*without haste, for God's sake, without haste*—tell me what to do. He who laughs may in the end suffer. I would have died with laughter if a month ago I had been told—that I could suffer as I now suffer, and happily suffer. Tell me, as an *honest person,*—do you wish to be my wife? Only if you can boldly say *yes* with all your soul, then you had better say no, if there is a shadow of doubt in you.

"For God's sake, examine your heart carefully.

"It will be dreadful for me to hear 'no,' but I foresee it, and I will find in myself the strength to bear it; but if as a husband I shall never be loved as I love, it will be terrible."

The ecstatic Sonya did not pause to read through this tortured analysis of a heart enthralled. Her eager eyes quickly discovered the question: "Do you wish to be my wife?" That was enough. On the other side of the locked bedroom door she heard Liza's frightened voice:—

"Sonya, what has the count written to you? Speak!"

Sonya remained silent, tightly gripping the precious letter.

"Speak at once! What has the count written you?" cried Liza again, a hysterical note in her voice.

"He has proposed to me," Sonya, with an effort, calmly answered.

"Refuse!" screamed Liza. "Refuse at once!" and she burst into sobs.

Tanya called her mother to quiet Liza. Sonya told her mother what had happened, and she was ordered to give Tolstoy her answer. She flew up the stairway, shot by the dining room, the drawing room, and ran into her mother's apartment. Tolstoy stood there, leaning agains the wall in the corner of the room, waiting for her. He took both her hands.

"Well, what?" he asked.

"Of course, yes."

In a few minutes the whole house knew what had happened.

6

Congratulations in the household were not unanimous. The news threw father Bers into a rage. He refused at first to give his consent, for he had expected Tolstoy to propose to his eldest daughter. But the mother's tactful diplomacy, Sonya's tears, and even Liza's generous pleading won a begrudging blessing from him.

Tolstoy's choice of Sonya, however, caused some embarrassment. The day after the proposal, the name-day of Sonya and her mother, was turned into an occasion for announcing the engagement to many visiting relatives and friends. Sonya and Liza, as usual, were dressed alike—lilac gowns with white *barège* trimmings, open collars, and lilac bows at the waist and on the shoulders. Both girls were pale and received the guests with tired eyes. To the customary name-day felicitations, the mother at first made the mistake of announcing to the guests that her daughter must also be congratulated on her engagement to Tolstoy. Many promptly turned to the crimson and suffering Liza with the customary exclamations. One of her old professors, even when apprized of the mistake, naïvely remarked: "It is a shame that it was not Liza; she was such a good student." Horror chilled Sonya when she saw in the throng the happy face of young Polivanov, resplendent in his new Guards uniform. Her brother perhaps prevented a scene by taking him aside and telling him the fatal news. Later, Sonya sought him out in an effort to explain. Her letter to Petersburg had not reached him.

"I knew," the unhappy Polivanov declared with tears in his eyes, "that you would forsake me; I felt it."

The only solace Sonya could offer her childhood sweetheart was that she could forsake him only for one man—Tolstoy.

"Bridegroom, gifts champagne," was Tolstoy's sole comment in his diary on this day of celebration. In his bliss he did not forget to write to Granny, that faithful friend whom he might have married, if she had only been "ten years younger." He informed her of his approaching marriage, and then with the pardonable exaggeration of the insensate lover, he added: "I would have to write volumes to give you any understanding of what she is like; I have never been so happy since I was born."

Whatever sense of personal loss Granny may have felt over this announcement, she rose nobly to the occasion, expressing her delight at the thought of acquiring "a charming granddaughter," and concluding: "There, now, our prodigal son is bound forever. I rejoice, rejoice, rejoice!"

Over the strenuous objections of mother Bers, Tolstoy demanded that the marriage take place as soon as possible. The trousseau and various other preparations he impatiently brushed aside as needless delays. Finally, a date just one week after his proposal was decided upon. Every day he visited Sonya. With the conviction that there should be no secrets between them, he turned over his diaries to her, and with the unwisdom of a girl of eighteen she allowed herself to peer into this history of his past excesses and moral lapses. "I remember," she wrote later, "how terribly shocked I was by the reading of these diaries that he gave to me before my marriage out of a sense of personal duty. I wept much upon glancing into his past, but to no purpose." Sonya forgave all, though she now feared to lose the love of this man.

Tolstoy had his own fears and doubts, the doubts that had tormented him from the moment he fell in love with Sonya. On the morning of his marriage day, September 23, he violated all proprieties by suddenly appearing at her home. He at once overwhelmed her with questions and doubts about her love for him. It seemed to her as though he were afraid of marriage. Sonya began to weep. Her mother scolded him for his behavior and he immediately left.[1] Later he wrote in his diary: "On the day of the marriage, fear, disbelief, and dislike of the ceremony."

The marriage was to take place in the evening in the Court church of the Kremlin. Sonya's attendants dressed her in her wedding gown and veil. Then they awaited the arrival of Tolstoy's best man to tell them that the bridegroom was at the church. The minutes passed and still no news. A terrifying thought flashed into Sonya's mind, prompted by her painful session with Tolstoy that morning, that he had actually run off. Finally, instead of the best man, Tolstoy's

[1] This whole incident, as well as others connected with his marriage, are faithfully retold in the marriage scene of Levin and Kitty in *Anna Karenina*.

faithful valet arrived with the agitated explanation that his master had no clean dress shirt. Everything had been packed and sent to the Bers house. A clean shirt was finally procured and after another long wait, the news came that Tolstoy was at the church.

The bridal party set out. Many people crowded the church which was brightly illuminated for the wedding. The priest in his sacerdotal headgear and vestments of heavy silver cloth met Tolstoy and his bride at the door and led them to the altar. Sonya's thin arms and shoulders emphasized her extreme youthfulness. Spectators whispered comments on it and on her weeping. Perhaps some said, as they did of Kitty in *Anna Karenina:* "What a darling the bride is, like a lamb decked for the slaughter." The beautiful Russian Orthodox ceremony, enhanced by the lovely music of the invisible choir that harmoniously filled the church from the windows to the vaulted roof, lasted a long time. After the marriage the party drove back to the bride's house where guests were provided with a bountiful repast and much champagne.

The new *dormeuse* (sleeping carriage) that Tolstoy had bought for the occasion waited outside. He was impatient to be off for Yasnaya Polyana. The tearful farewells between Sonya and her family were painfully prolonged. Finally tearing herself away with difficulty from her sobbing mother, Sonya entered the carriage and they began their journey. Burying herself in a corner, the bride, worn out from weariness and grief, did not cease to weep. Tolstoy was a bit hurt. An orphan for most of his life, he found it difficult to understand Sonya's copious tears on parting from her parents. He wrote cryptically of that night in the diary: "She is weepy. In the carriage. She knows everything and it is simple. . . . But she's afraid."

On the evening of the next day they arrived at Yasnaya Polyana. Tolstoy's brother Sergei welcomed them with the traditional hospitality of bread and salt, and Auntie Tatyana with an icon of the Virgin. Bride and groom bowed, kissed the image and then Auntie Tatyana. Their long and eventful life together at Yasnaya Polyana had begun, and under the most auspicious circumstances. The next day Tolstoy jotted down in his diary: "Incredible happiness! . . . It cannot be that all this will end only with life!"

PART THREE

"There is the Third Period . . .

in Which

I Lived a Correct,

Honorable Family Life . . ."

XVI

The Porcelain Doll

At times such bliss seemed unreal to the newly-made husband. Less than a week after the event, Tolstoy hurried off a letter to Granny: "As I write I hear from upstairs the voice of my wife, whom I love more than anything in the world; she is talking with my brother. I have lived to the age of thirty-four and did not realize that one may love so and be so happy." And two days later, as though amazed that such happiness could last a whole week, he jotted down in the diary: "I don't recognize myself. All my mistakes are clear to me. I love her just as much, if not more."

Back in Moscow Tatyanchik the Imp impatiently awaited news from her married sister, and when the letter arrived it was filled with the self-satisfaction of a happy bride. There were exclamations over the gracious reception accorded her by all and praise for the charming appointments of her new home. Sonya no doubt exaggerated for effect, for no special bridal furnishings had displaced the Spartan simplicity of the large bare rooms of Yasnaya Polyana. As for her husband, she only discreetly hinted at the immensity of his love for her, as though it had already become a hallowed subject. But she added a sophisticated touch for the benefit of her younger sister: "I'm afraid to think about the future, for now one does not dream as a virgin, but directly knows one's fate, only it is terrible to think of spoiling it. Being still a little girl, you do not understand this; when you are married, you will understand." Then putting aside the mystery and the burden of marriage for a moment, she asked Tanya to send her the warm boots and face powder that she had forgotten. Tolstoy tacked on a humorous postscript. "You see," he wrote to Tanya, "how all this is fine and touching, especially the thoughts about the future and the powder. . . . Farewell darling, and may God give you such happiness as I now enjoy. More does not exist."

A lyric ecstasy filled the letters and diaries of the happy couple during their honeymoon days. In his rosy frame of mind, Tolstoy could not resist a note to Fet, to whom he had not written since his quarrel with Turgenev. With that curious conviction of the lover that all humanity must be absorbed in his personal good fortune, he abruptly announced to his friend: "I've been married for two weeks and am happy, and a new, entirely new, man!" The new feelings that he was experiencing defied his passion for analysis. He tried to take an inventory of the reasons for his sensations and reactions, but he succeeded only in reducing them to trifles that in turn added up to something beyond his immediate powers of comprehension. In the diary he wrote: "I love her at night, or in the morning when I awake and see: she looks at me and loves. And no one, especially not I, prevents her from loving me in her manner, as she understands it. I love her when she sits close to me and we know that we love each other, as only we are able to, and she says: 'Lyovochka,' and then adds: 'Why are chimneys built so straight?' Or: 'Why do horses live so long?' etc. I love when we are alone, and I say: 'What are we to do? Sonya, what are we to do?' She laughs. I love when she gets angry with me, and in the twinkling of an eye, her thoughts and words sometimes sharp, she says: 'Let me be, you bore me.' In a moment she smiles timidly at me. I love when she does not see me and does not know that I love her in my fashion. I love her when she is a little girl in a yellow dress and sticks out her lower jaw and tongue at me. I love when I see her head tilted backwards, her serious, frightened, childish, and passionate face. I love when . . ."

2

If a full measure of felicity is taken for granted in a newly married couple, so also is the disintegrating effect annihilating time may have on it. The honeymoon ardor ran its course rather soon, and the disillusioning period of adjustment set in. Hardly a week had passed after their arrival at Yasnaya Polyana when the first tiff took place. Others followed in alarming succession, for both husband and wife were extremely sensitive, and each seemed bent on creating more than the usual number of difficulties that complicate early married life.

Sonya was immensely flattered with her new title of Countess and with being mistress of a large house. But even in these attractive circumstances, existence in the country soon became a trying matter. She was a city girl, only eighteen, accustomed to the theater, music, balls, and to merry parties of young folk. There was none of this at Yasnaya Polyana. Almost the only people she saw, besides the members of the household, were provincial neighbors and the uncouth wayfarers that her husband liked to bring home or the peasants he often took delight in talking to. Tolstoy tried to amuse her in the long autumn and early winter evenings. They read *Les Misérables* together, and he taught her English. She made clear copies of his manuscripts, and even attempted to help with his school, which still dragged on for a brief period.

Although Sonya was eager to take an active part in her husband's work in the country, she found it extremely difficult to adapt herself to this new way of life. Frequently she was left alone with no resources of her own to fall back on. Tolstoy would shut himself up in his study, or go hunting, or more often busy himself with the affairs of his estate. For at this time, perhaps because of the feeling that he would soon be a family man, he experienced anew a desire to expand and improve his property. He began the cultivation of bees, bought a herd of sheep, planted numerous fruit trees, and planned to set up a distillery to which Sonya and even her father objected as immoral. He plunged into these new enterprises with zeal, and Sonya tried to share his enthusiasm. She bravely declared her desire to work in the dairy, but the smell of the cowshed nauseated her. Tolstoy was annoyed by her city-bred squeamishness.

Over these first months of marriage after the honeymoon, the diaries of both husband and wife were turned into frank confessions of their quarrels, reconciliations, and painful efforts to build their love on a foundation of mutual understanding and self-sacrifice. This fact is all the more surprising since, by agreement, each had free access to the other's diary. There is a marked difference, however, in the uses to which they put their respective records. Tolstoy, as formerly, made his an impartial history of events and an inventory of his thoughts and feelings; Sonya, by her own admission, took to her diary when things went wrong, when she felt the need of seeking relief by pouring out her dissatisfactions and sorrow in its pages. The result is that her diary more frequently presents a dark, one-sided picture of her existence.

About two weeks after her marriage, Sonya expressed the gloomy conviction in her diary that Tolstoy did not believe in her love, and that she could not forget, as she ought to, her stupid, childish dreams of an ideal husband. Intellectually and emotionally jealous of Tolstoy's capacity for self-sufficiency, she was too young and inexperienced to accept him as she found him. It was hard to surrender her story-book notion of married love for the commonplace reality of daily life on a country estate. Then, too, her penchant for seeking misery in her happiness, her fondness for sitting, like Stephen, melancholy upon a stool, complicated the simple adjustments that any young bride has to make. "I'm terribly, terribly sad," began her entry on October 11. "I retire into myself more and more. My husband is ill, out of spirits, does not love me. I expected this but did not think it would be so awful. . . . No one knows that I'm unable to create happiness either for myself or for him."

Complaints about her inability to fill up the hours of the day ran like a litany through the early pages of Sonya's diary. Rather bitterly she wrote: "It is not difficult to discover an occupation; there are many of them. But one must first develop a liking for these trifling matters—winding up the clock, banging on the piano, reading many stupid things and very few fine ones, and pickling cucumbers. All this will come about, I know, when I manage to forget my idle girlhood life and get accustomed to the country."

Such a reformation came very hard. When Tolstoy was away, the house was like a tomb to her. "I live for him, by him," she protested, "and I wish him to be the same. It is oppressive for me here, and today I ran off, because everything and everybody had become disgusting to me. . . . I could hardly keep from laughing for joy when I ran softly out of the house. . . . If I do not absorb him, if I'm a doll, if I'm only a wife and not a human being, then I cannot live so and do not wish to. Of course I'm an idler, yes, but I'm not such by nature, and yet I do not know; chiefly I'm not convinced in what and where I'm to busy myself."

Tolstoy was fully aware of the trying period his young wife was going through, but he was not disposed to make many concessions. In his long bachelor existence he had fallen into ruts that were now not easy to climb out of. He had grown accustomed to being alone with his thoughts and work and could not, like a lovesick young swain, attach himself everlastingly to the skirts of his girl wife. Perhaps he expected her—the fate of so many wives of great husbands—to make herself over in his image and merge her individuality into his. At best, however, Sonya could never do much more than compromise with such a demand.

The disturbing doubts that tortured Tolstoy before his proposal returned more than once. "Today there was a *scene,*" he wrote in his diary only a week after marriage. "I was sad at the thought that we behave just like others. I told her that she had offended me in my feeling for her; I wept. She's charming. I love her even more. But is there not something false?" A few days later he listed two more disputes, but his love, he insisted, was stronger, although now different.

Yes, there was a palpable difference in Tolstoy's love and he had already begun to assay it. His state of mind at this juncture is faithfully reflected by the autobiographical Levin in *Anna Karenina.*[1] Shortly after his marriage Levin was happy, but not in the manner he had expected. At every turn he grew disillusioned with his former dreams only to discover unexpected new charms. During his bachelorhood he had regarded with some scorn the trifling cares, disputes, and jealousies of married couples, and he had convinced himself that nothing like this would exist in his own married life. He found, however, that insignificant trifles took on an unusual and indisputable importance. In a similar fashion, Tolstoy's search for family happiness forced him into endless compromises with trifles. He understood their significance, but he submitted with reluctance. His bachelor ideal of family happiness, like Levin's, vanished forever. If the compensations brought him much real joy, they also fettered the wings of his genius.

3

The ubiquitous ghosts and even the living images of women in her husband's past haunted Sonya and were the cause of much of their quarreling. She struck a note of protest on the very first page of her diary after marriage, and she con-

[1] See Part V, Chapter XIV.

tinued to strike it with morbid persistence. "All his past is so awful for me," she wrote, "that it seems I will never become reconciled to it." A precious part of him—his golden youth with its eager passion—had been forever lost to her. Her reactions were natural enough for a girl of eighteen: her own purity had been polluted by the many women who had preceded her. And her imagination insistently conjured up these predecessors: "He kisses me, and I think: I'm not the first to attract him. . . . I also have been captivated, but only in my imagination, whereas he has been fascinated by women, real, pretty, with characters, faces, and souls of their own, which he loved and by which he was captivated, just as he is captivated by me, at least for the present."

No doubt Sonya had in mind a particular woman—Tolstoy's recent peasant love, Aksinya. By chance less than three months after the marriage Aksinya was ordered to wash the floors of the manor house, and she was pointed out to Sonya as "that woman." The ardent lines devoted to Aksinya in Tolstoy's diary had stuck in Sonya's memory. That day she jotted down a few venomous ones of her own. "Sometimes I think I'll put an end to myself from jealousy," her diary reads. " 'I'm in love as never before!'[2] A simple wench, fat, fair; it is horrible! With what satisfaction I just now looked at a dagger, a gun. One blow—easy. While there's yet no child.[3] And she is right here, several steps away. I'm simply like an insane woman. I'm going for a drive. I can see her at this moment. How he loved her! If one could only burn his diary and all his past."

Here was the stuff of tragedy and a theme worthy the creative powers of her husband.[4] One can sympathize with the young wife's fury, although she knew that her husband had severed all relations with Aksinya shortly before his marriage. If she could only kill him and create him anew, Sonya reflected, she would do it with pleasure. Years later, after his death, she told his former secretary, and perhaps with Aksinya in mind, that in her first year of marriage she used to dress as a peasant girl and roam about the secluded forest paths near the house in the hope that Tolstoy would mistake her for his lover and hail her by the name she wished to ascertain. Aksinya continued to stalk her thoughts.

[2] A line in Tolstoy's diary about his love for Aksinya.
[3] Apparently Aksinya was pregnant by Tolstoy at this time.
[4] The manuscript of *The Devil,* the tale inspired by his relations with Aksinya, Tolstoy concealed from his wife.

She saw her in a terrible dream that she described in her diary. The peasant women of the village appeared in the garden, all dressed up as ladies of fashion. "The last to enter was Aksinya in a black silk dress," wrote Sonya. "I talked with her, and such a vicious feeling came over me, that I at once seized her child from somewhere and began to tear it into bits. In my fearful rage I ripped off feet, head —all. Lyovochka came; I told him that they would send me to Siberia. But he gathered up the legs, arms, all the parts, and said that it was nothing, only a doll. I looked, and in fact instead of a real body, there was only cotton-wool and leather. And this vexed me."

One need be neither a medieval necromancer nor a modern Freudian to read the proper interpretation into this horrific farrago from the world of dreams. However excusable was Sonya's jealousy of Aksinya, there was little sense to her childish fears about other women at this time. She complained bitterly because her husband liked to play duets with Olga Islenev, her cousin, who visited them at Yasnaya Polyana, and there were moments when even her younger sister Tanya fell under suspicion. And after reading the letters of Granny and Valerya to Tolstoy, she could not suppress a jealous pang over the part these two women had played in her husband's life. Perhaps just because of her intense love, she was jealous of everyone and everything that surrounded him. Her diary clearly shows that she tended to be hostile to any interest of her husband that did not immediately serve their mutual affection. Even the inner world of creative fancy that he liked to retire to often caused her qualms, for she feared he would find there support and sustenance independent of her love.

4

For the first three months at Yasnaya Polyana the Tolstoys rarely visited and had few callers. Late in December the couple packed themselves off to Moscow for the Christmas holidays. To her delighted sister Tanya, Sonya seemed pale and thin. She was already pregnant.

After the solitude of the country, the resumption of her former gay Moscow existence was not an unmixed blessing for Sonya. She now had to visit and be visited by Tolstoy's friends, often people she had never met before and of some of whom she stood in awe. It was a trial for the young bride. There were fashionable clothes and hats to buy, and a fastidious husband to please in the matter, for Tolstoy had very definite opinions about female attire, as he had about nearly everything. He came into the room suddenly when she was trying on a new hat, a modish creation, very high in front, covering the ears, and adorned with a chin strap.

"What!" he exclaimed in horror. "Is Sonya going to visit in this Babylonian tower!" She stuck to her choice. The visit was made. Sonya felt ill at ease, timid, and got cross with him for not paying sufficient attention to her. The sisters of his old friend Dyakov were present. Sonya imagined that they behaved in a patronizing and condescending manner to her. She was jealous of them, especially of his former love Alexandra Obolenski. Tolstoy, on the other hand, was immensely pleased that all seemed to like his young wife.

In the end Sonya preferred to let Tolstoy visit without her. She had become self-conscious about her pregnant condition. One evening he went off to call on the Sushkovs, and promised to return at twelve as usual. The irritated Sonya remained with her mother and Tanya and whiled away the evening with an account of her life at Yasnaya Polyana. With the natural instinct of the happy bride, she garnished her narrative with glamour and gladness. But here and there a peevishness peeped through. "You know, Tanya," she complained, "I sometimes get bored with being 'grown-up'; the silence in the house vexes me, and I feel an irresistible need for jollity and action. I leap about, run, and remember you when we used to cut up, and you used to say that I was 'off my head.' And then Auntie Tatyana laughs good-naturedly, and, looking at me, says: 'Be careful, softly, my dear Sonya; think of your baby.' "

The hours wore on with this chatter until midnight. But no Tolstoy. Sonya grew quiet, then angry, and somewhat hysterical by the time one o'clock struck. She imagined all manner of accidents that might have happened, and was sure that Alexandra Obolenski was at the Sushkovs'. With difficulty her mother restrained her from returning to her hotel alone. Shortly after one, Tolstoy entered. Sonya, her nerves at the breaking point, burst into tears. In consternation he tried to comfort her, begged her pardon, and fell to kissing her hand.

"Darling, sweet," he pleaded, "calm yourself. I was at the

Aksakovs', where I met the Decembrist Zavalishin;[5] he interested me so much that I did not notice how the time passed."

Scenes, tears, and reconciliations were a regular diet during the six weeks of their Moscow sojourn. "Every such quarrel, however insignificant, marks a diminution of love," Tolstoy noted in his diary. What he did not always perceive was that in this purging fire of doubts and uncertainties their love was gradually assuming a new aspect of greater calm and strength. Their diaries clearly reveal this slow transformation. He observed her morbid fear and jealousy, and compared her to other women to her disadvantage. "Since morning, dresses. She dared me to object and I did: tears, nonsense, explanations. . . . We made it up somehow. On these occasions I'm always dissatisfied with myself, especially with the kisses—this is a kind of sham cement. . . . At dinner the cement fell away; tears, hysterics. The best indication that I love her is that I did not get angry. It all grieved me, terribly grieved and saddened me. I went out to forget and distract myself. . . . To remain at home with her is painful. Without doubt much has begun insensibly to weigh on my heart. I feel that she suffers, but I suffer still more, and I can say nothing to her—for there is nothing to say. I'm simply cold, yet it is with warmth that I must comprehend everything. She will cease to love me; I'm almost convinced of this. The only thing that can save me is for her not to love anybody else. . . . 'You are good,' she says. I don't like to hear that; it makes me think that she does not love me." Two weeks later, however, he wrote: "On the very best of terms with my wife. The ebb and flow now do not surprise and frighten me. Although it is not so at present, I rarely have any fear now; she is young, and there is much she does not understand and does not love in me, and there is much in herself that she strangles for my sake, and all these sacrifices must instinctively be chalked up against me." By the time he returned to Yasnaya Polyana, he was able to reflect the happy feeling of complete reconciliation: "I feel fine, fine, and I love her so!"

[5] D. I. Zavalishin, one of the rebels exiled by Nicholas I for his part in the Decembrist Revolt of 1825. The records indicate that Zavalishin was not in Moscow at this time. He corresponded with Aksakov, however, and no doubt Tolstoy talked about him with Aksakov. Such a statement was perhaps incorrectly remembered by Tanya Bers, the authority for this incident.

5

If we may accept the evidence of her diary, Sonya was heartily glad to leave Moscow and return to Yasnaya Polyana. By now the purging fire had badly singed, if not utterly destroyed, some of her fine-feathered notions of married life. There was nothing in the world dearer to her than Lyovochka, she told herself. Only to be alone with him in the country, away from his exacting Moscow friends—that would be heaven. She now saw no reason why she could not create happiness for herself at Yasnaya Polyana. Thoughts of the coming child banished her former restlessness.

If quarrels were less frequent and love less strained, a worm of discontent did not cease to gnaw at Tolstoy over most of the period of his wife's pregnancy. He was an active, passionate man, and the passivity, even frigidity, of Sonya, now accentuated by her condition, preyed upon his mind. Not unlike many young brides, she evinced a fear and disgust for physical relations. About two weeks after marriage, she wrote in her diary: "All physical manifestations are so repugnant." And this common difficulty, requiring sympathetic understanding and delicate adjustments, was apparently magnified by his inordinate demands. The tension increased with the months of pregnancy, evoking a desperate protest from Sonya. "Lyova deserts me more and more," she noted in her diary. "The role of the physical side of love plays a great part with him. And that is awful. For me, on the contrary, it means nothing." At times she grew frantic at the thought that she would lose him. "I feel that I have become unendurable to him; now I have only one purpose—to leave him in peace, to take myself out of his life as much as possible. I can bring him no pleasure now because I'm pregnant."

Tolstoy curiously connected this sexual coldness with Sonya's pronounced inactivity and general lack of interest in everything that went on around her. He called her a doll, and in a letter to her sister Tanya he betrayed in a psychic manner his intense emotional dissatisfaction. The letter was a joint effort, indicating his intention that Sonya should read what he wrote. His part amounted to a short story, to which has actually been given the title, "The Tale of the Porcelain Doll." Although on the surface it claimed to be nothing more than a joking performance, composed to amuse Tanya and her parents, it was executed with all his literary skill and concealed a profound meaning. Sonya began it and then Tolstoy took hold. In a seriocomic vein he told how he fell asleep, and suddenly his wife entered the room. "I opened my eyes and I saw Sonya, not the Sonya whom we know, but a porcelain Sonya!" He then vividly described her appearance and his own consternation over this weird transformation. "She did not look at me," he continued, "but past me at her own bed; it was obvious that she wanted to lie down, and she swayed back and forth. I did not know whether I was standing on my head or my feet; I seized her and wanted to carry her to bed. My fingers did not press into her cold porcelain body, and what struck me even more was that she had become as light as an empty glass phial. And suddenly she seemed to shrink, as it were, and became tiny, smaller than the palm of my hand, although she still looked just the same." He placed her on a pillow, put out the light, and lay down beside her. Then he heard her voice: "'Lyova, why have I become porcelain?' I did not know what to answer. Again she spoke: 'Does it make any difference that I am porcelain?' I did not wish to grieve her and said that it did not matter. I felt her in the darkness —she was so cold and porcelain. But her belly was the same as when she was alive, protruding upwards in a cone shape, a little unnatural for a porcelain doll." After he had fondled the doll for a while, they both went to sleep. Tolstoy ended the story by relating that the next day Sonya became her own live self, but that every time they were alone, she turned into porcelain. "She is not dismayed by this," he concluded, "nor am I. To put it frankly, however strange it may be, I'm glad of this, and despite the fact that she is porcelain, we are very happy." It is difficult to believe that Sonya missed the point of the story, but she naïvely added to this letter to Tanya: "He has invented this that I am porcelain; such a rascal! But what does it mean— God knows."

Whatever amusement was intended—and the Bers family regarded the story only as a pleasantry—the letter unquestionably reflected a serious difficulty in the intimate relations between husband and wife. Yet it would be a mistake to construe his tale of the porcelain doll as evidence of a permanent lesion in their physical life together. Uneven as this was at the time, their life together was essentially a happy one. Only the day after his letter to Tanya, he noted in the diary: "I love her always more and more. Today is the fifth month, and I experience what I have not experienced for a long time—a feeling of frustration before her. She is so impossibly pure and fine and substantial for me. At these moments, I feel that I do not possess her; despite the fact that she gives herself entirely to me. I do not possess her, because I do not dare to; I do not feel myself worthy. I'm nervously irritated and therefore not *completely* happy. Something torments me. Jealousy of that person who would be completely worthy of her. I'm not worthy."

6

As Sonya's time approached, the couple were drawn still closer together in that mysterious community of feeling evoked by the unknowable future that they both awaited. "I, happy man, still live," Tolstoy wrote his sister. "I listen to my child's kicking in Sonya's belly." He planned the education of his unborn child, read medical books, and, as Sonya put it, "continually examines my abdomen" in an effort to determine exactly the eventful day. He would suddenly enter the room after reading an authority on obstetrics and abruptly announce to his wife: "He already has toe nails," to which Sonya would be on the point of replying: "Who?" before she recollected herself.

The uneventful country existence that had formerly seemed so dull to Sonya now cheerfully absorbed her with its numerous details. She no longer played with dolls, as Tolstoy jokingly wrote Fet, but had become his serious helpmate in the affairs of the estate. He had dismissed his steward and clerks on the theory that they were simply a hindrance to efficient management, and, singlehanded, directed the work while Sonya took charge of the office and accounts. Fet, paying a visit to Yasnaya Polyana at this time, found Tolstoy in working clothes busily directing the dragging of his pond and taking all possible care that the carp should not escape. Sonya came running down the path with a huge bunch of keys hanging at her waist. After gaily greeting Fet, she leaped over a low railing between the path and the pond, despite her "exceedingly interesting condition." At dinner that night, Fet remarked, some of the captured carp made their appearance at the table. All seemed merry and filled with hope, and kind old Auntie Tatyana beamed over the happiness of her *cher Léon.*

The eagerly expected first-born arrived on June 28, 1863, and was christened Sergei. One of the greatest scenes that Tolstoy ever wrote, the birth of Kitty's first child in *Anna Karenina,* was directly inspired by his emotional reaction to the birth of Sergei. How close his art could be to reality may be observed by comparing this scene in the novel with the rather full record of his experience in his diary. "At the crucial time," he wrote in this detailed account, "I was both agitated and quiet, occupied with trifles as before a battle or during a moment close to death. I was annoyed with myself that I felt so little." He held Sonya during her labor pains, "and I felt how her body trembled, stiffened, and she grimaced; and I never before experienced the feeling that her body conveyed to me, not even before marriage." He prepared for her the huge divan on which he himself had been born. "But in me," he continued, "there was always the same feeling of indifference and of self-reproach for it, and of irritation."

The birth of Sergei ended Tolstoy's preparatory period for the enjoyment of family life. There were some immediately stormy scenes, for his mother-in-law had descended on Yasnaya Polyana to be on hand for the arrival of her first grandchild. There were the usual sharp differences of opinion that sometimes developed into three-cornered battles on the care of infants. Sonya's mother and father took her side in the controversy that raged on the nursing of little Sergei. Because of Sonya's illness, the physician ordered her not to nurse the child herself. Tolstoy had obstinate and unreasonable ideas on this score, perhaps long ago suggested to him by his reading of Rousseau, and he demanded that the young mother should take complete charge of her infant. Although his son-in-law might be a master of language and literature, Dr. Bers angrily declared, he had no understanding of practical matters, and accordingly a wet nurse was engaged. Tolstoy believed Sonya capricious and wrote in his diary that she did not love him. But a little more thought on the matter and he realized his gross unfairness. In a penitent mood he wrote a confession of regret in her diary: "Sonya, forgive me; I know now that I have been at fault and how I've been at fault. There are days when you live, as it were, not by your own will, but subject to some external, irresistible law. Such I've been towards you these past days. I always thought I had many failings, but there is also a tenth part of feeling and magnanimity. I was rude and cruel, and to whom? To the one being who has given me the most happiness in life and who alone loves me. Sonya, I realize that this will not be forgotten or forgiven; but I know more than you and I understand all my own meanness, Sonya darling; I am at fault, and I am wicked. In me, however, there is an excellent man who sometimes sleeps. Love and do not blame him." Shortly after, in a fit of anger over some other offense, he crossed out all these fine sentiments. But soon one could see him trying to quiet the crying child by sticking a funnel in the infant's mouth and pouring milk into it with his large, trembling hand.

These tempests in the teapot, however, quickly passed. Despite his firm intention to share equally in all the cares connected with the bringing up of little Sergei, he soon manifested a father's indifference to his child in the infant stage. The baby interested him only as an essential part of the world that he dwelt in with his beloved wife.

And that world at last began to pay its premiums in family happiness. Soon after his marriage he had written to Granny: "I was getting weary of keeping accounts with myself, of continually turning over a new leaf (remember); I was growing accustomed to my vileness, and had begun to think of myself, if not absolutely, then as relatively good. Now I have renounced my past as I have never renounced it before. I feel my wickedness every moment; I compare myself to her, to Sonya, but 'I cannot wash out the mournful lines.' "[6] If he could not wash out the lines of his past, he discreetly drew a curtain between them and his present happiness. "Whoever is happy is right," he observed, and if thinking could make it so, he was happy now with his wife, his child, and with that golden vision of an ideal family life illuminating the path before him.

[6] A verse from Pushkin's "Recollections," one of Tolstoy's favorite poems.

XVII

An Epic Is Born

Tolstoy's spiritual quest was not compatible with any earthly ideal of happiness, for perfectibility did not exist this side of paradise for him. This kind of search the pleasures of marriage could interrupt but not terminate. Yet his spiritual existence was a part of him that his young wife imperfectly understood and always resented. Tolstoy realized that marriage had transformed the whole order of his life. He soon gave up his school and abandoned his pedagogical magazine, a release that once again turned his thoughts in the direction of creative writing. But a feeling of apathy in the midst of his happiness both saddened and irritated him. Less than a month after marriage he wrote in the diary: "Now I'm always occupied with matters that are dubbed practical. But this idleness is becoming burdensome to me. I cannot esteem myself. And therefore my relations with others are unsatisfactory and unclear. . . . All this annoys me, both my life and even hers. *I must work.*"

Tolstoy imagined that his spiritual and creative forces were being frustrated by the demands of his new existence, and this belief no doubt contributed somewhat to the periods of incompatibility of husband and wife. He wrote in the diary in a moment of distress over his inability to resume artistic work: "For the third time I've tried to write. It is frightful, terrible, insane to say that one's happiness is made up entirely of material circumstances: a wife, children, health, riches! Perhaps the poor idiot who runs the streets is right. One can have a wife, children, health, and the rest, but happiness is not in that. Lord, give me grace and aid me!"

Tolstoy's moody behavior in the early months of marriage often mystified Sonya, who complained that he was growing old, did not eat or sleep well, and spent most of his time wandering about the estate. In reality, however, marriage had little to do with his discontent and inability to write. This state of mind was a phase of his everlasting dualism that was subject to no order of life and was beyond the control of his own will. Even before his marriage, he had grown disillusioned with the educational work that he had undertaken more or less as an escape from what he thought was his failure as a literary artist. A similar confusion seems to have existed in Prince Andrei's mind in *War and Peace* when he blurted out to Pierre his bitter, misanthropic advice never to marry, at least, not until his life's work was done and he was an old man. No, the discontent was rooted in Tolstoy's own nature, and he confessed the fact in his diary: "I'm happy with her, but I am terribly dissatisfied with myself. I swing, swing under the mountain of death and scarcely feel strong enough to check myself. I don't wish to die, but I want and love immortality. There is no need to choose. The choice has long since been made. Literature, art, pedagogy, and the family. Inconsistency, timidity, laziness, weakness—these are my enemies."

Here Tolstoy realistically plumbed his state of mind. Not family concerns or the failings of Sonya stood in his way. On the contrary, the happiness that he at last found in marriage led him out of the impasse that had reached a crucial stage at about the time he became a frequent visitor at the Bers home. His emotional impulses had been localized, and the family ideal that he eventually realized temporarily resolved the inner struggle of his nature. His thoughts and energies once again had been freed for creative work.

2

Tolstoy was fond of saying that writing was just like childbirth; until the fruit had ripened it did not emerge, and when it did, it came with pain and labor. Yet he was as happy in producing novels as Sonya was in bringing forth children. In a creative ferment now, six months after his marriage he was impatient to rid his mind of all other concerns. The school and pedagogical magazine had irritated him by their lingering death. Even the manuscript of *The*

Cossacks that he owed to Katkov seemed like an obstacle, for his thoughts were spawning vaster designs. He had written the publisher to suggest that the agreement be canceled and he would refund the advance, for he saw no hope of finishing the novel. When he finally sent off the first part, he accompanied it with a note in which he gloomily wrote to Katkov: "Now, as always, I'm extremely dissatisfied with this tale, and I have corrected it again and again up to this very moment, but I do not feel it possible to work any more on it." And in the diary he tersely judged his performance: ". . . terribly weak. I suppose, therefore, that it will please the public." *The Cossacks* and *Polikushka,* which he had finished earlier, appeared in print at the beginning of 1863.[1]

Tolstoy's literary friends hailed his return to print after an absence of almost three years. Fet positively raved over *The Cossacks,* and Turgenev, still sulking like Achilles in his tent, emerged long enough to lavish generous praise. Dr. Bers, who had begun to take a keen parental interest in his son-in-law's literary work, wrote of his delight, amplifying it by a baffling professional observation that the nervous systems of the characters entirely corresponded to their muscular control. Tatyanchik the Imp, always a rabid partisan of Tolstoy, reported that everyone was in raptures over *The Cossacks,* but she quoted a letter from her fiancé, who informed her that readers in Petersburg "found the novel indecent and impossible to give to young girls. . . ."

Professional critics were not so uniformly enthusiastic. *Polikushka* went entirely unnoticed by them; *The Cossacks* they praised highly for its artistic worth, but all condemned the author's passionate protest against civilization. Tolstoy's intention had been to write a large work in three parts. However, the design of the novel had changed several times over the years that he had labored away at it, and perhaps because of his frequently interrupted efforts, a certain inconsistency is apparent in the characterization of the hero. Olenin changes from a world-weary youth who turns his back on civilization in the early sections to a philosophical reasoner who, at the end, searches for the personal happiness that was Tolstoy's own aim in 1862. Running through the story is a frank condemnation of society, and one may see in this a continuation of Tolstoy's hostility towards those critics who three years before had censored him for disregarding

[1] They were published in Nos. 1 and 2 of the *Russian Messenger.*

contemporary social factors in his writing. And once again a radical reviewer of the *Contemporary* flatly condemned Tolstoy's work because it lacked social content. The hero was brusquely dismissed as a "petty Hamlet," the contents as having no relation to the burning questions of the day, and the author as a willful exponent of the literature of escape.

Before his energies became entirely absorbed with the greatest creative effort of his life, Tolstoy, in the early months of 1863, tried his hand at a unique little tale, "Kholstomer," the story of a horse. The idea had long been in his mind. It will be remembered that once in the course of a walk with Turgenev, they had stopped before an old, broken-down jade, and the convincingness of Tolstoy's imaginary account of the sad-looking animal's thoughts and feelings had astonished and delighted his companion. With this inspiration, he now wrote his story based on the life of a real horse, Kholstomer, famous for his enormous stride and incredible speed.[2] He seemed to project himself into the consciousness of the poor, old piebald gelding of the tale as a great novelist might enter into the minds of the human beings he imagines. One is tempted to explain such artistic wizardry only in the words of Turgenev—that Tolstoy must at one time have been a horse himself. When Fet wrote to Tolstoy about his recent publications, he replied: "I live in a world so far removed from literature and its critics that upon receiving your letter my first feeling was one of surprise. Really who was it that wrote *The Cossacks* and *Polikushka*? And what is there to discuss about them? Paper endures anything and editors pay for and print anything. But this was only a first impression; afterwards I looked into the meaning of what you said, rummaged about in my head and found there in a corner, among old, forgotten rubbish, something obscure under the heading *Art*."

In fact, brief notes in the diary not long after his marriage hint at this renascence of the artistic urge to create something truly magnificent. A typical one reads: "Someone told me that I'm foolish not to use my time in writing. It is long since I remember having such a powerful desire, and a

[2] Dissatisfied with the results, Tolstoy put the manuscript aside. It was fished out twenty-two years later by his wife, who was then editing the first collected edition of his works and desired a new piece. After some urging, he agreed to print it, but not until he had thoroughly reworked the whole tale. It then appeared in 1886.

quiet, self-assured desire, to write." "The epic type would be a natural one for me," runs another entry. And shortly before the birth of his son, he jotted down: "I'm reading Goethe, and thoughts fairly swarm." Tolstoy's creative spirit was already prepared to grapple with the tremendous design of *War and Peace*.

3

In his letters and diary at the end of 1862 and the beginning of the next year, Tolstoy threw off various hints that he was contemplating a new novel. And in a letter to Granny in the autumn of 1863, his intention for the first time was declared in more definite language. She had gently reproved him in a letter for his long silence since his marriage. He was exactly like those novels, she had joked, that usually came to an end with the chapter about the marriage, that is to say, at the very moment life began to be most interesting. In his reply he described his happiness as a husband and father. "I do not burrow any more into my state of mind," he continued ". . . or into my feelings; I only feel and do not think in my family relations. This condition affords me tremendous mental scope. I have never felt my mental and even all my moral faculties so free and so ready for work. And this work now exists. It is a novel covering the years from 1810 to 1820, which has entirely occupied me since autumn. . . . Now I am an author with all my soul. I write and meditate as never before." He had at last embarked on the arduous creative path that led to *War and Peace*.

The gestation period of Tolstoy's great masterpiece was long and severe, and its birth was attended by much pain and labor. As early as 1856 he had contemplated a story, the hero of which was to be an exiled Decembrist.[3] And in a letter to Herzen, dated March 26, 1861, he informed him that he had actually begun this tale when abroad in the late autumn of 1860, but there is no further reference to any progress on the work. Now, in 1863, when he was casting about for a subject, he returned to this theme of the Decembrists. He selected 1856 as the time of the action of the novel, and for his hero a man who had returned home after having spent many years of exile in Siberia for his part in the abortive Decembrist Revolt of 1825.

[3] All the prefatory material, drafts and variants of *War and Peace* may be found in the Jubilee Edition (Vols. XIII-XIV).

After writing three chapters that contain an extraordinarily vivid picture of peasant life,[4] Tolstoy found himself involuntarily returning to the year 1825, when his hero's misfortunes began. Even at this time, however, the hero was a married man of mature age, and Tolstoy felt strongly that in order to understand him thoroughly he must study the period of his youth. Thus, putting aside all that he had written up to this point, he plunged into an investigation of the notable 1812 year. In this fresh beginning his hero receded more and more into the background and other figures, partly historical and partly of his own invention, took hold of his imagination. The logic of his expanding design drove him further down into the pages of Russian history until he reached the year 1805, at which point he made still a third beginning. By now the original hero and action had all but vanished. He could not seem to decide at what year to open the novel, but he finally settled on the period between 1805 and 1814.

It is clear that Tolstoy's final design comprehended an extensive trilogy, of which *War and Peace,* centered in the year 1812, was to be the first novel; the other two, connected but complete works in themselves, were to deal with the events of 1825 and 1856. Although the introductory chapters of the novel on 1856 exist, no manuscript drafts have come down to us concerning the theme of the Decembrist Revolt of 1825. Yet over the course of the next fifty years he never lost sight of his original desire to write a novel about the Decembrists.

Once Tolstoy had settled upon the external limits of *War and Peace,* the second and most difficult stage began—working out the plan and composition of the novel. When he started to write, he by no means had clearly in mind the succeeding course of events that would fill his vast canvas. Nor did the finished product six years later embody the artistic purpose with which he began. For the earliest outlines place the emphasis upon "peace." Historical events were intended to serve merely as a scaffolding or background for the development of a tale of family life among the gentry. The principal characters were to be subjected to a series of adversities that would undermine them spiritually, but in the end they would be regenerated and begin a

[4] These chapters have been published in the Jubilee Edition (Vol. XV); they have also been published in an English translation in René Fülöp-Miller's *Tolstoy* (N. Y., 1931).

quiet and happy life. The whole theme of "war" with its historical events and persons did not enter into the design of the novel until much later. Although this initial plan called for a kind of family novel in the spirit of Dickens, Tolstoy intended to charge it with an intense, contemporary appeal. This work was to serve as an answer to those critics who had so harshly condemned him for failing to treat in his fiction the burning problems of the day.

4

By September of 1863 Tolstoy was deep in *War and Peace*. The family circle and intimate friends buzzed with the news. Father Bers in Moscow enthusiastically acclaimed the project and sent his son-in-law batches of references to source material on Napoleon's invasion. Even the studious Liza, who by now had forgiven if not entirely forgotten her unrequited love, loyally answered an urgent request for aid: "I have fulfilled your commission dear friend Lyovochka; I have looked up the materials for your novel, and I'm sending you a list of books in which mention is made of the year 1812." There follows a long list carefully drawn up and meticulously annotated. At this point, the learned girl appears to have read much more on the subject than her brother-in-law. And from her detailed answers to his questions concerning these books, it is clear that at this stage Tolstoy was interested primarily in memoirs, letters, and human-interest stories. That is, he intended to place the emphasis upon the private lives of people rather than upon historical events.

At first this sudden, all-absorbing literary activity worried Tolstoy's wife. Besides, at the moment she was foolishly annoyed with him for an impulsive desire he had manifested to go off to war (Russian troops were being sent to put down a Polish rebellion). "What do you think of the Polish business?" he interpolated in a letter to Fet on other matters. "It looks bad! Shall we . . . not be obliged to take down our swords from their rusty nails? . . ." Sonya took this passing fancy seriously. Angrily she scribbled in her diary: "Now he's married, is pleased with himself, has a child, but he wants to throw it all over and go to war. . . . I don't believe in this love for the fatherland, in this *enthusiasm* at the age of thirty-five."

But her Lyovochka was really interested in another war, that of 1812, and he waged it on reams of paper, shut up in his study hours on end. "Where is he?" Sonya gloomily asked herself in the diary, and she answered, "The History of 1812. He used to tell me everything—now I'm unworthy. Formerly all his thoughts were mine. The minutes were happy, marvellous, now they are not."

As soon as Tolstoy had finished a small section of the novel, written in his nearly illegible handwriting, Sonya was promptly drafted to make a clear copy, and there began the long years of close association in his literary work. She developed into an invaluable assistant. With some justice she might have complained of the use that he made of her in this work. The poet takes the best out of his life and puts it into his writings, Tolstoy once declared, which is the reason his writing is beautiful and his life bad. However conscious Sonya may have been of the truth of this observation, and although she grew jealous at times of his complete absorption, she never ceased to take a passionate interest in his literary endeavors. She loved to copy *War and Peace,* she declared, and she copied a great deal of it as many as seven times. The consciousness of serving a genius and a great man gave her strength for anything, she wrote in her diary. As she copied the barely decipherable pages she felt uplifted, morally and spiritually. She was carried away into a world of poetry, and it seemed to her that it was not his novel that was so good but she who was so clever.

Not all of Tolstoy's material came out of books. His own life and the lives of many who made up his intimate world were drawn upon for *War and Peace,* as in the case of so many of his other works. Of particular importance at the moment was Tatyanchik the Imp. In the summer of 1863 she, her brother Alexander, her childhood sweetheart Kuzminski, and a certain Anatole, with whom she was carrying on a violent flirtation, were all invited to Yasnaya Polyana. The slim, supple, and graceful sixteen-year-old Tanya was original and attractive in appearance with her dark, slightly wavy hair, refined face, large mouth, and delicately tinted complexion. In her spontaneous nature that expressed itself in irresistible mirth, quick sensibility, and passionateness, Tolstoy found the model for his heroine Natasha Rostov, and he now observed Tanya's every movement.

The young people made Yasnaya Polyana ring from morn till night with their merrymaking. Tolstoy and his wife soon grew displeased with the sly, designing, handsome Anatole, and finally, offended by the impropriety of his conduct, they sent him packing. He reappeared again as the brilliant but calculating Anatole Kuragin in *War and Peace.*

Tanya, sad at losing Anatole, prolonged her stay several months after the others had left. A born coquette, however, she soon comforted herself by carrying on a flirtation with Tolstoy's brother Sergei, more than twice her age. He frequently visited Yasnaya Polyana. As the flirtation gave promise of becoming something more serious, despite Sergei's gypsy mistress and brood of illegitimate children, Tolstoy and Sonya grew disturbed. In vain Tolstoy warned her that a heart once given away cannot be taken back, and a tormented heart always bears a scar.

Tanya was devoted to Tolstoy; he seemed like a father to her and the one man, she said, who thoroughly understood her. When he looked at her with his penetrating eyes, she knew that she could keep no secrets from him. They were much together that autumn, often strolling through the paths of the ancient Zaseka woods that seemed to Tanya more majestic and beautiful than ever at sunset. She rode with him on the hunt, and in the evening sang for hours to his accompaniment on the piano.

In October the nobility of Tula gave a ball in honor of the young Tsarevitch, later Alexander III, who was visiting the city. The Tolstoys were invited. Sonya wept because illness would not permit her to attend; Tanya was in ecstasies, for Tolstoy promised to take her. All the fears, joys, triumphs, and breathless experiences of Tanya on that memorable night reappear in the unforgettable description of Natasha's first ball in *War and Peace.*

The next day Sonya pensively listened to her sister's rapturous account of the dance.

"Do you know, Tanya," she broke in, "I could not have gone even if I had been well."

"Why?"

"Surely you know Lyovochka's views. Could I dress in a ball gown with an open neck? This is entirely unthinkable. How often has he condemned married women who 'go naked,' as he expresses it."

There was truth in this—Tolstoy was extremely severe in such matters. He was even capable of grotesque fits of jealousy over the harmless attention that young men paid to his wife. There was also a twinge of jealousy, however, in

Sonya's reaction to Tanya's gala evening with her husband. Tolstoy continued to study Tanya's volatile nature, and he frequently engaged her in conversations about herself, while there gradually took shape in his imagination the charming image of Natasha Rostov.

5

In December, the Tolstoys, worried over the swift progress of Tanya's attachment for Sergei, took her back to Moscow. Sonya also required medical treatment in the city. During their stay of only a few days, Tolstoy visited literary friends, and with a nose keen for the scent of any material for the novel, he consulted the famous historian M. P. Pogodin. Katkov was also looked up in connection with the plans for the serial publication of *War and Peace*.

Upon his return to Yasnaya Polyana, Tolstoy sought relief from his labors on the novel by writing a comedy. The idea of doing a play had been in his mind since 1856, and several abortive attempts had been made. Perhaps the smoldering desire once again to pay off his critics among the radicals was behind this new and completed effort in five acts, *A Contaminated Family,*[5] for in it he depicted a typically vulgar group of representatives of the progressive movement of the 1860's. Among the principal characters was a landowner's daughter, with short hair, abbreviated skirt, spectacles, and a cigarette continually drooping from her mouth. In the jargon of the type, she regarded herself as an "emancipated woman," scorned the insignificance of the female provincial aristocratic rabble and the social web of prejudices, and while living off the substance of her wealthy uncle, she scorned him also. Then there was an ignorant, conceited radical student who imagined himself the most advanced of intellectuals. The characters were well individualized, and for all his own sympathies Tolstoy portrayed with commendable impartiality members of both the old and the new orders.

Father Bers in Moscow, delighted with this new literary venture of his son-in-law, busied himself with theatrical people in an effort to arrange for the production of the comedy. By the beginning of February, Tolstoy had finished

[5] This play is little known in English. It has been translated, under the title of *The Progressives,* in Fülöp-Miller's *Tolstoy.*

the play, and he and Sonya hurried up to Moscow, filled with the exciting prospect of seeing his first dramatic work on the stage. As an initial precaution, Tolstoy invited his friend, the celebrated dramatist A. N. Ostrovski, to hear him read *A Contaminated Family*. The growling, bearlike Ostrovski let Tolstoy off lightly with the terse remark that the play had too little action and ought to be reworked, but to Nekrasov he wrote a very unflattering comment: "It was so hideous that I positively had to stop my ears at his reading."

Tolstoy went blithely ahead and submitted the play for production. He was disappointed, for he was informed that it was too near the end of the season for the theater to attempt a new piece. He and Sonya returned to Yasnaya Polyana, and from a statement in a letter to his sister shortly after, it appears that he began to have doubts about his play, for he wrote: "Among other things I've done a comedy that I wanted staged at Moscow, but I had no success before Shrovetide, and the comedy, it seems, is poor; it was all written to ridicule the emancipation of women and the so-called nihilists." *A Contaminated Family* was never produced or printed in his lifetime,* but his interest in drama and the stage eventually bore rich fruit.

6

Tolstoy returned to his novel, but over the next six months there were periods when he wrote little. Much of his time was spent in hunting, or on business trips to the estates of his brother and sister. Sonya disliked his being away from home. She grew melancholy, and the fear that he would suddenly die haunted her. Her letters were cheerless accounts of daily tasks and of worries over her son. His answers were chatty, amusing, and comforting. To the charge that he had forgotten her, he wrote: "Not for a moment, especially when I'm with people. On the hunt, however, I do forget; I remember only about a particular woodchuck. . . ." In another, announcing his return home, he wrote: "Tomorrow morning I will be leaving, and by evening I will be feeling your watermelon and seeing your dear face." (Sonya was again far gone in pregnancy and gave birth to a daughter, Tatyana, on October 4, 1864.)

Auntie Tatyana used to say: "Our dear Tanya will come

*It was not published in Russian until 1928.

with the grasshoppers." And with the spring the Imp was back at Yasnaya Polyana. No doubt she hoped to see Sergei, to whom she was now engaged, but she had promised to wait a year before marriage because of her extreme youth. Sergei, however, was waging a losing battle with his conscience, for he could not get himself to abandon his gypsy mistress of sixteen years' standing. Tolstoy, fully aware of all the joy and grief in this affair, tried sympathetically to prevent a catastrophe. At the same time his creative imagination was transforming the love of Tanya and Sergei into that of Natasha and Prince Andrei in *War and Peace*.

In his diary on September 16, 1864, Tolstoy jotted down: "It's almost a year since I wrote in this book and it has been a good year. Relations between Sonya and me have been strengthened, consolidated. We love, that is to say, we are dearer to each other than all other people in the world, and we see each other clearly. We have no secrets, nothing on our conscience. Meanwhile, I've begun a novel; I've written about 120 printed pages, but now I find myself in a period of correction and alterations. This is painful. Pedagogical interests are far removed. My son is not very close to me."

About ten days later Tolstoy set off on horseback to visit a neighbor. Two of his hunting dogs trailed after him. Suddenly a hare was sprung and the dogs were after it in a flash. He could not restrain himself. "Sick 'em!" he yelled, and galloped after the dogs. The horse, unused to the hunt, stumbled and fell, and Tolstoy also went down, breaking his right arm. He lay there in agony for some time before he could attract the attention of a passing peasant, and he had himself carried to a hut in the village rather than home, for he feared to frighten his pregnant wife. The arm was soon set by a Tula physician, but for weeks after he continued to suffer severe pain. Finally, deciding that it had been badly set and that an operation might be necessary, he went to Moscow towards the end of November.

Tolstoy remained at his mother-in-law's home for a little more than three weeks. A painful operation was performed, and he eventually recovered full use of his arm. Before and after the operation, he crowded his days with activity, most of it in connection with work on *War and Peace*. He shopped in the bookstores for material, consulted authorities on history, and spent hours reading in the libraries. The amount of historical research that he did for the novel, however, has often been exaggerated. He made no attempt to exhaust such material, for he read only up to the point where it became clear to him what use he wished to make of his sources.

Liza and Tanya Bers served as eager amanuenses when Tolstoy was unable to write because of his injured arm. With a concentrated expression on his face, and supporting his bad arm with his hand, he dictated to Tanya while walking back and forth across the room. "No, it's trite, won't do," he would talk to himself, forgetting her presence. In dictating, his tone was imperious, there was impatience in his voice, and often he changed his phrasing three or four times. Occasionally he dictated quietly, smoothly, as though he had it all by heart, and then the expression on his face became calm. The awed Tanya felt that she was doing something immodest, that she had become the involuntary witness of his inner world, a world concealed from all. The periods of quiet cold dictation he distrusted. Without agitation, he told his wife, the business of writing just did not get on.

Nor at this time could Tolstoy resist the desire to test a few of the initial chapters of his novel by reading them to friends. An evening was arranged by papa Bers at the Perfilyevs'. Guests gathered in the large, murky drawing room, illuminated by two oil lamps. To the observant Tatyanchik the Imp, the preparations took on all the solemnity of a christening. The plump hostess in her tall cap spangled with ribbons, seated in the middle of a high-backed divan, looked like a stuffed museum piece expecting a miracle to bring her to life. Tolstoy began with some confusion, weakly, hesitantly. Tanya suffered for him. But he quickly gathered confidence, firmness, and soon his brilliant reading carried all with him. These guests, intimates of the Bers family, began to look furtively at each other as they recognized the living models of many of the characters he described. When Natasha was introduced, Varya Perfilyev broadly winked at the blushing Tanya. And Tanya was delighted to hear the description of her own doll Mimi, and the true story of how she had asked Boris to kiss the doll and made him kiss her instead. This was not life transposed by art; it was life itself. And as all the guests crowded around to congratulate him at the conclusion of the performance, Varya Perfilyev excitedly cried out to her mother:—

"Why, Mama, Marya Dmitrevna Akhrosimov is you; she resembles you exactly!"

"I don't know, I don't know, Varya," replied the charmed hostess, "I'm not worth describing."

Tolstoy smiled and said nothing, but papa Bers was in seventh heaven over the success of his son-in-law.

Tanya regretted that Sonya was not present at this triumph. Hardly a day passed during Tolstoy's brief absence, however, that letters or telegrams were not exchanged between husband and wife. As always, Sonya's correspondence was largely a record of domestic trivia—her daily tasks, the diarrhea and smallpox of the children, and the various illnesses of cows, pigs, and sheep. She worried over his seeming lack of concern for little Sergei and Tanya, and she overwhelmed him with well-intentioned advice on how to take care of himself in Moscow. The temptations of the city troubled her imagination, and she confessed to being jealous of the women he might meet. But throughout these letters her love and infinite concern for everything that made up his life shone forth brightly. She missed him terribly. "With you I feel myself an empress, without you I'm superfluous." She pleaded for every last detail about the operation on his arm and about his work in Moscow. "Lord, how I should like to see you, talk and sit with you," she wrote after he had been gone only five days. "You know me, you know how I love you and that I'm wretched without you."

Sonya envied and perhaps was a little jealous of the privilege enjoyed by her sisters in Moscow of taking dictation on the novel. Tolstoy had left her some sections to copy, and she eagerly applied herself to this task at night, after the children were asleep and the house quiet. "How I like everything about Princess Marya!" she excitedly wrote him. "You see her so clearly. Such a splendid, sympathetic character. I will always criticize you. Prince Andrei, in my opinion, is not yet entirely clear." He had written her of his bargaining with Katkov, from whom he had demanded, and finally obtained, twenty-five rubles a printed page for serial publication of *War and Peace*. With a suggestion of that business astuteness that she later displayed in the publication of her husband's works, his young wife warned him not to print serially. All who took the *Russian Messenger*, she observed, would not buy the book when it appeared in this form, and these were the very people who could afford to purchase the book.

Tolstoy wrote Sonya how proud he was of her praise of the novel. Love, deep and tender, ran through nearly all of his letters to her during these few weeks in Moscow; and for her frequent moods of depression and anger over household worries or his absence, he had only words of understanding and sympathy. He flattered her intellectual powers. She belonged, he wrote, to the "Black Bers," with her mother and Tanya. Their minds slumbered, but they could do things if they wished to, and they loved passionately. That he did not inquire always about the children, he explained, was no reason for her to suppose that he was not interested. But he did not love them, he admitted, as much as he loved her. "Yesterday I explained to Tanya," he wrote in another letter, "why it is easier for me to bear a separation from you than it would be if I were not writing. Along with you and the children (I feel, however, that as yet I do not love them enough), I have a continual love or care for my writing. If this were not so, I really feel that I could not spend a day without you; this you will surely understand, for what writing is for me the children must be for you."

At the first opportunity he returned home, but only after he had handed over to his publisher the first thirty-eight chapters of *War and Peace,* a surrender that saddened him, he wrote Sonya, because he could no longer correct and improve them.

7

Was this full, contented existence Tolstoy's youthful ideal of family happiness? He seemed to think so now. In January 1865, he wrote to Granny:—

> Do you remember I wrote you once that people are mistaken in expecting some happiness or other in which there is no work, no deceit, no grief, and all goes smoothly and pleasantly? I made a mistake then. Such happiness exists, and I have been living it for the third year now, and with every day it becomes smoother and deeper. And the material of which this happiness is made is most unlovely—children who (pardon me) befoul themselves and squall, and my wife, who nurses one and leads the other around and reproaches me because I do not see that both are on the brink of the grave, and the paper and ink by means of which I describe the events and feelings of people who never existed.

Life at Yasnaya Polyana now flowed smoothly along those well-grooved ruts prescribed by the petty obligations and pleasant amenities of a happy family existence. The Tolstoys lived modestly, and the contented inertia that often takes possession of congenial married people made them loath to leave their isolated estate. They visited and were visited by few friends, but these were close and dear—the Fets, the Dyakovs, and members of the family, such as his brother and sister, grandfather Islenev, and above all Tanya. Her engagement to Sergei was finally broken off, for in the end his conscience had obliged him to marry his gypsy mistress and legitimize their children. Two years later the restless Tanya married, much against Tolstoy's advice, her cousin and childhood sweetheart, A. M. Kuzminski. Tolstoy's sister, who was much abroad,[7] left her two daughters, aged fourteen and fifteen, at Yasnaya Polyana for long periods of time, and they contributed to the jollity of the household.

Sonya was rapidly and completely identifying herself with the sphere Kaiser Wilhelm allotted to women: *Kirche, Küche, Kinder,* a division of interest that once prompted her husband to wonder what could possibly be left for the men. At first she had been somewhat fearful of him and regarded everything through his eyes. Even the litter that he had allowed to accumulate around the outside of the house in his bachelor days she feared to complain of. But two years of intimacy brought courage and determination. The model housewife Sonya bravely ordered the surroundings cleaned up, the paths fixed, and flowers planted.

Upon surveying the results, her husband remarked with a trace of annoyance: "I don't understand why all this. We lived very well without it."

But gentle Auntie Tatyana came to Sonya's rescue. "My dear Léon," she observed, "Sonya has done well in tidying up around the house; it is so much pleasanter now to promenade." In fact, although he had a masculine weakness for old clothes and for preserving things as they always had been, he quickly took his wife's hint, and all were surprised one day to discover him painting the benches in the garden and cleaning and trimming the paths. This was not merely part of the business of learning to be a husband; it was also devotion to Sonya.

In the management of the estate the more practical wife

[7] Her husband, from whom she was separated, died in 1865, but before this she had married abroad a Swedish viscount.

again set the pace. The new enterprises that Tolstoy had initiated shortly after his marriage required careful attention. There was no place here for the altruism of his youth in agricultural improvements and in the rehabilitation of his peasants. Changed circumstances curiously brought out in him at this time that latent aspect of the aristocratic landowner who forgot his social ideals in the face of the present necessity of providing for a growing family. Bitterly he wrote to the governor of the province to demand protection against peasants who stole his livestock and produce. And in a letter to his wife, while visiting one of his properties, he remarked with obvious irony that he had spent the night "in the hut of a dear Russian peasant," and he concluded: "What swine and sluts they are!"

The happy family life that could so easily divorce Tolstoy from his youthful ideals had also created that disposition of soul so vital to the free functioning of his art. For the present the struggle between spiritual perfection and material well-being had ceased. When he was shut up in his study, no one dared to disturb him. He wrote with irritation, often with tears and pain, but always with the conviction, as his wife expressed it, that this greatest creation of his genius must be superb. The road ahead was long and hard, but he took fresh courage at the thought that the first section of *War and Peace* would soon be published. With a feeling of elation he wrote to Fet in January 1865: "Do you know what surprise I have in store for you? After a horse threw me to the ground and broke my arm, and just as I regained my senses, I said to myself that I am an author. And I really am an author, but an isolated, furtive author. In a few days the first half of Part I or 1805[8] will appear. Please, write me your opinion of it in detail. Your opinion is dear to me, even more so than the opinion of a man whom I love less the more I grow up—Turgenev. He *will understand*. What I have printed formerly, I now regard only as a trial of the pen and a kind of draft of an *opus*. What I now print, although I like it more than my former work, seems weak, as introductions must be. But what comes after—tremendous!"

[8] This first part was published under the title "Eighteen Hundred and Five," in the February and March numbers, 1865, of the *Russian Messenger*.

XVIII

War and Peace

No READER could have guessed from the first part of *War and Peace* the massive superstructure that would be raised on this rather slight foundation. Least of all could Tolstoy have guessed it at the beginning of 1865. Drafts of early plans called for a family novel with a historical background. There were no indications of the vast sweep, the concentration on war, and the elaborate philosophy of history in the final scheme.

Tolstoy's desire to transform his novel into a mighty epic of war was first suggested in a passage in his diary in March 1865. After going through the memoirs of one of Napoleon's marshals,[1] he jotted down: "I read with delight the history of Napoleon and Alexander. At once I was enveloped in a cloud of joy; and the consciousness of the possibility of doing a great thing took hold of my thoughts—to write a psychological novel of Alexander and Napoleon, and of all the baseness, phrases, madness, all the contradictions of these men and of the people surrounding them." There then followed a brief but vivid sketch of the two rulers. And succeeding entries in the diary reaffirmed his delight with this changed purpose and his determination to carry it out.

Now new plans ran through all the cracks and zigzags of Tolstoy's creative mind, but they still failed to crystallize into the intricate pattern of *War and Peace*. Four days after he had conceived the idea of a psychological novel on Napoleon and Alexander, he entered in the diary: "Wrote little this evening; but pretty well. I can. Yet all this time my new thoughts become more important and I'm dissatisfied with the old." During the autumn and winter of

[1] *Mémoires du maréchal Marmont, duc de Raguse.*

1865 he worked hard and the design of the novel gradually expanded. Art was long and life short, he dolefully told Fet in a letter in December, and he complained of his inability to fulfill more than a fraction of what he had planned. By the end of the year he had the third part ready for printing.

The growing conviction that he was engaged in a major effort soon led Tolstoy to follow Sonya's advice to publish the novel in book form instead of serially in a magazine. While in Moscow in January 1866, he contracted with M. S. Bashilov, an artist and relative of his wife's family, to do a set of illustrations for a separate edition. He returned to Yasnaya Polyana much elated and "very pregnant" with new material. Throughout all of 1866, not even excepting the summer, when he usually rested from writing, he kept at the novel. Although the design had become more complicated, the genre changed, and the historical aspects had assumed an entirely new significance, it was clear that he had not yet fully grasped the final conception of the work. For in a letter to Fet, dated May 1866, he wrote that he hoped to finish the novel by the autumn of 1867 and to publish it in a separate edition with illustrations, and under the title *All's Well That Ends Well.* Tolstoy had miscalculated by two years the time of completion, and he had not yet hit upon the actual title, which fact suggests that the final historical and philosophical purpose still evaded him.

Several compelling factors, however, were inevitably directing Tolstoy's mind towards the ultimate design and execution of *War and Peace*. During the 1860's in Russia the subject of philosophy of history was much discussed in intellectual circles. The two problems most frequently posed were the relation of individual freedom to historical necessity, and the factor of causality in history. Nowhere was the subject more debated than in the homes of Tolstoy's Moscow Slavophile friends. Chief among them were the historian M. P. Pogodin, Yu. F. Samarin, well-known author of social, religious, and philosophical works, and S. S. Urusov, a brilliant but cross-grained theorist on mathematics and military strategy, whose acquaintance Tolstoy had made in his Sevastopol days. Between 1866 and 1868 Tolstoy often went to Moscow, usually in connection with his novel, and on his visits he rarely failed to meet and discuss with these friends who were so deeply interested in historical problems. No doubt Proudhon's work, *La guerre et la paix,* then much talked about in Russia, was also a frequent subject for discussion. Pogodin suggested that Tolstoy look into his book, *Historical Aphorisms,* and he also read at this time works of Joseph de Maistre.[2] All these discussions and studies helped to turn his mind towards that ultimate and vaster conception of his masterpiece as a medium for the full expression of a philosophy of history.

In an early unpublished foreword, apparently intended for the novel as Tolstoy first designed it, he wrote: "The life of officials, merchants, students, and peasants does not interest me, and I only half comprehend it; the life of the aristocrats of that time, thanks to the monuments of the age, and for other reasons, I do understand, and it is interesting and dear to me." Now his new historical design obliged him to study also the profound influence of the peasantry on the events of 1812. The immediate result was the creation of one of the finest characters in the novel, Platon Karatayev, that symbolic personification of the simplicity and truth living in the great gray masses of Russia.

In March 1867 Tolstoy at last hit upon the title *War and Peace,* and by then the future course of the novel was finally decided. Three months later, having given up his notion of an illustrated edition, he signed a contract with a printer to issue the volumes separately just as soon as he completed them, and he employed P. I. Bartenev, editor of the *Russian Archive,* to serve as proofreader.[3] For this was an independent publishing venture, and Tolstoy, while accepting the risks, stood to make a large profit if the novel sold well.[4]

In September Tolstoy visited the battlefield of Borodino before he undertook to write his famous description of that engagement. He took for company Stepan Bers, the twelve-year-old brother of his wife. To his great regret he discovered that the caretaker of the monument on the field, an old veteran, from whom he hoped to obtain a firsthand account of the battle, had very recently died. Tolstoy carefully surveyed the terrain and drew up a plan of the battle

[2] *Correspondance diplomatique* and *Soirées de St. Pétersbourg.*

[3] Later, this task was assumed by Tolstoy's friend, S. S. Urusov, who read proof on the sixth volume.

[4] Tolstoy contracted for 4800 copies. The novel eventually ran to six volumes in this first edition and sold for 10 rubles a set. He agreed to advance 4500 rubles for the printing and promised 30 per cent of the gross profits to the printer and proofreader. If the edition sold out, he would realize a profit for himself of 29,100 rubles. The silver ruble was worth about 50 cents, and its purchasing power was several times greater than its equivalent today.

which he published in his novel. On his way home he wrote to Sonya: "I'm very, very satisfied with my trip. If God gives me health and peace of mind, I'll write such a description of the Battle of Borodino as was never written before. Always boasting!"

Tolstoy now worked so hard at the novel that he endangered his health. He continued to write later sections while correcting proof of the earlier parts which he then sent to Bartenev in Moscow for final inspection. Bartenev fell into despair over the author's numerous corrections. "God knows what you are doing!" he complained to Tolstoy in one of his letters. "At this rate we'll never finish with the corrections and printing. . . . More than half of your besmearing is unnecessary, and meanwhile the printing bill soars terribly." And the next day came another wail from him: "For God's sake, stop picking away at it!" Tolstoy replied: "I can't help messing it up. But I'm firmly convinced that this messing serves a great use. Therefore I'm not afraid of the printers who, I hope, will not be very captious. But no matter what you say, that which you like would be much worse if it were not scribbled over at least five times." The work did not give him a moment's rest, he declared to a friend, and he had spells of dizziness from writing constantly. By the end of 1867 he had the satisfaction of seeing three volumes of *War and Peace* published.

The new direction he had given the novel caused Tolstoy infinite trouble. He worried over what the critics, and particularly his Moscow Slavophile friends, would think of the antihistorical point of view he was developing. In a letter to Pogodin in March 1868, he earnestly defended his original approach.

> My thoughts about the limits of freedom and independence [he wrote], and my views on history are not a mere paradox that has occupied me in passing. These thoughts are the fruits of all the intellectual efforts of my life, and they are an inseparable part of that philosophy which I have achieved, God alone knows with what striving and suffering, and it has given me complete calm and happiness. Yet along with this I know and knew that in my book they will praise the sentimental scenes with my young ladies, the laughter over Speranski, and such rubbish. . . .

Despite fears, doubts, illness, and periods of deep despair, *War and Peace* moved irresistibly on. If he had many low moments in the course of its composition, there were also joyous compensations after a day well spent in the successful handling of a difficult scene. Then he would jauntily emerge from his study, happy, smiling, and declaring that he had just left a piece of his life in the inkwell. In March 1868, the fourth volume appeared, the fifth in March 1869, and the sixth and last in December of that year. It had taken him more than six years to write *War and Peace.*

2

Tolstoy was staying with the Bers family in Moscow at the time the first part of *War and Peace* appeared. On the morning of publication, before he got out of bed, he sent his young brother-in-law, a military student, for a copy of a newspaper in which he expected a review. The youth lagged, and Tolstoy impatiently shouted: "You wish to be a general of infantry? Yes? Well, I wish to be a general of literature! Run at once and bring me the paper!" Tolstoy was serious; he wanted to be a literary general, and *War and Peace* was intended to advance him to that rank. Further, the financial stake was considerable and now an important item in his mounting expenses.

Literary friends like Fet and Botkin lavished praise. With the first volume Turgenev showed himself a conscientious objector. "Positively bad, boring, and unsuccessful," he curtly declared. But as the successive volumes appeared he gradually, and it seems almost unwillingly, surrendered to the charm of *War and Peace.* Soon he lost all reserve in acclaiming those features of the work "that will not die as long as the Russian language lives." "For in this novel," he concluded in a letter to Fet's brother-in-law, "there are so many first-class beauties, such life and truth and freshness, that with the appearance of *War and Peace* Tolstoy has taken first place among all our contemporary writers." He became not a general, but a generalissimo of literature, and at the hands of the recognized leader—Turgenev.

There were detractors, of course, particularly among those adherents of the two extreme social and political parties—the patriotic conservatives and the cosmopolitan radicals. Both were indignant over the novel. The first group condemned Tolstoy's failure to perpetuate the notion of widespread patriotism in the Russian armies of 1812; the second group bitterly censured him for idealizing the nobility of that time and for manifesting sympathy with conservative tendencies.

On the whole, *War and Peace* caused a sensation; it quickly went into a second edition and was extolled in numerous reviews. The most thorough and discriminating criticism was contributed in a series of four articles by N. N. Strakhov, later a distinguished philosophical thinker and a close friend of Tolstoy. His final judgment of the novel was: "A complete picture of human life. A complete picture of the Russia of that day. A complete picture of what may be called the history and struggle of peoples. A complete picture of everything in which people find their happiness and greatness, their grief and humiliation. That is *War and Peace*." After reading this appraisal, Tolstoy, with the self-assurance of the genius who knows that he has scored, calmly remarked to his wife: "N. N. Strakhov has placed *War and Peace* on the pinnacle where it will remain in the opinion of society."

Tolstoy's philosophy of history was the feature of the novel most persistently objected to, as it is among modern readers. He had anticipated both objections and misunderstanding on this score, for in 1868, a year before the novel was actually finished, he had taken the precaution to publish an article explaining his views—"Some Words about *War and Peace*."[6] There he defended the artist's treatment of history as contrasted with that of the historian. The actions and speech of historical persons, he asserted, had been scrupulously reproduced without change. But he stoutly defended his contention that the great events of history in no sense depend upon the will of any individual such as Napoleon, rather they are predetermined. History, he explained, is not the slave of kings but kings are the slaves of history. Behind a historical event is never one reason but a whole series of reasons, and all of them are beyond the control of a single individual. Tolstoy's position naturally led him to distrust the historical approach of nearly everyone who had written about the period of Napoleon.

However much Tolstoy's views on historical necessity and causality may have been influenced by his Slavophile friends and by what he read at this time, their roots can be clearly discerned in his previous thought and writings. Opposition to traditional historical methodology and his intellectual

[6] This article appeared in *Russian Archive*, No. 3.

anarchy date from the period of his youth. And these tendencies were intensified by the evidence he found in the "whole library" of books that he read in preparation for *War and Peace*. For now his detailed knowledge of the facts behind the invasion of the French and of the consequences of the war began to convince him that governments and rulers do not work for the good of the people but for their harm. This growing conviction was reflected in a strange project that he formulated in 1868 for the formation of a society that would dedicate itself to work for the independence of all Russians. Any member, wrote Tolstoy, "who received a rank, decoration, or money from the government would be excluded from the society." They were to eschew luxury, live simple and moral lives, help their fellow members in all things, and try to increase the membership of the society.

In *War and Peace,* however, Tolstoy was too great an artist to allow his historical hobbyhorse to run away with the novel. Each of the more than five hundred active characters he placed on this vast stage of life has his own distinct personality and speaks his own language. Even the dogs, as Strakhov pointed out, are individualized. If many of these men and women were suggested by people he knew, and if he drew upon himself for those two central figures, Prince Andrei and Pierre, all were passed through the alembic of his art and transformed into creatures of his imagination. With some justice the radical critics could point out that he did not see the faults of the privileged classes and failed to portray the dark misery of the peasantry at that time, although he significantly recognized in the novel the historical mission of the people. In an interesting letter addressed but not sent to the author P. D. Boborykin, Tolstoy defended his avoidance of social problems. "The aims of art," he wrote, "are incommensurable (as they say in mathematics) with social aims. The aim of an artist is not to resolve a question irrefutably, but to compel one to love life in all its manifestations, and these are inexhaustible. If I were told that I could write a novel in which I could indisputably establish as true my point of view on all social questions, I would not dedicate two hours to such a work; but if I were told that what I wrote would be read twenty years from now by those who are children today, and that they would weep and laugh over it and fall in love with the life in it, then I would dedicate all my existence and all my powers to it."

However justifiable this conviction may be as an aesthetic aim, it is not a full explanation of Tolstoy's deliberate avoidance of the real social problems that played so large a part in the historical period he attempted to re-create. The fact is that he wrote *War and Peace* in an atmosphere of love and family happiness. The prevailing spirit of the book is an ecstatic love of life in all its manifestations. Lulled to contentment by his own happiness, he evaded the suffering and grief of people in the historical past and tried to see in life, as his character Karatayev did, only "a resplendent comeliness."

3

Daily grubbing in the garden of life was for Tolstoy a necessary and salutary escape from intense creative activity. While he was writing *War and Peace,* he also led the full existence of a family man; he busied himself with the cares of his estate, with hunting, visiting, and entertaining friends. The Tolstoy and Fet families exchanged visits over this period. He now felt closer than ever to Fet with whom he could share his inmost thoughts, and whose judgment of his novel was almost the only criticism he cared to solicit. "Without speaking of any others," he wrote him, "you are a man whose mind I value above that of all my acquaintances, and who alone in personal relations gives me that very bread without which a man will not be satisfied." On the other hand, Fet was incapable of returning his own full measure of devotion. He was a man of mind, not of heart, Tanya Bers keenly observed, a man who thought of himself first, and in speaking produced the impression always of listening to himself.

Joined more closely to him by those ties of feeling that Tolstoy valued most was the constant friend of his university days, D. A. Dyakov. His model estate was only a few miles from Nikolskoye, a property that Tolstoy had acquired after the death of his brother Nikolai. When Tolstoy visited Nikolskoye, he rarely failed to extend his trip to Dyakov's where he always received a warm welcome. Sometimes Tanya accompanied him and remained with the Dyakovs for long periods, for she was also the darling of this household. Indeed, after the early death of Dyakov's charming wife, Tanya seriously considered marrying the widower, a match which Tolstoy much preferred to that with her childhood sweetheart Kuzminski. Dyakov's kindness, unfailing good nature, and sense of humor endeared him to Tolstoy. There were a few other close friends at this time, such as the mathematically-minded Urusov who wished to reduce everything, even the death of kings, to exact laws.

When visitors arrived, Tolstoy became the demon contriver of household amusements, such as domestic balls and masquerades. Dressed in some outlandish costume, he held the center of the stage, entertaining all by singing tender gypsy songs to his own accompaniment on the guitar. Once on Sonya's name-day he prepared a surprise. When the guests were seated at the festive table on the terrace, suddenly from the garden came the sounds of music. One of Sonya's favorite pieces was being played. Tolstoy had secretly obtained the services of a regimental band in the neighborhood. The beaming expression of the surprised and delighted Sonya in her white dress and flowing ribbons was answered across the table by her Lyovochka's equally delighted grin. And the holiday spirits of the guests, especially of the young ladies, soared, for they knew that the presence of the band meant dancing after dinner.

Nor did Tolstoy hesitate to employ his literary talent on such occasions. In August 1866, when the Dyakovs were visiting Yasnaya Polyana, Tolstoy proposed to the young people that they do a little play instead of the customary charades. They at once importuned him to write something, and several days later he brought them the manuscript of a comedy in three acts called *The Nihilist*. The plot concerned a conventional married couple who were visited by a group of young people, one of whom was an attractive student filled with the new nihilist ideas. The husband imagined that the student had designs on his wife, but in the end all was satisfactorily explained. Sonya played the husband and Tanya his wife, and the other parts were acted by young guests. The role of a religious pilgrim was improvised for Tolstoy's sister, who acted it brilliantly. After much rehearsing and coaching by Tolstoy, the play was put on in the large dining room, to the huge enjoyment of an audience composed of older members of the household and neighbors.[6]

[6] A version of this comedy has been published in the Jubilee Edition (Vol. VII), and it has been translated in Fülöp-Miller's *Tolstoy*.

The little world of Yasnaya Polyana was complete and satisfying. It had the further advantage of being a private world of Tolstoy's own creating. The instinct for exclusiveness was strong within him; he suffered only occasionally from a lack of those advantages to which his cultural background had accustomed him. The theater, music, libraries, he wrote to father Bers, and conversations with intellectuals, were the only pleasures he missed in the country. Such deprivations were plentifully compensated during his trips to Moscow over this period. Two of these visits, in January 1866 and February 1868, on which occasions he was accompanied by his family, extended for more than a month each. On the first he studied sculpturing and modeled a horse and then a bust of Sonya, but he soon wrote to Fet that, although the work was agreeable, he was convinced that he would never be a sculptor. Many hours were spent in libraries reading books that provided material for his novel. The whole question of the Masons, for example, had to be thoroughly investigated, and at the end of his studies he came to the conclusion that it was too bad that all these Masons were such fools. And quite apart from the considerable amount of research for his novel, he managed to read much literature at this time.[7]

Tolstoy's visits to Moscow only made clearer to him how firm was his attachment to Yasnaya Polyana. The dust, crowds, and noises of the city disgusted him. When the business of the novel took him away from home, Sonya peevishly charged him with a fondness for city life. Patiently and sincerely he wrote her: "It is insupportable for me in the city, yet you say that I like to gad about. I only wish that you loved the country one tenth as much as I hate the idle vanity of the city."

4

In the summer of 1866, Tolstoy underwent an experience that he always remembered with chagrin and self-condemnation. Not far from Yasnaya Polyana an infantry regiment was stationed. One of its most insignificant members was Vasili Shibunin, who had been reduced to the ranks for some offense and now did clerical work. In his unhappiness

[7] Between 1865 and 1870, Tolstoy mentions that he read works of Cervantes, Montaigne, Goethe, Mérimée, Hugo, Sand, Dickens, Schopenhauer, Trollope, and Turgenev.

he took to drink, which aggravated a naturally irritable and moody disposition. His company commander, a cold, cruel, and meticulous Pole, took a sadistic delight in oppressing his men by means of calculated humiliations. Shibunin became the victim of his petty persecution. On one occasion the courage of vodka led Shibunin to protest his commander's unreasonable criticism of a battalion report that he had just copied. When he was ordered to the guardhouse for his effrontery, he lost control of himself and violently struck his commander. Shibunin was arrested and held for court-martial.

Two officers of the regiment, who were acquainted with Tolstoy, asked him to take upon himself Shibunin's defense, for the poor clerk was in imminent danger of being condemned to death. Tolstoy agreed. He visited Shibunin in his cell, but he found the gloomy, taciturn prisoner of little assistance. Shibunin accepted the situation as something ordained. He simply explained that he had hit the commander because he could no longer tolerate his unjust persecution.

Tolstoy decided to base his defense on the military law governing the crime. This law allowed a mitigation of sentence if it could be proved that the defendant exhibited positive insane tendencies. Tolstoy wrote out an elaborate plea[8] and delivered it before the military tribunal. He convinced only one of the officers that the punishment should be softened; the majority opinion condemned Shibunin to be shot.

Tolstoy at once wrote Granny to use her influence with the Minister of War to obtain a pardon from the Tsar. She hurried off a reply that the minister needed the name of Shibunin's regiment, which Tolstoy had neglected to indicate. This was a patent subterfuge. From the facts Tolstoy had supplied in his letter, it would have been very easy to look up the name of the regiment stationed near Yasnaya Polyana. Tolstoy complied at once, however, but vital time had been lost. The truth of the matter was that the minister had no intention of requesting a pardon.

Shortly after the trial Shibunin was marched out to an open field. All the troops were drawn up, and a number of peasants looked on anxiously. A priest gave the condemned man the last rites of the Church. Soldiers presented arms,

[8] It was later published.

the drums rolled, and the sentence was read aloud. Shibunin listened quietly with lowered eyes. At the conclusion of the reading the priest pressed a cross to the prisoner's lips. The troops shouldered arms, the drums rolled again, and Shibunin was led to a stake placed before a freshly dug grave. His eyes were covered, a shroud thrown over him, and he was tied to the stake. Twelve riflemen took up positions fifteen paces away. Amid the beating of the drums, the officer in charge waved a handkerchief and twelve shots rang out. The warm body was dropped into the hole and quickly covered over; the troops marched off past the grave to the strains of a regimental band. Some peasant women among the spectators fainted, others quietly sobbed.

Ever since Tolstoy had witnessed the execution of a criminal in Paris on his first trip abroad in 1857, he had entertained a horror of capital punishment. Yet, when he read through his speech defending Shibunin some forty years after the event, he felt only extreme disgust for himself and contempt for his reasoning at that time. He had based his plea for a human life on a man-made law instead of on the moral law and the law of God. On the other hand, he insisted that he had felt then, although in a very confused way, that this terrible deed ought not to have taken place, and that it was somehow connected with all the other errors and miseries of mankind.

5

Tolstoy jokingly wrote Fet that he loved his wife less than his novel—a kind of humor Sonya found it difficult to appreciate since she bore him four children before *War and Peace* was finished.[9] If the growth of his family kept pace with that of his novel, he had no cause for discouragement, for he too was growing artistically and morally and spiritually. It was a growth according to rule, he wrote Granny, like an apple tree, constantly trimmed and trained so that its roots would sink more deeply into the life-giving earth. "Never have I felt myself so entirely, so vividly all soul as I do now, when the impulses and passions are limited."

Sonya cared nothing for this internal illumination in her husband, but his dawning love for their oldest child, which she now began to observe, delighted her beyond measure.

[9] After Sergei and Tatyana, Ilya was born May 22, 1866, and Leo on May 20, 1869.

Not until little Sergei was approaching his second birthday did Tolstoy evince any affection. "I'm beginning to love him very much," he noted in the diary. "An entirely new feeling." A quiet and proud love for the baby took possession of him. Sonya wrote to her younger sister that her husband had grown very tender toward little Sergei and continually played with him, but that she was much hurt and offended because he paid not the slightest attention to his second child, Tanya. Before another year had passed, however, she could announce to her sister that Lyovochka had "simply gone out of his mind" over tiny Tanya.

Although the children were still too young for any formal education, the pedagogue in Tolstoy could not resist some speculation on this favorite theme. He attempted to prescribe certain clothes for the children and was opposed to giving them toys. In these matters he nearly always found himself a minority of one, defending his theories against the objections of Sonya, Auntie Tatyana, an old Russian nurse, and a recently employed young English governess.

Despite his belief that women were not the equal of men and acted and lived primarily by feeling, Tolstoy at this time willingly left the practical affairs of the household and the supervision of the children entirely in the hands of his wife. The children, she said, were her greatest happiness. Now, in contrast to the experience with her first child, when illness obliged her to employ a wet nurse, she grew furiously jealous and demanded that the substitute be sent away.

Entries in her diary over this period seem to indicate that Sonya's almost morbid love for her children was an unconscious attempt to compensate for what she believed to be Tolstoy's loss of affection for her. The intellectual differences that separated them she magnified into an unbridgeable chasm, and it made her feel lonely and deserted. Lyovochka, she noted, had such a powerful will, and was so occupied and independent. "I feel that he is life, power," she wrote in March 1865. "But I'm only a worm that crawls and gnaws at him. I'm afraid to be weak." This curious self-abasement alternated with a possessiveness that sprang from her consuming love for him as a husband, a love that came first in her world before his talent, moral worth, or literary activity. Any defection on his part, real or imagined, worried her excessively.

Sonya's feeling of insufficiency fed her jealousy. She noticed that he went out frequently for walks. "I began to think," she noted in the diary almost three years after marriage, "does he not go to Aksinya? This tortured me the whole day." She grew angry with her sister Tanya for occupying so much of Tolstoy's time. Their excursions together aroused her suspicions. "They've gone shooting in the woods alone," she jotted down. "God knows what comes into my head."

A good wife may contemplate everything through her husband's eyes save women, and there were few women in Tolstoy's past or present life who still failed to provoke Sonya's jealousy. While he was on a trip in 1869, a letter to him from Granny came to Yasnaya Polyana. Sonya did not hesitate to open it and summarize the contents in a letter to her husband. "She writes you many tender things and it annoys me," Sonya reported. "I think that it would have been better if you had married her. . . ." Sonya could never become quite reconciled to Granny, although this kind friend had recently written to both of them, but particularly for Sonya's benefit, that whatever may be an old woman's charm, she will forever be a spent candle, no longer harmful to anyone. Tolstoy had made the mistake of praising Granny too highly to Sonya.

Instead of the whole masculine arsenal, women have but one single moral weapon—love, and Sonya lived to record Tolstoy's every response to her love. "Today Lyovochka became more affectionate," she entered in her diary. "He kissed me, which has not happened for a long time. I've been poisoned by the thought that it has been a long time since he lived with me." If she protested too much her insignificance, she also proudly itemized her contributions to his literary labors. When the well-known writer V. A. Sollogub, who visited Yasnaya Polyana in August 1866, told her that she was the ideal wife of an author, because she was the nurse of her husband's talent, she readily agreed and carefully wrote down this observation in her diary. Sometimes he discussed his literary plans with her and acted upon her criticism, and this made Sonya "terribly happy."

In Tolstoy's own diary[1] over this period, both the debits and the credits of married life were faithfully listed. Entries or quarrels were balanced with loving reconciliations, or with such declarations as: "We are so happy together, as

[1] Beginning with 1865, Tolstoy ceased to keep his diary, with the exception of a few random jottings, for the next thirteen years.

happy as only one couple out of a million can be." Although his trips were rather brief, they missed each other very much and absence often forced passionate expression of the love and tenderness that were buried during their daily existence together. "Today it seemed so terrible for me to sleep alone," wrote Sonya, "that I put our little girl in your place. . . ." Joyfully she described how she had shown his picture to little Sergei who exclaimed "Papa!" "I love you terribly!" she concluded another letter. "I want to kiss your hand and you, and tell you how dear and charming you are."

Tolstoy's letters to Sonya might be the letters of any husband to any wife. Conjugal epistolary commonplaces were now rarely brightened by the humor and verbal playfulness of his letters to her shortly after their marriage. Only his deep and ever-fresh feeling of love lends significance to these letters. "Farewell, my soul, my darling," he ended one. "Know and remember that I've thought of you no less than you of me; and I think of you now and will think." He kissed her eyes, he wrote, and her neck and hand. While staying at her parents' house in Moscow, he hurried off a letter to tell her: "I always love you more when I'm parted from you. . . . How dear you are to me; for me you are better, purer, more precious and desirable than anything in the world. I gaze on your childhood portraits and rejoice." He anxiously awaited her answers and read them at once. "I cannot describe," he declared, "the tenderness even to tears that I feel for you and not only now, but every minute of the day. My soul, my darling, the best in the world! For God's sake, do not fail to write me every day. . . ."

Tolstoy had been married almost five years when he wrote this. For some husbands the springs of love dry up with the passing of time and are displaced by habit sanctified by duty. For Tolstoy, time brought a deeper, more spiritual meaning to his love for Sonya. She and his children had become the center of his being, and apart from fulfilling his consuming need to love, they gave added purpose to his life and broadened the whole frame of his existence.

6

In his state of complete happiness, it is not surprising that Tolstoy lost contact with the world outside of Yasnaya Polyana. Throughout this whole period there are few indications of the sensitiveness to human misery and injustice that had inspired his search for spiritual truth in the past. Exceptions to this indifference were rare. In the summer of 1865, when he was on the way to his property at Nikolskoye, the fearful effects of a prevailing drought over the surrounding countryside and its forewarning of famine for the peasantry drew from him an anxious letter to Fet, in which he expressed his pain and puzzlement over the contrast of the well-to-do and the poor victims of calamity. "Lately I've been satisfied with my private affairs," he wrote, "but the general course, that is the impending misery of famine, torments me more and more every day. It is so strange, and even good and terrible. We have rosy radishes on our table, yellow butter, and well-baked soft bread on a clean tablecloth; the garden is green and our young ladies in muslin dresses are happy that it is both hot and shady; while out there that evil devil hunger is already at work covering the fields with gooseweed, cracking the withered earth, chafing the hard heels of the peasants, and of their women, and splitting the hoofs of the cattle; and all of them scold and murmur, I dare say, against us who, under our shady lime trees and in muslin dresses, can have creamy yellow butter on a painted dish."

It is curious that this faint awareness of peasant discontent should suddenly take the form, two months later, of a remarkable statement, entirely unconnected with the famine, on the future social revolution. For in his notebook on August 13, 1865, Tolstoy wrote down what he claimed was a dream, and it stands as an uncanny anticipation of his later position on private property. "The universally national task of Russia," he declared, "is to endow the world with the idea of a social structure without landed property. *'La propriété c'est le vol'* will remain a greater truth than the English constitution as long as the human family exists. This is an absolute truth, but out of it emerge relative truths—application. The first of these relative truths is the view of the Russian people on property. The Russian people refuse to believe that land is the most stable form of property, because it is least dependent upon labor and hampers the acquisition of property by others. This truth is not a dream—it is a fact expressed in general among peasants and *Cossacks*. The learned Russian understands this truth, and equally so the peasant who says: Let them inscribe us as Cossacks, and the land will be free. This idea has a future. The Russian revolution can be based on this only. The Russian revolution will not be against the Tsar and despotism, but against landed property. It will say: Take from me, from man, what you wish, but leave all the land to us. The autocracy will not prevent but will facilitate this order of things."[2]

These political and social observations, however, did not reflect any practical interest in such matters. During the writing of *War and Peace* Tolstoy remained severely aloof from the important events that were taking place in the nation. After the Polish rebellion had been put down, he wrote Granny in November 1865 that he felt neither sympathy nor anger over the edict that prohibited the Poles from speaking their own language. And he coldly declared that he would not condemn the brutality with which the rebels were crushed. "It is all the same to me," he wrote, "who strangles the Poles, takes Slesvig-Holstein, or speaks in the assembly of the Zemstvos. Butchers fell the oxen we eat, but I'm not obliged to accuse them or sympathize with them." The rising clamor for reform, and the intense political and social activity that made these years among the most significant in the country's history were simply ignored by him. If he bothered to notice events outside his estate, it was only to ridicule them, as his scornful charge to Fet that the national hero worship of the peasant who had saved Alexander II from an assassin's bullet in 1866 was stupid in the extreme.

7

Had the search then ended? Was Tolstoy finally at peace with himself? For during the last few years in which he had worked on *War and Peace* Tolstoy, the seeker after material success, had found it in his literary labors and in family happiness. But had that incessant voice of spiritual discontent also been stilled? On the contrary, various facts suggest that the great spiritual crisis of his later life had its roots in this period of the 1860's. In a nature divided against itself, material success simply intensified the struggle between

[2] The only thing revolution does not change, it would seem from this statement, is the government. Forty-three years later Tolstoy came upon this forgotten note among his papers, read it, and exclaimed with wonder and delight over this signal proof that he had anticipated by many years his theory on private property. His consistency, he felt, showed that the life of the spirit in a man was not temporal but existed in him always.

good and evil. He wanted to believe that flesh and blood alone could build up the happiness and morality of life, but in his heart he knew that they could not save the spirit.

A man who can love can do all things, Tolstoy wrote Granny, but was he not thinking of a selfish, fleshly love? The thought troubled him. At times, throughout this whole period, he heard the small voice of conscience telling him that there existed a good higher and more worthy than family happiness. In one of these self-lacerating moods, recalling so clearly the anxieties of his youth, he wrote to his sister-in-law Tanya on February 20, 1865: "Here is what I've been deliberating upon now for the second day: that it is very sad that the world is made up entirely of egoists, of whom I'm the first. I'm not blaming anyone, but I think that it is very disgusting, and that between husband and wife there is no egoism only when they love each other."

In this rarefied atmosphere of spiritual needs, Tolstoy had to walk alone. Sonya had her own world of thoughts, feelings, and desires, and at bottom it was entirely different from his. With little success he turned to Fet for spiritual communion. And in an unusual letter to his friend Samarin in January 1867, Tolstoy's spiritual loneliness and despairing hunger for a kindred spirit who would understand are pathetically evident. He began by declaring that he urgently needed the moral and intellectual companionship of a man like Samarin who loved truth more than anything else. "I also am such a man," he continued. "I have my weaknesses, habits of vanity, and warm ties, but up to now—I shall soon be forty—I have loved truth more than anything; I do not despair of finding it, and I am still searching and searching. At times, and precisely this year more than ever before, I have failed to raise a corner of the curtain to take a peep there—but I'm alone, and it is hard and terrible, and it seems that I have lost my way."

Tolstoy was right; he had lost his way, and brief periods of deep depression and mental groping testify to his struggle to find the road once again to spiritual perfection. Rare and unexplained fits of anger threw the household into consternation and were outward manifestations of his inner ferment. On one occasion and for no apparent reason he roared at Sonya to get out of his room, and in an uncontrollable rage he smashed a tray of dishes on the floor.

Behind his disturbed state of mind was the phantom of death that seemed to mock his happiness. Perhaps his thoughts were more often turned to the subject because over this period there died the wife of his close friend Dyakov, the critic Botkin, his father-in-law, Granny's beloved sister, and his own sister's former husband. He wrote of the latter to Granny: "He died quite lonely at Lipetsk. That is the worst of death—it is impossible to atone for the wrong one has done a man who is dead now or to do him some good still. It is said: Live in a way that makes you always fit for death. I myself should have said: Live in a way that anyone may die and you have nothing to repent of."

If death were but the end of his happiness, Tolstoy wondered, then of what use was this happiness? At one point in his notebook at this time he even imagined that death was a desirable end, a release and comfort. "I have desired and desire something now. What is it?" he asked himself. "I desire something that is not here in this world. But it is somewhere, because I desire it. Where, then? I must be reborn in order to be content, and to be content with the best that is in me. To be reborn is to die. That is the only contentment that I desire and what we all desire."

Such a thought was a passing fancy, and death as the end of everything he loved terrified Tolstoy; yet its image haunted him, and on one occasion appeared before him with fearful reality. At the end of August 1869, he set out on a journey to Penza Province to look over an estate that he contemplated buying. On the road he wrote to Sonya that he had had a terrible experience one night, the details of which he would tell her later. What happened that night he probably described accurately in his autobiographical *Notes of a Madman* some twelve years afterwards.

On his trip he reached the town of Arzamas and spent the night in a little house. He lay down on the divan and dozed. In a short time he awoke and the room was dark. He tried in vain to go to sleep again. "Why have I come here?" he asked himself. "Where am I going? From what and whither am I fleeing? I am running from something terrible, and I cannot run. I am always with myself and I torment myself. I am he, I am always there. Neither Penza Province nor any estate will add or take away anything from me. I am bored with myself, insupportable, and torment myself. I wish to sleep, to forget—and I cannot. I cannot get away from myself."

He went out into the corridor, hoping to escape from

what tormented him. But it pursued him and obscured everything.

"What is this stupidity?" he said to himself. "What am I distressed over? What do I fear?"

"Me," answered the voice of death. "I am here!"

Tolstoy in horror struggled with the phantom. But death, like some physical presence, murdered his sleep and filled his mind with thoughts of dissolution and of the end of all he held dear. He prayed and closed his eyes, but the phantom remained to torment him until he finally was obliged to wake his servant and leave.

In time, Tolstoy forgot this harrowing experience at Arzamas. But in the depths of his thoughts there still lurked the terrible specter of death that he had seen, and in a few years it reappeared to demand an answer to its incessant question.

XIX

Creative Interlude

TOLSTOY TOLD FET that the hours seemed dead after his prolonged effort on *War and Peace.* He read and wrote nothing and simply felt himself agreeable and stupid. Nerves had been stretched to the breaking point, and his physician warned him of the danger of a collapse. His creative imagination and intellect, however, could never lie fallow for long. Whole poems, novels, and philosophical theories, he wrote Granny, marched through his brain continually. Turgenev once remarked that the hounds of thought hunted Tolstoy's head to exhaustion. Even while working on *War and Peace,* he requested historical material from his friend Bartenev for a new novel on the reign of Paul I, a design that never materialized. And he had already plunged into a special study of philosophy before his masterpiece was fairly out of the way. Hegel's works struck him as an "empty collection of phrases," but in August 1869 he wrote Fet: "Do you know what this summer has been for me? An endless ecstasy over Schopenhauer, and a series of mental pleasures such as I've never experienced before. I have bought all his works and have read and am reading them (as well as Kant's). And assuredly no student in his course has learned and discovered so much as I have during this summer. I do not know whether I shall ever change my opinion, but at present I'm confident that Schopenhauer is the greatest genius among men." And he concluded with an offer to collaborate with Fet on a translation of Schopenhauer.

Philosophy was an intellectual brew that Tolstoy always stirred the wrong way. He was hostile to systems of thought or to systems of any sort. He now pondered much and painfully over philosophical problems, and he talked endlessly, but the net result was always a headache. His speculations filled him with gloom and thoughts of death, whereas a faith was what he really hoped to find. "They reproach me with fatalism," he declared to Sonya, "but no one could be more believing than I. Fatalism is a subterfuge for those who do ill; but I believe in God, in the expression of the Gospel that not one hair falls unless willed by the Lord. Therefore, I say that all is predestined."

Drama quickly displaced Tolstoy's zeal for philosophy. Over the winter of 1870 he read plays of Shakespeare, Molière, Goethe, Pushkin, and Gogol, and he contemplated writing a comedy. "During this whole winter," he told Fet, "I've been, in general, busy only with drama. . . . I lie in bed (sick), and characters for tragedy or comedy begin to act. And they present themselves very well."

Sonya saw that he was not really serious about this new endeavor, and he actually confessed to her that after having wrestled with a subject of epic proportions, it was difficult and hardly worth while to concern himself with a drama. In fact, with another epic subject in mind, he now turned to explore the age of Peter the Great. The period excited him with its rich, thrilling activity and colorful figures. Jottings on this reading in his notebook for April 1870 plainly indicate the preliminary massing of material for a historical novel on the time of Peter. An opening chapter was drafted, and in November he wrote Fet: "You cannot imagine how difficult is this preliminary labor of ploughing deeply the field that I intend to sow. I ponder and change my mind continually over what may happen in the lives of all the future people of this huge projected work, and I think of the million possible combinations which make the selection of one so hard."

Less than a month later, however, Fet was bewildered to receive the following information from Tolstoy: "I got your letter a week ago but have not answered because from morn to night I'm learning Greek. I'm writing nothing, only learning; and to judge by information reaching me from Borisov, your skin—to be used as parchment for my Greek diploma—is in danger." He then went on to relate that he could already read Xenophon at sight and Homer with a dictionary. "But how glad I am that God sent this folly upon me! In the first place I enjoy it, and secondly, I have become convinced that of all that human language has produced truly and simply beautiful, I knew nothing—like all the others who know but do not understand; and thirdly, because I have ceased to write, and never more will write wordy rubbish. I'm guilty of having done so, but by God I won't do so any more!" And he finally expressed the conviction that "without a knowledge of Greek there is no education."

The proposed novel on Peter the Great was quite submerged under this new enthusiasm. He applied himself to Greek with all that ardor and concentration that he gave to any subject or cause that excited his admiration and interest. He says that he learned to read the language with some ease in three months. His claim astonished a Moscow professor of Greek whom he visited the following winter. To test him, the professor proposed that they read something at sight. They differed on the meaning of several difficult passages, but after some discussion the professor agreed that Tolstoy's interpretations were correct. Like an arrogant schoolboy, he boasted to friends that he read Plato and Homer in the original, and to Fet he wrote that he was living in Athens and at night spoke Greek in his sleep. Sonya listened to all the wearying details of his progress. Her principal worry was that his intense application would undermine his health.

In the early months of 1871 Tolstoy's health did break down. Although his Greek studies were no doubt one cause, other factors contributed. There were organic disturbances—fever and rheumatic pains, but these were accompanied by insomnia, nervous exhaustion, and depressed spirits. He wrote to Urusov: "Never have I experienced such misery; I do not wish to live." And to Fet he complained of failing powers, an expectation of death, and an absence of spiritual peace.

The feverish and fruitless activities of Tolstoy after the completion of *War and Peace* were not so much a cause as a symptom of his physical and spiritual breakdown. For to pause meant always to examine himself, to concentrate upon his own fate and historical mission. Now, as in periods of inactivity in the past, he sought to escape from himself. These swift thrusts into philosophy, drama, and Greek studies were unconscious attempts to arrest his mind with some all-absorbing task. But his studies did not distract him from the intense self-analysis that nearly always brought him to the point of spiritual despair.

Tolstoy's low state at this time was aggravated by a serious quarrel with his wife. On May 20, 1869, another son, Leo, had been born. After this fourth child in less than seven years of married life, Sonya, with perhaps justifiable querulousness, noted in her diary: "With every child I deny myself more of life and grow reconciled under the burden of cares, illness, and years." Nevertheless, on February 12, 1871, a fifth child, Marya, arrived, and after this birth Sonya suffered an illness that almost proved fatal. The prospects of another pregnancy frightened her, and she made known her fears to her husband. With his strict views on marriage, such an attitude deeply offended him and brought about a temporary coldness in their relations that intensified his spiritual loneliness. His poor health became so alarming that he was advised to go to Samara for a *kumys* cure.

2

Tolstoy went first to Moscow where he decided that he would set out for that part of Samara which he had visited in 1862. His young brother-in-law, Stepan, who had grown to worship him ever since their excursion together to the battlefield of Borodino, joyfully agreed to accompany him on this trip. On June 10 they took the train to Nizhni Novgorod. Travel by rail, which had only recently been introduced into Russia, seemed to Tolstoy one of the more dubious benefits of civilization. When he had to use this form of locomotion, he preferred to go third class, for he liked to chat with the peasants.

At Nizhni Novgorod they boarded a Volga steamer and proceeded to the town of Samara. Tolstoy had received a tender, solicitous letter from Sonya. She implored him to think more of himself and of his health and less of the family he had left behind at Yasnaya Polyana. "I feel that I have a solace in the children," she wrote, "you have your inner, spiritual life. For God's sake, do not give way to fear, grief, and disquietude." He replied that his health was unusually good. Indeed, the river trip boosted his spirits. With his unfailing interest in people, he was soon on the friendliest terms with all on the boat, especially with the sailors with whom he slept in the fore part of the vessel.

From Samara Tolstoy made a journey of some eighty miles on horseback to the village of Karalyk. There his old friends the Bashkirs gave him a warm welcome. Soon he settled in a tent in the open steppe and applied himself to his cure—a diet restricted to *kumys* and meat. Living conditions were extremely primitive. A few days after his arrival, he wrote Sonya that he would be happy if he were only well. He looked upon everything as though he were a corpse, the sort of attitude he hated in other people, he remarked. "As formerly, I do not see through things with love. If I happen to be in a poetical mood, then it is most bitter, tearful—I want to weep."

Tolstoy's low spirits did not last long in these picturesque surroundings, although the state of his health fluctuated considerably. In the neighborhood were several other Russians who had come to regain their health. Tolstoy's genial disposition banished dull care among these melancholy invalids. The group grew gay and lively. An ancient teacher vied with him in skipping rope; an attorney's clerk insisted on showing his ignorance in futile debates on literature and philosophy; a young farmer quickly fell into wide-eyed idolatry. In a near-by village Tolstoy came upon the religious sect of Molokans or Milk-Drinkers, who based their faith on the Bible, rejecting all the traditions of the Russian Orthodox Church. He admired their honesty and industry, and frequently discussed with them in an effort to discover their points of difference with the Orthodox faith.

There were hunts on the steppes and a visit to a fair held at Buzuluk, sixty miles away. Tolstoy circulated among the motley crowd, chatting and laughing with them, but he became indignant over a drunken peasant who, in an excess of affection, sought to embrace him. He saw real poetry in the simple easy life of the Bashkirs, readily adapted himself to their ways, and even took an interest in their Mohammedan faith (on his way home he bought a copy of the Koran to read). To Fet, he wrote: "As is proper when one is taking a *kumys* cure, I'm drunk and sweat from morn to night, and I find pleasure in it. It is very good here, and were it not for homesickness, I should be quite happy. Were I to begin describing, I should fill a hundred pages with this country and my own occupations. I'm reading Herodotus, who describes in detail and with great accuracy these same milk-consuming Scythians among whom I'm living." In truth, he had reverted to his Greek again, reading it with the ancient teacher among the *kumys*-drinking invalids. But this passion was running low, and after they had been there some time, young Bers had no difficulty in getting Tolstoy's permission to press leaves between the pages of his huge Greek lexicon.

In letter after letter Sonya implored him to abandon these hateful Greeks. "Not to no purpose is this language dead," she warned, "for it brings a man to a dead state of mind." But her chief plaint was his absence. Despite all the visitors and amusements at Yasnaya Polyana, "without you it is without its soul," she wrote. "You alone are able to inject poetry and charm in all and over all . . . for me all is dead without you."

Her letters, Tolstoy good-naturedly parried in one reply, were probably more harmful to him than Greek, "because of the agitation they throw me into. More so when I receive them unexpectedly; I cannot read them without tears, and I tremble all over and my heart thumps. Though you write anything that comes into your head, to me every word is significant, and I read them all over and over again. . . . At this moment I love you so that I wish to weep." Indeed, he was impatient to return home, so much did he miss his family, and at the end of six weeks he was back again at Yasnaya Polyana, although not much improved in health. His stay on the steppes, however, suggested the purchase of land in Samara, for he saw a possibility of realizing a handsome profit on horse raising.

3

N. N. Strakhov's brilliant review of *War and Peace* had originally attracted Tolstoy to him. Soon after that, he felt impelled to write him an unusual letter, inspired by Strakhov's magazine article, "The Feminine Question," which had been prompted by a recent Russian translation of John Stuart Mill's treatise, *The Subjection of Women.* In his article Strakhov opposed the feminist movement and held up woman as God's most perfect creation. But she should cling to her natural calling of wife and mother, he declared, for in competing with men in their activities and careers, she forfeited that which she should value most—her femininity.

Tolstoy, in his letter, enthusiastically supported Strakhov's position. He went further and maintained that not even unmarried women should enter the professions. Then he introduced a strange line of reasoning. "You will perhaps be astonished," he wrote, "when I say that in the list of honorable callings I include that of the 'Magdalen.' For when I consider the present state of society, I am bound to do so. These unfortunates have always existed, and will always exist. In my opinion it would be monstrous to suppose that God made a mistake, as it were, when He created this order of being; and was our Saviour in error when He pardoned the woman who was a sinner?" Tolstoy justified his argument by pointing to the crowded conditions of modern cities which made prostitution necessary if the family was to survive. Prostitutes were indispensable, he insisted, and their number should be in proportion to the population. "Should we permit promiscuous sexual intercourse, as many 'liberals' wish to do?" he asked. "Impossible! It would be the ruin of family life. To meet the difficulty, the law of development has evolved a 'golden bridge' in the form of the prostitute. Just think of London without its 70,000 prostitutes! What would become of decency and morality, how would family life survive without them? How many women and girls would remain chaste? No, I believe the prostitute is necessary for the maintenance of the family."

Perhaps a lurking sense of the unwisdom of his argument prevented Tolstoy from sending this letter to Strakhov. The stand he took, one commonly held by certain cultivated people in Russia at that time, was obviously determined by his conviction that the family and family life must be protected at any cost. In later years a clearer understanding of the problem of prostitution made him see the error of his position, and he eventually repudiated it.

Several months after this surprising letter (that he never sent) Tolstoy replied to a request from Strakhov to contribute to his magazine, *Zarya*. He politely declined, but he concluded with the warmest expressions of friendship and a pressing invitation to Strakhov to pay a visit to Yasnaya Polyana. At their first meeting the following summer, shortly after Tolstoy's return from Samara, these two men discovered at once how much they had in common spiritually, and Strakhov's boundless esteem for Tolstoy was very flattering to him.

After Strakhov's departure, Tolstoy replied kindly to his letter of thanks, but he could not refrain from injecting a paternal note. In touching upon Strakhov's future career, he strongly advised him to drop journalism. At this time the whole subject of journalism was much on Tolstoy's mind. He was childishly proud of the fact that for over a year he had not looked at a newspaper or magazine. "The newspaper and magazine business," he wrote one editor who had solicited an article, "is an intellectual brothel from which there is no escape."

Strakhov, far from being offended by this well-intentioned advice, was rather pleased by Tolstoy's expressed interest in his career. Until his death in 1896, Strakhov rarely failed to visit Yasnaya Polyana in the summer, and Tolstoy looked forward to his coming with impatience. His favorite path in the garden where he often paced up and down in philosophical meditation was dubbed "Strakhov's Walk" by the children. Tolstoy had almost a blind faith in his critical judgment, but he could not always accept his philosophical views. Perhaps the secret of their close friendship was Strakhov's ability to return in kind the devotion that Tolstoy gave so readily to the few people he sincerely loved. Yasnaya Polyana was his Mecca, Strakhov declared. He did not flatter—Tolstoy scorned this in a friend—but he criticized without offense and appreciated with insight. With sincerity and truthfulness, he could express their mutual feeling in these words: "Well, how soon and where will you find a man who would love and understand you as I do?"

In his search for a program of work after his return from Samara, Tolstoy finally reverted to an old interest—pedagogy. The subject had never ceased to concern him, as occasional observations in his diary and statements in his letters indicate. And the future prospect of the education of his growing family naturally directed his thoughts along these lines. He wrote to Granny as early as 1865: "I'm always thinking a great deal about education, and I impatiently await the time when I can begin to teach my own children. I intend then to open a new school and to write a résumé of all that I know about education and about what no one knows or with which no one agrees." And buried among a spate of material on *War and Peace* in one of the notebooks, dated 1868, there is the following announcement: "First book for reading and a primer for families and schools, with directions to teachers, by Count L. N. Tolstoy." Accompanying this is a detailed plan for what later became his well-known *ABC Book*.

In the autumn of 1871, Tolstoy turned to this plan in real earnest. His new effort filled him with joy. All his energies were concentrated on the task, and every letter carried an excited reference to the work. Sonya was pressed into service again as an amanuensis. The visit of Eugene Schuyler, an American consular official at Moscow, was turned into an inquisition on methods of education in the United States, and he was importuned to furnish data on the teaching of reading in American schools. Tolstoy pored over endless collections of Russian proverbs, medieval legends, and the folk tales of a dozen different countries. He worked out problems in arithmetic and physics, and for the section on astronomy he stayed up all night to observe the stars. There were hurried trips to Moscow to arrange for the printing, and long hours over proofs that never satisfied him. He grew disgusted with his Moscow printer and transferred the publishing to a Petersburg firm, securing the valuable services of Strakhov there as a proofreader.

In the summer of 1872 Tolstoy went for a rest to a recently acquired estate in Samara,[1] but his anxiety over the *ABC Book*, which was then going through the press, was so intense that he returned home sooner than he had intended. Finally the *ABC Book* appeared. Shortly after publication, he wrote in all seriousness to Granny that he had put into it more work and love than on anything else he had done, and that he knew that this was the one important matter of his life.

The *ABC Book* comprised a complete curriculum for beginning pupils. There were sections on reading and writing with drawings, exercises, and various typographical devices to aid in spelling and pronunciation; there were also sections on natural sciences and arithmetic. Detailed directions for teachers were included. Tolstoy realized the importance of effective examples and exercises, and his selections are original and often reveal profound artistic judgment. The frame of reference was restricted by the limitations of the students and their daily lives. "From the natural sciences," he wrote Strakhov, "I did not choose what may be found in books or anything that I by chance knew or what appeared to me necessary to know, but only that which was clear and beautiful; and when it seemed to me insufficiently clear and beautiful, I tried to express it in my own way."

In the reading selections of the book, Tolstoy the artist is everywhere in evidence. He labored over the style of many of the folk tales, legends, and historical narratives that he translated from various foreign languages. No doubt the

[1] In August 1871, Tolstoy had purchased 6750 acres in Samara, in the Buzuluk district, for 20,000 rubles.

models that he had discovered in his studies of Greek literature influenced his stylistic purpose. He strove for clarity and simplicity and achieved them to a remarkable degree. Already he was beginning to believe that the language of sophisticated literature was less effective than the language of the people, and the tales and poetry of the folk he ranked, artistically, above the works of educated writers. At this time he became one of the co-founders of the Society of Lovers of Russian Folksongs. A number of the stories in the *ABC Book* are Tolstoy's own, and they are told with much of the fetching artlessness of folk tales. He composed charming adventures of his favorite dogs, Milka and Bulka, admirable in their simplicity and in the sincerity of the feelings conveyed. Two of his stories, "A Prisoner of the Caucasus" and "God Sees the Truth but Waits" which he also published separately, he later regarded as the best of all his works.

The *ABC Book,* based upon the pedagogical theories that Tolstoy had developed and put into practice in his own village school, was designed, as he said, for the teacher who loved both his calling and his pupils. The work firmly eschews useless or erudite knowledge or facts beyond the comprehension or experience of beginners. A pupil who imagines that the earth stands in water with fish in it, declared Tolstoy, judges much more healthily than one who believes that the earth spins and is not able to understand and explain this fact. For the chief significance of teaching, he maintained, was not in the assimilation of a known quantity of information, but in awakening in students an interest in knowledge.

Tolstoy hardly dared to hope for an agreeable reception of the *ABC Book,* although he was confident of its worth and convinced that it had few if any faults. Letters to Granny and Strakhov at the time of publication were filled with foreboding, yet he anxiously wished for success which would have signalized acceptance of his precious educational theories. He was not left long in doubt, for the storm broke swiftly. The innovations infuriated pedagogues, and a deluge of sharp, even vicious, reviews resulted. In the first few months only four hundred copies were sold.

Tolstoy was bitterly disappointed. He had deliberately tried to avoid extremes in his theorizing in the *ABC Book,* for he had learned a lesson from his past educational controversies, but the reviewers decided that the work was really an attack on the accepted methods. Tolstoy had opposed to a pedagogical system of reason one of faith, to a system of science one of instinct and imagination, and to a system of conviction and ideas one of moral principles. In particular, the critics dealt severely with his theory for overcoming illiteracy and his notions of teaching arithmetic, all of which, they charged, were backward.

Tolstoy's first impulse was to turn fiercely upon his critics, but he contented himself in the end with a rather mild letter to the editor of a periodical, in which he answered the frequent charge that he was ignorant of the popular oral method of teaching reading. Inwardly he scorned the official type of city education, and he had an equal contempt for the new frills introduced from Western Europe by the intelligentsia. He was an aristocratic agrarian, opposed to city civilization, and more than ever he now felt the need of harmony with the peasants.

With a feeling of relief Tolstoy turned once again to teaching the peasant children of the district. The school served as a proving ground for the methods he had advocated in his *ABC Book*. Classes began in January 1872. Sonya helped, and so did eight-year-old Sergei and his sister Tanya, one year younger. They made up a merry company, with some thirty-five peasant youngsters attending class daily. Lessons were gay and lively, the children did pretty much as they pleased, and answered questions all together. What Tolstoy liked most was the picturesqueness and originality of the language of these peasant boys and girls. He once stopped a boy who was running into the next room.

"Where are you off to?" he asked.

"To uncle, to bite off a piece of chalk."

"Cut along, cut along! It's not for us to teach them, but for them to teach us," he said to someone when the boy was gone. "Which of us would have expressed himself like that? You see, he didn't say to 'get' or to 'break off' but to 'bite off,' which is right, because they do literally 'bite' off the chalk from the lump with their teeth, and don't 'break' it off."

4

With the *ABC Book* out of the way, Tolstoy returned to the subject of a historical novel on the time of Peter the Great. Throughout 1872 his letters reflect mounting interest and finally complete absorption in this theme. He envisaged a novel of the epic dimensions of *War and Peace*. Fet and Granny were informed of the big new work and of the joy, timidity, and doubt with which he approached the subject. Friendly historians were importuned for aid; a whole library of books was assembled and studied, and an acquaintance living in a district near the Sea of Azov was asked to obtain topographical details concerning Peter's campaign there. He even planned a trip to the distant Solovetski island in the White Sea in order to secure material on that infamous ancestor of Peter's day, P. A. Tolstoy, who had been banished to a monastery there, but in the end he was unable to make the journey. Scribbled notes from his reading grew more and more bulky. Customs, habits, clothes, weapons, maps, and popular sayings of this past age were investigated —all was grist for his mill. So zealous was he in this research that he once dashed home early from a hunt because he suddenly remembered a minor detail of seventeenth-century costume that he wished to check. "What an epoch for an artist!" he wrote Strakhov.

The instinct of the scholar was strong in Tolstoy. He enjoyed historical research, but he never forgot that it was only a means towards an artistic end. Yet, after months of intensive study of the period of Peter the Great, he found it extremely difficult to start writing. He strained at one beginning after another but all were cast aside. At night, after the children had gone to bed, he talked enthusiastically to Sonya over his vast plans for the novel and then grew gloomy because nothing had been done.

The months wore on into the next year and still the novel remained a mass of unrealized plans. His failure literally made him ill, and so frayed were his nerves that he became unbearable to all around him. In all he made some twenty beginnings. By March of that year, his letters clearly indicated that at last he had grown reconciled to the fact that he would never write a novel on the period of Peter the Great. Once he had admitted this to himself, he was able to put the project, on which he had expended so much effort, entirely out of his mind.

Years later, in recalling his attempt, Tolstoy decided that he had failed because he could not re-create this historical past in his imagination. It was too remote, he said, and hence he was unable to enter fully into the spirit of the people and of the times. Further, his study of the period had altered his initial enthusiasm for Peter. Intimate historical facts and documents drove him to the conclusion that the Tsar possessed no qualities of real greatness and was "simply a drunken fool."[2]

5

When Tolstoy returned home from Samara in the summer of 1872, he found that a bull had fatally injured his herdsman. With officious zeal, the local examining magistrate, a young man, placed Tolstoy under technical arrest. That is, he obtained a promise that Tolstoy would not leave his estate until the whole matter could be brought up at court.

These proceedings infuriated Tolstoy, and worry over the impending examination deprived him of any judicious perspective in this occurrence. With a feeling of outraged dignity, he wrote to Granny for sympathy and perhaps because he deliberately wished to wound the sensibilities of this aristocratic woman who always remained in his eyes a symbol of the governmental proprieties that he scorned. The wrong done him was infamous, he protested. "It is intolerable to live in Russia—intolerable for a man like me, a man with a gray beard, six children, with the consciousness of a useful, industrious life, with my firm conviction that the fault cannot be with me, with the contempt I cannot help feeling for these newfangled tribunals as I know them, and with my sole wish to be left alone, just as I let the entire universe alone; it is intolerable, I say, to live in dread of some silly youngster, displeased with my nose, who is able to make me sit down in the prisoner's dock and send me to jail afterwards." He had decided, he told Granny, to go to England, where everybody's freedom and dignity were assured. Sonya agreed and the children would benefit. He would sell off all his property and find a good healthy place on the English coast. At this point in his letter that exclusive pride of family, never far beneath the surface, emerged. "To live pleasantly in England," he declared, "one must be acquainted with fine, aristocratic families. In this you can help me, and I ask you to do it. . . . Two or three letters of introduction will open to us the doors of some good English

[2] This fragmentary material has been published completely for the first time in the Jubilee Edition (Vol. XVII). A fragment of the novel has been translated into English in Fülöp-Miller's *Tolstoy*.

circle. It is indispensable because of the children who are to be brought up there." Then he concluded: "It is a current argument that the law affords security. It is just the reverse with us. I have adapted my life to the utmost security. I am contented with very little; I seek and wish for nothing but peace. I am loved and honored by the peasantry. Thieves even respect me; I enjoy perfect security, but not on the part of the law."

Tolstoy's frequently expressed dislike for Europe and his contempt for the kind of educational value that children obtained from association with aristocratic families were momentarily forgotten in the rage that prompted this letter. On the other hand, whenever his life, as now, had come in contact with the arbitrariness of the law or abuses of society, the instinct to revolt always flared forth. Nothing could be more consistent than his growing intolerance for all manifestations of man-made civilization. It was the anarchy of extreme individualism. Shortly before this affair and after a visit to Moscow, he had written Granny of his disgust with the idleness, luxury, and ill-gotten wealth of these well-to-do city dwellers. The rottenness spreading into every social stratum shocked him. He threatened never to set foot in the city again and dreaded the future when his daughters would be grown up and exposed to all this.

The incident passed off harmlessly enough, for the authorities soon wrote to excuse their precipitate action, and Granny also to twit him for his unreasonable attitude. His feeling of resentment, however, did not die easily, and he felt obliged to answer Granny that in a matter of this sort he would always adhere to his expressed opinion that it was best for a man who esteemed himself "to turn from this dreadful sea of obtrusive triviality, of disgusting idleness, this lie, lie, lie that from all sides floods the tiny island of honest and industrious life that I have built up for myself. Away to England, for there only is personal freedom protected from every kind of outrage, and there alone is it possible to lead a tranquil and independent life!" This incident added fuel to a flame that was soon to become a bonfire and consume the last ties binding him to man's social order.

6

England as the domicile of the future exponent of civil disobedience had something of the ludicrous about it. Only in

Russia could Tolstoy be moderately contented, or perhaps it would be better to say, only on that plot of land with which he had so completely identified himself—Yasnaya Polyana. However uncertain his spiritual happiness may have been at this time, in the bosom of his blooming family he still thoroughly enjoyed life, despite frequent tribulations.

In March 1872, Tolstoy wrote in a jocular vein to Granny and compared himself to an old, gray-haired, toothless creature. "My life," he added, "is the same as ever, and I could not wish it better. There are a few great intellectual joys—as few as I have it in my power to experience—and a fat fund of *silly joys,* for instance: to teach reading to peasant children, to break in a colt, to admire the large room that has just been built on the house, to calculate the income from a newly purchased estate, to translate a fable of Aesop well, to work at a symphony with my niece, playing four hands, to have fine calves, all of them heifers, and so on. The great joys—that means an extremely happy family, all the children lively, healthy, and, I'm almost convinced, clever and unspoiled, and then work."

There was nothing more to add to the silly joys and great joys of Tolstoy's self-contained existence at this time. Happy people, he remarked, had no history, and at Yasnaya Polyana they were all happy. In September 1873, he mentions the eleventh anniversary of his marriage in a letter to Fet, and finds nothing to comment on, save that his children are learning, that his wife assists in teaching them, and that he is sitting for his portrait by Kramskoi, the distinguished Russian artist.

The children—a sixth, Petya, had been born on June 13, 1872—had each finally won an individual place in the affection of their father. Their sprouting natures fascinated him and he swiftly gained their confidence, not as a father, but as a big brother who knew all the secrets of their little hearts. Another letter to Granny, in October 1872, reveals how deeply he had pondered over these tiny personalities. The oldest, Sergei, he wrote, was somewhat weak and patient in expression, and gentle. "Whenever he laughs, his laugh does not prove contagious, but whenever he cries, I find it difficult to refrain from tears." He had brains, was artistically receptive, learned to perfection, and was clever at jumping and gymnastics, but for the rest, awkward and inattentive. Ilya, the second boy, was a bad pupil and always thought of what he had been forbidden to think about. Original in all things, he was also ardent, violent, and ever ready to strike. When he cried, he was peevish and furious but when he laughed he made the world laugh with him. Forbidden things proved particularly enticing to him, and he was very apt at finding them out. "While quite a little fellow," Tolstoy wrote, "he once overheard somebody saying that my wife had felt the quickening of her child; after this it became his favorite sport for a long time to push a cushion under his smock, to stroke it with his outstretched hand, and to murmur with a smile: 'That's baby.' " Eight-year-old Tanya was already thinking of having children of her own, and graceful Leo did everything skillfully and well. Of Masha, two years old, he remarked with surprising prescience: "She is going to be enigmatical. She will suffer and search and never find. She is always going to search for the unattainable." Petya, the sixth, he set down as quite a colossus but protested his inability to understand or love children under two years of age.

A little more than a year later (November 9, 1873) this same Petya, when seventeen months old, died from a sudden illness. It was the first death in the family. Tolstoy drew comfort from the fact that if one of the eight members of the family had to go, it was better that it should be the youngest. Sonya, however, grieved deeply over the loss of her child, and her husband sympathized with this sorrow of a mother's heart, that wonderful and highest manifestation of Divinity on earth, as he declared.

Sorrows at Yasnaya Polyana, however, were few during these halcyon days. Informality prevailed in the household, although a few aristocratic traditions clung to the daily routine like grandmother's fine old lace on a modish wedding gown. An editor from Moscow arrived on business. Presently a door in the rear opened and a man, a bit above middle height, appeared. He had a full sandy beard and hair and wore common boots and a worker's dark gray blouse pulled together by a leather belt. The editor took him for a servant and asked for the count. The "servant" enjoyed the mistake and risked a rebuke for his impertinence before announcing that he was Count Tolstoy. At once he changed into the gracious host. Those deep blue eyes under the bushy brows lit up with curiosity. There was something electric about this personality that shocked a visitor into an immediate awareness that he was in contact with the great.

A devotion to work was one of the rules of Tolstoy's life. All the family assembled at breakfast, and the master's jokes and quips rendered the conversation more gay and lively. Finally, he would get up with the words, "It's time to work now," and he would disappear into his study, usually carrying off a glass of strong tea with him. No one dared disturb him. When he emerged in the early afternoon, it was to take his exercise, usually a walk or a ride. At five he returned for dinner, ate voraciously, and when he had satisfied his hunger he would amuse all present by vivid accounts of any experience he had had on his walk. After dinner he retired to his study to read, and at eight he would join the family and any visitors in the living room for tea. Often there was music, reading aloud, or games with the children.

The children came in for a good deal of attention from both their parents. As one might expect, the democratic educational principles that Tolstoy formulated for peasant youngsters were in good part abandoned in the case of his own children out of deference to the prevailing views of the social circle in which later they would have to move. When the children were old enough, they were placed under the care of foreign governesses and tutors from whom they learned English, French, and German. But the parents kept a strict watch over them. Sonya taught them reading, writing, and music, and Tolstoy arithmetic. The children were not allowed to select only the subjects they were interested in, as had been the case in Tolstoy's peasant school, but they were not punished for failure in their lessons and were rewarded when they did well. Politeness to servants as well as to members of the family was insisted upon, and kindness to animals.

For the children, their father was the greatest man in the world and they loved to be in his company. He divined their inmost thoughts, and there was nothing they could conceal from him. In their games he was one of them, and they eagerly vied with him in gymnastics, skating, swimming, and riding. Frequently they accompanied him on long walks through the woods when he tried to impress upon them the beauties of nature that he understood and appreciated so well. With an unusual sense of childish fun, he invented games or banished their tears or sulks with some spontaneous outburst of tomfoolery. When all the children would be sitting quietly in the living room, after the departure of some dull visitor, he would suddenly jump up from his chair, raise one hand, and run around the table at a hopping gallop. All the children flew after him, hopping and waving their hands in imitation. After several gallops around the table, they would fall panting in their chairs, the flat atmosphere having been cleared and gay spirits recovered. He called this restorer of happy spirits his "Numidian Cavalry."

On holidays the house was turned over to the children. At Christmas, for example, all was a beehive of activity as the grownups arranged various amusements for the youngsters. Tolstoy always took a leading part in these festivities. The children were gathered around the tree one holiday, fingering their presents. Suddenly an old man appeared leading a bear on a rope. The children screamed with delight. At their demand the bear growled, crawled, danced, and lay down on one side and turned slowly over. Only when the children noticed the absence of their father, who had been there a moment before, did they discover that he was the bear in a fur coat turned inside out.

In the summers Tolstoy spent much time with his children and took them on visits to his sister's or to his other estates. In June 1873, the whole family made the long journey to their new property in Samara. The novel sights and strange Bashkirs provided endless excitement for the youngsters, but the primitive living conditions vastly annoyed their mother. To make matters worse, there was a bad failure of crops in the province of Samara that summer. The peasants faced a terrible famine. Tolstoy made an investigation in the district, sent a letter to a Moscow newspaper in which he effectively described the disastrous situation of the peasants, and appealed for funds. He contributed a hundred rubles, and solicited the aid of friends, among them Granny, who interested the Empress in the matter. As a result, almost two million rubles were raised, much grain contributed, and the worst consequences of a famine averted.

The fame of Tolstoy's name had a good deal to do with the initial success of this undertaking. It was his first, but would not be his last, public service of this nature. His sensibilities rarely failed to respond to human suffering, especially among the peasants. Though he might call them swine and sluts, this born aristocrat never ceased to feel a deep, underlying kinship with the peasants.

XX

Anna Karenina

SHORTLY AFTER the completion of *War and Peace,* the hounds that indefatigably coursed Tolstoy's brain had turned up a fine quarry, but the game had escaped because of various false scents. For in February 1870, Tolstoy had mentioned to Sonya a new theme for a novel; it would concern a married woman in high society who had lapsed morally. "His problem," he said, "was to represent this woman as not guilty but merely pitiful. . . ."

Tolstoy had actually hit upon the theme of his next great novel—*Anna Karenina,* but the various occupations described in the preceding chapter had crowded the project out of his mind. Three years later, impelled by a curious circumstance, he suddenly returned to the theme. One day his son Sergei had been reading to his old aunt from Pushkin's *Tales of Belkin.* The book was left lying around. Tolstoy picked it up, thumbed through it, read bits to Sonya, and was delighted with the narrative skill. The opening sentence of a fragmentary tale in the collection caught his eye: "The guests arrived at the country house."

"How charming that is!" he exclaimed. "That's the way for us to write. Pushkin enters directly into the matter. Another would begin to describe the guests, the rooms, but he jumps into the action at once." That very night, under the inspiration of his reading Pushkin, he began *Anna Karenina.*[1] Sonya noted in her diary that he started the novel on the nineteenth or twentieth of March, 1873.

[1] The story has often been repeated that the direct sentence of Pushkin, "The guests arrived at the country house," gave Tolstoy his cue for the opening of *Anna Karenina,* the second sentence of which reads, "Everything was upset in the Oblonskis' house." But the actual beginning of the novel in the first draft was something quite different.

As usual the family circle hummed with excitement over the beginning of a new work of fiction, and his letters at this time testify to his own enthusiasm. Interruptions occurred. In May, the five-year-old daughter of Tanya Kuzminski died. This child of his sister-in-law was a general favorite with the Tolstoys, and he wrote the grieving mother a curious, condoling letter. Religion alone, he declared, could comfort her. "Why does a child live and die?" he asked. "This is a terrible problem. But for me, there is only one explanation: *It is better off*." And he advised Tanya to read every day and learn by heart the 130th Psalm.

By March 1874, Tolstoy had the first part of his novel ready for printing, but four months later he wrote to a friend that *Anna Karenina* was "repulsive and disgusting" to him. In truth, he had already put the novel aside, for once again the restless urge to be doing something that seemed really worth while had run afoul of his creative spirit. What that something was he explained in a letter to Granny: "I find myself in my summer disposition of soul, i.e. not occupied with poesy, and I have given over printing my novel; I'm so displeased with it that I wish to abandon it; I now occupy myself with practical matters, and precisely with pedagogy. . . ."

2

A sense of unfulfillment in his educational work troubled Tolstoy. Intellectual pride as well as the conviction that he had a public service to perform made it difficult for him to admit defeat after years of effort. And the recent failure of his *ABC Book* still rankled. He had taken up the cudgels again as early as June 1873, when he wrote a letter to a Moscow newspaper to argue against some phases of the German *Lautiermethode,* a phonetic system that had been widely adopted by Russian pedagogues in teaching children to read. And three months later he gathered around him at Yasnaya Polyana a group of village schoolteachers in an effort to induce them to employ his own methods of teaching. Sonya wrote angrily to her sister Tanya of the consequences of this reversion to pedagogy: "The novel is entirely forgotten, and this vexes me."

The first important result of Tolstoy's new drive was that the Moscow Committee on Literacy accepted his invitation to appear before them to explain his educational ideas. It was a bold gesture for he was always ill at ease in such large gatherings. The meeting took place in January 1874. About a hundred people were present, for Tolstoy's name attracted many eminent pedagogues. But the eagerly anticipated battle did not take place, for Tolstoy bluntly refused to give an exposition of his method; he offered merely to answer questions. When the head of the committee asked him how he taught the letters of the alphabet, Tolstoy replied that he drew them in large size on the board, pointed to them and named them, and the pupils repeated them after him. He went through the whole alphabet in one lesson, he explained, and the next day the children knew it perfectly. The assembled pedagogues were naturally confused, for in part Tolstoy obviously employed the very oral method that he professed to scorn. Further questions, however, soon elicited the real nature of his opposition, for he drifted into an explanation of his theory of teaching. His sole aim, he said, was to teach children to read and write what they needed to read and write, not to develop them. His explanations failed to convince, and he agreed to a practical demonstration of the efficiency of his method. He was sure, he told his wife, that it would prove nothing, for they were all "too stupid and stubborn." And the practical demonstration which took place in a Moscow school attached to a factory turned out to be inconclusive. The Committee on Literacy then suggested an extensive test of both methods.

Two groups of illiterate Moscow children of similar ages and social background were provided. An expert in the prevalent phonetic system was designated to teach one group, and P. V. Morozov, an old instructor in the Yasnaya Polyana school, agreed to instruct the other group by Tolstoy's method. The experiment lasted for seven weeks. Tolstoy coached his teacher, followed the competition with close interest, and even journeyed to Moscow to visit the school and offer practical suggestions to Morozov.

At the conclusion of the experiment six members of the Committee on Literacy examined both groups of students. Although there was no unanimity among the examiners, a majority decided that the pupils taught by Tolstoy's opponent had excelled in all three subjects—reading, writing, and arithmetic. Shortly after, a full meeting of the committee was held to appraise the results of the tests. Tolstoy was present and objected that the experiment had failed to prove anything, for it had been conducted under the worst possible conditions. He pointed out that most of the pupils were too young and that the constant presence of visitors had prevented the teachers from holding the children's attention. On this occasion, he went into considerable detail about the system of teaching that he employed, which, he maintained, he had learned from the peasants themselves and not from the pedagogues. After all, he argued, the schools must satisfy the needs of the people and not what theory-ridden educationalists think they need. His vigorous defense did not convince more than one member of the committee, who was half convinced anyway by the results of the experiment. Whether it was out of consideration for the personal prestige of Tolstoy, or because their own minds had been befuddled by the inconclusiveness of the experiment, the committee finally voted to leave the question open.

Tolstoy decided to put his educational views before a larger public. Strakhov, appalled at this extravagant waste of creative genius on what he considered a lost cause, kindly but firmly remonstrated. Tolstoy testily replied that he valued his pedagogical work more highly than his artistic productions. With a keen sense of publicity he suggested to his old friend Nekrasov, with whom he was now scarcely on speaking terms, that something be done on the educational question in his new and very popular periodical, *Notes of the Fatherland*. The editor, hoping to secure the famous author as a regular contributor, eagerly offered to accept anything he cared to write on pedagogy. This was exactly what Tolstoy desired, for he had already begun work on an extensive article, "On National Education." It appeared in Nekrasov's periodical in September 1874.

This article, which takes the form of a letter addressed to the head of the Committee on Literacy, is largely a reaffirmation of the views Tolstoy expressed in the pages of his own pedagogical magazine twelve years before. With ruthless dogmatism he condemned outright both methods of teaching—the phonetic and the visual—then used in Russian elementary schools. And those native teachers who burned incense to German pedagogical theory he sharply criticized for failing to understand or respect the educational needs of the Russian masses. All a teacher had to know, he maintained, was what to teach and how to teach. To find out what to teach, one must go to the people, to the students and their parents. At present, he asserted, the people demanded that their children learn how to read and write and to cipher.

Until they demanded something more, teachers had no right to teach more. As for how to teach, he summed it up in his old phrase: the only criterion for pedagogy was freedom, the only method was experience.

The article created a great stir among the public, infinitely more so than all of Tolstoy's publications on educational themes in the past. To be sure, the work was attractively written, but now it had also come from the pen of the famous author of *War and Peace,* and he had had the good sense to print it in a widely read and authoritative periodical. In a real sense his efforts suddenly made the public pedagogically minded and inspired a surprisingly large number of articles and letters in a variety of magazines. Although the experts, with few exceptions, vigorously attacked him as a pedagogical nihilist, his views elicited widespread sympathetic response among laymen. After years of striving he at last had the satisfaction of knowing that his theories had reached the public.

With such encouragement, Tolstoy felt impelled to try for further success. In February 1875, he published his *New ABC Book*. It was shorter, cheaper, more practical, and, as he remarked in the foreword, adaptable to any method of teaching. Here, too, he now won success, for the Ministry of National Education recommended the work. It was widely adopted by the schools and ran into many large editions (100,000 copies were printed in the 1900 edition).

At the same time Tolstoy published four children's *Readers,* which contained mostly material taken from his first *ABC Book*. The excellence and variety of the selections, the artistic simplicity of the narratives, and no doubt the inexpensive price, gained an enormous market for these little books, and over the years they sold in tens of thousands.

Tolstoy's former dream seemed on the point of realization —he was beginning to exercise a pronounced influence on the course of elementary education in Russia. The dream now expanded. Vaster projects crowded his brain. He wanted to take a prominent place in the larger field of national education, and he wrote to the Minister to inquire whether the government would consider a detailed program that he was contemplating on instruction in the schools and another for training teachers. Although the reply was favorable, it was delayed so long that the impatient Tolstoy had already charged off in another direction. Breaking a long rule he had established, he allowed himself to be nominated for the County Council, and when elected, he accepted an appointment to the Education Committee.

One naturally thinks of the poet Matthew Arnold, inspector of schools in England at this time. With Arnold, however, the post was a means of livelihood and a most unpoetic business; Tolstoy, in his more restricted sphere, found a world of poetry in the work of inspecting the local schools. "Whatever I may do," he wrote to Granny in December 1874, "I at least always feel convinced that forty centuries look down upon me from the heights of the pyramids, and that the world will perish if ever I stand still. . . . I have now jumped out of abstract pedagogy into the practical on one side and the abstract on the other—the work of the schools in our district. And I straightway began to love these thousands of children with whom I'm concerned, as I did fourteen years ago. I keep asking people why we want to instruct the population, and there are five answers to it. Do tell me yours. Here is mine: I do not argue about it, but whenever I enter a school and see this multitude of ragged children, thin, dirty, with bright eyes and so often with angelic expressions, I am seized with the anxiety and terror I would experience in seeing people drown. Ah, how to drag them out, and who is to be first, who next! And the thing about to perish is precisely the most precious, most spiritualized, and the most striking thing to be found in children." He next mentioned the lack of progress on *Anna Karenina,* and then added: "But I cannot tear myself away from living creatures to bother about imaginary ones."

Sonya by no means shared his new enthusiasm, and she feared that the novel would never be finished. He had been offered the handsome rate of over thirty rubles a page for *Anna Karenina,* and yet, Sonya complained to her sister, he spent all his time in school or with district teachers in his study. The writing of novels she adored, but all these primers, arithmetics, and grammars she scorned. "I look with perplexity on all this," she wrote her brother, "and I regret the efforts he expends on such occupations, instead of composing a novel, and I do not understand to what degree it is useful, since this activity is restricted to a tiny corner of Russia—the Krapivenski district."

Tolstoy paid little attention to this domestic opposition. His reforming zeal in educational matters had taken complete possession of him. He agitated with some success for inexpensive instruction in the district, and he launched his pet project of establishing at Yasnaya Polyana a teachers' training seminary, for he wished to train peasant teachers to take their place in the milieu in which they had grown up and to provide the kind of education for peasant children that would not instill in them alien desires or render them unfit for the performance of duties to which they would be called by their position in life. This was to be, he remarked, a "university in bast shoes."

In 1876 the Ministry of National Education approved of Tolstoy's carefully prepared plan for a teachers' training seminary at Yasnaya Polyana. And his request to the Tula government for financial assistance in return for a certain number of tuition-teaching scholarships was granted. A good deal of renovating was done on one wing of the manor house at Yasnaya Polyana that was to be used for classrooms, and many other preparations were made for the opening in September 1877. For some unexplained reason, perhaps because the educational centers in the Tula government did not favor the idea, only twelve candidates applied for the courses. This poor showing discouraged Tolstoy, and he refused to open his "university in bast shoes." It was his last constructive effort to improve formal education in Russia. A long and arduous chapter in the history of Tolstoy's civic conscience had come to an end.

3

No doubt Sonya felt relieved at the demise of her husband's pedagogical passion. Now he could finish *Anna Karenina*. In December of 1874 he had sold the serial rights to Katkov for the magnificent sum of 20,000 rubles, and a little more than three parts had appeared in 1875 in the early numbers of the *Russian Messenger*. Then work on the novel was interrupted until the next year. Fet egged him on, and Strakhov wrote him of the ecstatic praise going the rounds of Petersburg over the early parts. Family worries, periodic feelings of repugnance for the novel, and a trip to Samara —at the end of which he gloomily wrote Fet that he had not soiled his hands with ink or his heart with thoughts—were used as excuses for his failure to keep at *Anna Karenina*. Several more parts were published in 1876, but only under considerable stress and with such a conviction that the writing was poor that he begged Strakhov not to praise his efforts. Two laudatory reviews that Strakhov sent he burned without reading. As he reached the end, however, he took new courage and expended greater effort. The final parts appeared in 1877 in the first four issues of the *Russian Messenger*. But the eighth and last part Katkov refused to publish because Tolstoy would not change unpatriotic allusions to Russian volunteers who were at that time aiding the Serbs against the Turks. Accordingly, Tolstoy published this last part separately. The whole novel, considerably corrected with Strakhov's aid, appeared in book form the following year.

Tolstoy had built the story of his novel, as that of *War and Peace,* out of the stuff of life, and its greatness rests on those qualities that he thought most important in art—simplicity, goodness, and truth. After eight years of respectable married life to a cold and pompous husband, the warm-hearted and attractive Anna falls in love with Vronski, a passion that is sincerely returned. Her husband, conventional society, and her own moral nature are sacrificed to this consuming love which becomes the only thing left in life for Anna. In her frantic efforts to protect and sustain her love, she becomes egotistic and possessive, and jealousy eventually transforms into hate the love for which she had given up everything. There is only one escape, and Anna's suicide in the end fulfills the epigraph of the novel: "Vengeance is mine, I will repay."

Parallel with the story of Anna and Vronski runs the account of the love of Kitty and Levin. Tolstoy drew heavily upon himself for the character of Levin, and the latter's brother Nikolai is modeled on Tolstoy's dead brother Dmitri. Indeed, the whole story of Levin and Kitty—their courtship, marriage, and family existence—is in many respects the story of Tolstoy and his wife. Scenes from his own life are transformed by art into the magnificent drama of fiction—the birth of Levin's first child, the death of his brother, the unsurpassable mowing scene; and even the tragic suicide of Anna under the wheels of the train was suggested by the similar fate of the jealous mistress of one of Tolstoy's neighbors.

If *Anna Karenina* has nothing of the epic sweep of *War and Peace,* it gains artistically by virtue of its compactness and inner unity. As art it is perfection, Dostoyevsky remarked, and he felt that there was nothing in European literature that could be compared with it. Tolstoy had never probed more deeply the mystery of human fate nor presented more arrestingly the dependence of human happiness on the immutable laws of nature. Anna defied these laws, and nature that neither forgets nor pardons quietly and dispassionately exacted retribution.

With the appearance of *Anna Karenina* the reputation of Tolstoy as Russia's greatest novelist was secure. Almost without exception, the enthusiastic reviews accorded him the leading position. Even abroad, Turgenev, in a foreword to a French translation of the *Two Hussars,* generously declared Tolstoy's pre-eminence. From Petersburg Strakhov maintained a running commentary in his letters to Tolstoy on the reaction of the reading public as the parts of the novel appeared. People were in ecstasies; they wept over the unforgettable and pathetic scenes of little Seryozha, and haunted the bookshops for fear of losing out on the next installment. Nearly everyone recognized, as Henry James did some twenty years later in America, that Tolstoy's fiction represented perfection in the art of depicting human life.

4

Meanwhile, death continued to stalk the premises at Yasnaya Polyana throughout the period in which *Anna Karenina* was written. In June 1874, Auntie Tatyana, almost eighty years of age, died. Although it was expected, Tolstoy could not fail to be deeply affected by the passing of this foster mother of his childhood, the constant solace and confidante of his youth and manhood, the woman who had taught him "the spiritual happiness of love." "She was a wonderful being," he wrote to Granny, ". . . for fifty years she lived here, and not only did no evil, but not even a disagreeable thing to anyone. Yet she was afraid of death; she did not say she was afraid, but I saw it. What does this signify? I think it is humility. I lived with her all my life, and it will be terrible without her."

The next year, on February 21, Tolstoy's ten-months-old son, Nikolai, died from a sudden illness. He had been born only five months after the death of little Petya, and was so like him that the parents involuntarily called him "Petya." Both Tolstoy and his wife were grief-stricken. Sonya was soon pregnant again, however, and at the end of 1875, falling desperately ill, she gave premature birth to a daughter who lived less than two hours. And very shortly after this, at the end of December, Tolstoy's ancient aunt, Pelageya, who had recently come to live with the family, also died. For some mysterious reason the loss of this last link with his mother and father, his protectress during his Kazan student days, profoundly affected and haunted him for some time. It is little wonder that he wrote to Fet: "Fear, horror, death, the children's jollity, food, vanity, doctors, falseness, death, horror. It was all terribly oppressive."

Death, however, could not absorb for long the interests of a family in which births had become so frequent: a ninth child, Andrei, was born to the Tolstoys on December 6, 1877. With this brood Sonya's tasks were endless. She made their clothes, tended them in all their illnesses, played games with them, and despite the employment of various governesses and tutors, she also gave lessons to the children. And at night, if guests were not present, she made neat copies of her husband's untidy manuscripts. To her sister Tanya she wrote: "I teach, and nurse like a machine from morn to night, from night to morn."

Tolstoy felt keenly his duty towards the children, particularly in the matter of their education. When they were old enough, he taught them Latin and Greek. After explaining the alphabet, he would set them to reading Xenophon at once, completely ignoring the grammar. Ilya, the second son, surprised all the masters at his school examination by his ability to translate the classics at sight with comparative ease, although he knew no grammar. At night Tolstoy would sometimes read to them romantic fiction, such as the tales of Jules Verne, and on one occasion they were all delighted with the illustrations he drew for one of these stories.

The children always looked forward to the summer, for then their father ordinarily rested from his labors and spent more time with them. In June 1875, he once again took the whole family with him to his Samara estate. On this visit he arranged a horse race that attracted hordes of people from the surrounding countryside. There was much feasting, music, and wrestling, at which the Bashkirs excelled. The horse race was finally run, and Tolstoy presented prizes. After two days of festivities, the guests departed. Tolstoy was delighted with the good order preserved by all, and without the presence of a policeman. The next summer Tolstoy again went to Samara, this time without the family. He proceeded to Orenburg to buy horses, for he wished to develop a large stud farm. At one time he had as many as four hundred horses, but eventually the project failed.

As Tolstoy's creative and pedagogical work demanded more and more of his time, he easily fell into the habit of letting Sonya assume most of the responsibility for their growing family of children. The tense moments when his overcharged sensitivities reacted violently to childish misbehavior grew more frequent. The "nasty face" of little Ilya, he wrote his wife, on one of the rare occasions when she was away from home, literally tortured him all day. When he finally overcame his indecision and talked to the child, he wept with his son. He had praised all his children to Granny, but in a letter four months later he wrote wearily: "I have felt so much and thought so much about them, and made such efforts—and to what end? In order that at best they may grow up neither too bad nor too stupid. It's a strangely ordained world, and, as my friend Fet says, the longer I live in it, the less I understand." He was beginning to realize the truth of the Russian proverb: "Few children—few cares, more children—more cares."

Apart from his excursions to Samara in the summers, Tolstoy absented himself from Yasnaya Polyana with more and more reluctance. Trips to Moscow on the business of publishing *Anna Karenina* were unavoidable, but he never remained in the city any longer than necessary. Now, not even Moscow's cultural attractions could detain him. In December 1876, however, he felt a hurried business visit to the city well rewarded, for he made the acquaintance of the great composer Tchaikovsky. From his youth, Tchaikovsky had been an enthusiastic admirer of Tolstoy's works, which he felt had been written by an author with a superhuman power for probing the human heart. After their first meeting Tchaikovsky wrote a friend that he had been completely enchanted by Tolstoy's ideal personality. Tchaikovsky induced N. G. Rubinstein, then Director of the Moscow Conservatory, to give a musical evening solely for Tolstoy's benefit. When Tchaikovsky's "Andante in D Major" was played, Tolstoy burst into tears, not an unusual occurrence when he was deeply affected by music. Tchaikovsky admitted that his vanity as a composer had never been so flattered. After Tolstoy returned home, he wrote Tchaikovsky that his literary efforts had never been so wonderfully rewarded as on that musical evening, and he sent him a collection of folk songs taken down in the Yasnaya Polyana district in the hope that Tchaikovsky would make use of them, he remarked, "in a Mozart-Haydn style and not in the

Beethoven-Schumann-Berlioz artificial manner!" Tchaikovsky did not think much of the songs, and it is rather strange that this acquaintance, begun with such ardor and lofty mutual regard on both sides, should have quickly cooled. Later evidence indicates that Tchaikovsky rather resented that Tolstoy, this searcher of souls in his novels, was in real life a simple fellow who had no interest in probing his soul and merely wanted to chat with him about music.

5

During the period in which *Anna Karenina* was written, Sonya enjoyed and had earned the right to bask in the reflected glory of her husband's genius, but like any practical-minded woman, there were times when she would have willingly exchanged the reflected glory for some commonplace fun. She was still an attractive young woman, and the long winters at remote Yasnaya Polyana provided her with no stage on which to shine. The summer with its visitors and festivities was always an eagerly anticipated season in a year of isolation, but now Tolstoy, exhibiting a moodiness strange for him, wrote to Fet that these visitors bored him.

Sonya confided her rebellion largely to the pages of her diary. "I hate those people," she wrote, "who tell me that I'm beautiful; I never thought this, and now it is already too late. And what good would beauty do me, what do I need it for? . . . Lyovochka would grow accustomed to the most hideous face, if only his wife were quiet, worshipful, and lived the kind of life that he had selected for her." And in another passage she complained gloomily: "This excessively isolated country existence has finally become insupportable to me. A sad apathy, an indifference to everything; today, tomorrow, the months, the years are all the same to me." At this charming time of their life together, why, she suspiciously asked, did he so willingly leave her for a trip to Samara? She used the excuse of collecting material for his biography to pore over his old diaries, and once again, after almost fifteen years of married life, these records of his old sins of the flesh filled her with brooding jealousy. Passages of fiercely expressed hatred for herself and her daily existence alternated with such pathetic declarations as "I'm much concerned with my own external appearance, and I begin to dream about another life than that which I am now leading. That is, I want to read much, to be educated, to be intellectual. I want to be beautiful, to think about clothes, and stupid things."

No doubt a series of illnesses contributed greatly to Sonya's frayed disposition at this time and kept her husband in a state of constant worry. "What situation can be more terrible for a healthy husband than the illness of a wife," he wrote to a friend in the spring of 1876. "This year I've experienced and continue to experience this situation. My wife has been dangerously ill. All winter she was unwell, grew weak, and is now again in bed. . . . For me, this situation is grievous, especially because I do not believe in doctors or in medicine. . . ." He thought of taking her abroad, but instead he sent her for treatment to a distinguished Petersburg physician in January 1877. And with deep concern he hastened off a letter to Granny in that city, asking her to watch out for his wife and give him an absolutely faithful report of her health. It was the first meeting between these two—the wife and the woman of whom Sonya could never dispel a twinge of jealousy because of the part, however innocent, that she had played in her husband's past. Granny, as might be expected from this aristocratic lady of exquisite breeding, wrote Tolstoy a warm letter concerning his wife's charms. Sonya was more restrained in her reaction to Granny. The comforting report of the doctor was that he had never seen lungs so sound and strong (they had feared consumption). He found nothing organically wrong and attributed most of her illness to nerves. His concluding advice to husband and wife was that they should live in a normal and philosophic manner.

Tolstoy and his wife, however, had reached a point where life together in a normal and philosophic manner had become quite impossible. Something had quietly and unobtrusively dropped out of the happy harmony of their married existence. It had been caught in the ebb and flow of the ceaseless conflict in his soul, in the throb and stress of a gigantic disharmony. Outwardly, all remained as before, but a mutual dissatisfaction was felt. Nor could Tolstoy interest himself so wholeheartedly in family matters as formerly, and Sonya observed this defection. Tolstoy's mind was now full of thoughts on life and death. He had once again returned to the path that he had stumbled along and had been repeatedly diverted from all his life. He was never again to leave it. The questions that had intermittently tormented him for years must now be answered. The spiritual crisis had been reached. His confused and persistent spiritual quest made for coldness and disharmony in the family. Poor Sonya did not understand this soul-sickness; it depressed her and evoked protest. And she would continue to protest for the next thirty years.

XXI

The Crisis

ALL HIS LIFE Tolstoy had been searching for God, often in ways that evaded his own consciousness. Instead of sinning his way to God, like Dostoyevsky, he had to reason his way to Him. What was about to take place in his spiritual life did not represent a change or a break with the past, but rather an intensification of a development that had been proceeding slowly ever since his youth. He had had moments of spiritual crisis in the past, when he had confronted the riddle of existence, but always the material concerns of life had intervened. The experience is a common one and is usually dismissed, either because man cannot be bothered or because he lacks the courage to probe to the bottom.

Marriage, with its hope of family happiness, had saved Tolstoy from a period of deep despair that had seemed crucial. What he did not realize, however, was that his fifteen happy years of marriage were a transition period—they had not cured his despair, but had merely diverted it. Shortly after marriage the same gnawing self-examination began again, quietly at first, but with a constantly rising tempo. Innumerable family cares and tremendous creative efforts momentarily lulled him in periods of spiritual agony. As he himself said, he was like a sick man who pays no attention to the first slight signs of an indisposition; then these signs reappear more and more often and merge into one uninterrupted period of suffering; the suffering increases, and before the sick man realizes it, what he took for a mere indisposition has become more important to him than anything in the world—it was death! This was a disease family happiness could no longer cure. Indeed, as the ideal existence he liked to consider it, his family happiness had ended forever.

An observation in Tolstoy's notebook suggested that even as early as 1865 he had begun to notice the slight signs of the "indisposition" that soon developed into intense spiritual suffering. "Everyone knows and experiences in a dream," he wrote, "the conscious feeling of helplessness and at the same time a sense of the possibility of power, when you wish to run or strike a blow and your legs fail you or you hit powerlessly and softly—this feeling of captivity (I am unable to describe it in any better fashion) is momentarily undergone by the best of us even in our conscious state. In the most enduring, happy, and poetic moments, in moments of joyous, satisfied love, one feels even more strongly that there is much that is lacking, that something is cut out, that one's legs will not move, that one's blows are soft and futile." This sense of futility grew like a malignant cancer and slowly began to paralyze all Tolstoy's activities. He experienced moments of perplexity when life seemed to stand still, and he felt dejected for he did not know what to do or how to live. These moments of perplexity passed, but they returned more and more frequently, and they were always expressed by the question: "What is it for? What does it all lead to?"

At first, Tolstoy thought these were rather stupid and childishly simple questions to which everyone knew the answers. But when he tried to solve them, he became convinced that they were the most important and deepest of life's questions. Now he had to know *why* he did anything —why he built up his estate, bettered the lot of his peasants, educated his children, or wrote novels. He found no satisfactory answer. Life came to a standstill; it had become meaningless. There was nothing ahead, he wrote, but suffering and real death—complete annihilation.

Tolstoy confessed to himself at this time that he had everything to live for—a loving wife, family, wealth, fame, and good health. Yet life seemed stupid, a spiteful joke that someone had played on him. After nearly fifty years of existence he had achieved almost everything man could wish for, but he stood on the summit of life like an archfool, seeing plainly that there was nothing in life, that there had been and would be nothing. And meanwhile someone watched and was amused by it all. He imagined himself clinging to the branch of life, yet knowing that the dragon of death inevitably waited to devour him. His love of family happiness and of art had ceased to be sweet to him. Death waited; all else was false.

2

The question that brought Tolstoy to the verge of suicide at the age of fifty was, as he expressed it himself, the simplest of questions lying in the soul of every man: Why should I live, why wish for anything, or do anything? In short, has life any meaning that the inevitable death awaiting one does not destroy? And to free himself of this dilemma, he experienced an almost irresistible urge to commit suicide. So strong was this inclination to self-destruction that he had to be wily with himself. He took a cord out of his room lest he be tempted to hang himself from the crossbeam, and he avoided hunting for fear that he would take this easy way out to shoot himself. One cannot doubt the reality of the forces that almost brought him to take his life, but his inquiring mind first imposed upon him the necessity of searching every possible source for a solution to this question. And his *Confession,* which he probably drafted in 1879, contains the remarkable record of this extensive inquiry.

The exact sciences, Tolstoy found, did not deal with the question at all, whereas the speculative sciences, culminating in metaphysics, dealt with it but supplied no satisfactory answer. He read and thought, and the more he read and thought the further he felt from his goal. He could get no answer from the materialists. The answers of all the pure philosophers and great thinkers he consulted may be summed up in the words of Socrates: "The life of the body is an evil and a lie. Therefore the destruction of the life of the body is a blessing and we should desire it." What these profound minds had declared, Tolstoy concluded, had also been thought by millions upon millions of people. One could not be deceived—all was vanity! Science and philosophy failed to provide him with solace and faith in his hour of spiritual need, and the experience left him forever with the firm conviction that they fail to answer the basic questions of life.

In his search Tolstoy next turned to an inquiry into the lives of the men of his own class, and he decided that they met the problem that beset him in one of four ways. The first way was that of ignorance; some people, mostly women or the very young or dull, did not understand this question of life to which he could not close his eyes. The second way was that of the Epicureans, the majority of the men of his circle, who, because of their leisure, comfort, and all the favorable but accidental circumstances of their position, would not think of the inevitability of sickness, age, and death, which would destroy all their pleasures.

The third way out, Tolstoy saw, was that of strength and energy, an escape that he wished to adopt himself, for it was suitable only for a few exceptional people who understood that life was an evil and must be destroyed. The last way out was that of the weak people, who saw the truth of the situation and yet clung to life as though they still hoped to obtain something from it. And sadly he realized that he belonged to this category.

The fact that he could reach such conclusions and not act upon them puzzled Tolstoy. If he really believed that life was a stupid joke, then why not get rid of it? Other people were contented and liked what they were doing, so why bother them with this conviction that life was repulsive and dull? His very failure to act convinced him that something was radically wrong with his reasoning and he turned his thoughts in a new direction.

3

One runs the risk of suggesting that there was something of the amateur philosopher about Tolstoy's setting down in cold-blooded and logical fashion the progressive stages of his spiritual travail. But he did not live by reason alone. The quality of sheer feeling, so prevalent in his artistic productions, constantly warred against his rational convictions and tormented him to the point of physical suffering. Reason might prove to him, as it had to many others, that life was a long disease of which sleep was the only alleviation and death the only cure, but a feeling deep within him told him that there was something more, some ineluctable answer beyond the power of reason to divine.

Tolstoy had found no answer to his doubts either in knowledge or in the personal solution of the social class to which he belonged. Something now obliged him to turn for light to the peasantry. In his *Confession* he related that suddenly he instinctively felt that if he wished to live and to understand the meaning of life, he must seek this meaning not among those who had lost it—his own social class—

but among those millions who knew it and who supported the burden of their own existence. Upon examination he saw that the peasantry had a knowledge of the meaning of life, and that that knowledge was their faith in God. This simple faith of the peasant, however, his reason at first rejected.

Tolstoy's dilemma was more terrible than ever. He could find nothing along the path of reasonable knowledge except a denial of life, and in faith he could find nothing but a denial of reason. Yet he quickly realized that it was a mistake to expect finite things to supply a meaning to life, for the finite has no ultimate meaning apart from the infinite. The two must be linked together before an answer to life's problems could be reached. And he at last began to see that however unreasonable might be the replies given by faith in God, they had an advantage in that they introduced a relation between the finite and the infinite, without which no reply was possible.

Religion had hovered on the periphery of Tolstoy's mind for years, and on several occasions, such as during his stay in the Caucasus, at Sevastopol, and in France when his brother Nikolai died, the subject had entirely absorbed his thoughts. But only in the first half of 1870 did religion, with all its unreasonableness, begin to appeal consistently as the most profound expression of the wisdom of humanity. Although religion is illogical, he wrote to Fet in January 1873, "there is something in it." And the next year he jotted down in his notebook his intention (never fulfilled) to write an article on that "something by which people live," and the "something," he indicated, was religion.

Tolstoy saw at this time that religion gave meaning to life, but the Church itself was an insult to his reason. Only faith, however, could make life possible for him, for if a man lived, he must believe in something. His problem now was to reconcile faith and the Church that preached it, for he was willing to accept any faith if only it did not demand of him a direct denial of reason.

Tolstoy next began a detailed investigation of religions—Buddhism, Mohammedanism, and especially Christianity. He studied them in books, and he eagerly sought information from learned people, theologians, and monks. Even the popular "New Christians" of that time, the Evangelicals, who professed salvation by faith in the Redemption, were sympathetically considered. Tolstoy knew followers of Lord

Radstock, the ardent and persuasive English Evangelical preacher, who traveled in Russia. One of them, Count A. P. Bobrinski, Minister of Ways of Communication, visited him in February 1876, and he wrote to Granny of this prominent Radstockite: "No one ever spoke better to me about faith than Bobrinski. He is irrefutable because he does not offer evidence, he simply believes, and you feel that he is happier than those who do not have his faith, and you chiefly feel that it is impossible to acquire this happiness from faith by the power of reason; one must obtain it by a miracle. And this I desire."

But Tolstoy's searching intellect and instinctive hatred of insincerity quickly led him to condemn the Evangelicals, who hoped to make him their spokesman in Russia. He required a faith much more intelligible than the scheme of Redemption by the blood of Jesus. God pouring down grace on aristocratic members of the English Club and well-fed boards of stockholders seemed to him silly and immoral. The faith he sought had to face the facts of life, and he imagined that it could be won only through work and suffering. In a later letter to Granny he wrote: "It is strange and awful to say, but I believe in nothing that is taught by religion. And what is more, I not only hate and despise atheism, but I can see no possibility of living, and still less of dying, without faith. . . . As to the exigencies of my brain and the answers of the Christian faith, I find myself in the position of two hands wanting to clasp each other, but the fingers of which resist uniting."

Throughout 1876 and part of the next year Tolstoy's letters to close friends revealed his attempts, now in passionate outbursts, now in closely reasoned speculation, to reconcile the God of revealed religion with his reason and his demand for a faith that made life worth living. To the ordinarily sympathetic Granny, this complex, tortured searching seemed futile. It had never occurred to her that there was any choice in the matter of religious faith. Why did he not accept the salvation offered him by the Russian Orthodox Church? And she attributed his persistent ratiocination on this theme to false shame. The charge angered him. "The religious problem for me," he replied, "is exactly like the problem of a shipwrecked man: he looks out for something to seize in order to save himself from the imminent danger that he feels with all his being. And now for two years religion has held out to me this possibility of salvation; therefore false shame is utterly out of the question. The fact is that every time I seize this plank of salvation, I am drowned with it; I seem somehow able to float along if I do not catch hold of the plank."

His mind aglow with radiant thoughts that were constantly darkened by doubts, Tolstoy doggedly kept up the search for religious truth. "It is the first time you have spoken to me about the Deity—God," he eagerly wrote Fet in April 1877. "And I have long been thinking about that chief problem. But do not say that one cannot think about it. One not only can, but must! In all ages the best, the real people, have thought about it. And if we cannot think about it *as they did,* we must find out *how.*"

4

Tolstoy's prolonged and profound spiritual struggle seemed to effect a transformation in his whole character. Sonya noted in her diary how the religious spirit in him grew stronger every day; and she wrote to her sister Tanya that his eyes were often fixed and strange; that he hardly talked at all and had quite ceased to belong to this world. His health suffered under the strain and his ebullient nature grew meek and humble. The very thought that he had a single enemy in the world became painful to him. In this temper of mind he remembered his long-standing feud with Turgenev and promptly sent him a letter to Paris, in which he recalled their old friendship and his initial literary indebtedness to him, and concluded: "Sincerely, if you can forgive me, I offer you all the friendship of which I am capable. At our time of life there is only one good—loving relations with people, and I will be very happy if they exist between us." Turgenev was touched and joyfully accepted the offer of reconciliation, promising to visit Tolstoy that summer. The dangerous fascination of the younger for the older writer had never really ceased, and Turgenev had followed closely, though critically, every step of Tolstoy's career during the whole course of their rupture of seventeen years.

True to his promise, Turgenev visited Yasnaya Polyana in the summer of 1878. The whole household bubbled with excitement, for most of its members had never seen the famous author. They were much impressed by his appearance—his huge frame and noble head with its full white beard and shock of hair. Both men seemed delighted to see each other. Turgenev thought Tolstoy had grown quiet and mature. Much of the time was spent in Tolstoy's study in philosophical and religious discussions. Turgenev charmed the family with his conversation, played chess with young Sergei, and read to all of them one of his tales, "The Dog," which, however, failed to impress his listeners. Despite his years, he was still very active and accompanied Tolstoy and the children in a walk about the estate. Coming across a seesaw that had been set up to amuse the youngsters, the two authors were tempted. The sixty-year-old Turgenev mounted one end of the board and the fifty-year-old Tolstoy the other, and they seesawed while the children gleefully looked on.

Returning to his own estate Turgenev wrote: "I cannot help repeating to you once more what a fine and agreeable impression my visit to Yasnaya Polyana made on me, and how happy I am that the misunderstanding that existed between us has vanished without a trace, as though it had never been." Yet not even Tolstoy's newly discovered humility could entirely eradicate his suspicion of his rival's sincerity. For in subsequent letters to Fet, Tolstoy complained that Turgenev had not changed, and that it was better to "keep farther away from him and from sin," for he was "an unpleasant sort of quarrel-maker."

The new direction Tolstoy's thoughts were taking was reflected in his attitude towards war. In 1876 Russian volunteers hastened to the aid of Serbia and Montenegro in their hopeless struggle against Turkey, whose relations with Russia became seriously strained. In November, Tolstoy went to Moscow to hear about the war. "This whole affair disturbs me greatly," he wrote to Fet. "It is well for those to whom it is clear, but I am frightened when I reflect on the complexity of the conditions amid which history is made, and on how some Madame A.—with her vanity and false sympathy for something indefinite—becomes an indispensable cog in the machine!" In the last part of *Anna Karenina,* he had expressed his doubts about the self-sacrificing character of the Russian volunteers and the purity of the patriotism of the press. Levin exposes the hypocrisy of the press and condemns the chauvinistic sentiment that leads to war.

When war actually broke out between Russia and Turkey, in April 1877, Tolstoy was torn by conflicting emotions. His own experience with war in the past had left him with a sense of horror over its utter futility. Neither this, however, nor his growing conviction of the sinfulness of war could save him from the wave of patriotic enthusiasm that now swept the country. He followed the course of events with anxious expectancy, and the moral question involved was quickly displaced by a mounting anger over the lack of success of Russian arms. In fact, so agitated did he become over defeats that he began to write an article on the reasons behind these military failures.[1]

Throughout this period Tolstoy's distraught state of mind made literary work extremely difficult and at times impossible, although it is clear that he found a kind of refuge in creative efforts. Frequently he had lost sight of *Anna Karenina* in this religious mist, and he apparently gained comfort from the work only in describing Levin's painful search for spiritual values that reflected so strikingly his own quest. Towards the end of the novel, however, in 1877, Tolstoy returned to the design of *The Decembrists* which some fourteen years before he had laid aside in favor of *War and Peace*.

This old project, a logical sequel to *War and Peace,* and long conceived of as the second of a great trilogy of novels, aroused Tolstoy's sluggish creative powers. He had in mind a work as prodigious as *War and Peace,* and he now turned to it with something of his former zeal. Historical materials were collected and investigated; old Decembrists were visited and their memories of years of proud suffering in exile were ransacked at his request; and he went to Petersburg to inspect the dungeons of the Petropavlov Fortress, where some of the rebels had been confined—he was told politely that he could see every part of the prison except the dungeons, which only three persons in the whole Empire, the Emperor, the commandant, and the chief of the gendarmes, could leave after having once entered. His interest continued until January 1879, when he once again dropped the subject. His decision was no doubt prompted partly by the fact that the authorities refused him permission to study material in the State Archives, and partly because he lost sympathy with the rebels when he learned that their movement was not a purely national one but had been inspired by French ex-

[1] A body of Turkish prisoners, held at a place not far from Yasnaya Polyana, interested Tolstoy. Struck by the fact that each captive had a copy of the Koran in his kit, he conversed with the Turks on religion.

ample and thought. On the other hand, it is also clear that a resurgence of his spiritual unrest and his preoccupation with another work at this time—his *Confession*—helped turn him away from the theme.

Indeed, war or novel writing or practical affairs could not contend successfully with the spiritual ferment in his soul. With a sense of relief he wrote to Fet in April 1879: "Heaven knows where my Decembrists are now. I do not think about them, and were I to do so and to write, I flatter myself that my breath alone, of which the story would smell, would be unendurable to those who shoot men for the good of humanity. . . . But I should mention that even now I conscientiously abstain from reading newspapers and consider it a duty to wean everyone from that pernicious practice."

The growing intensity of Tolstoy's spiritual search for a religious faith that would solve all his doubts was gradually drawing him away from the material concerns of life. In March 1876, Sonya had written of her husband in her diary: "Today he says that he cannot live long in this terrible religious struggle in which he has been buried over these last two years, and now he hopes that he is close to the time when he may become an entirely religious man." He extracted a curious comfort from the *Pensées* of Pascal, a book that he eagerly read and wrote about to Granny and Fet. It was not, however, the dogmatic theology of the great Frenchman that pleased him, but the consuming and dramatically expressed doubts about life and death that drove Pascal on in his quest for religious faith.

Since the faith of worldly theologians and of the people of his own class repelled him, Tolstoy turned to believers among the poor, simple, unlettered folk: pilgrims, monks, sectarians, and peasants. Pilgrims he sought out on the highway, on their long plodding trips to holy places; peasants he stopped to converse with on their way to and from work; and hermits and monks he visited in their retreats and monasteries. In the summer of 1877, accompanied by Strakhov, he traveled to the famous Optina Monastery in the Kaluga district. There he held long religious discussions with the Elder, Father Ambrose, and was impressed by his wisdom. In June 1879, he visited the catacomb monastery at Kiev, but he gained little spiritual sustenance from this trip.

Tolstoy found a great deal of superstition mixed with Christian truths among these simple people, but the deeper he pondered the more convinced he became that they possessed a faith that was necessary to them and gave their life real meaning. Their days were passed in labor, and whereas people of his own social level were terrified of suffering and death, he observed that these poor folk lived and suffered and approached death with tranquillity. The better he came to know them, the more he loved them, and the easier it was for him to go on living. Under their influence he was conscious of a change taking place in him, a change that had long been preparing and the promise of which had always been in him. The life of his own spoiled and rich circle had lost all meaning for him, but the life of laboring people, of the great masses of mankind that produce life, now appeared to him in its true light.

Tolstoy had by no means won his spiritual battle, for he saw clearly enough that the mainspring in the lives of these simple people was their faith in God, and this fact once again accentuated his own search for God. He went through endless and tortuous arguments with himself over the cause of causes, but he derived no comfort from the fact that men had persistently denominated "God" the first cause of all. He realized that the conception of God was something that he could evoke or refrain from evoking in himself at will.

The process of fluctuating between belief and unbelief induced in Tolstoy an awareness of something that had hitherto escaped his attention. He noticed that when he believed in God, life seemed worth living; when he forgot Him or disbelieved in Him, he had no further interest in life. "What more do you seek?" a voice exclaimed within him. "This is He. To know God and to live is one and the same thing. God is life. Live seeking God and then you will not live without God."

This experience drove all thoughts of suicide from his head. He recognized that the strength of life that now returned to him was not new; it had belonged to his earliest childhood and youth. He had simply reverted to the belief that the Will that produced him desired something of him—it desired a belief in God, in moral perfecting, and in a tradition transmitting to us the meaning of life.

The humble people of Russia had led Tolstoy to an understanding of the meaning of life and to a belief in God, and like them he felt that he must live "godly," and that he must renounce all the pleasures of life, must labor, humble himself, suffer, and be merciful. He realized that the essence of the peasant's faith in God, like the essence of every faith, consists in its giving life a meaning that death does not destroy. But he still had his exacting reason to contend with. Although he strove with all his soul to mingle with the people and fulfill the ritual side of their religion, his reason rebelled. For a time he accepted the dogma of the Church on the principle that truth reveals itself to love, and if you do not submit to the ritual of the Church, you transgress against love, and by transgressing against love, you deprive yourself of the possibility of recognizing the truth.

Accordingly, Tolstoy humbled his reason, faithfully attended the Russian Orthodox services, fasted, and prepared for communion. This kind of playing bopeep with God by observing religious ceremonies, the sincerity and truth of which his reason denied, soon revolted him. When the priest at communion made him say that he believed that what he was about to swallow was the true flesh and blood of the Lord, he felt a pain in his heart. He knew that he was lying and thus destroying his relation to God and losing all possibility of believing.

V. I. Alekseyev, an atheistically inclined tutor whom Tolstoy took into his house at this time, expressed surprise that a man of his intellect and sincerity could pray and observe the rites of the Church. It was a winter morning and they were discussing such questions in the drawing room at Yasnaya Polyana. The sun's slanting rays were striking the frosty tracery on the window. Tolstoy called Alekseyev's attention to the fact that in the wonderfully illuminated flower patterns he saw only the sun's reflected rays, but knew that afar off it was the real sun that produced the effect. The people, continued Tolstoy, saw only a reflected image of religion, but he himself looked further and saw—or at least knew—that very far away there existed the source from which all light comes. But the difference between him and the people, he pointed out, need not prevent their common brotherhood, for both looked at the source of light, only their reason penetrated it to different depths. Yet at times Tolstoy, upon returning from church, admitted that he could stand it no longer. The peasants chatting unconcernedly on everyday affairs at the most solemn moments of the service proved to him that their relation to religion was one of complete unconsciousness.

Fasting also troubled Tolstoy. When his doctor warned

him that he was injuring his health, he made a pilgrimage to the Monastery of St. Sergius, some miles from Moscow, to consult the famous monk Leonid. He solved the problem, however, in his own way. One day his wife served up fast-food to all the household save the tutors, who, by their own request, received regular meals. A dish of the tutors' cutlets was left on the window sill. Tolstoy asked Ilya to pass him this dish, and he ate the cutlets with more than ordinary relish. From that time on he gave up fasting.

In the end, Tolstoy was obliged to confess to himself that belief in Orthodoxy was impossible. He wondered why the priests of his own Church considered the beliefs of all others heretical. Because of the conflicting interpretations of various churches, the teaching of Christ that promised to unite all in one faith and love had ended in destroying what it sought to create. When he asked a theologian why these sects should not unite on the main points on which all could agree, he was told that such concessions would bring reproach on the spiritual authorities for deserting the faith of their forefathers.

This was the last straw. Tolstoy was seeking faith, the power of life, and the priests were seeking the best way to fulfill before men certain human obligations. His disillusion was completed when he studied the relation of the Church to war and executions, for by now he had forsworn patriotism as an irrational state of mind. Killing was evil and repugnant to him, yet the teachers of the faith prayed for the success of Russian arms and sanctified murder in war.

Tolstoy did not leave the Church at this time, for he still felt its truth, but he no longer doubted that there was much in it that was false. What deeply concerned him, however, was: Where did the truth and falsehood come from? Both, he was convinced, were contained in the Scriptures and holy tradition and had been handed down by the Church. This conviction led him to a study and investigation of these writings and traditions, for he recognized that somehow a knowledge of the meaning of life was inseparably connected with the religious doctrine of Christianity. He knew that the explanation of everything, like the commencement of everything, must be concealed in infinity. The limits of the intellect he accepted, but he wished to understand in such a way that everything that was inexplicable should present itself to him as being necessarily inexplicable, and not as something he was under an arbitary obligation to believe.

Tolstoy ended his *Confession* on this promise to write a future work—an examination of Christian theology—in an effort to determine what is true and what is false. He had come a long way from *War and Peace* and *Anna Karenina.* The *Confession,* however, is one of the noblest and most courageous utterances of man, the outpourings of a soul perplexed in the extreme by life's great problem—the relation of man to the infinite—yet executed with complete sincerity and high art. In it he dared to tell the cynical unbelievers that religion contained the only explanation of the meaning of life, and to the believers in dogmatic and popular religion he declared that the very foundations of their faith were erroneous. And in *Confession* he uncompromisingly turned his back on fifty years of his existence with all their joys and sorrows, all their fame and magnificent artistic achievements, and bravely looked forward to a new way of life of a man seeking moral perfection in service to God and humanity.

In his diary, which he had resumed again after some thirteen years of interruption, he wrote in October 1879: "There are worldly people, heavy and wingless. Their activity is on the ground. There are strong ones among them: Napoleon. They leave terrible traces among men and cause a commotion, but it is all on earth. There are those whose wings grow equally and who slowly rise and fly: monks. There are light people, winged, who rise easily from among the crowd and again descend: good idealists. There are powerfully-winged ones who, drawn by carnal desires, descend among the crowd and break their wings. Such am I. Then they struggle with broken wings, flutter desperately, and fall. If my wings heal I will fly high. God grant it. There are those who have heavenly wings, and purposely—from love to men—descend to earth (folding their wings) and teach men to fly. When they are needed no more, they fly away: Christ."

Russian Transliteration Table

(*Based on the New Russian Orthography*)

Nota Bene: –

1. Russian Christian names (Петр, Александр, etc.) that have common English equivalents (Peter, Alexander, etc.) retain their English form, except when they appear in the titles of books or articles.

2. The family names of a few Russian authors that have acquired fixed spellings in English (Gorky, etc.) retain their popular English spellings, except when they appear in the titles of books or articles.

Russian	English	Note
А а	A a	
Б б	B b	
В в	V v	
Г г	G g	(in the genitive endings его and ого, г=v)
Д д	D d	
Е е	E e	(when initial and after ь, ъ and all vowels, except ы, – е = ye; after ы, е = ie)
Ё ё	Yo yo	(after ж and ш, ё = o)
Ж ж	Zh zh	
З з	Z z	
И и	I i	(after ь, и = yi)
Й й	I i	(the combinations ий = i and ый = y)
К к	K k	
Л л	L l	
М м	M m	

Russian	English	Note
Н н	N n	
О о	O o	
П п	P p	
Р р	R r	
С с	S s	
Т т	T t	
У у	U u	
Ф ф	F f	
Х х	Kh kh	
Ц ц	Ts ts	
Ч ч	Ch ch	
Ш ш	Sh sh	
Щ щ	Shch shch	
ъ	(omitted)	
ы	y	
ь	(omitted)	
Э э	E e	
Ю ю	Yu yu	(after ы, ю = iu)
Я я	Ya ya	(after ы, я = ia)

❧ i ☙

Index

Ernest J. Simmons was born in Lawrence, Massachusetts, December 8, 1903, and educated at Harvard, where he received his Ph.D. in 1928. Although English literature and European folklore were his major interests through graduate work, a period of research in the Soviet Union, 1928–9, turned his attention to Russian literature with extraordinary significance both for himself and for the development of Russian studies in the United States. He returned to Harvard as an instructor in the English Department, 1929–36; and became assistant professor and Chairman of the Board of English Tutors, 1936–9. For 1941–6 he was associate professor of English and Russian literature at Cornell University, becoming Chairman of the Department of Slavic languages and literature in 1942. For 1946–58 Professor Simmons was Chairman of the Department of Slavic languages and has been Professor of Russian literature at the Russian Institute of Columbia University. Between 1946 and 1950 he was managing editor of *The American Slavic and East European Review.* He was also a member of the Executive Committee of the Modern Languages Association, 1953–4, and of the Board of Trustees of Sarah Lawrence College, 1956–8. Professor Simmons has done further research in the Soviet Union in 1932, 1935, 1937, 1947, and 1958, having three times been awarded the Milton grant for foreign travel. He has been on the Joint Committee on Slavic Studies of the American Council of Learned Societies and Social Science Research Council since 1947. Professor Simmons has been an associate editor of *The English Slavonic Review* and general editor of *The Columbia Slavic Studies* since 1949. His numerous books include *Pushkin* (1937), *Dostoevski: The Making of a Novelist* (1940), *Russian Fiction and Soviet Ideology: Introduction to Fedin, Leonov, and Sholokhov* (1958); he has lectured widely, contributed articles to numerous journals, and edited a variety of scholarly volumes. His *Leo Tolstoy* was originally published in 1946. Professor Simmons is married and has one son; he lives in Jaffrey Center, New Hampshire.

This book *is set on the Linotype in Granjon, a type named in compliment to Robert Granjon, but neither a copy of a classic face nor an entirely original creation. George W. Jones based his designs upon the type used by Claude Garamond (1510–61) in his beautiful French books, and more closely resembles Garamond's own than do any of the various modern types that bear his name. The book was composed, printed, and bound by* THE COLONIAL PRESS INC., *Clinton, Massachusetts. Paper manufactured by* S. D. WARREN COMPANY, *Boston. Cover design by* MILTON GLASER.

Vintage Russian Library

R-1001A *Leo Tolstoy: The Years of Development, 1828-1879* BY *Ernest J. Simmons*

R-1001B *Leo Tolstoy: The Years of Maturity, 1880-1910* BY *Ernest J. Simmons*

R-1002 *The Kremlin and World Politics: Studies in Soviet Policy and Action* BY *Philip E. Mosely* (A VINTAGE ORIGINAL)

R-1003 *Stalin: A Political Biography* BY *Isaac Deutscher*

R-1004 *How the Soviet System Works* BY *Raymond A. Bauer, Alex Inkeles, and Clyde Kluckhohn*

R-1005 *The Thief,* A NOVEL BY *Leonid Leonov*

R-1006 *The Soviets in World Affairs* BY *Louis Fischer* (Fall 1960)

R-1007 *Years of Childhood* BY *Serge Aksakov* (Fall 1960)

R-1008 *Early Joys,* A NOVEL BY *Konstantin Fedin* (Fall 1960)

R-1009 *Pan-Slavism* BY *Hans Kohn* (Fall 1960)

R-1010A *The Vintage Turgenev* (VOLUME I) *Smoke, Fathers & Sons, First Love* (Fall 1960)

R-1010B *The Vintage Turgenev* (VOLUME 2) *On the Eve, Rudin, A Quiet Spot, Diary of a Superfluous Man* (Fall 1960)

Vintage Books

K-1 *The Art of Teaching* BY *Gilbert Highet*
K-2 *The Stranger* BY *Albert Camus*
K-3 *Death in Venice & Seven Other Stories* BY *Thomas Mann*
K-4 *A Short History of Music* BY *Alfred Einstein*
K-5A *Democracy in America* BY *Alexis de Tocqueville,* VOL. I
K-5B *Democracy in America* BY *Alexis de Tocqueville,* VOL. II
K-6 *In Search of Theater* BY *Eric Bentley*
K-7 *Howards End* BY *E. M. Forster*
K-8 *The Immoralist* BY *André Gide*
K-9 *The American Political Tradition* BY *Richard Hofstadter*
K-10 *Stephen Crane: Stories and Tales* EDITED BY *R. W. Stallmann*
K-11 *Lectures on Psychoanalytic Psychiatry* BY *A. A. Brill,* M.D.
K-12 *Poetry and the Age* BY *Randall Jarrell*
K-13 *James Joyce's Ulysses* BY *Stuart Gilbert*
K-14 *Moses and Monotheism* BY *Sigmund Freud*
K-15 *Hawthorne's Short Stories* EDITED BY *Newton Arvin*
K-16 *No Exit & Three Other Plays* BY *Jean-Paul Sartre*
K-17 *Freedom and Responsibility* BY *Carl L. Becker*
K-18 *The Life of Henri Brulard* BY *Stendhal*
K-19 *The Captive Mind* BY *Czeslaw Milosz*
K-20 *The Armed Vision* BY *Stanley Edgar Hyman*
K-21 *The Death of the Heart* BY *Elizabeth Bowen*
K-22 *The Law of Civilization and Decay* BY *Brooks Adams*
K-23 *The Plumed Serpent* BY *D. H. Lawrence*
K-24 *Poems and Essays* BY *John Crowe Ransom*
K-25 *The Vintage Mencken* GATHERED BY *Alistair Cooke*
K-26 *The American Democrat* BY *James Fenimore Cooper*
K-27 *Strait Is the Gate* BY *André Gide*
K-28 *Five Stories* BY *Willa Cather*
K-29 *Stories* BY *Frank O'Connor*
K-30 *The Rebel* BY *Albert Camus*
K-31 *Rendezvous with Destiny* BY *Eric F. Goldman*
K-32 *The Hero* BY *Lord Raglan*
K-33A *Gide Journals* EDITED BY *Justin O'Brien,* VOL. I (1889–1924)

K-33B *Gide Journals* EDITED BY *Justin O'Brien*, VOL. II (1924–1949)

K-34 *The Autobiography of Michel de Montaigne* EDITED BY *Marvin Lowenthal*

K-35 *Forces in Modern British Literature* BY *William York Tindall*

K-36 *Short Stories of Katherine Mansfield* EDITED BY *Elizabeth Bowen*

K-37 *The American Character* BY *D. W. Brogan*

K-38 *The Critical Performance* EDITED BY *Stanley Edgar Hyman*

K-39 *Poetics of Music* BY *Igor Stravinsky*

K-40 *The American Essays of Henry James* EDITED BY *Leon Edel*

K-41 *The Future of the Novel—Essays by Henry James* EDITED BY *Leon Edel*

K-42 *The Economic Basis of Politics* AND RELATED WRITINGS BY *Charles A. Beard*, COMPILED BY *William Beard*

K-43 *The Coming of the French Revolution* BY *Georges Lefebvre*

K-44 *The Anatomy of Revolution* BY *Crane Brinton*

K-45 *The Good Soldier* BY *Ford Madox Ford*

K-46 *Flaubert and Madame Bovary* BY *Francis Steegmuller*

K-47 *The Classical Tradition in Poetry* BY *Gilbert Murray*

K-48 *The House in Paris* BY *Elizabeth Bowen*

K-49 *The Selected Letters of Gustave Flaubert* EDITED BY *Francis Steegmuller*

K-50 *Eleanor of Aquitaine and the Four Kings* BY *Amy Kelly*

K-51 *The Philosophy of Literary Form* BY *Kenneth Burke*

K-52 *Virgin Land* BY *Henry Nash Smith*

K-53A *The Social History of Art* BY *Arnold Hauser*, VOL. I (PREHISTORIC, ANCIENT-ORIENTAL, GREECE AND ROME, MIDDLE AGES) ILLUSTRATED

K-53B *The Social History of Art* BY *Arnold Hauser*, VOL. II (RENAISSANCE, MANNERISM, BAROQUE) ILLUSTRATED

K-53C *The Social History of Art* BY *Arnold Hauser*, VOL. III (ROCOCO, CLASSICISM, ROMANTICISM) ILLUSTRATED

K-53D *The Social History of Art* BY *Arnold Hauser*, VOL. IV (NATURALISM, IMPRESSIONISM, THE FILM AGE) ILLUSTRATED

K-54 *Some People* BY *Harold Nicolson*

K-55 *Essays* BY *Thomas Mann*

K-56 *The White Goddess* BY *Robert Graves*

K-57 *Archetypal Patterns in Poetry* BY *Maud Bodkin*

K-58 *H. L. Mencken: Prejudices—A Selection* MADE BY *James T. Farrell*

K-59 *Under the Volcano* BY *Malcolm Lowry*

K-60 *The Declaration of Independence* BY *Carl L. Becker*

K-61 *Where Angels Fear to Tread* BY *E. M. Forster*

K-62 *The Novel in France* BY *Martin Turnell*

K-63 *Confessions of Zeno* BY *Italo Svevo*

K-64 *The Natural History of Nonsense* BY *Bergen Evans*

K-65A *Great Operas* BY *Ernest Newman,* VOL. I

K-65B *Great Operas* BY *Ernest Newman,* VOL. II

K-66 *Two Legends* BY *André Gide*

K-67 *A History of Russian Literature* BY *D. S. Mirsky* EDITED BY *Francis J. Whitfield*

K-68A *Great Issues in American History,* VOL. I, 1765–1865 EDITED BY *Richard Hofstadter*

K-68B *Great Issues in American History,* VOL. II, 1864–1957 EDITED BY *Richard Hofstadter*

K-69 *The Spirit of Liberty* BY *Learned Hand* EDITED BY *Irving Dilliard*

K-70 *The Myth of the Birth of the Hero* AND OTHER WRITINGS BY *Otto Rank,* EDITED BY *Philip Freund*

K-71 *St. Mawr* AND *The Man Who Died* BY *D. H. Lawrence*

K-72 *The Road to Reunion* BY *Paul H. Buck*

K-73 *Economics and the Art of Controversy* BY *John Kenneth Galbraith*

K-74 *The Mentality of Apes* BY *Wolfgang Köhler*

K-75 *The Myth of Sisyphus* AND OTHER ESSAYS BY *Albert Camus*

K-76 *The Tree of Culture* BY *Ralph Linton*

K-77 *The Far Side of Paradise* A BIOGRAPHY OF F. SCOTT FITZ-GERALD BY *Arthur Mizener*

K-78 *The Folded Leaf* BY *William Maxwell*

K-79 *Stories* BY *Elizabeth Bowen*

K-80 *Seven Men and Two Others* BY *Max Beerbohm*

K-81 *The Road to Xanadu* BY *John Livingston Lowes*

K-82 *Verdi* BY *Francis Toye*

K-83 *Kings and Desperate Men* BY *Louis Kronenberger*

K-84 *The American Experience* BY *Henry Bamford Parkes*

K-85 *Poems by Wallace Stevens,* A SELECTION BY *Samuel French Morse*

K-86 *The Transposed Heads* BY *Thomas Mann*

K-87 *God's Country and Mine* BY *Jacques Barzun*

K-88 *Opera as Drama* BY *Joseph Kerman*

K-89 *William Blake* BY *Mark Schorer*

K-90 *The Power of Blackness* BY *Harry Levin*

K-91 *They Came Like Swallows* BY *William Maxwell*

K-92 *Catherine of Aragon* BY *Garrett Mattingly*

K-93 *Four Metaphysical Poets* BY *Joan Bennett*

K-94 *Alternative to Serfdom* BY *John Maurice Clark*

K-95 *The Age of Reform* BY *Richard Hofstadter*

K-96 *Lafcadio's Adventures* BY *André Gide*

K-97A *Modern French Painters* BY *R. H. Wilenski,* VOL. I

K-97B *Modern French Painters* BY *R. H. Wilenski,* VOL. II

K-98 *The Mind of The South* BY *W. J. Cash*

K-99 *The Inside Story* BY *Fritz Redlich* AND *June Bingham*

K-100 *Beethoven* BY *J. W. N. Sullivan*

K-101 *H. L. Mencken on Politics, A Carnival of Buncombe* EDITED BY *Malcolm Moos*

K-102 *The Jacksonian Persuasion* BY *Marvin Meyers*

K-103 *Domestic Manners of the Americans* BY *Mrs. Trollope* EDITED BY *Donald Smalley*

K-104 *Beyond the Mexique Bay* BY *Aldous Huxley*

K-105 *Anthropology of Folk Religion* EDITED BY *Charles M. Leslie* (Fall 1960)

K-106 *Charlemagne, From the Hammer to the Cross* BY *Richard Winston* (Fall 1960)

K-107 *Wagner as Man and Artist* BY *Ernest Newman* (Fall 1960)

K-108 *The Shape of Content* BY *Ben Shahn* (Fall 1960)

K-109 *Adventures of the Mind,* FROM The Saturday Evening Post (Fall 1960)